DENMARK

T0291317

FISHING AND AQUACULTURE
INDUSTRY HANDBOOK

VOLUME 1
STRATEGIC INFORMATION, REGULATIONS, OPPORTUNITIES

International Business Publications, USA
Washington DC, USA- Denmark

DENMARK
FISHING AND AQUACULTURE INDUSTRY HANDBOOK
VOLUME 1 STRATEGIC INFORMATION, REGULATIONS, OPPORTUNITIES

UPDATED ANNUALLY

We express our sincere gratitude to all government agencies and international organizations which provided information and other materials for this handbook

Cover Design: International Business Publications, USA

**2017 Edition Updated Reprint International Business Publications, USA
ISBN 978-1-5145-1855-7**

For additional analytical, business and investment opportunities information,
please contact Global Investment & Business Center, USA
at (703) 370-8082. Fax: (703) 370-8083. E-mail: ibpusa3@gmail.com
Global Business and Investment Info Databank - www.ibpus.com

Printed in the USA

For additional analytical, business and investment opportunities information,
please contact Global Investment & Business Center, USA
at (703) 370-8082. Fax: (703) 370-8083. E-mail: ibpusa3@gmail.com
Global Business and Investment Info Databank - www.ibpus.com

DENMARK

FISHING AND AQUACULTURE INDUSTRY HANDBOOK
VOLUME 1
STRATEGIC INFORMATION, REGULATIONS, OPPORTUNITIES

TABLE OF CONTENTS

For additional analytical, business and investment opportunities information,
please contact Global Investment & Business Center, USA
at (703) 370-8082. Fax: (703) 370-8083. E-mail: ibpusa3@gmail.com
Global Business and Investment Info Databank - www.ibpus.com

For additional analytical, business and investment opportunities information,
please contact Global Investment & Business Center, USA
at (703) 370-8082. Fax: (703) 370-8083. E-mail: ibpusa3@gmail.com
Global Business and Investment Info Databank - www.ibpus.com

For additional analytical, business and investment opportunities information,
please contact Global Investment & Business Center, USA
at (703) 370-8082. Fax: (703) 370-8083. E-mail: ibpusa3@gmail.com
Global Business and Investment Info Databank - www.ibpus.com

STRATEGIC AND DEVELOPMENT PROFILES

Capital and largest city	Copenhagen 55°43′N 12°34′E55.717°N 12.567°E
Official languages	Danish
Recognised regional languages	• Faroese • Greenlandic • German
Demonym	• Danish • Dane
Government	Unitary parliamentary constitutional monarchy
- Monarch	Margrethe II
- Prime Minister	Helle Thorning-Schmidt
Legislature	Folketing
Establishment	
- Consolidation	c. 10th century
- Democratisation (Constitutional Act)	5 June 1849
- Danish Realm	24 March 1948
Area	
- Denmark	42,915.7 km^2 (133rd) (16,562.1) sq mi
- Greenland	2,166,086 km^2 (836,330 sq mi)
- Faroe Islands	1,399 km^2 (540.16 sq mi)
Population	
- July 2014 estimate	5,639,719 (113th)
- Greenland	56,370
- Faroe Islands	49,709
- Density (Denmark)	131/km^2 339.3/sq mi
GDP (PPP)	2013 estimate
- Total	$211.321 billion (52nd)
- Per capita	$37,794 (19th)
GDP (nominal)	2013 estimate
- Total	$324.293 billion (34th)
- Per capita	$57,998 (6th)
Gini	▲28.1 low
HDI	▲0.900 very high · 10th
Currency	Danish krone (DKK)
Time zone	CET (UTC+1)
- Summer (DST)	CEST (UTC+2)
Drives on the	right
Calling code	+45
ISO 3166 code	DK
Internet TLD	.dk

Denmark is a Nordic country in Northern Europe, located southwest of Sweden and south of Norway, and bordered to the south by Germany. The Kingdom of Denmark comprises Denmark and two autonomous constituent countries in the North Atlantic Ocean, the Faroe Islands and Greenland. Denmark has an area of 43,094 square kilometres (16,639 sq mi), and a population of around 5.64 million inhabitants. The country consists of a peninsula, Jutland, and the Danish archipelago of 443 named islands, of which around 70 are inhabited. The islands are characterised by flat, arable land and sandy coasts, low elevation and a temperate climate. A Scandinavian nation, Denmark shares strong cultural and historic ties with its overseas neighbours Sweden and Norway. The national language, Danish, is very closely related and mutually intelligible with Swedish and Norwegian.

The unified kingdom of Denmark emerged in the 10th century as a proficient seafaring nation in the struggle for control of the Baltic Sea. Danish rule over the personal Kalmar Union, established in 1397, ended with Swedish secession in 1523. The following year, Denmark entered into a union with Norway until its dissolution in 1814. Denmark inherited an expansive colonial empire from this union, of which the Faroe Islands and Greenland are remnants. Beginning in the 17th century, there were several cessions of territory; these culminated in the 1830s with a surge of nationalist movements, which were defeated in the 1864 Second Schleswig War. Denmark remained neutral during World War I. In April 1940, a German invasion saw brief, military skirmishes while the Danish resistance movement was active from 1943 until the German surrender in May 1945. An industrialized exporter of agricultural produce in the second half of the 19th century, Denmark introduced social and labour-market reforms in the early 20th century, making the basis for the present welfare state model with a highly developed mixed economy.

The Constitution of Denmark was signed on 5 June 1849, ending the absolute monarchy which had begun in 1660. It establishes a constitutional monarchy—the current monarch is Queen Margrethe II—organised as a parliamentary democracy. The government and national parliament are seated in Copenhagen, the nation's capital, largest city and main commercial centre. Denmark exercises hegemonic influence in the Danish Realm, devolving powers to handle internal affairs. Denmark became a member of the European Union in 1973, maintaining certain opt-outs; it retains its own currency, the krone. It is among the founding members of NATO, the Nordic Council, the OECD, OSCE, and the United Nations; it is also part of the Schengen Area.

Danes enjoy a high standard of living and the country ranks highly in numerous comparisons of national performance, including education, health care, protection of civil liberties, government transparency, democratic governance, prosperity and human development. Denmark is frequently ranked as the happiest country in the world in cross-national studies of happiness. The country ranks as having the world's highest social mobility, a high level of income equality, has one of the world's highest per capita incomes, and has one of the world's highest personal income tax rates. A large majority of Danes are members of the National Church, although the Constitution guarantees freedom of religion.

Background: Once the seat of rapacious Viking raiders and later a major power in northwestern Europe, Denmark has evolved into a modern, prosperous nation that is participating in the political and economic integration of Europe. So far, however, they have opted out of some aspects of the European Union's Maastricht Treaty including the new monetary system launched on 1 January 2003.

GEOGRAPHY

Location: Northern Europe, bordering the Baltic Sea and the North Sea, on a peninsula north of Germany

Geographic coordinates: 56 00 N, 10 00 E
Map references: Europe

Area: *total:* 43,094 sq km

land: 42,394 sq km
water: 700 sq km
note: includes the island of Bornholm in the Baltic Sea and the rest of metropolitan Denmark, but excludes the Faroe Islands and Greenland

Area—comparative: slightly less than twice the size of Massachusetts
Land boundaries:
total: 68 km
border countries: Germany 68 km
Coastline: 7,314 km

Maritime claims:
contiguous zone: 4 nm
continental shelf: 200-m depth or to the depth of exploitation
exclusive economic zone: 200 nm
territorial sea: 3 nm

Climate: temperate; humid and overcast; mild, windy winters and cool summers
Terrain: low and flat to gently rolling plains
Elevation extremes:
lowest point: Lammefjord -7 m
highest point: Ejer Bavnehoj 173 m
Natural resources: petroleum, natural gas, fish, salt, limestone, stone, gravel and sand

Land use:
arable land: 60%
permanent crops: 0%
permanent pastures: 5%
forests and woodland: 10%
other: 25%

Irrigated land: 4,350 sq km

Natural hazards: flooding is a threat in some areas of the country (e.g., parts of Jutland, along the southern coast of the island of Lolland) that are protected from the sea by a system of dikes

Environment—current issues: air pollution, principally from vehicle and power plant emissions; nitrogen and phosphorus pollution of the North Sea; drinking and surface water becoming polluted from animal wastes and pesticides

Environment—international agreements:
party to: Air Pollution, Air Pollution-Nitrogen Oxides, Air Pollution-Sulphur 85, Air Pollution-

Sulphur 94, Air Pollution-Volatile Organic Compounds, Antarctic Treaty, Biodiversity, Climate

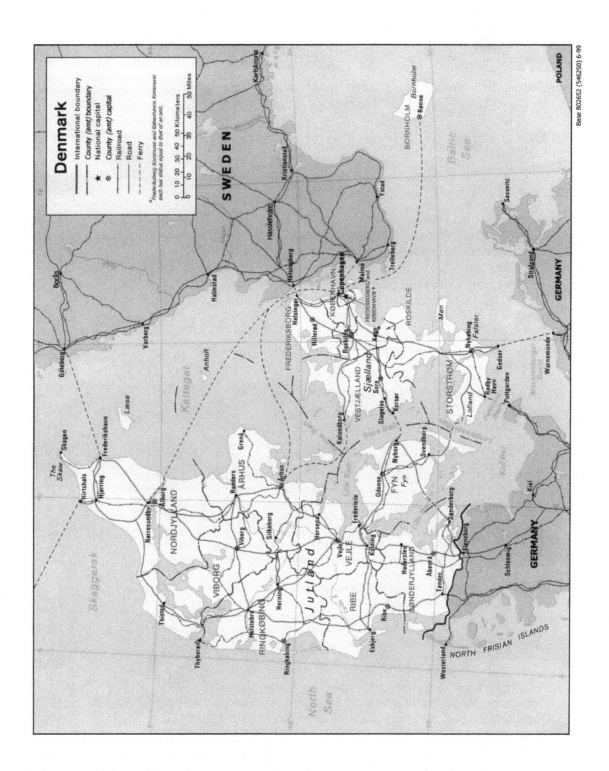

For additional analytical, business and investment opportunities information,
please contact Global Investment & Business Center, USA
at (703) 370-8082. Fax: (703) 370-8083. E-mail: ibpusa3@gmail.com
Global Business and Investment Info Databank - www.ibpus.com

Change, Desertification, Endangered Species, Environmental Modification, Hazardous Wastes, Marine Dumping, Marine Life Conservation, Nuclear Test Ban, Ozone Layer Protection, Ship Pollution, Tropical Timber 83, Tropical Timber 94, Wetlands, Whaling
signed, but not ratified: Air Pollution-Persistent Organic Pollutants, Antarctic-Environmental Protocol, Climate Change-Kyoto Protocol, Law of the Sea

Geography—note: controls Danish Straits (Skagerrak and Kattegat) linking Baltic and North Seas; about one-quarter of the population lives in Copenhagen.

PEOPLE

Population: 5,356,845

Age structure:
0-14 years: 18% (male 504,182; female 478,547)
15-64 years: 67% (male 1,811,445; female 1,765,038)
65 years and over: 15% (male 331,207; female 466,426)

Population growth rate: 0.38%
Birth rate: 11.57 births/1,000 population
Death rate: 10.97 deaths/1,000 population
Net migration rate: 3.22 migrant(s)/1,000 population

Sex ratio:
at birth: 1.05 male(s)/female
under 15 years: 1.05 male(s)/female
15-64 years: 1.03 male(s)/female
65 years and over: 0.71 male(s)/female
total population: 0.98 male(s)/female

Infant mortality rate: 5.11 deaths/1,000 live births

Life expectancy at birth:
total population: 76.51 years
male: 73.83 years
female: 79.33 years

Total fertility rate: 1.62 children born/woman

Nationality:
noun: Dane(s)
adjective: Danish

Ethnic groups: Scandinavian, Eskimo, Faroese, German
Religions: Evangelical Lutheran 91%, other Protestant and Roman Catholic 2%, other 7% (1988)
Languages: Danish, Faroese, Greenlandic (an Eskimo dialect), German (small minority)

Literacy:
definition: age 15 and over can read and write
total population: 99%
male: NA%
female: NA%

For additional analytical, business and investment opportunities information, please contact Global Investment & Business Center, USA at (703) 370-8082. Fax: (703) 370-8083. E-mail: ibpusa3@gmail.com
Global Business and Investment Info Databank - www.ibpus.com

GOVERNMENT

Country name:
conventional long form: Kingdom of Denmark
conventional short form: Denmark
local long form: Kongeriget Danmark
local short form: Danmark

Data code: DA
Government type: constitutional monarchy
Capital: Copenhagen

Administrative divisions: metropolitan Denmark—14 counties (amter, singular—amt) and 2 kommunes*; Arhus, Bornholm, Fredericksberg*, Frederiksborg, Fyn, Kobenhavn, Kobenhavns*, Nordjylland, Ribe, Ringkobing, Roskilde, Sonderjylland, Storstrom, Vejle, Vestsjalland, Viborg
note: see separate entries for the Faroe Islands and Greenland, which are part of the Kingdom of Denmark and are self-governing administrative divisions

Independence: first organized as a unified state in 10th century; in 1849 became a constitutional monarchy

National holiday: Birthday of the Queen, 16 April (1940)

Constitution: 1849 was the original constitution; there was a major overhaul 5 June 1953, allowing for a unicameral legislature and a female chief of state
Legal system: civil law system; judicial review of legislative acts; accepts compulsory ICJ jurisdiction, with reservations
Suffrage: 18 years of age; universal

Executive branch:

chief of state: Queen MARGRETHE II (since 14 January 1972); Heir Apparent Crown Prince FREDERIK, elder son of the monarch (born on 26 May 1968)

head of government: Prime Minister Helle THORNING-SCHMIDT (since 3 October 2011)

cabinet: Council of State appointed by the monarch

elections: the monarchy is hereditary; following legislative elections, the leader of the majority party or the leader of the majority coalition usually appointed prime minister by the monarch

Legislative branch:

unicameral People's Assembly or Folketing (179 seats, including 2 from Greenland and 2 from the Faroe Islands; members elected by popular vote on the basis of proportional representation to serve four-year terms unless the Folketing is dissolved earlier)

elections: last held on 15 September 2011 (next to be held by September 2015)

election results: percent of vote by party - Liberal Party 26.7%, Social Democrats 24.9%, Danish People's Party 12.3%, Social Liberal Party 9.5%, Socialist People's Party 9.2%, Unity List 6.7%,

Liberal Alliance 5%, Conservative People's Party 4.9%, other 0.8%; seats by party - Liberal Party 47, Social Democrats 44, Danish People's Party 22, Social Liberal Party 17, Socialist People's Party 16, Unity List 12, Liberal Alliance 9, Conservative People's Party 8; note - does not include the two seats from Greenland and the two seats from the Faroe Islands

Judicial branch: Supreme Court, judges are appointed by the monarch for life

Political parties and leaders: Social Democratic Party Poul Nyrup RASMUSSEN; Conservative Party Torben RECHENDORFF; Liberal Party Uffe ELLEMANN-JENSEN; Socialist People's Party Holger K. NIELSEN; Progress Party Kirsten JAKOBSEN; Center Democratic Party Mimi JAKOBSEN; Social Liberal Party Marianne JELVED; Unity Party no leader; Danish People's Party Pia KJAERSGAARD; Radical Liberal Party Margrethe VESTAGER; Conservative People's Party Torben RECHENDORFF; Christian People's Party Jann SJURSEN

International organization participation: AfDB, AsDB, Australia Group, BIS, CBSS, CCC, CE, CERN, EAPC, EBRD, ECE, EIB, ESA, EU, FAO, G- 9, IADB, IAEA, IBRD, ICAO, ICC, ICFTU, ICRM, IDA, IEA, IFAD, IFC, IFRCS, IHO, ILO, IMF, IMO, Inmarsat, Intelsat, Interpol, IOC, IOM, ISO, ITU, MTCR, NATO, NC, NEA, NIB, NSG, OECD, OPCW, OSCE, PCA, UN, UNCTAD, UNESCO, UNHCR, UNIDO, UNIKOM, UNMIBH, UNMOGIP, UNMOP, UNMOT, UNOMIG, UNPREDEP, UNTSO, UPU, WEU (observer), WHO, WIPO, WMO, WTrO, ZC

Diplomatic representation in the US:
chief of mission: Ambassador Knud-Erik TYGESEN
chancery: 3200 Whitehaven Street NW, Washington, DC 20008
telephone: 1 (202) 234-4300
FAX: 1 (202) 328-1470
consulate(s) general: Chicago, Los Angeles, and New York

Diplomatic representation from the US:
chief of mission: Ambassador Edward E. ELSON
embassy: Dag Hammarskjolds Alle 24, 2100 Copenhagen
mailing address: PSC 73, APO AE 09716
telephone: 45 35 55 31 44
FAX: 45 35 43 02 23

Flag description: red with a white cross that extends to the edges of the flag; the vertical part of the cross is shifted to the hoist side, and that design element of the Dannebrog (Danish flag) was subsequently adopted by the other Nordic countries of Finland, Iceland, Norway, and Sweden.

ECONOMY

This thoroughly modern market economy features a high-tech agricultural sector, state-of-the-art industry with world-leading firms in pharmaceuticals, maritime shipping and renewable energy, and a high dependence on foreign trade. Denmark is a member of the European Union (EU); Danish legislation and regulations conform to EU standards on almost all issues. Danes enjoy a high standard of living and the Danish economy is characterized by extensive government welfare measures and an equitable distribution of income. Denmark is a net exporter of food and energy and enjoys a comfortable balance of payments surplus, but depends on imports of raw materials for the manufacturing sector. Within the EU, Denmark is among the strongest supporters of trade liberalization. After a long consumption-driven upswing, Denmark's economy began slowing in 2007 with the end of a housing boom. Housing prices dropped markedly in 2008-09 and, following a short respite in 2010, have since continued to decline. Household indebtedness is still relatively high at more than 275% of gross disposable income in the first half of 2013. The global financial crisis has exacerbated this cyclical slowdown through increased borrowing costs and lower export demand, consumer confidence, and investment. Denmark made a modest recovery in 2010, in part because of increased government spending; however, the country experienced a technical recession in late 2010-early 2011.

Historically low levels of unemployment rose sharply with the recession and have remained at about 6% in 2010-13, based on the national measure, about two-thirds average EU unemployment. An impending decline in the ratio of workers to retirees will be a major long-term issue. Denmark maintained a healthy budget surplus for many years up to 2008, but the budget balance swung into deficit in 2009, where it remains. In spite of the deficits, the new coalition government delivered a modest stimulus to the economy in 2012. Nonetheless, Denmark's fiscal position remains among the strongest in the EU with public debt at about 46% of GDP in 2013. Despite previously meeting the criteria to join the European Economic and Monetary Union (EMU), so far Denmark has decided not to join, although the Danish krone remains pegged to the euro.

GDP (purchasing power parity):

$211.3 billion (2013 est.)
country comparison to the world:
55

$211.1 billion (2012 est.)
$211.9 billion (2011 est.)
note:data are in 2013 US dollars

GDP (official exchange rate):

$324.3 billion (2013 est.)

GDP - real growth rate:

0.1% (2013 est.)
country comparison to the world:
195

-0.4% (2012 est.)
1.1% (2011 est.)

GDP - per capita (PPP):

$37,800 (2013 est.)
country comparison to the world:
32

$37,800 (2012 est.)
$38,100 (2011 est.)

For additional analytical, business and investment opportunities information,
please contact Global Investment & Business Center, USA
at (703) 370-8082. Fax: (703) 370-8083. E-mail: ibpusa3@gmail.com
Global Business and Investment Info Databank - www.ibpus.com

note:data are in 2013 US dollars

Gross national saving:

24.1% of GDP (2013 est.)
country comparison to the world:
54

22.6% of GDP (2012 est.)
23.3% of GDP (2011 est.)

GDP - composition, by end use:

household consumption:
49.1%
government consumption:
28.8%
investment in fixed capital:
17.7%
investment in inventories:
0.2%
exports of goods and services:
53.4%
imports of goods and services:
-49.2%
(2013 est.)

GDP - composition, by sector of origin:

agriculture:
1.5%
industry:
21.7%
services:
76.8% (2013 est.)

Agriculture - products:

barley, wheat, potatoes, sugar beets; pork, dairy products; fish

Industries:

iron, steel, nonferrous metals, chemicals, food processing, machinery and transportation equipment, textiles and clothing, electronics, construction, furniture and other wood products, shipbuilding and refurbishment, windmills, pharmaceuticals, medical equipment

Industrial production growth rate:

1.1% (2013 est.)
country comparison to the world:
143

Labor force:

2.795 million (2013 est.)
country comparison to the world:
106

Labor force - by occupation:

agriculture:
2.6%
industry:
20.3%
services:
77.1% (2011 est.)

Unemployment rate:

6% (2013 est.)
country comparison to the world:
59

6% (2012 est.)

Population below poverty line:

13.4% (2011)

Household income or consumption by percentage share:

lowest 10%:
1.9%
highest 10%:
28.7% (2007)

For additional analytical, business and investment opportunities information,
please contact Global Investment & Business Center, USA
at (703) 370-8082. Fax: (703) 370-8083. E-mail: ibpusa3@gmail.com
Global Business and Investment Info Databank - www.ibpus.com

Distribution of family income - Gini index:

24.8 (2011 est.)
country comparison to the world:
137

24.7 (1992)

Budget:

revenues:
$181.4 billion
expenditures:
$189.7 billion (2013 est.)

Taxes and other revenues:

55.9% of GDP (2013 est.)
country comparison to the world:
8

Budget surplus (+) or deficit (-):

-2.5% of GDP (2013 est.)
country comparison to the world:
103

Public debt:

47% of GDP (2013 est.)
country comparison to the world:
75

45.6% of GDP (2012 est.)
note:data cover general government debt, and includes debt instruments issued (or owned) by government entities other than the treasury; the data include treasury debt held by foreign entities; the data include debt issued by subnational entities, as well as intra-governmental debt; intra-governmental debt consists of treasury borrowings from surpluses in the social funds, such as for retirement, medical care, and unemployment; debt instruments for the social funds are not sold at public auctions

For additional analytical, business and investment opportunities information,
please contact Global Investment & Business Center, USA
at (703) 370-8082. Fax: (703) 370-8083. E-mail: ibpusa3@gmail.com
Global Business and Investment Info Databank - www.ibpus.com

Fiscal year:

calendar year

Inflation rate (consumer prices):

0.8% (2013 est.)
country comparison to the world:
18

2.4% (2012 est.)

Central bank discount rate:

0.75% (31 December 2011 est.)
country comparison to the world:
133

0.75% (31 December 2010 est.)

Commercial bank prime lending rate:

3.6% (31 December 2013 est.)
country comparison to the world:
162

3.6% (31 December 2012 est.)

Stock of narrow money:

$147.6 billion (31 December 2013 est.)
country comparison to the world:
26

$150.4 billion (31 December 2012 est.)

Stock of broad money:

$180.2 billion (31 December 2013 est.)
country comparison to the world:
42

For additional analytical, business and investment opportunities information,
please contact Global Investment & Business Center, USA
at (703) 370-8082. Fax: (703) 370-8083. E-mail: ibpusa3@gmail.com
Global Business and Investment Info Databank - www.ibpus.com

$174.3 billion (31 December 2012 est.)

Stock of domestic credit:

$675 billion (31 December 2013 est.)
country comparison to the world:
22

$664.5 billion (31 December 2012 est.)

Market value of publicly traded shares:

$NA (31 December 2012 est.)
country comparison to the world:
31

$179.5 billion (31 December 2011)
$231.7 billion (31 December 2010 est.)

Current account balance:

$19.6 billion (2013 est.)
country comparison to the world:
16

$17.44 billion (2012 est.)

Exports:

$106 billion (2013 est.)
country comparison to the world:
37

$104.9 billion (2012 est.)

Exports - commodities:

machinery and instruments, meat and meat products, dairy products, fish, pharmaceuticals, furniture, windmills

Exports - partners:

Germany 15.9%, Sweden 13.5%, UK 9.6%, US 6.6%, Norway 6.3%, Netherlands 4.6%

Imports:

$98.45 billion (2013 est.)
country comparison to the world:
35
$96.77 billion (2012 est.)

Imports - commodities:

machinery and equipment, raw materials and semimanufactures for industry, chemicals, grain and foodstuffs, consumer goods

Imports - partners:

Germany 21.2%, Sweden 13.5%, Netherlands 7.5%, China 6.4%, Norway 6.3%, UK 5.6% (2012)

Reserves of foreign exchange and gold:

$89.5 billion (31 December 2013 est.)
country comparison to the world:
24

$89.7 billion (31 December 2012 est.)

Debt - external:
$586.7 billion (31 December 2012 est.)
country comparison to the world:
24
$571.4 billion (31 December 2011)

Stock of direct foreign investment - at home:

$146 billion (31 December 2013 est.)
country comparison to the world:
31

$147.1 billion (31 December 2012 est.)

Stock of direct foreign investment - abroad:

$248.3 billion (31 December 2013 est.)

For additional analytical, business and investment opportunities information,
please contact Global Investment & Business Center, USA
at (703) 370-8082. Fax: (703) 370-8083. E-mail: ibpusa3@gmail.com
Global Business and Investment Info Databank - www.ibpus.com

country comparison to the world:
21
$241.7 billion (31 December 2012 est.)

Exchange rates:

Danish kroner (DKK) per US dollar -
5.695 (2013 est.)
5.7925 (2012 est.)
5.6241 (2010 est.)
5.361 (2009)
5.0236 (2008)

ENERGY

Electricity - production:
33.71 billion kWh
country comparison to the world:
63

Electricity - consumption:
33.56 billion kWh
country comparison to the world:
60

Electricity - exports:

10.71 billion kWh
country comparison to the world:
20

Electricity - imports:

15.92 billion kWh
country comparison to the world:
13

Electricity - installed generating capacity:

13.71 million kW
country comparison to the world:
48

Electricity - from fossil fuels:

63% of total installed capacity
country comparison to the world:
129

Electricity - from nuclear fuels:

0% of total installed capacity
country comparison to the world:
75

Electricity - from hydroelectric plants:

0.1% of total installed capacity
country comparison to the world:
150

Electricity - from other renewable sources:

36.9% of total installed capacity
country comparison to the world:
2

Crude oil - production:

207,400 bbl/day
country comparison to the world:
39

Crude oil - exports:

155,200 bbl/day
country comparison to the world:
32

Crude oil - imports:

55,010 bbl/day (2010 est.)
country comparison to the world:
54

Crude oil - proved reserves:

805 million bbl
country comparison to the world:
43

Refined petroleum products - production:

For additional analytical, business and investment opportunities information,
please contact Global Investment & Business Center, USA
at (703) 370-8082. Fax: (703) 370-8083. E-mail: ibpusa3@gmail.com
Global Business and Investment Info Databank - www.ibpus.com

145,300 bbl/day
country comparison to the world:
62

Refined petroleum products - consumption:

160,200 bbl/day
country comparison to the world:
64

Refined petroleum products - exports:
104,400 bbl/day
country comparison to the world:
43

Refined petroleum products - imports:

124,100 bbl/day
country comparison to the world:
45

Natural gas - production:
6.412 billion cu m
country comparison to the world:
50

Natural gas - consumption:

4.994 billion cu m
country comparison to the world:
63

Natural gas - exports:

2.983 billion cu m
country comparison to the world:
39

Natural gas - imports:

254 million cu m
country comparison to the world:
68

Natural gas - proved reserves:

42.98 billion cu m
country comparison to the world:
67

For additional analytical, business and investment opportunities information,
please contact Global Investment & Business Center, USA
at (703) 370-8082. Fax: (703) 370-8083. E-mail: ibpusa3@gmail.com
Global Business and Investment Info Databank - www.ibpus.com

Carbon dioxide emissions from consumption of energy:

46.66 million Mt

COMMUNICATIONS

Telephones - main lines in use:
2.431 million
country comparison to the world: 53

Telephones - mobile cellular:
6.6 million
country comparison to the world: 97

Telephone system:
general assessment: excellent telephone and telegraph services
domestic: buried and submarine cables and microwave radio relay form trunk network, multiple cellular mobile communications systems
international: country code - 45; a series of fiber-optic submarine cables link Denmark with Canada, Faroe Islands, Germany, Iceland, Netherlands, Norway, Poland, Russia, Sweden, and UK; satellite earth stations - 18 (6 Intelsat, 10 Eutelsat, 1 Orion, 1 Inmarsat (Blaavand-Atlantic-East)); note - the Nordic countries (Denmark, Finland, Iceland, Norway, and Sweden) share the Danish earth station and the Eik, Norway, station for worldwide Inmarsat access (2011)

Broadcast media:
strong public-sector TV presence with state-owned Danmarks Radio (DR) operating 4 channels and publicly owned TV2 operating roughly a half dozen channels; broadcasts of privately owned stations are available via satellite and cable feed; DR operates 4 nationwide FM radio stations, 15 digital audio broadcasting stations, and about 15 web-based radio stations; approximately 250 commercial and community radio stations (2007)

Internet country code:
.dk

Internet hosts:
4.297 million
country comparison to the world: 25

Internet users:
4.75 million
country comparison to the world: 48

TRANSPORTATION

Airports:
80
country comparison to the world:

Airports - with paved runways:

---

total: 28
over 3,047 m: 2
2,438 to 3,047 m:
7
1,524 to 2,437 m: 5
914 to 1,523 m: 12
under 914 m: 2

Airports - with unpaved runways:

total: 52
914 to 1,523 m: 5
under 914 m: 47 (2013)

Pipelines:
condensate 11 km; gas 4,377 km; oil 647 km; oil/gas/water 2 km

Railways:

total: 2,667 km
country comparison to the world:
62
standard gauge: 2,667 km 1.435-m gauge (640 km electrified)

Roadways:
total:
73,929 km
country comparison to the world:
63
paved: 73,929 km (includes 1,143 km of expressways) (2012)

Waterways:

400 km
country comparison to the world:
88

Merchant marine:
total: 367
country comparison to the world:
27

by type: bulk carrier 4, cargo 48, carrier 1, chemical tanker 125, container 94, liquefied gas 4, passenger 1, passenger/cargo 40, petroleum tanker 36, refrigerated cargo 3, roll on/roll off 8, specialized tanker 3
foreign-owned: 27 (Germany 9, Greenland 1, Norway 2, Sweden 15)
registered in other countries: 582 (Antigua and Barbuda 20, Bahamas 69, Belgium 4, Brazil 3, Curacao 1, Cyprus 6, Egypt 1, France 11, Gibraltar 7, Hong Kong 42, Isle of Man 30, Italy 4, Jamaica 1, Liberia 8, Lithuania 8, Luxembourg 1, Malaysia 1, Malta 34, Marshall Islands 7, Moldova 1, Netherlands 27, Norway 7, Panama 41, Philippines 2, Portugal 4, Saint Vincent and the Grenadines 9, Singapore 149, Sweden 4, UK 43, Uruguay 1, US 31, Venezuela 1, unknown 4)

For additional analytical, business and investment opportunities information, please contact Global Investment & Business Center, USA at (703) 370-8082. Fax: (703) 370-8083. E-mail: ibpusa3@gmail.com
Global Business and Investment Info Databank - www.ibpus.com

Ports and terminals:

major seaport(s):
Baltic Sea - Aarhus, Copenhagen, Fredericia, Kalundborg; North Sea - Esbjerg,
river port(s):
Aalborg (Langerak)
dry bulk cargo port(s):
Ensted (coal)
cruise port(s):
Copenhagen

MILITARY

Military branches:
Defense Command: Army Operational Command, Admiral Danish Fleet, Arctic Command,
Tactical Air Command, Home Guard

Military service age and obligation:
18 years of age for compulsory and voluntary military service; conscripts serve an initial
training period that varies from 4 to 12 months according to specialization; reservists are
assigned to mobilization units following completion of their conscript service; women
eligible to volunteer for military service
Manpower available for military service:
males age 16-49: 1,236,337
females age 16-49: 1,224,182 (2010 est.)
Manpower fit for military service:
males age 16-49: 1,014,560
females age 16-49: 1,003,921

Manpower reaching militarily significant age annually:
male: 37,913
female: 35,865
Military expenditures:
1.41% of GDP

country comparison to the world: 71
1.35% of GDP (2011)
1.41% of GDP (2010)

TRANSNATIONAL ISSUES

Disputes - international:
Iceland, the UK, and Ireland dispute Denmark's claim that the Faroe Islands' continental
shelf extends beyond 200 nm; Faroese continue to study proposals for full independence;
sovereignty dispute with Canada over Hans Island in the Kennedy Channel between
Ellesmere Island and Greenland; Denmark (Greenland) and Norway have made
submissions to the Commission on the Limits of the Continental Shelf (CLCS) and Russia
is collecting additional data to augment its 2001 CLCS submission

Refugees and internally displaced persons:
stateless persons: 3,623 (2012)

For additional analytical, business and investment opportunities information,
please contact Global Investment & Business Center, USA
at (703) 370-8082. Fax: (703) 370-8083. E-mail: ibpusa3@gmail.com
Global Business and Investment Info Databank - www.ibpus.com

GREENLAND

Capital (and largest city)	Nuuk (Godthåb) 64°10′N 51°44′W64.167°N 51.733°W
Official language(s)	Greenlandic (Kalaallisut)
Ethnic groups	88% Inuit (including Inuit-Danish mixed) 12% Europeans, mostly Danes
Demonym	Greenlander, Greenlandic
Government	Parliamentary democracy within a constitutional monarchy
- Queen	Margrethe II
- High Commissioner	Mikaela Engell
- Prime Minister	Kuupik Kleist
Autonomy	within the Kingdom of Denmark
- Norwegian sovereignty	1261
- Contact re-established	1721
- Ceded to Denmark	14 January 1814
- Status of amt	5 June 1953
- Home rule	1 May 1979
- Further autonomy and self rule	21 June 2009*
Area	
- Total	2,166,086 km^2 (12th) 836,109 sq mi
- Water (%)	83.1
Population	
- January 2011 estimate	56,615*
- Density	0.027/km^2 (241st) 0.069/sq mi
GDP (PPP)	2007 estimate
- Total	$2.122 billion (n/a)
- Per capita	$37,517 (n/a)
HDI (1998)	0.927* (very high) (n/a)
Currency	Danish krone (DKK)
Time zone	GMT (UTC+0 to −4)
Drives on the	right
ISO 3166 code	GL
Internet TLD	.gl
Calling code	+299

Greenland (**Kalaallisut**: *Kalaallit Nunaat* meaning "Land of the **Greenlanders**"; Danish: *Grønland*) is an **autonomous country** within the **Kingdom of Denmark**, located between the **Arctic** and **Atlantic Oceans**, east of the **Canadian Arctic Archipelago**. Though **physiographically** a part of the **continent** of **North America**, Greenland has been politically and culturally associated with **Europe** (specifically **Norway** and **Denmark**) for about a millennium. The largest island in Greenland is also named *Greenland*, and makes up most of the country's land area.

Greenland has been inhabited, though not continuously, by Inuit peoples via Canada for 4500-5000 years. In the 10th century, **Norsemen** settled on the uninhabited southern part of

Greenland. In the 13th century, the **Inuit** arrived, and in the late 15th century the **Norse colonies** were abandoned. In the early 18th century contact between **Scandinavia** and Greenland was re-established and Denmark established rule over Greenland.

Greenland became a Danish colony in 1814 after being under the rule of **Denmark-Norway** for centuries. With the **Constitution of Denmark** of 1953, Greenland became a part of the Kingdom of Denmark in a relationship known in Danish as *Rigsfællesskabet* (Commonwealth of the Realm).

In 1979 Denmark granted **home rule** to Greenland, and in 2008 Greenland **voted** to transfer more power from the **Danish royal government** to the local **Greenlandic** government. This became effective the following year, with the Danish royal government in charge of foreign affairs, security (defence-police-justice), and financial policy, and providing a subsidy of **DKK** 3.4 billion, or approximately $11,300 per Greenlander, annually.

Greenland is, by area, the **world's largest island** that is not a **continent**. With a population of 56,615 (January 2011 estimate) it is one of the **least densely populated dependencies or countries in the world**

GEOGRAPHY AND CLIMATE

Greenland lies between latitudes **59°** and 84°N, and longitudes **11°** and **74°W** and is the third largest country in North America. The Atlantic Ocean borders Greenland's southeast; the **Greenland Sea** is to the east; the Arctic Ocean is to the north; and **Baffin Bay** is to the west. The nearest countries are Canada, to the west across Baffin Bay, and Iceland, east of Greenland in the Atlantic Ocean. Greenland also contains the **world's largest national park**, and is the world's largest island and the **largest dependent territory** by area in the world. However, since the 1950s, scientists have postulated that the **ice sheet** covering the country may actually conceal three separate island land masses that have been bridged by glaciers over the last geologic **cooling period**. The average annual temperatures of Nuuk, Greenland vary from -9 to 7 °C (16 to 45 °F)

The total area of Greenland is 2,166,086 km^2 (836,330 sq mi) (including other offshore minor islands), of which the **Greenland ice sheet** covers 1,755,637 km^2 (677,855 sq mi) (81%) and has a volume of approximately 2,850,000 km^3 (680,000 cu mi). The highest point on Greenland is **Gunnbjørn Fjeld** at 3,700 m (12,139 ft). The majority of Greenland, however, is less than 1,500 m (4,921 ft) in elevation.

The weight of the massive Greenland ice sheet has depressed the central land area to form a basin lying more than 300 m (984 ft) below **sea level**. The ice **flows** generally to the coast from the centre of the island.

All **towns and settlements of Greenland** are situated along the ice-free coast, with the population being concentrated along the west coast. The northeastern part of Greenland is not part of any municipality, but is the site of the world's largest national park, Northeast Greenland National Park.

At least four scientific expedition stations and camps had been established on the ice sheet in the ice-covered central part of Greenland (indicated as pale blue in the map to the right): **Eismitte**, **North Ice**, North GRIP Camp and The Raven Skiway. Currently, there is a year-round station, **Summit Camp**, on the ice sheet, established in 1989. The radio station **Jørgen Brønlund Fjord** was, until 1950, the northernmost permanent outpost in the world.

The extreme north of Greenland, **Peary Land**, is not covered by an ice sheet, because the air there is too dry to produce **snow**, which is essential in the production and maintenance of an ice sheet. If the Greenland ice sheet were to **melt** away completely, the world's sea level would rise by more than 7 m (23 ft).

Between 1989 and 1993, U.S. and European **climate** researchers drilled into the summit of Greenland's ice sheet, obtaining a pair of 3 km (1.9 mi) long **ice cores**. Analysis of the layering and chemical composition of the cores has provided a revolutionary new record of climate change in the **Northern Hemisphere** going back about 100,000 years, and illustrated that the world's **weather** and **temperature** have often shifted rapidly from one seemingly stable state to another, with worldwide **consequences**.

The glaciers of Greenland are also contributing to a rise in the global sea level at a faster rate than was previously believed. Between 1991 and 2004, monitoring of the weather at one location (Swiss Camp) showed that the average winter temperature had risen almost 6 °C (11 °F). Other research has shown that higher snowfalls from the **North Atlantic oscillation** caused the interior of the ice cap to thicken by an average of 6 cm or 2.36 in/yr between 1994 and 2005.

However, a recent study suggests a much warmer planet in relatively recent **geological times**:

> Scientists who probed 2 km (1.2 mi) through a Greenland glacier to recover the oldest plant DNA on record said that the planet was far warmer hundreds of thousands of years ago than is generally believed. **DNA** of trees, plants and insects including butterflies and spiders from beneath the southern Greenland glacier was estimated to date to 450,000 to 900,000 years ago, according to the remnants retrieved from this long-vanished boreal forest. That view contrasts sharply with the prevailing one that a lush forest of this kind could not have existed in Greenland any later than 2.4 million years ago. These DNA samples suggest that the temperature probably reached 10 °C (50 °F) in the summer and −17 °C (1.4 °F) in the winter. They also indicate that during the last **interglacial** period, 130,000–116,000 years ago, when temperatures were on average 5 °C (9 °F) higher than now, the glaciers on Greenland did not completely melt away

In 1996, the American Top of the World expedition found the world's northernmost island off Greenland: **ATOW1996**. An even more northerly candidate was spotted during the return from the expedition, but its status is yet to be confirmed.

In 2007, the existence of a new island was announced. Named "**Uunartoq Qeqertaq**" (English: *Warming Island*), this island has always been present off the coast of Greenland, but was covered by a glacier. This glacier was discovered in 2002 to be shrinking rapidly, and by 2007 had completely melted away, leaving the exposed island.

The island was named Place of the Year by the Oxford Atlas of the World in 2007. Ben Keene, the atlas's editor, commented: "In the last two or three decades, global warming has reduced the size of glaciers throughout the **Arctic** and earlier this year, news sources confirmed what climate scientists already knew: water, not rock, lay beneath this **ice bridge** on the east coast of Greenland. More islets are likely to appear as the sheet of frozen water covering the world's largest island continues to melt."

Some controversy surrounds the history of the island, specifically over whether the island might have been revealed during a brief warm period in Greenland during the mid-20th century.

For additional analytical, business and investment opportunities information,
please contact Global Investment & Business Center, USA
at (703) 370-8082. Fax: (703) 370-8083. E-mail: ibpusa3@gmail.com
Global Business and Investment Info Databank - www.ibpus.com

TOPOGRAPHY

About 81% of Greenland's surface is covered by the Greenland ice sheet. The weight of the ice has depressed the central land area into a basin shape, whose base lies more than 300 m (984 ft) below the surrounding ocean. Elevations rise suddenly and steeply near the coast.

GREENLAND ECONOMY

Rank	186rd out of 227rd
Currency	1 Danish krone (DKr) = 100 øre
Fiscal year	calendar year
Trade organisations	none
Statistics	
GDP	$1.989 billion
GDP growth	-2%
GDP per capita	$36,500
GDP by sector	agriculture: industry: services:
Population below poverty line	9.2%
Gini index	NA%
Labour force	28,240 (January 2009)
Labour force by occupation	agriculture: 4.9% industry: 31.9% services: 63.2%
Unemployment	6.8%
Main industries	fish processing (mainly shrimp and Greenland halibut); Oil, gold, niobium, tantalite, uranium, iron and diamond mining; handicrafts, hides skins, small shipyards
External	
Exports	$485 million
Export goods	fish and fish products 72%, metals 10%, Other 10%, Oil 8%
Main export partners	Denmark 63.7%, 15.7% Other, Japan 12.1%, China 8.5%
Imports	$867 million
Import goods	machinery and transport equipment, manufactured goods, food, petroleum products
Main import partners	Denmark 59.5%, Sweden 20.8%, Other 13.1%, UK 6.6% (2010)
Public finances	
Public debt	$58 million
Revenues	$1.47 billion
Expenses	$1.51 billion , including capital expenditures of $83 million
Economic aid	• $512 million subsidy from Denmark

The **Economy of Greenland** can be characterized as small, mixed and vulnerable.* The present economy consists of a big **public sector** and comprehensive foreign trade, which has resulted in an economy with periods of strong growth, considerable inflation, unemployment problems and extreme dependence on capital inflow from **Denmark** and use of outside, mainly Danish, skilled labour.*

The economy is critically dependent on exports of **fish,*** **whaling** and **textiles** and substantial support from the Danish Government, which supplies about half of government revenues.

Unemployment remains very high and GDP per capita is similar to the average European economies.

The effective starting point of the modern economy of **Greenland** was the mercantile expedition led by missionary **Hans Egede**, sent by the **Kingdom of Denmark** in 1721. This established the settlement of **Godthåb** and re-established Danish sovereignty in Greenland. The Danish government was initially very protective of what it considered a fragile Greenlandic culture, effectively sealing it off from international commerce and maintaining a strict monopoly on Greenlandic trade, allowing only small scale barter (**troaking**) with Scottish whalers.

RECENT HISTORY

After **World War II**, reforms of the Greenlandic economy were proposed. The G-50 Report was presented in 1950 by the Danish grand commission. The commission comprised Landsrådene (the highest Greenlandic council) and Danish economists. The report outlined a program to transform Greenland from a **subsistence economy** to a modern **welfare state**. The state would be based on the Danish model, and would be sponsored by Denmark. Following this report, Greenland was made an equal part of the Danish Kingdom in 1953, and Home Rule was granted in 1979.

Greenland left the **European Economic Community** in February 1985,mostly due to EEC fishery policy and partly due to the EEC-wide ban on sealskin products. Effectively the only ties Greenland now has with the **EU** are via Denmark; most EU laws do not apply to Greenland. However Greenland enjoys preferential access to EU markets.

During the 1950s and 1960s the Danish government introduced an urbanization and modernization program, aimed at creating an urban economic environment in Greenland, by expanding the coastal towns. People from the surrounding small settlements were rehoused in hastily built houses, such as the infamous **Blok P**, and modern fishing practices were introduced. The program was intended to reduce costs by improving access to education and health care, and by providing employees for the cod fisheries, which grew rapidly during the early 1960s but have since effectively collapsed. This **urbanization** has resulted in continuing social problems, such as unemployment and alcoholism.

The Greenland economy shrank in the early 1990s, but since 1993 has grown again. The Greenland Home Rule Government (GHRG) has pursued a tight fiscal policy since the late 1980s which has helped the public budget and lowered inflation. From 1990, Greenland registered a foreign trade deficit following the closure of the Maarmorilik **lead** and **zinc** mine.

SECTORS OF THE ECONOMY

The Greenland economy is extremely dependent on exports of fish and on support from the Danish Government, which supplies about half of government revenues. The public sector, including publicly-owned enterprises and the municipalities, plays the dominant role in the economy.

OIL AND NATURAL RESOURCES

Deposits of many metals are known to exist. These include gold, nickel, platinum group elements, copper, lead, zinc, molybdenum, iron, niobium, tantalum, uranium, and specialty metals including rare earth elements; as well as coal and diamonds.[*] Prospectors are currently seeking commercially viable deposits. The BMP (Bureau of Minerals and Petroleum) is promoting

Greenland as an attractive destination for prospectors.* Greenland was formerly the world's premier source of natural **cryolite**, but by the late 1980s the reserves at Ivittuut had been depleted. However, with advances in mining technology and increases in mineral prices, previously closed mines are being reopened, such as the lead and zinc mine at Maarmorilik, and the gold mine at Nalunaq.

Companies are exploring **hydrocarbon** and **mineral** deposits. There have been several offshore licensing rounds since 2002, with a number of successful bids by multinational oil companies in partnership with **NUNAOIL** the state oil company for blocks. Press reports in early 2007 indicated that two international **aluminum** companies were considering building **smelters** in Greenland using local hydroelectric power.

While the GHRG (Greenland Home Rule Government) has primary sovereignty over mineral deposits on the mainland, as laid down in the 2008 treaty, oil resources are within the domain of the Danish exclusive economic zone. **Exploring for oil** has been ongoing since the 1970s, when a series of five dry wells were drilled, and there was a further dry well in the early 2000s. In 2010 British petrochemical company Cairns Oil reported "the first firm indications" of commercially viable oil deposits.

TOURISM

Tourism has some near-term potential, but this is limited by the short summers and high costs. **Air Greenland** and **Continental Airlines** had direct flights from the U.S. east coast from May 2007 to April 2008, but these are now discontinued.

AGRICULTURE, HORTICULTURE AND FORESTRY

Agriculture is presently of little importance in the economy, but **climate change** has enabled its expansion, by obtaining higher production of existing crops, introducing new ones, and extending the cultivated areas.Roughly 1% of the total land area can be used for growing crops. Presently 10% of all potatoes consumed in Greenland are produced locally, with a projection of 15% by 2020. Due to the lengthening of the productive season new crops have been introduced, such as apples, strawberries, broccoli, cauliflower, cabbage and carrots. In southern Greenland the growing season is mid-May through to mid-September, on average three weeks longer than a decade ago.

IMPORTANT INFORMATION FOR UNDERSTANDING DENMARK

PROFILE

Geography*
Area: 43,094 sq. km. (16,639 sq. mi.); slightly smaller than Vermont and New Hampshire combined.
Cities: *Capital*--Copenhagen (pop. 538,031 in Copenhagen and 1,697,490 in the Capital Region, October 2010). *Other cities*--Aarhus (310,653), Aalborg (198,501), Odense (190,147).
Terrain: Low and flat or slightly rolling; highest elevation is 173 m. (568 ft.).
Climate: Temperate. The terrain, location, and prevailing westerly winds make the weather changeable.

*Excluding Greenland and the Faroe Islands

People

Nationality: *Noun--*Dane(s). *Adjective--*Danish.
Population: 5,557,709.
Annual population growth rate (2010): 1%.
Ethnic groups: Scandinavian, Inuit, Faroese, Turkish, German, Polish, Iraqi, Lebanese, Bosnian, Pakistani, Yugoslav (former), Somali, Iranian, Vietnamese, British, Afghan-.
Religious membership: Danish National Evangelical Lutheran Church 80.7%; Muslim about 4%. *Other--*majority consisting of Protestant denominations and Roman Catholics; also 19 Muslim, 3 Jewish, 6 Buddhist, and 8 Hindu religious communities recognized by the state.
Languages: Danish, Faroese, Greenlandic (Inuit dialect), some German. English is the predominant second language.
Education: *Years compulsory--*9. *Attendance--*100%. *Literacy--*99%.
Health*: *Infant mortality rate* (2009)--3.6/1,000. *Life expectancy--*men 76.5 years, women 80.8 years.
Work force: 2.69 million. Employment: *Industry, construction, and utilities--*20%; *government--*33%; *private services--*44%; *agriculture and fisheries--*3%.

*Excluding Greenland and the Faroe Islands

Government
Type: Constitutional monarchy.
Constitution: June 5, 1953.
Branches: *Executive--*queen (head of state), prime minister (head of government), cabinet. *Legislative--*unicameral parliament (Folketing). *Judicial--*appointed Supreme Court.
Political parties (represented in parliament): Venstre (Liberal), Social Democratic, Danish People's, Social Liberal, Socialist People's, Unity List, Liberal Alliance, Conservative.
Suffrage: Universal adult (18 years of age).
Administrative subdivisions: 5 regions and 98 municipalities.

Economy
 Agriculture, fisheries, and extractive industries (4.5% of GDP, 2010): *Products--*meat, milk, grains, seeds, hides, fur skin, fish and shellfish.
Industry (19.1% of GDP): *Types--*industrial and construction equipment, food processing, electronics, chemicals, pharmaceuticals, furniture, textiles, windmills, and ships.
Natural resources: *North Sea--*oil and gas, fish. *Greenland--*fish and shrimp, potential for hydrocarbons and minerals, including zinc, lead, molybdenum, uranium, gold, platinum. *The Faroe Islands--*fish, potential for hydrocarbons.
Trade (2010, goods): *Exports--*$96.744 billion: industrial production/manufactured goods 73.3% (of which machinery and instruments were 21.4%, and fuels, chemicals, etc. 26%); agricultural products and others for consumption 18.7% (meat and meat products were 5.5% of total export; fish and fish products 2.9%). *Imports--*$84.409 billion: raw materials and semi-manufactures 37.4%; consumer goods 17.9%; capital equipment 21.7%; transport equipment 9.7%; fuels 8.0%. *Major trade partners, exports--*Germany 16.8%, Sweden 13.3%, U.K. 7.8%, U.S. 6.6%, Norway 6.3%, Holland 4.4%. *Major trade partners, imports--*Germany 20.8%, Sweden 13.3%, Holland 7.1%, U.K. 6.0%, China 7.6%, Norway 3.9%, U.S. 3.2%.
Official exchange rate (average): 5.62567 kroner=U.S. $1.

PEOPLE AND HISTORY

The Danes, a homogeneous Gothic-Germanic people, have inhabited Denmark since prehistoric times. Danish is the principal language. English is a required school subject, and fluency is high. A small German-speaking minority lives in southern Jutland; a mostly Inuit population inhabits Greenland; and the Faroe Islands have a Nordic population with its own language. Education is compulsory from ages seven to 16 and is free through the university level.

For additional analytical, business and investment opportunities information,
please contact Global Investment & Business Center, USA
at (703) 370-8082. Fax: (703) 370-8083. E-mail: ibpusa3@gmail.com
Global Business and Investment Info Databank - www.ibpus.com

Although religious freedom is guaranteed, the state-supported Evangelical Lutheran Church has a membership of 80.7% of the population. Several other Christian denominations, as well as other major religions, find adherents in Denmark. Islam is now the second-largest religion in Denmark, with the number of Muslims in Denmark estimated at 3.6% of the population.

During the Viking period (9th-11th centuries), Denmark was a great power based on the Jutland Peninsula, the Island of Zealand, and the southern part of what is now Sweden. In the early 11th century, King Canute united Denmark and England for almost 30 years.

Viking raids brought Denmark into contact with Christianity, and in the 12th century, crown and church influence increased. By the late 13th century, royal power had waned, and the nobility forced the king to grant a charter, considered Denmark's first constitution. Although the struggle between crown and nobility continued into the 14th century, Queen Margrethe I succeeded in uniting Denmark, Norway, Sweden, Finland, the Faroe Islands, Iceland, and Greenland under the Danish crown. Sweden and Finland left the union in 1520; however, Norway remained until 1814. Iceland, in a "personal union" under the king of Denmark after 1918, became independent in 1944.

The Reformation was introduced in Denmark in 1536. Denmark's provinces in today's southwestern Sweden were lost in 1658, and Norway was transferred from the Danish to the Swedish crown in 1814, following the defeat of Napoleon, with whom Denmark was allied.

The Danish liberal movement gained momentum in the 1830s, and in 1849 Denmark became a constitutional monarchy. After the war with Prussia and Austria in 1864, Denmark was forced to cede Schleswig-Holstein to Prussia and adopt a policy of neutrality. Toward the end of the 19th century, Denmark inaugurated important social and labor market reforms, laying the basis for the present welfare state.

Denmark remained neutral during World War I. Despite its declaration of neutrality at the beginning of World War II, it was invaded by the Germans in 1940 and occupied until liberated by the Allied forces in May 1945. Resistance against the Germans was sporadic until late 1943. By then better organized, the resistance movement and other volunteers undertook a successful rescue mission in which nearly the entire Jewish population of Denmark was shipped to Sweden (whose neutrality was honored by Germany). However, extensive studies are still being undertaken for the purpose of establishing a clearer picture of the degree of Danish cooperation--official and corporate--with the occupying power. Denmark became a charter member of the United Nations and was one of the original signers of the North Atlantic Treaty.

Cultural Achievements
Denmark's rich intellectual heritage has made multifaceted contributions to modern culture. The discoveries of astronomer Tycho Brahe (1546-1601), the work of geologist, anatomist, and bishop Blessed Niels Steensen (1639-86--beatified in 1988 by Pope John Paul II), and the contributions of Nobel laureates Niels Bohr (1885-1962) to atomic physics and Niels Finsen (1860-1904) to medical research indicate the range of Danish scientific achievement. The fairy tales of Hans Christian Andersen (1805-75), the philosophical essays of Soeren Kierkegaard (1813-55), and the short stories of Karen Blixen (pseudonym Isak Dinesen; 1885-1962) have earned international recognition, as have the symphonies of Carl Nielsen (1865-1931). Danish applied art and industrial design have won many awards for excellence, with the term "Danish Design" becoming synonymous with high quality, craftsmanship, and functionalism. Among the leaders in architecture and design was Arne Jacobsen (1902-1971), the "father of modern Danish design." Georg Jensen (1866-1935) was known for outstanding modern design in silver, and "Royal Copenhagen" is among the finest porcelains. Entertainer and pianist Victor Borge (1909-2000), who emigrated to the United States under Nazi threat in 1940 and became a naturalized U.S. citizen, had a worldwide following.

The Danish Film Institute, one of the oldest in Scandinavia, holds daily public screenings of Danish and international movies in their original language and works to maintain and restore important archival prints. Movie directors who have won international acclaim include Gabriel Axel (Babette's Feast, 1987 Oscar for Best Foreign Film), Bille August (Buster's World, 1984; Pelle the Conqueror, 1988 Oscar for Best Foreign Film; The House of the Spirits, 1993), Lars von Trier (Breaking the Waves, 1996; Dancer in the Dark, 2000 Cannes Golden Palm; and Antichrist 2009, Nordic Council's Film Prize 2009), and Susanne Bier (In a Better World, 2011 Golden Globe for Best Foreign Language Film). Danes became involved early on in the "Dogma film" genre's development, in which small, hand-held digital cameras permitted greater rapport between director and actor and gave a documentary film feel to increasingly realistic works. Examples of the Dogma concept include von Trier's The Idiots (1998) and Dogville (2003, starring Nicole Kidman), Thomas Vinterberg's The Celebration (1998 Cannes Special Jury prize), Soeren Kragh-Jacobsen's Mifune's Last Song (1999 Berlin Silver Bear award), and Lone Scherfig's Italian for Beginners (2000 Berlin Silver Bear award). Mads Mikkelsen is one of Denmark's best-known actors internationally, with film roles in King Arthur (2004), Casino Royale (2006), After the Wedding (2006, which was nominated for an Oscar), and Clash of The Titans (2010).

The Louisiana Museum north of Copenhagen, "Arken" south of Copenhagen, and the North Jutland Art Museum in Aalborg showcase international collections of modern art. The State Museum of Art and the Glyptotek, both in Copenhagen, contain masterpieces of Danish and international art. Denmark's National Museum building in central Copenhagen holds most of the state's anthropological and archeological treasures, with notable prehistoric and Viking Age collections; two of its best satellite collections are the Viking Ship Museum in Roskilde west of the metropolis and the Open Air Museum in a nearby northern suburb, where buildings have been transported from their original locations around the country and reassembled on plots specially landscaped to evoke the original site. The Museum of Applied Art and Industrial Design in Copenhagen exhibits the best in Danish design. The internationally-known Royal Copenhagen Porcelain Factory exports worldwide. Danish ceramic designers have included Bjoern Wiinblad, whose whimsical creations first appeared in the 1950s, Gertrude Vasegaard, and Michael Geertsen.

Denmark has a number of impressive castles, many of which have been converted to museums. Frederiksborg Castle, on a manmade island in a lake north of Copenhagen, was restored after a catastrophic fire in the 1800s and features important collections and manicured gardens. Kronborg (or Hamlet's) Castle in Helsingoer (Elsinore), which once exacted tribute from passing ships, holds furniture and art collections of the period and hosts touring summer productions of Shakespearean works. Copenhagen's Rosenborg Castle, with public gardens in the heart of the city, houses the kingdom's crown jewels.

For American readers, probably the best-known contemporary Danish writer is Peter Hoeg (Smilla's Sense of Snow; Borderliners). Poems by poet, novelist, playwright, and screenwriter Klaus Rifbjerg and by poet, short-story writer, and composer Benny Andersen have been translated into English by Curbstone Press. Suzanne Broegger's works focus on the changing roles of women in society. Kirsten Thorup's "Baby" won the 1980 Pegasus Prize and was printed in English by the University of Louisiana Press. The psychological thrillers of Anders Bodelsen and political thrillers by Leif Davidsen also appear in English.

In music, Hans Abrahamsen and Per Noergaard are two well-known composers, and Abrahamsen's works have been performed by the National Symphony Orchestra in Washington, DC. Other international names are Poul Ruders, Bo Holten, and Karl Aage Rasmussen. Danes such as bass player Niels Henning Oersted Petersen have won broad international recognition, and the Copenhagen Jazz Festival held each year in July attracts international jazz enthusiasts. Rock and roll band Metallica's drummer, Lars Ulrich, is Danish.

The Royal Danish Ballet specializes in the work of Danish choreographer August Bournonville (1805-79). Danish dancers also feature regularly on the U.S. ballet scene, notably Peter Martins as head of New York City Ballet.

Cultural Policy

The Ministry of Cultural Affairs was created in 1961. Cultural life and meaningful leisure time were then and remain now subjects of debate by politicians and parliament as well as the general public. The democratization of cultural life promoted by the government's 1960s cultural policy has come to terms with the older "genteel culture;" broader concepts of culture now generally accepted include amateur and professional cultural, media, sports, and leisure-time activities.

Denmark's cultural policy is characterized by decentralized funding, program responsibility, and institutions. Danish cultural direction differs from that of other countries with a Ministry of Culture and a stated policy in that special laws govern each cultural field--e.g., the Theater Act of 1990 (as amended) and the Music Law of 1976 (as amended).

The Ministry of Cultural Affairs includes among its responsibilities international cultural relations; training of librarians and architects; copyright legislation; and subsidies to archives, libraries, museums, literature, music, arts and crafts, theater, and film production. During 1970-82, the Ministry also recognized protest movements and street manifestations as cultural events, because social change was viewed as an important goal of Danish cultural policy. Danish governments exercise caution in moderating this policy and practice. Radio and TV broadcasting also fall under the Ministry of Culture.

Government expenditures for culture totaled just over 1.0% of the public budget in 2008 and government expenditures for culture totaled 0.33% of gross domestic product (GDP). Viewed against the government's firm objective to limit public expenditures, contributions are unlikely to increase in the future and have remained about $1.2 billion for the last couple of years. Municipal and county governments assume a relatively large share of the costs for cultural activities in their respective districts, 57% to the government's 43%. Most support goes to libraries and archives, theater, museums, arts and crafts training, and films.

Foundations

Large, private foundations play an important part in supporting the spectrum of cultural activities from supporting struggling young artists to paying for large-scale restoration work, operating museums, and supporting scientific research. Private organizations such as the New Carlsberg Foundation, the Velux Foundation, and the Augustinus Foundation enjoy an almost semi-public stature due to their long records of working for the public good. U.S.-style corporate sponsorship of the arts is very limited in Denmark.

DEMOGRAPHICS

According to 2009 figures from Statistics Denmark, 90.5% of Denmark's population of over 5.4 million was of **Danish** descent. Many of the remaining 9.5% were immigrants—or descendants of recent immigrants—from **Bosnia and Herzegovina**, neighbouring countries, South Asia, and Western Asia. Many have arrived since the "Alien law" (*Udlændingeloven*) was enacted in 1983, which allows for the immigration of family members of those who had already arrived. There are also small groups of **Inuit** from Greenland and **Faroese**.During recent years, anti mass-immigration sentiment has resulted in some of the toughest **immigration laws** in the European Union. The number of residence permits granted related to labour and to people from within the **EU/EEA** has increased since implementation of new immigration laws in 2001. The number of immigrants allowed into Denmark for family reunification decreased 70% between 2001 and 2006

For additional analytical, business and investment opportunities information,
please contact Global Investment & Business Center, USA
at (703) 370-8082. Fax: (703) 370-8083. E-mail: ibpusa3@gmail.com
Global Business and Investment Info Databank - www.ibpus.com

to 4,198.(see **24 year rule**) During the same period the number of asylum permits granted has decreased by 82.5% to 1,095, reflecting a 84% decrease in **asylum seekers** to 1,960.

Denmark's population is 5,475,791, giving Denmark a population density of 129.16 inhabitants per km² (334.53 per sq mi). As in most countries, the population is not distributed evenly. Although the land area east of the **Great Belt** only makes up 9,622 km² (3,715 sq mi), 22.7% of Denmark's land area, it has 45% (2,465,348) of the population. The average population density of this area is 256.2 inhabitants per km² (663.6 per sq mi). The average density in the west of the country (32,772 km²/12,653 sq mi) is 91.86/km² (237.91 per sq mi) (3,010,443 people) (2008).

The **median** age is 39.8 years, with 0.98 males per female. 98.2% of the population (age 15 and up) is literate. The **birth rate** is 1.74 children born per woman (2006 est.). Despite the low birth rate, the population is still growing at an average annual rate of 0.33%. An international study conducted by Adrian White at Leicester University in 2006 showed that the population of Denmark had the highest life satisfaction in the world.

Danish is the **official language** and is spoken throughout the country. English and German are the most widely-spoken foreign languages.

A total of 1,516,126 Americans reported **Danish** ancestry in the 2006 American Community Survey. According to the 2006 census, there were 200,035 Canadians with **Danish** background.

RELIGION

Church of Denmark			
year	population	members	percentage
1984	5,113,500	4,684,060	91.6%
1990	5,135,409	4,584,450	89.3%
2000	5,330,500	4,536,422	85.1%
2005	5,413,600	4,498,703	83.3%
2007	5,447,100	4,499,343	82.6%
2008	5,475,791	4,494,589	82.1%
2009	5,511,451	4,492,121	81.5%
2010	5,534,738	4,479,214	80.9%
2011	5.560.628	4,469,109	80.4%

statistical data 1984–2002, 1990–2009 and 2010-2011. Source Kirkeministeriet

According to official statistics from January 2011, 80.4% of the population of Denmark are members of the **Danish National Church** (*Den Danske Folkekirke*), a **Lutheran** church that was made the official state religion by the **Constitution of Denmark**. This is down 0.6% compared to the year earlier and 1.2% down compared to two years earlier. Article 6 of the Constitution states that the **Royal Family** must belong to this Church, though the rest of the population is free to adhere to other faiths. About 15% of the Danes do not belong to any denomination.

Denmark's **Muslims** make up less than 2% of the population and is the country's second largest religious community. As per an overview of various religions and denominations by the Danish Foreign Ministry, other groups comprise less than 1% of the population individually and approximately 2% when taken all together.

According to the most recent **Eurobarometer Poll** 2005, 31% of Danish citizens responded that "they believe there is a God", whereas 49% answered that "they believe there is some sort of

For additional analytical, business and investment opportunities information, please contact Global Investment & Business Center, USA at (703) 370-8082. Fax: (703) 370-8083. E-mail: ibpusa3@gmail.com Global Business and Investment Info Databank - www.ibpus.com

spirit or life force" and 19% that "they do not believe there is any sort of spirit, God or life force". According to a 2005 study by Zuckerman, Denmark has the third highest proportion of **atheists** and agnostics in the world, estimated to be between 43% and 80%.

For more than a hundred years after the Reformation, Lutheranism was the only legal religion in Denmark, but in 1682 the state recognised three other faiths: **Roman Catholicism**, **the Reformed Church** and **Judaism**. Until the recent immigration of Muslims, these three were practically the only non-Lutheran religions practiced in Denmark. As of 2005, 19 Muslim communities have been officially recognised. **Forn Siðr** (English: Old Custom), based on the much older, native pagan religion, gained official recognition in November 2003.

Religious societies and churches do not need to be state-recognised in Denmark and can be granted the right to perform weddings and other ceremonies without this recognition.

EDUCATION

The Danish education system provides access to **primary school**, **secondary school** and most kinds of higher education. Attendance at "**Folkeskole**" or equivalent education is compulsory for a minimum of 9 years (aged 7 to 16). Equivalent education could be in private schools or classes attended at home. About 99% of students attend primary school, 86% attend secondary school, and 41% pursue **further education**. All college education in Denmark is free; there are no tuition fees to enroll in courses. Students in secondary school or higher and aged 18 or above may apply for student support which provides fixed financial support, disbursed monthly.

Primary school in Denmark is called "**den Danske Folkeskole**" ("Danish Public School"). It runs from the introductory "kindergarten class"/0'th grade ("børnehaveklasse"/ "0. Klasse") to **10th grade**, though 10th grade is optional. Pupils can alternatively attend "free schools" ("Friskole"), or private schools ("Privatskole"), i.e. schools that are not under the administration of the **municipalities**, such as **Christian schools** or **Waldorf schools**. The **Programme for International Student Assessment**, coordinated by the **OECD**, ranked Denmark's education as the 24th best in the world in 2006, being neither significantly higher nor lower than the OECD average.

Following graduation from *Folkeskolen*, there are several other educational opportunities, including *Gymnasium* (academically oriented upper secondary education), **Higher Preparatory Examination (HF)** (similar to *Gymnasium*, but one year shorter), **Higher Technical Examination Programme (HTX)** (with focus on **mathematics** and engineering), and **Higher Commercial Examination Programme** (HHX) (with a focus on trade and business), as well as **vocational education**, training young people for work in specific **trades** by a combination of teaching and **apprenticeship**.

Gymnasium (STX), HF, HTX and HHX aim at qualifying pupils for higher education in universities and colleges. Denmark also teaches the **IB Diploma**.

Denmark has several **universities**; the largest and oldest are the **University of Copenhagen** (founded 1479) and **Aarhus University** (founded 1928). There are thirteen **Danish Nobel laureates**.

Danish universities and other Danish higher education institutions also offer international students a range of opportunities for obtaining an internationally recognised qualification in Denmark. Many programmes are taught in English, including Bachelor's, Master's, PhD, exchange and summer school programmes

Folkehøjskolerne, ("Folk high schools") introduced by politician, clergyman and poet **N.F.S. Grundtvig** in the 19th century, are social, informal education structures without tests or grades but with an emphasis on communal learning, self-discovery, enlightenment and learning how to develop your own opinions through open debate. Grundtvig helped to develop an understanding of the relationship between individual and society, and he has had a significant influence on the didactic ideas underlying Danish education

GOVERNMENT

Denmark is a constitutional monarchy. Queen Margrethe II has largely ceremonial functions; probably her most significant formal power lies in her right to appoint the prime minister and cabinet ministers, who are responsible for administration of the government. However, she must consult with parliamentary leaders to determine the public's will, since the cabinet may be dismissed by a vote of no confidence in the Folketing (parliament). Cabinet members are occasionally recruited from outside the Folketing.

The 1953 constitution established a unicameral Folketing of not more than 179 members, of whom two are elected from the Faroe Islands and two from Greenland. Elections are held at least every 4 years, but the prime minister can dissolve the Folketing at any time and call for new elections. Folketing members are elected by a complex system of proportional representation; any party receiving at least 2% of the total national vote receives representation. The result is a multiplicity of parties, none of which holds a majority. Electorate participation normally is around 80%-85%.

The judicial branch consists of 22 local courts, two high courts, several special courts (e.g., arbitration and maritime), and a Supreme Court of 15 judges appointed by the crown on the government's recommendation.

Since a structural reform of local government was passed by the Folketing in 2004 and 2005, Denmark is divided into five regions and 98 municipalities. The regions and municipalities are both led by councils elected every 4 years, but only the municipal councils have the power to levy taxes. Regional councils are responsible for health services and regional development, while the municipal councils are responsible for day care, elementary schools, care for the elderly, culture, environment, and roads.

The Faroe Islands enjoy home rule and Greenland has expanded "self-rule," with the Danish Government represented locally by high commissioners. These local governments are responsible for most domestic affairs, with foreign relations, monetary affairs, and defense falling to the Danish Government.

Principal Government Officials

Cabinet of Helle Thorning-Schmidt II	3 February 2014 (Incumbent)	Social Democrats Danish Social Liberal Party	SR Cabinet

Portfolio	Minister	Took office	Left office	Party
Prime Minister's Office				
Prime Minister	Helle Thorning-Schmidt	3 February 2014	Incumbent	Social Democrats

Deputy Prime Minister, Minister of Economy and Interior	Margrethe Vestager	3 February 2014	2 September 2014	Social Liberals
	Morten Østergaard	2 September 2014	Incumbent	Social Liberals
Ministry of Foreign Affairs				
Minister for Foreign Affairs	Martin Lidegaard	3 February 2014	Incumbent	Social Liberals
Minister for Trade and Development Cooperation	Mogens Jensen	3 February 2014	Incumbent	Social Democrats
Ministry of Finance				
Minister for Finance	Bjarne Corydon	3 February 2014	Incumbent	Social Democrats
Ministry of Justice				
Minister for Justice	Karen Hækkerup	3 February 2014	Incumbent	Social Democrats
Ministry of Defence				
Minister for Defence	Nicolai Wammen	3 February 2014	Incumbent	Social Democrats
Ministry of Culture				
Minister for Culture and Church	Marianne Jelved	3 February 2014	Incumbent	Social Liberals
Ministry of Taxation				
Minister for Taxation	Morten Østergaard	3 February 2014	2 September 2014	Social Liberals
	Benny Engelbrecht	2 September 2014	Incumbent	Social Democrats
Ministry of Science, Innovation and Higher Education				
Minister for Research, Innovation and Higher Education	Sofie Carsten Nielsen	3 February 2014	Incumbent	Social Liberals
Ministry of Economic and Business Affairs				
Minister for Business and Growth	Henrik Sass Larsen	3 February 2014	Incumbent	Social Democrats
Ministry of Housing, Urban and Rural Affairs				
Minister for the City, Housing and Rural Affairs	Carsten Hansen	3 February 2014	Incumbent	Social Democrats
Ministry of Employment				
Minister for Employment	Mette Frederiksen	3 February 2014	Incumbent	Social Democrats
Ministry of Education				
Minister for Education	Christine Antorini	3 February 2014	Incumbent	Social Democrats
Ministry of Social Affairs				
Minister for Integration and	Manu Sareen	3 February	Incumbent	Social

Social Affairs		2014		Liberals	
Ministry of Food, Agriculture and Fisheries (Denmark)					
Minister for Food, Agriculture and Fisheries	Dan Jørgensen	3 February 2014	Incumbent	Social Democrats	
Ministry of Climate and Energy					
Minister for Climate and Energy	Rasmus Helveg Petersen	3 February 2014	Incumbent	Social Liberals	
Ministry of Transport					
Minister for Transport	Magnus Heunicke	3 February 2014	Incumbent	Social Democrats	
Ministry of Health					
Minister for Health and Prevention	Nick Hækkerup	3 February 2014	Incumbent	Social Democrats	
Ministry of the Environment					
Minister for the Environment	Kirsten Brosbøl	3 February 2014	Incumbent	Social Democrats	

Ambassador to the United States--Peter Taksoe-Jensen
Ambassador to the United Nations--Carsten Staur

Denmark maintains an embassy at 3200 Whitehaven Street NW, Washington, DC 20008-3683 (tel. 202-234-4300). Danish consulates general are located in Chicago and New York.

POLITICAL CONDITIONS

Political life in Denmark is orderly and democratic. Political changes occur gradually through a process of consensus, and political methods and attitudes are generally moderate. Growing numbers of immigrants and refugees throughout the 1990s, and less than successful integration policies, however, have led over the last decade to growing support for populist anti-immigrant parties in addition to several revisions of already-tight immigration laws, with the latest revision taking effect August 10, 2009. However, the left-of-center government that took office October 3, 2011 has indicated it will seek to ease immigration requirements.

The Social Democratic Party, historically identified with a well-organized labor movement but today appealing more broadly to the middle class, held power either alone or in coalition for most of the postwar period except from 1982 to 1993. From February 1993 to November 2001, Social Democratic Party chairman Poul Nyrup Rasmussen led a series of different minority coalition governments, which all included the centrist Social Liberal Party. However, with immigration high on the November 2001 election campaign agenda, the Danish People's Party doubled its number of parliamentary seats; this was a key factor in bringing into power a new minority right-of-center coalition government led by Liberal Party chief Anders Fogh Rasmussen (no relation to Nyrup Rasmussen).

Parliamentary elections held November 13, 2007 returned the coalition to government for another term of up to 4 years. In April 2009, after Anders Fogh Rasmussen was elected Secretary General of NATO, he was succeeded as Prime Minister by Lars Loekke Rasmussen (no relation). The coalition consisted of the Liberal Party ("Venstre") and the Conservative Party, holding 63 of 179 seats in the Folketing, and had the parliamentary support of the Danish People's Party, holding another 23 seats.

Following the September 15, 2011 general election, Social Democratic Party leader Helle Thorning-Schmidt formed a three-party minority coalition government with the centrist Social Liberal Party and the leftist Socialist People's Party. The coalition controls 77 of the seats in the Folketing (SDP 44, SLP 17, and SPP 16) and enjoys parliamentary support from the 12 seats held by the far-left Unity List (aka Red-Green Alliance). The opposition Liberal Party holds 47 seats, the Danish People's Party 22 seats, the Liberal Alliance 9 seats, and the Conservative People's Party 8 seats.

Denmark's role in the European Union (EU) remains an important political issue. Denmark emerged from two referenda (June 2, 1992 and May 18, 1993) on the Maastricht Treaty on the European Union with four exemptions (or "opt-outs"): common defense, common currency, EU citizenship, and certain aspects of legal cooperation, including law enforcement. The Amsterdam Treaty was approved in a referendum May 28, 1998, by a 55% majority. Still, the electorate's fear of losing national identity in an integrated Europe and lack of confidence in long-term stability of European economies run deep. These concerns were at the forefront of the September 28, 2000 referendum on Denmark's participation in the third phase of the Economic and Monetary Union (EMU), particularly the common currency, the Euro; more than 53% voted "no," and Denmark retained its "krone" currency unit.

The new government has positioned itself as more openly enthusiastic about the EU than its predecessor. It has promised to hold a referendum on eliminating the defense and justice and home affairs opt-outs, replacing the latter with an opt-in agreement. Denmark is preparing to hold the EU presidency during the first half of 2012. However, the referendum will not be held before the end of the country's EU presidency.

Denmark's relatively quiet and neutral role in international affairs abruptly changed when the Danish newspaper Jyllands-Posten printed 12 caricatures of Mohammed on September 30, 2005. Islamic law prohibits any visual portrayal of Mohammed, and Muslims viewed the caricatures as offensive. In early 2006 Muslims worldwide became infuriated with the Danes, began a boycott of Danish products, and burned Danish flags and the Danish embassies in Damascus and Beirut. The Danish Government sought during the crisis to defend freedom of expression even as it chastised the newspaper for insensitivity toward a religious minority. Jyllands-Posten refused to apologize but expressed regret if anybody felt offended by the cartoons. Several Danish newspapers reprinted the cartoons in a show of support of freedom of expression. The newspaper Politiken later apologized to anyone offended by its decision to reprint one of them. The Danish Government repeatedly reiterated its support for freedom of religion, but some animosity toward Denmark within the international Islamic community lingers.

ECONOMY

Currency	Danish krone (DKK, kr)
Fiscal year	calendar year
Trade organisations	EU, OSCE, WTO, OECD and others
	Statistics
GDP	$313.825 billion (2010 forecast) (nominal; 31st) $200.796 billion (2010 forecast) (PPP; 50th)
GDP growth	-0.4% (2012 est.)
GDP per capita	$36,336 (PPP; 17th)
GDP by sector	agriculture: 4.5%; industry: 19.1%; services: 76.4%
Inflation (CPI)	1.3% (2009)
Population below poverty line	N/A
Gini coefficient	24.7
Labour force	2.92 million
Labour force by occupation	agriculture: 2.5%; industry: 20.2%; services: 77.3% (2005 est.)

Unemployment	8.0%
Average gross salary	4,047 € / 5,464 $, monthly
Average net salary	2,390 € / 3,226 $, monthly
Main industries	petroleum and gas, iron, steel, nonferrous metals, chemicals, food processing, machinery and transportation equipment, textiles and clothing, electronics, construction, furniture and other wood products, shipbuilding and refurbishment, windmills, pharmaceuticals, medical equipment
Ease-of-doing-business rank	4th

External

Exports	$91.49 billion (est.) 33rd
Export goods	machinery and instruments, meat and meat products, dairy products, fish, pharmaceuticals, fashion apparel, furniture, windmills, Christmas trees, potted plants, mink and fox skin, salt, various specialty niche products
Main export partners	Germany 15.9% Sweden 13.5% United Kingdom 9.6% United States 6.6% Norway 6.3% Netherlands 4.6%
Imports	$84.74 billion
Import goods	machinery and equipment, raw materials and semimanufactures for industry, chemicals, grain and foodstuffs, consumer goods
Main import partners	Germany 20.8% Sweden 13.3% Netherlands 7.4% China 6.3% Norway 6.2% United Kingdom 5.6%
Gross external debt	$607.4 billion

Public finances

Public debt	45.3% of GDP
Revenues	$175.4 billion
Expenses	$175.6 billion
Economic aid	ODA, $2.13 billion
Credit rating	AAA (Domestic) AAA (Foreign) AAA (T&C Assessment) (Standard & Poor's)
Foreign reserves	US$86.560 billion

Denmark's industrialized market economy depends on imported raw materials and foreign trade. Within the European Union, Denmark advocates a liberal trade policy. Its standard of living is among the highest in the world, with a GDP per capita of $58,500 making Denmark the 18th richest country in the world in 2010. In 2010, Denmark devoted 0.91% of gross national income (GNI) to foreign aid to less developed countries, including for peace and stability purposes, refugee pre-asylum costs, and environmental purposes in central and eastern Europe and developing countries, making Denmark one of the few countries that are contributing more than the UN goal of 0.7% of GNI to aid. In 2011, Denmark is expected to devote a similar percentage. The new government has said it wants to raise official development assistance to 1% of GNI.

Denmark is a net exporter of food and energy. Its principal exports are machinery, instruments, and food products. The United States is Denmark's largest non-European trading partner, accounting for 5.0% of total Danish goods trade in 2010. Aircraft, computers, machinery, and instruments are the major U.S. exports to Denmark. Among major Danish exports to the United States are industrial machinery, chemical products, furniture, pharmaceuticals, canned ham and pork, windmills, and plastic toy blocks (Lego). In addition, Denmark has a significant services trade with the U.S., a major share of it stemming from Danish-controlled ships engaged in container traffic to and from the United States (notably by Maersk-Line). There were 436 U.S.-owned companies operating in Denmark in 2008, not including financial service companies.

Like the rest of the world, Denmark was affected by the 2008-2009 global economic crisis. Most local observers agree that Denmark is on the path to a slow recovery, with economic growth from the third quarter of 2009 onward. Gross unemployment averaged 6.0% in 2010, up from 2.7% in 2008, and is expected to average 6.2% in 2011; the average length of the unemployment period has increased. Unemployment is not anticipated to decrease before the end of 2012. Private consumption has contracted significantly and is still below pre-crisis levels. The same goes for industrial production, which was pushed to the lowest level in over a decade. Exports fell dramatically--about 20%--also due to the devaluation of trading partners' currencies, especially those of Sweden, Norway, and the U.K. In 2010 exports regained some of the loss with 10% growth; they exceeded pre-crisis levels in the spring of 2011. Export growth has led much of the recent GDP growth but has slowed in the second half of 2011 due to a slowdown in global economic activity. The government estimates GDP growth of 1.3% in 2011 and 1.8% in 2012. The budget surplus of 2008 became a deficit of $8.5 billion in 2009 (2.7% of GDP) and is forecast to be $12.6 billion in 2011 (3.8% of GDP), exceeding the 3% limit set by the Economic and Monetary Union of the EU (EMU).

The 2012 estimate shows a growing deficit of $15.7 billion (4.6% of GDP), while the 2011 deficit will likely be worse than estimated. The government has proposed plans for fiscal consolidation to bring the deficit below 3% of GDP by 2013; as of January 2011, the EU Commission said that Denmark's responses to remedy the budget deficit had been adequate. Following the renewed financial turmoil in the second half of 2011, the fiscal plan may no longer be sufficient. Public debt reached 43.7% of GDP in 2010 but remains well within the 60% limit set by the EMU. It is estimated to increase to 44.4% in 2011.

In addition to the global crisis, Denmark has underlying growth challenges and is projected to have one of the lowest productivity growth rates among Organization for Economic Cooperation and Development (OECD) countries in the decade to come; it dropped from sixth to twelfth place among the richest OECD nations from 1997 to 2007. Denmark is facing demographic challenges that could lead to labor supply shortages by 2015 according to some estimates. Denmark has maintained a stable currency policy since the early 1980s. The krone, formerly linked to the Deutschmark, has been pegged to the Euro since January 1, 1999. The Greek financial crisis has affected Denmark to some extent--as the Euro falls in value, the krone also falls, making Danish exports more competitive. Denmark's contribution to the EU financial support package to Greece was 1.2 billion Euro (approx. $1.6 billion). It is expected that as of 2011, Denmark will not meet the economic convergence criteria for participating in the EMU due to its public deficit rising above the allowed 3% of GDP, but the Danish Government remains committed to meeting the criteria. Prior to the Greek financial crisis, opinion polls showed a majority in favor of the EMU, but with the continued turmoil in the Euro zone, polling at the end of the third quarter of 2011 showed record high support for a "no" vote in the event of a referendum on joining the Euro zone (57% against versus 36% in favor).

No referendum on the EMU/Euro is expected during the life of the current parliament, which could run until 2015, and not until polling shows a significant majority supporting Denmark's entry into the common currency.

Danes are generally proud of their welfare safety net, which ensures that all Danes receive basic health care and need not fear real poverty. However, there is a growing political debate about how government policy should be reformed in order to preserve and strengthen the system. The portion of working-age Danes (16 to 66-year-olds) living mostly on government transfer payments amounts to 24% (2010). The heavy load of government transfer payments burdens other parts of the system. Health care, other than for acute needs, and care for the elderly and children have suffered, while taxes remain among the highest in the world. About one-third of the labor force is employed in the public sector.

Greenland

On June 21, 2009, Greenland assumed increased autonomy under a Self Rule Act, deepening the "home rule" that had been in effect since 1979. Under self rule, the Greenlandic government (Naalakkersuisut) and the Danish Government are recognized as equal partners and Kalaallisut, the Inuit dialect, becomes the official language of Greenland. The Greenland Government intends to take responsibility for additional government functions gradually, such as prisons, criminal justice, courts of law, family law, passports, and mineral resources. The Danish Government freezes its annual block grant at the 2007 level of 3.2 billion kroner ($570 million, 2010 exchange rate). That grant will be adjusted for Danish inflation, though not the often higher Greenlandic inflation, meaning the value in real terms is expected to shrink in coming years. However, Greenland gains rights to its mineral, oil, and natural gas resources: the first 75 million kroner ($13.3 million) from mineral/oil/gas revenues would go to Greenland, with further revenues split equally between the two governments, and with Denmark's share being subtracted from the annual block grant. Once the block grant is eliminated, any additional revenue would be subject to renegotiation between the Danish and Greenlandic governments.

The public sector in Greenland, including publicly-owned enterprises and the municipalities, plays the dominant role in the economy and employs roughly 50% of the workforce. A large part of government revenues still comes from the Danish Government block grant--46% in 2009. The block grant remains an important supplement to GDP. About one-third of government revenue came from taxes in 2009.

Greenland's economy has been relatively unharmed by the global economic crisis. The main sources of income for Greenland are transfers from abroad, the value of fish production, and the direct and indirect effects of mineral exploration. Transfers from abroad are contained in agreements and will not be influenced by international trends, while the value of fisheries and mineral resource exploration is influenced by international economic developments. According to the Greenlandic Economic Council, real GDP is estimated (the most recent national account statistics are from 2007) to have contracted by 1.0% in 2009, followed by a recovery of 2.0% growth in 2010 and 3.0% growth in 2011.

The outlook for 2012 is for zero GDP growth. The recovery was primarily driven by hydrocarbon and mineral exploration and exploitation investments, as well as high levels of construction activity in the capital Nuuk in 2010-2011 and the 2010-2011 increase in the price of fish and shrimp, Greenland's main export. The 2012 outlook is highly uncertain depending on continued exploration activities. A commercial find of hydrocarbons or minerals could add significantly to activities, while disappointments could lead to contraction. Unemployment rose in 2008-2010 after an extended period from 2003 with lower unemployment. Unemployment now seems to have stabilized at the 2010 level. Structural reforms are still needed in order to create a broader business base and economic growth through more efficient use of existing resources in both the public and the private sectors.

Due to its continued dependence on exports of fish (mainly shrimp), which make up 85% of goods exports, Greenland's economy remains sensitive to foreign developments. Greenland has registered a growing foreign trade deficit since the closure of the last remaining lead and zinc mine in 1989. The trade deficit reached $391 million, or 24% of GDP, in 2010. International interest in Greenland's mineral wealth is increasing. International consortia are increasingly active in exploring for hydrocarbon resources off Greenland's western coast; in November 2010, seven exclusive licenses for exploration and exploitation of oil and gas were awarded.

There are international studies indicating the potential of oil and gas fields in northern and northeastern Greenland. The U.S. Geological Survey estimates that up to 17 billion barrels of oil and gas are present in the area between Canada and Northwest Greenland. Cairn Energy carried out three exploration drillings in Greenland in 2010, the first exploration drilling in Greenland in 10 years, and discovered gas and oil-bearing sands in one of the drillings. Drilling continued in 2011 but without significant finds. The U.S. aluminum producer Alcoa in May 2007 concluded a memorandum of understanding with the Greenland Home Rule Government to build an aluminum smelter and associated power generation facility in Greenland to take advantage of abundant hydropower potential, although progress on that project has been delayed. It is estimated that, upon completion, the Alcoa investment would be worth approximately $2.5 billion. Tourism also offers another avenue of economic growth for Greenland, with increasing numbers of cruise lines now operating in Greenland's western and southern waters during the peak summer tourism season.

Faroe Islands
In early 2008, the Faroese economy began to show signs of an impending slowdown. The main difficulty lay with the fishing industry coming under pressure from smaller catches combined with historically high oil prices. Reduced catches, especially of cod and haddock, strained the Faroese economy in 2008-2009. GDP grew 24% (in current prices) between 2004 and 2008 but then contracted by 0.8% in 2008 and by 1.6% in 2009. According to the Governmental Bank of the Faroes (Landsbanki Foroya), the Faroese economy changed from a downturn to growth in 2010, and it is estimated that nominal GDP increased by 3.4% in 2010. The bank predicts that there are prospects for nominal economic growth in 2011 (3.1%) and 2012 (3.5%), but developments in 2011 have brought these estimates down from 5% annually. The main drivers of growth are considerably higher output levels in the fisheries sector and expectations for increased private spending. As households gradually become secure enough to increase consumption further, revenues from tax and duties may increase faster than GDP. These economic developments would reduce government deficits to some extent. This is desirable if the public deficit is to remain at a level where the Faroe Islands can sustain economic fluctuations without losing the confidence of both citizens and international creditors.

The temporary slowdown in the Faroese economy followed a strong performance since the mid-1990s, with annual growth rates averaging close to 6%, mostly as a result of increased fish landings and salmon farming and high and stable export prices. Positive economic development had helped the Faroese Home Rule Government produce increasing budget surpluses that in turn helped to reduce the large public debt, most of it to Denmark. Most of the Faroese who emigrated in the early 1990s (some 10% of the population) due to an economic recession have returned. Unemployment had been low since 2003 and practically non-existent at its lowest level of 1.2% in April 2008, but has since increased sharply, with average unemployment of 5.7% in 2010 and rising to above 7% in early 2011. Unemployment is expected to decrease slightly in 2012 as the economy improves. The currency of the Faroe Islands is the Foroyska kronan. However, it is not an independent currency. Faroese bank notes are Danish bank notes that feature Faroese motifs. There are no Faroese coins.

Initial discoveries of oil in the Faroese area give hope for eventual oil production, which could lay the basis for a more diversified economy and thus less dependence on Danish economic assistance. Aided by an annual subsidy from Denmark corresponding to about 6% of Faroese GDP, the Faroese have a standard of living comparable to that of the Danes and other Scandinavians.

Politically, the present Faroese Home Rule Government has initiated a process toward greater autonomy from Denmark, if not complete secession. In that respect, agreement on how to phase out the Danish subsidy plays a crucial role.

NATIONAL SECURITY

Although Denmark remained neutral during the First World War, its rapid occupation by Nazi Germany in 1940 persuaded most Danes that neutrality was no longer a reliable guarantee of security. Danish security policy is founded on its membership in NATO. Since 1988, Danish budgets and security policy have been set by multi-year agreements supported by a wide parliamentary majority, including government and opposition parties. In 2009, Danish defense expenditures were 1.4% of GDP.

Denmark has been a member of NATO since its founding in 1949, and membership in NATO remains highly popular. There were several serious confrontations between the U.S. and Denmark on security policy in the so-called "footnote era" (1982-88), when a parliamentary majority forced the government to adopt specific national positions on nuclear and arms control issues that were at variance with Alliance policy. With the end of the Cold War, however, Denmark has been an active and supportive member of the Alliance.

FOREIGN RELATIONS

Danish foreign policy is founded upon four cornerstones: the United Nations, NATO, the EU, and Nordic cooperation. Denmark also is a member of, among other organizations, the World Bank and the International Monetary Fund; the World Trade Organization (WTO); the Organization for Security and Cooperation in Europe (OSCE); the Organization for Economic Cooperation and Development (OECD); the Council of Europe; the Nordic Council; the Baltic Council; and the Barents Council. It is a member of the Arctic Council and chaired the organization during 2009-2011. Denmark emphasizes its relations with developing nations. It is a significant donor and one of the few countries to exceed the UN goal of contributing 0.7% of GNP to development assistance.

In the wake of the Cold War, Denmark has been active in international efforts to integrate the countries of Central and Eastern Europe into the West. It has played a leadership role in coordinating Western assistance to the Baltic states (Estonia, Latvia, and Lithuania). The country is a strong supporter of international peacekeeping. Danish forces were heavily engaged in the former Yugoslavia in the UN Protection Force (UNPROFOR), as well as in NATO's Operation Joint Endeavor/Stabilization Force in Bosnia and Herzegovina (IFOR/SFOR), and currently in the Kosovo Force (KFOR). It also participates in UNIFIL (Lebanon) and has twice commanded a NATO maritime task force against piracy off the coast of Somalia. It was an early and very active participant in air operations over Libya in 2011, including ground strike missions.

Danes have at times had a reputation as "reluctant" Europeans. When they rejected ratification of the Maastricht Treaty on June 2, 1992, they put the European Community's (EC) plans for the European Union on hold. In December 1992, the rest of the EC agreed to exempt Denmark from certain aspects of the European Union, including a common defense, a common currency, EU citizenship, and certain aspects of legal cooperation. On this revised basis, a clear majority of Danes approved continued participation in the EU in a second referendum on May 18, 1993, and again in a referendum on the Amsterdam Treaty on May 28, 1998. Denmark has, however, at times also shown strong leadership within the European Union, as it did during its 2002 European Union presidency, when Denmark took a lead role in successful negotiations for the EU's inclusion of 10 new members from Central and Eastern Europe.

For additional analytical, business and investment opportunities information, please contact Global Investment & Business Center, USA at (703) 370-8082. Fax: (703) 370-8083. E-mail: ibpusa3@gmail.com Global Business and Investment Info Databank - www.ibpus.com

Since the September 11, 2001 terrorist attacks in the United States, Denmark has been highly proactive in endorsing and implementing United States, UN, and EU-initiated counter-terrorism measures, just as Denmark has contributed substantially to NATO's International Security Assistance Force (ISAF) in Afghanistan. It currently has about 750 soldiers in Afghanistan, operating without caveat and concentrated in Helmand province. In 2003, Denmark was among the first countries to join Operation Iraqi Freedom (OIF), supplying a submarine, a Corvette-class ship, and military personnel to support OIF's coalition in Iraq. Denmark in the end provided 500 troops to assist with stabilization efforts in Iraq. Denmark withdrew most of its troops from Iraq in August 2007, when Iraqi forces took over security responsibilities in the Basra area where Danish troops had been concentrated. Denmark maintains a small residual troop contingent that supports the NATO Training Mission in Iraq.

U.S.-DANISH RELATIONS

Denmark and the United States have long enjoyed a close and mutually beneficial relationship. Denmark and the United States consult closely on European and other regional political and security matters and cooperate extensively to promote peace and stability well beyond Europe's borders. Denmark largely shares U.S. views on the positive ramifications of NATO enlargement. Danish troops support ISAF-led stabilization efforts in Afghanistan. President George W. Bush made an official working visit to Copenhagen in July 2005, and Prime Minister Anders Fogh Rasmussen also met with President Bush at Camp David in June 2006 and in Crawford, Texas in March 2008. President Barack Obama met with Prime Minister Lars Loekke Rasmussen on October 2, 2009 in Copenhagen and in December 2009 at the Copenhagen climate summit COP-15. Prime Minister Rasmussen visited President Obama in the White House on March 14, 2011.

Denmark's active liberal trade policy in the EU, OECD, and WTO largely coincides with U.S. interests. There are differences of opinion between the U.S. and the EU on how to manage and resolve the global crisis, but not on the importance of action. The U.S. is Denmark's largest non-European trade partner with 5.0% of Danish merchandise trade. Denmark's role in European environmental and agricultural issues and its strategic location at the entrance to the Baltic Sea have made Copenhagen a center for U.S. agencies and the private sector dealing with the Nordic/Baltic region.

American culture--and particularly popular culture, from jazz, rock, and rap to television shows and literature--is very popular in Denmark. More than 300,000 U.S. tourists visit Denmark annually.

The U.S. Air Force (USAF) base and early warning radar facility at Thule, in northwest Greenland, serves as a vital link in Western and NATO defenses. In August 2004, the Danish and Greenland Home Rule governments signed agreements allowing for an upgrade of the Thule early warning radar in connection with a role in the U.S. ballistic missile defense system. The same agreements also created new opportunities for both sides to enhance economic, technical, and environmental cooperation between the United States and Greenland.

Principal U.S. Officials
Ambassador-- Rufus Gifford

Deputy Chief of Mission--Stephen Cristina
Ambassador OMS--Christine Kucera
DCM OMS--Michelle Stokes
Political/Economic Counselor--Richard Bell
Economic Officer--Shawn Waddoups
Political Officer--Edward Messmer
Public Affairs Officer--Robert Kerr

Consul--Robert Jachim
Management Officer--Jonathan Bayat
Environment, Science, Technology, and Health Officer--Edward Canuel
Agricultural Attache--Mary Ellen Smith (resident in The Hague)
Senior Commercial Officer--Frank Carrico (resident in Stockholm)
Defense Attache--Capt. Christopher McDonald, USN
Army Attache--MAJ Michael Cullinane, USA
Air Attache--Lt. Col. John Culton, USAF
Office of Defense Cooperation--Col. Clifford Puckett, USAF
Drug Enforcement Administration--Timothy Moran
Department of Homeland Security (ICE)--J. Michael Netherland
Regional Security Officer--Dimas Jaen
Legal Attache--Gregory Cox

The U.S. Embassy is located at Dag Hammarskjolds Alle 24, 2100 Copenhagen Ø, Denmark (tel. +45 33-41-71-00). The website contains links to U.S. Government agencies at the Embassy and provides a wealth of information on U.S.-Danish relations.

TRAVEL AND BUSINESS INFORMATION

Travel Alerts, Travel Warnings, Trip Registration
The U.S. Department of State's Consular Information Program advises Americans traveling and residing abroad through Country Specific Information, Travel Alerts, and Travel Warnings. **Country Specific Information** exists for all countries and includes information on entry and exit requirements, currency regulations, health conditions, safety and security, crime, political disturbances, and the addresses of the U.S. embassies and consulates abroad. **Travel Alerts** are issued to disseminate information quickly about terrorist threats and other relatively short-term conditions overseas that pose significant risks to the security of American travelers. **Travel Warnings** are issued when the State Department recommends that Americans avoid travel to a certain country because the situation is dangerous or unstable.

For the latest security information, Americans living and traveling abroad should regularly monitor the Department's Bureau of Consular Affairs Internet web site at **http://travel.state.gov**, where current **Worldwide Caution**, **Travel Alerts**, and **Travel Warnings** can be found. The travel.state.gov website also includes information about **passports**, tips for **planning a safe trip** abroad and more. More travel-related information also is available at **http://www.usa.gov/Citizen/Topics/Travel/International.shtml**.

The Department's **Smart Traveler** app for U.S. travelers going abroad provides easy access to the frequently updated official country information, travel alerts, travel warnings, maps, U.S. embassy locations, and more that appear on the travel.state.gov site. Travelers can also set up e-tineraries to keep track of arrival and departure dates and make notes about upcoming trips. The app is compatible with iPhone, iPod touch, and iPad (requires iOS 4.0 or later).

The Department of State encourages all U.S. citizens traveling or residing abroad to register via the **State Department's travel registration** website or at the nearest U.S. embassy or consulate abroad (a link to the registration page is also available through the Smart Traveler app). Registration will make your presence and whereabouts known in case it is necessary to contact you in an emergency and will enable you to receive up-to-date information on security conditions.

Emergency information concerning Americans traveling abroad may be obtained by calling 1-888-407-4747 toll free in the U.S. and Canada or the regular toll line 1-202-501-4444 for callers outside the U.S. and Canada.

Passports

The **National Passport Information Center** (NPIC) is the U.S. Department of State's single, centralized public contact center for U.S. passport information. Telephone: 1-877-4-USA-PPT (1-877-487-2778); TDD/TTY: 1-888-874-7793. Passport information is available 24 hours, 7 days a week. You may speak with a representative Monday-Friday, 8 a.m. to 10 p.m., Eastern Time, excluding federal holidays.

FISHING AND AQUACULTURE IN DENMARK - STRATEGIC INFORMATION AND DEVELOPMENTS

BASIC INFORMATION

The fishing industry in Denmark operates around the coastline, from western **Jutland** to **Bornholm**. While the overall contribution of the fisheries sector to the country's economy is only about 0.5 percent, Denmark is ranked fifth in the world in exports of fish and fish products. Approximately 20,000 Danish people are employed in fishing, aquaculture, and related industries.

Fishing is an important industry in Denmark. There are about 2,700 fishing vessels, crewed by approximately 1,900. There are about 8,000 people employed in the fishing industry as a whole. The total annual catch value is approximately DKK 3.0 billion (€ 0.4 billion). The value of exported fishery products (incl. products based on imported raw material) is DKK 20.5 billion (€ 2.7 billion).

Denmark's coastline measures about 7,300 kilometres (4,500 mi) in length, and supports three types of fishery industries: for **fish meal** and **fish oil**, pelagic fishery for human consumption, and the **demersal fishery** for **white fish**, **lobster** and deep water **prawns**.[2] The key ports for demersal fishing are **Esbjerg**, **Thyborøn**, **Hanstholm**, **Hirtshals**, and **Skagen**. The **North Sea** and **Skagen** account for 80% of the catches.

The Danish **fishing fleet** is noted for its **economic democracy**: the value of the catch is shared by everyone on the ship according to a pre-set scale, and this system unites the whole crew's interest in returning the largest possible catch. Fish waste is sold to **Danish mink farmers**. The mink pelts are sold at the world's largest fur auctions, held annually in Copenhagen.

Ranking sixth in the world's leading exporters of fish products, Denmark has a strong position in fish production and aquaculture has a long and well established tradition in the country. The main product produced is rainbow trout from freshwater ponds and mariculture units, the latter also producing roe as an important by-product. Eel is farmed in recirculated freshwater tank systems; mussels and oysters are produced in minor quantities and turbot fry is exported for further ongrowing. A variety of other species are raised primarily for restocking which represents an increasing share of total turnover.

Total annual aquaculture production in Denmark was around 40 000 tones, or 3.3 percent of the total fish production in Denmark, worth 20 percent of the total value of fish produced. Earnings from the aquaculture sector were about US$ 114 million, making it worth more than the economically important Danish cod fisheries; about 90 percent of production goes for export. More than 800 people are directly employed in production (just above 600 being full-time employees), mainly in traditional fish farming. In addition, a significant number of people are employed in associated industries such as processing and smoking.

Danish aquaculture is strictly regulated by environmental rules, with the exception of full recirculation eel farms, all Danish fish farms have to be officially approved in accordance with the Danish Environmental Protection Act. A fixed feed quota is assigned to each individual farm in addition to specific requirements including feed conversion ratios, water use and treatment, effluents, removal of waste and offal, etc.

The North American rainbow trout (Oncorhynchus mykiss) has been farmed in Danish freshwater ponds for more than 100 years, since the 1950s it has also been produced in offshore cages and since the 1970s in land-based marine aquaculture units. Also during the 1970s, eel (Anguilla anguilla) farming in recirculated freshwater tanks was developed which also lead to the creation of a niche market for the export of Danish recirculation technology for use in aquaculture for a range of species.

With growing environmental awareness, strict environmental regulations have been introduced for Danish aquaculture since 1987. At a national level, maximum values were stipulated for effluents such as nitrogen (N), phosphorus (P) and organic substances (O) produced from freshwater as well as marine aquaculture. These regulations, based on fixed feed quotas for each individual farm, virtually caused a halt to any further increases in production for Danish trout farming, except for the effects of developing improved feed composition and feeding techniques. Theoretically, documented evidence of N, P and O effluent levels below the individual farm limit might overrule its feed quota, but since no effective measuring techniques were available, the feed quotas, once given, could not be changed.

However, the feed quotient (kilos of feed required to produce one kilo of fish) have been improved by 25 percent since 1987. Furthermore, in freshwater aquaculture, water treatment and recirculation techniques have continually developed, so on the whole, local environmental requirements have been complied with while on a national level, effluent levels have been reduced by around 50 percent during the period.

In accordance with EU regulations, several areas have been assigned as habitat areas, bird protection and/or Ramsar (the Ramsar Convention on Wetlands) areas. In accordance with a national regulation, no approval shall be granted for the construction of new or modification or expansion of existing saltwater fish farms and marine aquaculture establishments if to do so could bring about deterioration of the habitat types or habitats of species on the site or cause disturbance that would have significant consequences for the species for which the site is designated.

No licences have been issued for new freshwater fish farms since the introduction of environmental regulations. Around 40 percent of the freshwater fish farms have since closed, mainly as a result of county buy-ups and the abolition of farms in order to improve environmental and fish passage conditions in the adjacent streams. Approvals and feed quotas are assigned to the individual farm and can not easily be transferred to others. At its peak in 1995, the production from Danish freshwater ponds reached just above 36 000 tonnes, by 2003, production had fallen to about 24 500 tonnes, worth US$ 63 million, from 337 farms. All of these farms are located in Jutland, the western peninsula of Denmark.

Since the introduction of environmental regulations, only one licence for a new Danish marine fish farm has been issued in 2004. Besides environmental regulations production is very much dependent on weather conditions and can sometimes be disturbed by oil pollution resulting from the shipping industry. Fluctuating from one year to another, production peaked in 1993 at about 7 900 tonnes from 30 farms with offshore cages and about 1 500 tonnes from 10 land-based salt water farms. In 2003, production was about 7 200 and 900 tonnes from 24 and 10 farms, worth US$ 24 and US$ 3 million,

For additional analytical, business and investment opportunities information,
please contact Global Investment & Business Center, USA
at (703) 370-8082. Fax: (703) 370-8083. E-mail: ibpusa3@gmail.com
Global Business and Investment Info Databank - www.ibpus.com

respectively[1] .

Eel farming has not been subject to setbacks due to environmental regulations, but during the 1990s was affected by heavy competition in the market for glass eels (European eel, Anguilla anguilla). On top of a decreasing influx of glass eels from the Atlantic Ocean, a growing proportion of the glass eel catches that were not used directly for human consumption in the Southern European market were bought by Asian fish farmers (mainly from China) for ongrowing at steadily increasing prices. In addition, the import into the EU of final eel products from Asia has led to strong competition in that market.

Production from Danish eel farming peaked in the late 1990s at about 3 000 tonnes a year from a total of 30 farms. Subsequently, most of the farms have been closed and the 2003 production dropped to 2 000 tonnes, worth US$ 17 million from 11 farms. However, Danish eel aquaculture as an industrial sector is sustaining a developing industry for recirculation technology that has an important export market.

In Denmark considerable numbers of farmed fish are released each year into natural water bodies, for example, marshes, lakes, streams and marine water areas. The release of fish is undertaken mainly to compensate for the lack of natural spawning possibilities or recruitment and to improve conditions for recreational fishing. Finally, fish are released when restoring lakes – so-called biomanipulation – and as a method of rehabilitating stocks of endangered fish species.

The main financial contributor to fish releases is a fund administered by the Ministry of Food, Agriculture and Fisheries. Anglers and spare-time fishermen (fishing for home consumption) pay for annual licences that generate more than US$ 5 million a year, which helps to finance restocking projects and research supplemented by funding from other public authorities and private organisations. In the beginning, fish restocking in Denmark mainly concentrated on salmon, however, in recent years the area of attention has broadened to include many fish species, among which eel is very important.

Danish shellfish production, which historically has depended on fisheries, is now second in the EU as a result of the favourable conditions for shellfish production found in shallow Danish waters. The main product produced is blue mussel, which is also, along with oysters, a priority for the rapidly growing Danish shellfish farming industry, albeit it is still in its infancy. Production in 2003 was at just 11 tonnes, by 2004 a total of 44 licences had been granted and about the same numbers of applicants were awaiting completion of their application. To help in the promotion of the development in this sector, the Danish Shellfish Centre has been established and aided by regional, national and EU funding.

In general the development of Danish commercial aquaculture production has been slow for about 15 years, however, following the recommendations from advisory committees (2002, 2003 and 2004), adjustments to the regulations are being considered for both marine and freshwater farming and to some extent new optimism is growing in the industry. Also working in this direction is the new strategy, introduced by the EU Commission in 2002, for sustainable development of European aquaculture which is aiming at an annual growth of 4 percent

The fishing industry in Denmark is a main source of income to households. While fishing is a practice noted from the Medieval times, particularly in the coastal area of Denmark for eel fishing with woven traps, the earliest innovation in fisheries wasn't recorded until 1849 when the **Danish seine** or anchor seine technique of fishing was introduced resulting in unprecedented quantities of fish catch from the **Limfjord**.[4]

During 1856, the Danish Royal Trade Monopoly that was practiced since 1709 was annulled. In 1872, the first fishing vessels started operating in East Iceland when ship made of steel made in England replaced the wooden vessels.[5] This created many new opportunities for the Faroese, and played an important part in the development of the Faroese fishing industry. This method of fishing spread to **Esbjerg** on the south-west **Jutland** coast in 1880 when transportation using rail links facilitated export to **Europe**. Esbjerg became a popular site for all Danes for fishing **plaice** in early 1900 when motorized boats were also introduced for the operations.[4] During 1939-40, the **Tórshavn Shipyard** in Faroes built the 'Vónin' (Hope) which was the first ship of Denmark.[5] From 1920 to 1950, the fishing vessels known as the blue ships of Denmark were conspicuously plied for deep-sea fishing in the North Sea. Now, Danish seine is considered a major fishing technique in the world. In the 20th century, deep sea fishing came to dominate the scene. However. this has not discouraged the use of **long line fishing** technique with use of several hooks on short lines that are attached to a main line.[4]

In 1903, the fishery limit for the **Faroe Islands** was 3 nautical-miles under an agreement signed between Denmark and **Great Britain**. In 1959, it was extended to 12 nautical miles and Denmark officially implemented this policy from 1964. In 1978, the 200-nautical mile limit came into force, which is now in vogue, on the same lines as adopted by **North Atlantic** nations.[5]

FISHING CATEGORIES

Three broad categories of fishing in Denmark are industrial fishery, fishery for human consumption (also known as pelagic fishing), and **demersal** fishery. Industrial fishing is for industrial use of producing fish oil and fish meal. Initially, Industrial fishing using trawlers began in the 1940s with **herring** fishing in the **North Sea**. Over time, other fish species included **sand eel**, **Norway pout**, **blue whiting** and **sprat** (sprat in **Skagerrak/Kattegat** and in the **Baltic Sea**). By 1993, the percentage of **sand eel** was about 70%, when the total industrial fish catch was 1.2 million tons. However, in terms of cash value, **cod** fish was a better catch.[6] This type of fishing is also found to be overall remunerative as it contributes to 27% in financial value from 77% of catch.[3]

For human consumption, the fish species caught are cod, **plaice** and **herring** and also species such as **hake**, **dover sole**, and **turbot**. In deep waters, fish species caught are **Norway lobster**, **deep water prawn**, and common **mussels**. In terms of financial value, the fish species of interest, in the order of precedence, are **cod**, **sand eel**, **plaice**, **herring** and **Norway lobster**. Stocks of **eel** has declined since 1970. Method of fishing in this type of fishing practice involves use of stationary or dredging gear, **gillnets** and **pound nets**, **traps** and **hooks** while for catching mussels special **dredgers** are adopted.[3]

In **demersal fishery**, the species fishes caught are white fish (cod, hake, **haddock**, **whiting**, **saithe**), flatfish (**sole**, plaice, **flounder** and so forth), **lobster** and deep water prawns. One feature which needs consolidation is the uniting of small fishing operators of Denmark into one viable major sector, as at present the Norwegians have held this position. As the Danish industrial and cod fisheries role is a major factor in the North Sea, the resource position of a few species is not definite.[7]

For additional analytical, business and investment opportunities information,
please contact Global Investment & Business Center, USA
at (703) 370-8082. Fax: (703) 370-8083. E-mail: ibpusa3@gmail.com
Global Business and Investment Info Databank - www.ibpus.com

The key ports for fishing in the above types of fishing operations are **Esbjerg**, **Thyboren**, **Hansholm**, **Hirtshals**, and **Skagen**. The **North Sea** and **Skagen** account for 80% of the catches.[3] Much of the fishing industry is also located in Greenland and Faroe Islands which are self-governing dependencies of Denmark.[8]

PROCESSING INDUSTRIES

As it provides processing links with many other countries, Denmark imports fish for this activity and its own fishing produce from the sea is exported. One feature which needs consolidation is the uniting of small fishing operators of Denmark into one viable major actor, as at present the Norwegians have held this position.[7] The waste of the many fish industries are fully utilized in mink pelt production which now a well-established revenue earner to the state.[7]

Use of machinery in fishing operations is well developed in Denmark. The number of fishing vessels in operation is 3400 with a crew of crewed of about 5.400. The people employed in this activity are 6.500 people.[9] Democratic values are practiced in the fishing with trawlers, as the fleet involved with the operations shares the catch value equally among all the members of the ship, which is an incentive to every fisherman to bring in more catch[3]

There are prescribed rules and quotas for purchase of fishing vessels. Danish fishing companies are permitted to own vessels provided their the fishermen or fishing companies are residents of Denmark. This rule applies to EU or EEC citizens also. One ship owner is permitted to own only four vessels with a combined capacity of GT of 5,000. Fishing volume in one pelagic vessel is restricted to a maximum of 10% of the Danish herring in the North Sea. The quota for mackerel fish is also the same on one vessel. Additional sprat quota/sandeel quota may be purchased for Baltic Sea sprat and Norway pout fishing.[10][11]

The type of vessels forming the fishing fleets are; trawlers, gill netters and poundnets (50% in this category but with capacity of less than 5GT mostly gill netter);trawlers and purse seiners of 150 GT. A substantial part of the fleet operate under depths of 24 m.[12]

RECENT DEVELOPMENTS

After a few prosperous years for Denmark's fishing industry, figures for 2012 were not so good with profits falling to some DKK 600 million from DKK 900 million per annum previously. The fall is attributed mainly to reductions in **sand eel** and **mackerel** catches while the prices of cod, herring and lobster were also expected to fall.[13] Further falls of around 9% were recorded in the consumer figures for the first quarter of 2013 when catches fell to 103,000 tons. Consumer prices also fell some 17% in comparison with 2012. By contrast, industrial fishing prospered with a price rise of 34% which, despite lower catches, brought an increase in profits of 31%.[14]

NATIONAL POLICY AND LAWS

Danish fishing industry has patterned its fishing policy based on the European Union's Fisheries Policy (CFP-2002) with adaptations to suit its national needs. A quota management system has been introduced. Individual owners are also permitted to have higher fishing rights, and it is in consonance with the policy followed for pelagic and industrial fisheries. The fleet and fleet capacity have been restricted to conform to the EU Policy, which provides for a rigid entry-exit system, and individual transfer of capacity rights has also been allowed. With this policy the export of fish recorded in 2005 was 1.03 million metric tonnes.[15]

National legislation in fishing has been adopted with due quota allocations done under the EU policy with technical rules that are framed on the basis of scientific studies which are carried out regularly. The 1999 Fisheries Act, with a few amendments made in 2002, is in vogue and it relates to fish stocks, specific rules for commercial and recreational fishing and first hand marketing and duties. A new national strategy along with a new plan of action for fisheries was also developed to meet the requirements of the EU's European Fisheries Fund as a 7-year programme.[15] EU regulations are also a hindrance by the fishermen as biological balance has not been achieved and EU control has led to more wastage.[7]

Another policy aspect is that according to biologists the number of fishermen in the field are quite large and the resources available may not be adequate to sustain all of them to be at par with the national average income level and this would call for greater efficiency of operations with less of wastage.

Over all, the policy Instruments address issues concerning vessel catch limits (could be on monthly basis), individual Transferable quotas (applicable only for herring), limits on number of days per month, Days at sea, time closures (such as during weekends, summer), licenses for limited and not limited access), lower limit of landing sizes (could be more than those set under CFP in some cases), debarring use of specific gear types in specified areas, limitation on engine power in specified areas, to notifying the fisheries control before landing and satellite monitoring.[12]

The Ministry of Food, Agriculture and Fisheries ensures that a sustainable development of the sector is effectively followed in both fisheries and aquaculture activities.[1] The proactive role played by the Ministry covers regulation and inspections, assistance in research activities, assistance in development activates related fisheries, the fish industry, fishery harbours and aquaculture; and in facilitating licenses for fish management and for recreational fisheries.

HUMAN RESOURCES

Table 1. Number of employees in Danish aquaculture in 2003

–	Freshwater	Offshore	Marine, land-based	Re-circulation	Others	Total
Male full-time	372	45	9	45	13	484
Female full-time	19	4	1	3	2	29
Male part-time	98	2	3	10	2	115
Female part-time	22	0	0	3	1	26
Male, season	36	72	3	3	8	122
Female, season	13	30	–	–	–	43
Total	560	153	16	64	26	819

Notes: Full-time employment: At least 90 percent of a normal working year.
Part time employment: At least 30 percent but less than 90 percent of a normal working year.

Season employment: Less than 30 percent of a normal working year.Source of information: Danish Directorate of Fisheries, Aquaculture Register 2003.

FARMING SYSTEMS

All freshwater fish farms in Denmark are located on Jutland in the western part of the country which possesses the most abundant flowing streams.

The land based marine farms are located in Ringkjøbing Fjord on Jutland.
All Danish offshore farms are located in the inner marine waters. Offshore farms cover in total 1-2 square kilometres, equalling about 0.02 percent of Danish marine territory.
About 90 percent of Danish farmed eel production takes place in Jutland.
Shellfish farms are almost exclusively located in the Limfjord, the strait dividing the northernmost part of Jutland.

FRESHWATER AQUACULTURE

Denmark was among the European pioneers in systematic pond farming of rainbow trout (**Oncorhynchus mykiss**) around the beginning of the 20th century. In 1914 Denmark had about 140 trout farms, primarily producing for export. Production fell drastically during and between the two great wars, but then began to flourish again. In 2003 there were 337 freshwater pond farms owned by about 200 farmers.

Today, the greater part of the Danish freshwater trout production is sold for processing at a "portion size" of 250–350 grams weight. Fish juveniles are also produced in specialised hatcheries and sold for further ongrowing in freshwater ponds and mariculture units, or for restocking purposes. A small but growing amount is sold for "put-and-take" angling.

In recent years the feed and feeding techniques have been improved to such a degree that the average feed conversion ratio in Danish fish ponds has been reduced to about 0.95 (= one kilo feed required for the production of a one kilo fish). This development has been dependent on the use of high-quality fish meal and fish oil, primarily produced from Danish sandeel fisheries in the North Sea.

Danish pond farming is subject to a variety of environmental regulations aimed at securing the water quality of rivers and lakes and reducing eutrophication of the open sea. A particular departmental order stipulates a number of requirements for the establishment and operation of freshwater farms. Counties assign individual limits to the fish farms on the annual amount of feed it can use and effluents it is allowed to produce, in addition to specific requirements regarding feed conversion ratios, water treatment, taking samples, keeping of operational records, filtering ponds and canals, removal of waste and offal etc.

There is a growing need for investment in measures required to meet the tightening environmental regulations which has resulted in economic strains being placed on fish farmers. One of the problems is that there has not yet been an efficient, reliable and cost-effective method developed for analysing the amount of N, P and organic effluents entering into the rivers. The 'model farm' concept, however, introduced by the recommendations of an advisory committee on freshwater aquaculture has created some degree of optimism within the industry.

MARINE AQUACULTURE

The first Danish mariculture installations were developed in the 1950s using cages located close to land, with the development of technology during the 1970s offshore cages were introduced. By 2003 Denmark had 24 offshore marine fish farms and 10 land based plants, pumping sea water through tanks ashore.

The main product from offshore cages as well as from land-based units is large rainbow trout, 2–5 kilos each. An essential by-product is the roe, which is salted and marketed as 'caviar', this is exported mainly to Japan and contributes substantially to the Danish mariculture economy. Competition, however, is increasing in this market and prices are decreasing.

Danish land-based seawater aquaculture usually follows the same production pattern as offshore farms. The land based system has some environmental advantages, however, since it is possible to filter the water, at least in part, before it is released back to the sea. Costs for establishing as well as running land-based seawater farms are higher than for freshwater ponds and offshore mariculture which renders them less attractive in a market where there is severe competition on product prices.

In recirculated seawater tanks, small quantities of turbot fry are produced for export for further ongrowing, mainly in Southern Europe; in addition, some plaice are produced for restocking purposes.

Apart from small quantities produced for restocking, Denmark has no salmon farms, in recent years, world production of farmed salmon has increased drastically, followed by a subsequent reduction in prices. Danish fish farmers have suffered because of this, since salmon and large trout would be competing directly in the low price end of the market.

EEL FARMING

Eel (**Anguilla anguilla**) farming is a relatively new activity only in existence for about the last 25 years, but the recirculation technology is now well established and also suitable for a number of other species. Denmark currently has 11 eel farms.
There is still room for development of a feed that is better suited for the specific requirements of eels that are being cultured. Not least because many details relating to eel reproduction remain to be fully understood, in spite of many years of research it is not yet possible to produce eel fry in captivity, however, there is some optimism that progress is being made in this area.

With recirculation technology requiring the water to be filtered and rinsed, Danish eel farming has had no difficulty in complying with environmental regulations. Danish eel farming technology is of a high standard and there is a considerable level of export of this technology and know-how.

SHELLFISH FARMING

Blue mussels (**Mytilus edulis**) and the European flat oyster (**Ostrea edulis**) have been farmed from time to time in small quantities within the Danish fjords, in 2003, production totalled 11 tonnes. Farmed mussels grow quicker than wild mussels and have a higher 'meat percentage', as a result of this, they are used primarily for direct consumption and are sold at higher prices than wild caught mussels.
A steady increase in Danish shellfish farming is expected in the future, following recommendations from a special committee (2004), 44 licences have been granted, mainly for farms in the Limfjord in Northern Jutland, and new facilities are being

For additional analytical, business and investment opportunities information,
please contact Global Investment & Business Center, USA
at (703) 370-8082. Fax: (703) 370-8083. E-mail: ibpusa3@gmail.com
Global Business and Investment Info Databank - www.ibpus.com

established.

Danish coastal marine areas and the Wadden Sea provide very good conditions for shellfish production in the shallow, relatively calm waters. By filtering the water during feeding, the shellfish are removing nutrients and thereby contributing towards counteracting the effects of eutrophication. Cultivating shellfish in the water column accelerates the growth considerably compared to bottom culture, and regular harvest /thinning further accelerates the growth of the remaining shellfish.

From time to time, algal blooms arise due to eutrophication giving rise to a risk of toxin accumulation in the shellfish, however, strict veterinary precautions are taken in accordance with EU and national regulations. Specific shellfish production areas are assigned and are subject to requirements relating to water quality, regular control of the products, etc., and the problems with algal blooms do not usually cause serious harm to the industry.

CULTURED SPECIES

Table 2. Danish aquaculture production in 2003 by volume and value

Species	Production	
	Tonnes	US$ million
rainbow trout	33 440	89.763
eel	2 011	17.233
brook trout	226	1.020
trout, not specified	79	0.840
salmon	16	0.800
brown trout	97	0.562
pike	...	0.141
blue mussel	11	...
turbot	5	...
pikeperch	6	...
Total	35 891	110.360

Note: Excluding values of eggs and roe, which were not categorised.
Source of information: Danish Directorate of Fisheries, Aquaculture Register

AQUACULTURE SYSTEM DEVELOPMENTS

Aquaculture in fresh water ponds and in salt water marshes are also finding increased attention of the government by breeding more species.[1]

Since 2004 new rules are in force for fresh water and saltwater fishing as an aquaculture practice under specific organic labeling. Fresh water fishing in ponds is notable for **rainbow trout** (*Oncorhynchus mykiss*); this species is also adopted to land based marine aquaculture. Eel farming is also popular where water is recirculated in fresh water tanks. Other varieties of fish adopted in fresh water fishing are mussels, **oysters** and **crayfish**. **Turbot** from which is mostly exported is also a species raised under aquaculture.

Many species are also raised for stocking. Shell fish has also been produced and its yield has was a record 280 metric tonnes between 2004 and 2005. Approval process involves clearance from the Department of Fisheries under the Danish Environment Protection Act; recirculated eel farms are exempt under this Act.

AQUACULTURE IN DENMARK

Netto production from aquaqulture farms grouped by species
Quantity is in tonnes, value in 1,000 DKK and price pr. kilo is in DKK

Species	Production		
	Weight	Value	Price pr. kg
European perch	1	...	...
Sea trout	115	7,775	127.84
Blue mussel	2,221	10,521	4.74
Chars nei	217	...	...
Northern pike	0	...	...
European whitefish	0	...	...
Noble crayfish	0	56	695.86
Brook trout	93	2,988	31.96
Common carp	0	...	...
Atlantic salmon	1,289	44,674	34.65
European flat oyster	0	...	...
Rainbow trout	31,087	751,725	24.18
Pike-perch	144	...	...
European flounder	0	...	...
Sturgeons	3	...	...
Eel	1,067	85,850	80.43
Total	36,239	920,488	

Table 3. Danish aquaculture: Number of farms and facilities of different types

–	Number of						
	Farms	Ponds	Canals	Tanks	Cages	Mussel wires	Others
Freshwater	337	7 504	497	3 719	40	0	31
Mariculture, offshore	24	0	0	0	186	0	0
Mariculture, land based	10	50	54	7	0	0	1
Recirculation	30	133	6	752	0	0	318
Others	13	6	0	0	4	52	149
Total	414	693	557	4 478	230	52	499

SOURCE OF INFORMATION: DANISH DIRECTORATE OF FISHERIES, AQUACULTURE REGISTER

Freshwater aquaculture

The majority of freshwater farms have traditional ponds dug into the ground water is taken into the ponds from a stream via a channel, usually assisted by a small dam in the stream. The water is then channelled through an array of ponds, each of which typically measures 25–35 x 5–7 metres and is 0.7 metres deep. From the pond outlets the water is then guided through a back channel which is also used for rearing fish, before it is output back into the stream thorough a precipitation basin, about 1 metre deep.

Normally, the water is oxygenated either by a central pump or by floating devices in the ponds. An increasing number of farms are recirculating the water after being first passed though micro filters and biological filters, thereby reducing the water intake and the discharge of nutrients from the farm.

The trout are harvested when they reach 'portion size' at about 250–350 grams weight, gutted and frozen or smoked for sale. A substantial amount, however, are exported alive, mainly to the German market.

MARICULTURE

In a typical Danish mariculture unit, trout at about 1 kilo in weight in spring (March–April) are transferred from freshwater ponds to offshore net cages. Feed is administered by feeding machines that distribute the feed over the cages from a boat, or from a platform via hoses to each of the cages.
In autumn/early winter (October–December) the fish are harvested at a size of about 2–5 kilo, gutted and frozen or filleted and smoked.

Due to the risk of ice during cold winters, the sea around Denmark is not suitable for mariculture all year around, so at the end of the season, the cages are taken ashore for maintenance and repair and also for storage until the following spring.

Production methods used in land-based aquaculture using sea water resemble those used for freshwater aquaculture, however, the water has to be pumped both in and out of the farm. The trout produced are of the same size as in offshore farming.

EEL FARMING

Fry (glass eels) caught from natural waters are the raw material for eel farming, the eels are reared in indoor tanks using tap water at 20–25 °C. The water is continually recirculated through mechanical and biological filters, oxygenated and disinfected using ultraviolet treatment. Feed is administered manually or by automatic feeding machines. A proportion of the production is sold as fingerlings for restocking purposes; however, the majority is grown on and exported for human consumption at about 100–200 grams each. Smaller amounts are grown to a size of 300–800 grams.

SHELLFISH FARMING

Mussels are usually cultivated on vertical ropes or in socks hanging from suspended lines ('longline' systems) tied to floating buoys which are anchored to the bottom. Mussel 'seed' (larvae) settle naturally on the hanging ropes in spring time. Almost all Danish waters carry plenty of mussel seed. The growing mussels are usually transferred from the ropes to socks in the autumn and harvested the following summer at a size about 45–55 mm.

Oyster seed is produced and cultivated most successfully in tanks, at a size of 30–40 mm the small oysters are transferred to the sea in baskets or trays hanging from suspended lines or lying on the bottom. Ongrowing takes place for 1.5–2 years before reaching a harvest size of 70–100 grams.

SECTOR PERFORMANCE

MARKET AND TRADE

The main income from the Danish export[*] of aquaculture products is derived from smoked trout, including fillets. In 2003 exports were 3 850 tonnes worth US$ 42 million. These exports predominantly go to Germany (73 percent), Switzerland (7 percent) and Belgium (6 percent).
Exports of gutted, chilled and frozen trout (including fillets) in 2003 were just over 8 700 tonnes worth US$ 39 million, mainly to Germany but also to The Netherlands, Sweden and Belgium.

Exports of live trout (portion size) from freshwater farms in 2003 were 5 100 tonnes, worth US$ 18 million, mainly to Germany.
Salted trout roe and 'caviar' is exported almost exclusively to Japan, in 2003 the export amounted to 544 tonnes worth US$ 5 million.

Export figures for Danish farmed eels are not easily extracted from the official statistics which include also export of wild caught eels. However, around 80 percent of the eels from Danish aquaculture are exported live to The Netherlands for harvesting and smoking. In 2003, this amounted to approximately 1 600 tonnes worth just over US$ 13 million.

CONTRIBUTION TO THE ECONOMY

The total aquaculture production in 2003 was estimated at 36 000 tonnes or 3.3 percent of the total national fish production and worth 20 percent of the total value of fish produced. However, the earnings from the aquaculture sector at about US$ 114 million, made it worth more than the economically important Danish cod fisheries. Over 90 percent of aquaculture production goes for export. It is estimated that 800 people are directly employed in production, however, a significant number of people are employed in associated industries such as processing and smoking.

For additional analytical, business and investment opportunities information, please contact Global Investment & Business Center, USA at (703) 370-8082. Fax: (703) 370-8083. E-mail: ibpusa3@gmail.com
Global Business and Investment Info Databank - www.ibpus.com

SECTOR MANAGEMENT AND STRUCTURE

THE INSTITUTIONAL FRAMEWORK

Though being an integrated part of the Danish fisheries sector and as such covered by the Fisheries Act under the Ministry of Food, Agriculture and Fisheries, the Danish aquaculture industry is mainly governed through the implementation of environmental regulations.

The Ministry of the Environment is in charge of administrative and research activities in the area of environmental protection and planning, the Ministry has three agencies, one corporate management centre and two independent research institutes. Two independent appeal boards and one Environmental Assessment Institute are also linked to the Ministry.

THE GOVERNING REGULATIONS

The **Fisheries act (2004, as amended)** regulates the management, control and development of fisheries and aquatic resources in Denmark. Chapter 13 addresses ocean farming and establishes a licensing system governing the establishment and operation of mariculture facilities. The Act grants the Minister of Food, Agriculture and Fisheries general power to make regulations with regard to the issuing of licences for the establishment and operation of ocean farms. The Regulation on the establishment and operation of ocean farms (1991)[1] sets forth more detailed rules on the licensing system of mariculture facilities. The issuing of licences has been delegated to the Danish Directorate of Fisheries.

For aquaculture facilities taking in fresh water, facilities that are placed on land taking in marine water, and for the fish farming of mussels, oysters etc., no regulations have been issued pursuant to the Fisheries act (2004) concerning licensing. For fish farming that requires feed, however, an approval according to the **Environment protection act (2001)** is required. For the fish farming of mussels, oysters etc., an application for a licence shall be filed with the Directorate of Fisheries in accordance with the Instruction on Applications for Bivalve Aquaculture in the Limfjord (2003).

RESEARCH, EDUCATION AND TRAINING

Applied research in relation to aquaculture in Denmark is primarily undertaken by the Danish Institute for Fisheries Research (DIFRES) under the Ministry of Food, Agriculture and Fisheries as well as a few other government-run research institutions. They are financed by basic funding from the ministry, linked to 'result contracts', as well as by allocations from different sources on the basis of specific research projects. Each of the institutions has a governing board to whom the director refers and to a great extent they set their own research priorities within the framework of the contract.

DIFRES carries out research and investigations relating to sustainable exploitation of live marine and freshwater resources, including aquaculture. Further, DIFRES acts as a counsellor to the Minister of Food, Agriculture and Fisheries, to other authorities, international commissions, the fishing industry and fishery organisations. DIFRES is managed by a director referring to a Governing Board with representation from the fishing industry including aquaculture, professional and industrial bodies, national research councils and members of the staff.

DIFRES has four research departments, one of which being the Department of Marine Ecology and Aquaculture. A main area of research is nutritional physiology in fish larvae and the use of live feed, which are critical parameters in aquaculture. This field is central to efforts to develop total production concepts applying to all life cycle stages from egg to the final product and promoting the use of alternative species of fish and shellfish in aquaculture.

Another DIFRES department deals with processing and improvement of the quality of fish products as well as quality assurance in the fish industry, covering raw material, process and product, microbiology and hygiene.

DIFRES cooperates with Danish universities in high level education within the scientific areas of the institution. There is no official Danish education specifically related to aquaculture, either at university or at lower levels, however, the Danish Aquaculture Organisation is working on proposals for an institutionalised education, following recommendations from the special committees on freshwater and marine aquaculture.

Working with documentation of the effects of recirculation technologies in freshwater aquaculture, the Department of Marine Ecology and Aquaculture cooperates with the National Environmental Research Institute (NERI) under the Ministry of Environment. Within the area of aquaculture systems, methods and environmental effects, this cooperation contributes to developing new technologies primarily in freshwater aquaculture, minimising the use of electricity, oxygen and feed, and reducing effluent levels of nutrients and traces of medicines and ancillary materials.

NERI undertakes scientific consultancy work, the monitoring of nature and the environment as well as applied and strategic research, its task being to establish a scientific foundation for environmental policy decisions. NERI also investigates the turnover and effects of N and P, the effects of selected hazardous substances, sustainable utilisation of water resources and the restoration of lakes and watercourses.

A number of DIFRES and NERI research projects relating to aquaculture actively involve the Danish Aquaculture Organisation which unites all branches in the industry (freshwater and marine aquaculture, eel farming, feed producers as well as processing and export).

The Danish Institute for Food and Veterinary Research is a governmental research institute under the Ministry of Family and Consumer Affairs. The Department of Poultry, Fish and Fur Animals performs research, diagnostics and advisory services concerning diseases and zoonoses in poultry, fish, fur animals, wildlife and pets. The research focuses on the development of methods for detection of pathogenic and zoonotic agents, as well as on the interaction between host and pathogens aimed at prevention and treatment of disease.

The diagnostic and consultancy services of the Department of Poultry, Fish and Fur

Animals support livestock producers, veterinarians and authorities, and are part of the veterinary contingency plan for infectious diseases. The department is a national reference laboratory for infectious diseases in poultry, fish and fur animals, as well as the EU and OIE reference laboratory for fish diseases.

The Danish Shellfish Centre (DSC) is a research and development organisation in Northern Jutland, sustained by regional funding and national funding for R&D projects. The objectives of the centre are to promote sustainable shellfish culture, fisheries and processing by exploiting the natural resources of plants and animals in coastal waters, thereby benefiting the industry, the public and the environment, converting new knowledge into industrial practice.

DHI Water & Environment is an independent, international consulting and research organization approved as an authorized technological service institute by the Ministry of Science, Technology and Innovation. Over a number of years, DHI has been consulting on aquaculture and environment topics; the main DHI services in this field are impact assessment, operational forecasting, modeling of production and clean technology.

TRENDS, ISSUES AND DEVELOPMENT

Since the introduction in Denmark of strict environmental regulations in the late 1980s, no licence has been issued for any new freshwater fish farms and only one licence for a new marine fish farm has been given (2004). Approvals and feed quotas are strictly tied to the individual farm and can not easily be transferred to others. Many freshwater farms have in fact been closed in order to improve environmental conditions in streams. On the whole, production has declined over the period.

Against the international background of increasing potential for aquaculture production, given the increasing pressure on marine catches, Denmark has had special committees looking into the potential for this sector. The freshwater and saltwater aquaculture committees in 2002 and 2003 respectively, recommended increasing the production efforts within a sustainable framework, stimulated by economic incentives. For both sub-sectors, a prerequisite for development has been a change to the present regulation system which is based on fixed feed quotas.

One concrete result of the recommendations is the 'model farm' plan with a strong link between investment in production, investment in equipment and management for environmental purposes. The plan makes it possible for the individual freshwater farm to more than double its production (up to +130 percent). So far, the implementation of the plan shows that the perspectives of increased production, improved environment and fish passages in the streams go together in a way that has attracted considerable interest among Danish and European aquaculturists.

For marine aquaculture, the main potential is connected with locating offshore cages in areas with optimum conditions for diluting and spreading emissions from the cages. An integrated mapping of Danish marine waters showing the different restrictions and potentials has been carried out to promote this development. The environmental rules for marine fish farming are in a process of readjustment to provide for a flexible regulation system based on documentation of environmental effects rather than stiff production limits by way of fixed feed quotas.

Further, an ad hoc advisory shellfish board was established in 2003 mainly along the same lines (also including the potential for shellfish fisheries) in order to optimise the total exploitation of Danish shellfish resources, primarily Blue mussel and European oyster. Based on interim recommendations from the committee, certain areas of the Limfjord (in the northern part of Jutland) were assigned to shellfish production and licensing began in early 2004. The recommendations of the board (2004) among others include transferable five-year licences and the establishment of a permanent advisory committee in order to integrate all relevant commercial and environmental aspects in the administration and the development of the industry. Amendments to the Fisheries Act in part implementing the recommendations are underway.

In 2004, a new Regulation on Organic Aquaculture came into force for a voluntary red Danish 'Organic' label. Farmed fish for organic labelling may be treated with antibiotics only once, and no genetically modified or biologically treated fish are allowed on the farm. The 'organic' label can only be used for fish from the family Salmonidae (salmon and trout) and European eel. The label has attracted some attention, but production still is very small.

There has been growing concern as to the status of wild stocks of European eel, catches have been decreasing for decades, for adult eels as well as for glass eels and many natural biotopes are considered as being endangered. Glass eel prices have exploded due to increasing international exports outside Europe. In order to secure the stocks and continued glass eel supplies for farming, Danish eel farmers in cooperation with European colleagues in the 1990s suggested to the EU Commission that measures should be taken to this effect. Following advice from biologists, the Commission is now working on proposals in order to protect and develop the European eel stock[+] .

The prevailing hope in the Danish aquaculture industry is that international as well as EU pressure for development of the industry will lead to quick changes in the direction of realistic environmental regulations that do not handicap the industry as a worthy competitor in the national and international market.

GREENLAND NATIONAL FISHERIES MANAGEMENT SYSTEM –

Introduction

Given the immense economic importance of fisheries to Greenland – an industry that accounts for approximately 92% of Greenland's total exports, the requirement for a well-solidified legal framework and stellar administrative system is paramount. The Greenland Home Rule Government's Fisheries Act is precisely the legislation, which constitutes Greenland's legal framework and administrative underpinnings by which the Executive Branch manages fisheries policies. The government has continually sought to achieve well-established relationships and well-endowed trust between local trade organizations and the fishing operations they represent, as well as the government-owned seafood operation, Royal Greenland, in order to align domestic fisheries policies and legislative acts with the domestic and international interests of these parties. Provided the Home Rule's administration of 18 companies, including Royal Greenland, the counterbalancing of the administration's authority with these monopolistic and, in many instances, wholly owned or only partially-privatized enterprises' profitability can be exceptionally conflicting. Therefore, a need for transparency and full-disclosure in the governments' interactions with enterprise is pivotal.

The manifestation of the Fisheries Act has enabled continual alignment of legislation and management policies to be further aligned with current conditions and external influences. The underlying foundations of Greenland's management of living marine resources are established by the Fisheries Act, which encompasses act specifications, rights and obligations, and other administrative declarations. The Fisheries Act specifies that utilization of fish stocks and resources must be carried out in a biologically acceptable manner, which the Home Rule Government has clearly delineated and fortified in administration of the Act. Furthermore, the administration of the Act solidifies the preeminence of *conservation* and *reproduction* with regard to maintaining and sustaining the longevity of these sovereign resources in the Greenlandic society.

For several decades the practical exercise of authority of Greenland's fisheries management system has been maintained in two different ways. The first of these methods is by means of inspection and license control. Inspections are managed in tandem by the "Grønlands Kommando" (the naval inspection fleet stationed at Grønnedal, South Greenland, as well as their aircraft based in Narsarsuaq) and the Fisheries License Control, the Home Rule government's designated fishing licensing and monitoring authority. These operations include practical inspection of fishing vessels' catch and fishing gear exclusively when they are at sea with onboard patrols. The second important – and more political – means of authority has traditionally been through the management of fish processing plants. In most cases, by limiting the time periods of purchase are allowed, these authoritative methods have enabled restrictions on fisheries with very short notice. These activities are a means of promulgating processing to be harmonized and in total congruence with resource management concerns.

OVERVIEW OF ECONOMIC ACTIVITIES IN GREENLAND

4. Among the four pillars of the Greenlandic economy (fisheries, raw materials, tourism and other land-based business), fishing and refinery processing of seafood products is the primary industry of Greenland. It accounts for 25% of total employment and 92% of exports --of which shrimp exports account for approximately 60% of total export revenues. Fisheries accounts for almost one quarter (~25%) of total employment, with 60% employed in fisheries and 40% employed in fish processing. Despite the vital contribution to national economy from fisheries, an export value of approximately DKK 2 billion (EUR 268.9 million according to the exchange rate from October 4,2004 of DKK 7.43779 = EUR 1), the value of income generated by fishermen is less than 10% of the total taxable income generated by the Greenlandic economy annually. The following table summarizes revenues and tonnage of seafood and non-seafood exports from 2000 to 2002:

Table 1. Catch Volumes and Gross Export Revenues

	2000		2001		2002		
	Tons	M DKK	Tons	M DKK	Tons	M DKK	M Euro*
Total	103 193	2 202	115 639	2.233	124 217	2 140	287.7
Shrimp, In Total	51 534	1 344	51 795	1.234	58 574	1 193	160.4
Cooked, Peeled & Frozen Shrimp	13 582	559	12 526	506	13 460	512	68.8
Industry and Frozen Shrimp	37 426	783	39 269	728	45 114	667	89.7
Other Shrimp Products	526	2	-	33	-	14	1.9

Cod, In Total	1 708	43	1 152	26	3 298	70	9.4
Frozen Cod	36	6	186	2	1 699	21	2.8
Cod, Salted and Dried/ Dried and Salted	290	46	499	10	443	8	1.1
Cod Filets, Frozen	1 382	-	444	14	1 086	39	5.2
Other Cod Products	-	-	23	-	70	1	0.1
Greenland Halibut, In Total	13 107	365	12 833	367	10 412	317	42.6
Halibut, Fresh, Frozen and/or Salted	12 557	327	12 065	323	9 701	278	37.4
Halibut, Smoked	23	37	529	42	361	36	4.8
Other Halibut Products	527	1	239	2	350	4	0.5
Redfish, Whole or Filet, Frozen	2 338	32	830	9	1 602	17	2.3
Snow Crabs	4 266	229	5 568	256	5 168	216	29.0
Other Fish Products, In Total	27 888	47	38 249	25	41 379	37	5.0
Trout, Frozen or Smoked	-	-	-	-	-	-	-
Fish Meat, Chopped - Miscellaneous	-	-	-	-	-	-	-
Atlantic Halibut, Frozen	383	8	7	-	26	-	-
Other Fish Products	27 505	39	38 242	25	41 353	37	5.0
Scallops, Frozen/ Dried/ Salted, In Total	527	37	541	46	535	42	5.6
Smoked/ Fresh/ Cooled/ Frozen/ Salted	-	-	-	-	-	-	-
Other Products - Non-Seafood Exports	1 761	85	4 671	248	3 249	203	27.3
*currency exchange rate for 2002 figures in Euros (DKK 7.43779 DKK=EUR 1)							

Considering that the fishing industry is exceptionally dependent on fish stocks and market prices internationally, income levels can be exceptionally variable and continually unstable. The composition of TAC volumes has changed drastically over the past two decades – 110 600 tons shrimp versus 5 000 tons cod in 2004 (only 4 400 tons cod allocated to Greenlandic fishing operations) shared between West and East Greenland excluding quotas allocated to Norway and Russia; whereas, previously cod fisheries were predominant and the preeminent revenue source in the 1980s. Moreover, fishing quotas for shrimp have been steadily increasing during the last years (85 000 tons in 2002 increased to 100 000 tons in 2003, and subsequently to 134 000 tons in 2004 – of which 27 000 tons are discounted due to allocation of 4 000 tons to the European Union and the remaining 23 000 tons attributable to conversion factor regulations) following scientific advice. However, due to stagnating market prices and escalating oil prices, the revenue base has markedly decreased and has suffered from the implications of destabilizing market effects. Snow Crabs have developed to become a valuable catch in recent years (catches doubled from 2000 to 2001 and revenue correspondingly multiplied by approximately 300%); however, stocks have been unstable and lack

of scientific research on the stocks precludes substantial fishing operations dedicated to this fishery. Consequently, the revenue base and TAC allocations have fallen in rather epic proportions since the beginning of 2002. Additionally, redfish seem to have migrated en masse irrefutably from Iceland to Greenland and could become a future revenue generator. The Home Rule Fisheries Ministry has submitted a list of potential other species to the Council, which may imply a more pervasive diversification in the of fishing activities in the foreseeable future.

For additional analytical, business and investment opportunities information,
please contact Global Investment & Business Center, USA
at (703) 370-8082. Fax: (703) 370-8083. E-mail: ibpusa3@gmail.com
Global Business and Investment Info Databank - www.ibpus.com

In general, in order to maintain the local and regional infrastructure, as well as employment in remote areas, the Home Rule allocates 13.5% (per the government's total budget from financial year 2002) of its current expenditure in the form of direct subsidies to Home Rule enterprises and through additional service contract arrangements with these companies. The direct financial support accounts for 6 – 6.5% of the total budget, which entails 88% allocated to the first pillar, namely fisheries, hunting and agriculture. However, whereas the subsidies are used for the development of the other business pillars (oil and minerals, tourism and other land-based activities), only 3% of the subsidies are used for development activities of the fisheries sector. In 2002 and 2003, the government allocated DKK 2.4 million (EUR 322 676), DKK 13.4 million (EUR 1.8 million) and DKK 9.4 million (EUR 1.3 million) to research, management services, and control and monitoring services, respectively, to the fisheries sector. Additionally, the fisheries sector benefits from additional service contracts and reduced pricing structures for water, heat and electricity, which amount to roughly DKK 60 million per year (EUR 8.1 million). The government's fall session in 2004 will further address potential reductions in this indirect subsidy for water, heat and electricity, which potentially may be reduced on a linear basis from the beginning of 2005 to the culmination of 2009 by approximately DKK 6 million per year (EUR 806 691 per year), a debate that will confront a long-standing liberal and socialistic principle of solidarity and equality for all citizens and communities in Greenland.

The dependence on fisheries makes the economy inherently exposed to external shocks. Further to some favorable years (especially 1998-1999) with a real GDP annual growth rate of more than 7%, the 2001-2002 figures represent a slowdown in the economy with a growth rate of 1-2%. This is unequivocally an implication of depressed market prices for shrimp with persistent high prices for oil. In 2001, though exports of shrimp had increased, the value of the export fell by DKK 110 million (EUR 14.8 million based on today's current exchange rate) in 2001. The market prices on shrimp decreased by 14.25% between 2001 and 2002 followed by a further decrease of nearly 5% in 2003. The Greenland halibut export value decreased with 5% and crab fishing, which had increased in previous years, decreased by 38% due to falling stocks and lack of scientific knowledge about the state of the stocks in 2001 and 2002. The land-based industry and trade sector has continued to stagnate incontrovertibly thronged by an increase in bankruptcies and decrease in investments. Delays in public expenditure and lack of substantive planning in further development of critical infrastructure – expansion of ports, further build-out of air transport infrastructure and consolidation of processing facilities – has been to the detriment of significantly higher export revenues as a per cent of GDP.

BACKGROUND ON THE GREENLANDIC FISHERIES

8. Greenland carries out extensive research via the modern Grønlands Naturinstitut (Greenland Institute of Natural Resources), and is also traditionally supported by scientific guidance primarily from NAFO (Northwest Atlantic Fisheries Organization) and ICES (International Council for the Exploration of Sea). The scientific advice is traditionally first presented in June each year, but the guidance for shrimp and snow crab is generally presented towards the end of November each year. According to the fishing legislation, it is the Home Rule Government that, based on the respective data, establishes the following year's total allowable catch (TAC) at the end of each calendar year for the subsequent calendar year. It is the quota order that is issued on this occasion, and the following quantities were stipulated for 2004 for offshore and coastal fisheries in respective order, including representation of allocations to Greenland's major trading partners and respective international agreements:

Table 2. Offshore Fisheries, 2004 Quotas

Notes:		Total Quota (Tons)	Allocation of Quotas by Country/ Countries					
			Greenland	European Union	Faroe Islands	Iceland	Norway	Russia
	West Greenland							
5)	Shrimp	78 100	74 100	4 000	-	-	-	-
5) 6) 12)	Greenland Halibut (Southwest)	5 500	2 150		150	-	1 450	1 200
12)	Greenland Halibut (Northwest)	4 000	3 600		150	-	-	250
	Snow Crab	1 405	1 000	-	-	-		
6)	Grenadiers	4 150	2 700	1 035	-	-	315	100
	Redfish	1 000	1 000	-	-	-	-	-
6)	Atlantic Halibut	1 200	1 000	-	-	-	200	-
	Catfish	1 000	1 000	-	-	-	-	-
	Capelin	25 000	25 000	-	-	-	-	-
	East Greenland							
5) 6)	Shrimp	12 400	6 725	1 695	1 350	-	2 830	-
5) 6)	Greenland Halibut	23 000	12 875	8 050	150	-	1 325	600
6)	Grenadiers	6 525	4 525	1 715	-	-	285	-
8)	Redfish (both Bottom & Pelagic)	17 500	1 000	(19 770)	-	-	100	-
6)	Atlantic Halibut	2 000	600	800	-	-	550	50
	Catfish	1 000	1 000	-	-	-	-	-
1)5)6)8)9)	Capelin	335 000	11 055	-	19 690	270 420	33 835	-
	Blue Whiting	40 000		-	-	-	-	-
11)	Bi-catch Quota	-	-	-	225	-	-	-
	Cod	5 000	4 400	-	-	-	600	-
5)6)7)9)10)				(max 14 270)	4 500	-	5 955	4 300
13)	Bi-catch Quota	-	-	2 000	-	-	150	max 10%
	Norway							
	Cod	1 900	1 900	-	-	-	-	-
	Haddock	330	330	-	-	-	-	-
	Saithe (North)	925	925	-	-	-	-	-
2)	Bi-catch Quota (North)	150	150	-	-	-	-	-
	Saithe (South)	1 000	1 000	-	-	-	-	-
3)	Bi-catch Quota (South)	100	100	-	-	-	-	-
	Russia							
	Cod	3 140	3 140	-	-	-	-	-
	Haddock	680	680	-	-	-	-	-
	Bi-catch Quota	max 10%	max 10%	-	-	-	-	-
	Faroe Islands							
4)	Bottom Fish	500	500	-	-	-	-	-
	Herring	3 100	3 100	-	-	-	-	-
	International							
	Herring	5 000	5 000	-	-	-	-	-
	Shrimp:							

NAFO-region 3M: 515 fishing days
NAFO-region 3L: 1 344 tons shared with the Faroe Islands
Svalbard (in close proximity to Norway): 643 fishing days

Notes to Table 2 pertaining to TAC allocations for offshore fisheries: 1) The preliminary TAC for capelin is established in June of each year for the quota year June 20th-April 30th for the following year (10 months) – capelin fishing in East Greenland is reserved during the period of May through June. The final TAC figure is solidified at the end of the fishing season. The aforementioned quota figures are established for the fishing season 2003/ 2004.

2) The bi-catch quota of other species (specifically redfish and Atlantic halibut) up to 150 tons in Norwegian territory north of 62° N.

3) The bi-catch quota other species up to 100 tons in Norwegian territory south of 62° N.

4) Maximum 20% cod and haddock. The bottom fish quota of 500 tons can be caught in either of the Faroe Islands' fishing regions referred to as "indre fiskedageområde" or "ydre fiskedageområde".

5) The European Union reached agreement with the Faroe Islands that the Faroe Islands would receive the EU's quota in this case, which implies 150 tons Greenland halibut to be fished within West Greenland waters, as well as 1 150 tons shrimp, 150 tons Greenland halibut, 500 tons pelagic redfish and 4 670 tons capelin to be fished in East Greenland waters.

6) The European Union reached agreement with Norway that Norway would receive the EU's quota in this case, which entails 800 tons Greenland halibut, 315 tons grenadiers and 200 tons Atlantic halibut to be fished in West Greenland waters, as well as 2 830 tons shrimp, 800 tons Greenland halibut, 285 tons grenadiers, 200 tons Atlantic halibut, 7 035 tons capelin and 5 230 tons pelagic redfish to be fished in East Greenland waters.

7) Maximum of 14 270 tons of the EU's quota can be derived by pelagic trawl (specifically pelagic redfish).

8) The European Union reached agreement with Iceland that Iceland would receive 14 070 tons of the EU's quota in this case. 9) The Faroe Islands can fish 4.000 tons pelagic redfish within Greenland's fishing territories from the allotted NEAFC quota for 2004. Greenland

and the Faroe Islands are in agreement to revise the distributions dated July 5th, 2004 and August 2nd, 2004 if feasible given catch-regulated considerations is possible. On that basis, additional quota will be granted in weeks 28 and 32 to the Faroe Islands consisting of 600 tons per week. 10) The 500 tons that the Faroe Islands has permission can only be caught in East Greenland fishing waters. Bottom trawling and pelagic trawling

catch volumes must be reported individually and clearly differentiable at the time of reporting. 11) Greenland will grant permission to a maximum of 3 trawlers and/ or line fishing vessels from the Faroe Islands access to experimental fisheries

in East Greenland waters – including cod, torsk/ tusk/ cusk and catfish/ spotted sea cat – for a consolidated 100 fishing days. The total allowable bi-catch of Atlantic halibut and Greenland halibut pertaining to the experimental fishing efforts may not exceed a maximum of 225 tons. 12) 500 tons of the European Union's quota can be caught either in the Northwest region or Southwest region upon agreement with Greenland. 13) The European Union's total bi-catch quota of cod, catfish/ spotted sea cat, skate/ thornback ray, ling, and torsk/ tusk/ cusk may not exceed

2 000 tons on a consolidated basis. Bi-catch of cod, specifically, may not exceed 100 tons.

Table 3. Coastal Fisheries, 2004 (Shrimp and Snow Crab)

	Total Quota (Tons)
Shrimp (*)	55 900
Snow Crab	4 200
Scallops - Nuuk region	720
Scallops - Mudderbugten region	-

Scallops - Attu region (**)	100
Scallops - Sisimiut region	-
Scallops - South - Saqqaq region	400
Scallops - North - Kangaarsuk region	700
Scallops - Nordre (Northern) Strømfjord region	300
Total Scallops Quota (***)	2 220

Comments:

Shrimp: This part of the total shrimp fishing quota is reserved for vessels which land the whole catch to a land production facility (with the exception of vessels with onboard processing approvals from the government - currently 4 vessels with 25% onboard processing permission and one vessel with 30% onboard processing permission), and is traditionally designated as the 'coastal quota'. Forty-three (43) percent of the total TAC for shrimp is allocated to coastal fishing vessels.

*** Outside of the restricted/ closed zone for the Attu region.*

**** TAC is allocated by geographic region for the coastal scallop fisheries.*

MODERNISATION AND OPTIMISATION OF THE FISHERIES

The main policy expressed by the newly established coalition government in 2002, and subsequently further restructured in 2003, is to make the fisheries sector financially viable. Considering that the most significant sector of Greenland's fisheries is shrimp fisheries, the structural reforms have mainly been concerned with this sector. Further to a restructuring of the offshore fisheries in the 1990s with a reduction of the fleet from 52 to 15 trawlers, a reform of the quota system was introduced with the introduction of the ITQ system. The offshore fisheries sector is now precluded from subsidies and, in fact, contributes additional marginal tariffs, though a program administered by the Home Rule's Tax Authority, which generates approximately DKK 7.5 million (EUR 1 milion) annually in income for the government.

With guidance from the report commissioned by the Enoksen Committee -- established by the Greenland Home Rule government with representation from the administration as well as external stakeholders, the introduction of efficiency criteria into the realm of restructuring the coastal shrimp fisheries has been underway since 2001 and is nearing a point of successful culmination. These consolidation efforts have been comprehensive in their overarching objectives to consolidate the fleet structure in the coastal fisheries concentrated on shrimp fisheries with approximately 60 vessels between

16.2 BRT and 810 BRT in 2001 – 5 of which have production capacity onboard and a respective requirement to deliver 25% of their total catch to processing plants onshore – to approximately 33 vessels in 2004. Further optimization of this fleet is being contemplated through a variety of methods, including additional calibration of the quota system aligned specifically with the individual vessels' fishing capacity and equipment, as well as achievement of profitability.

11. The Home Rule has allocated through the proposed Finance Act of 2005 coverage for additional restructuring efforts in the coastal shrimp fisheries and Greenland halibut fisheries amounting to DKK 27.4 million annually between 2005 and 2008 (EUR 3.7 million annually or EUR 14.7 million over the respective 4-year period). Approximately 50% of the coastal shrimp fleet vessels can be characterized as over 20 years old, and consequently modernisation and optimisation of the fleet is immensely critical to maintain profitable ventures. In conglomeration with these substantial capital appropriations in the Finance Act, the agreement, Protocol IV, with the EU stipulates investments required in the future totaling approximately EUR 101 million to secure the following in the next 10 years:

a) Procurement of 25 shrimp trawlers of steel with a 60 Tons capacity, which will necessitate an investment of around EUR 67 million

b) Procurement of 50 Greenland Halibut boats with 5 Tons capacity requiring an investment of EUR 20 million;

c) And, other fisheries investment: EUR 13.5 million.

12. In retrospect, the public expenditure for fisheries incorporated in the 2004 Finance Act provides for administration of fisheries and fisheries-related budgetary coverage of approximately 10,5M Euro – excluding salaries to employees, as well as exclusion of loan disbursements and income generated from the Erhvervstøtteordning, or Business Support Governance Fund. This can divided into the following items:

Shipping school in Paamiut: EUR 1.57 million

Fishing industry school, ATI EUR 1.10 mllion

Restructuring funds for shrimp and GL halibut fisheries EUR 0.54 million

Control and inspections (excluding salaries and overhead) EUR 1.90 million

Fisheries Conference 2004 (re: fortification of policies) EUR 0.13 million

Direct subsidies to shrimp fisheries EUR 3.29 million

NAFO, NEAFC, NASCO, ICES EUR 0.13 million

Experimental Fishing Projects EUR 0.67 million

Special Assistance Fund EUR 0.40 million

Information and Education Fund EUR 0.27 million

Greenland Institute of Natural Resources EUR 0.50 million

In accordance with the Home Rule Government's holistic approach to fisheries and overarching ambition for eventual full-scale administration of all facets of government to be assumed from the

Danish state – and the long-term aspiration of independence within the Danish realm, the government is increasingly focusing efforts on sustainability through administration. These objectives require an amalgamation of efforts in every facet of government and intensified involvement from both publicly-held enterprises and private corporations to ensure maximum GDP growth and substantive progress in export to alleviate the burdens of large-scale imports. Engagement from the entire population – principally federal and local municipal governmental branches working in close collaboration with private enterprises – will be of immense importance in securing Greenland's long-term economic self-sufficiency and sustainability.

Given the federal government's current budget of DKK 5.32 billion (EUR 715.1 million) allocated to federal, regional and local expenditures and operations expenses coupled with income of DKK 5.34 billion (EUR 718.2 million), the government manages a negative annual balance of approximately DKK 23.3 million (EUR 3.1 million) per year. Based on these figures, if one were to extrapolate what percentage of the government's budget is allocated specifically to direct governmental financial transfers to industry and non-profit organizations, the government allocates 32% of its total budget to GFTs (government financial transfers).

Of the aforementioned annual federal budget, Greenland currently receives DKK 2.95 billion, or EUR 396.9 million, annually, which constitutes the block grant agreement with the Danish state to fund Greenland's Home Rule administration in a budgetary capacity. Additionally, Greenland also receives DKK 319.4 million, or EUR 42.95 million, annually via the Protocol IV agreement with the European Union culminating at the end of 2006, which will be renegotiated in a newly established agreement, Protocol V, taking effect on January 1st, 2006. These financial commitments and external economic support – amassing a grand total of DKK 3.27 billion, or EUR 439.9 million, annually -- shed substantial light on the immense dependence on outside investment.

In that respect, Royal Greenland A/S, the 100% government-owned international seafood conglomerate and largest corporation in terms of earnings in Greenland, is a strong indicator of the dire need for increased international expansion of business interests and lack of economic self-sufficiency at the present time. Royal Greenland alone, which in the fiscal year 2001/2002 ending on September 30, 2002 achieved group turnover of DKK 3.46 billion (EUR 465.3 million) and pre-tax profit of DKK 101 million (EUR 13.6 million) following extraordinary restructuring items, generates barely enough gross turnover to cover the necessary external investment from the Danish state and the Protocol IV agreement funding from the European Union. Consequently, the need for broadening of ties internationally and innovative business practices to solidify other viable sources of income and enhanced GDP figures will be time consuming activities for Greenland to further secure its interests in eventual independence. Fisheries will unequivocally play a vital economic role in providing economic self-sufficiency and laying further groundwork for international accords and multilateral trade agreements.

STRUCTURE AND OVERVIEW OF THE FLEET

16. The Greenlandic fishing fleet is comprised of an amalgamation of old and new vessels and has lately been going through a restructuring exercise. The offshore fleet is modern and was financed by guarantees from the Greenland Treasury in the 1990s. The coastal fleet is generally quite antiquated with vessels dating back as far as the 1960s. The fishing fleet can be divided in three segments:

a.

Below 5 GRT -mainly dinghies with outboard motors, around 5 000 since commercial fisheries began. Less than 15% of the value of the former sales stem from this group; nevertheless, plays a seemingly dominant role in connection with the informal sector of the economy.

b.

From 5 to 80 GRT, up to 20 tons. With around 350 vessels, these dominate the small-scale fisheries. These would normally be limited to one-day operations and restricted to a specific operating radius; however, when a 80 Ton limit was introduced by the authorities to prevent the largest vessels from competing with coastal fishermen, several 79-tons boats were built for use in both offshore and coastal fisheries.

c.

Above 80 GRT, mostly far above this level. These boats are equipped for long-distance fisheries and most can do processing on board with the average sailing time offshore of approximately one month. These are primarily preoccupied with shrimp fisheries with the

license condition that 25% are delivered to land-based processing facilities and the remainder can, at the vessel owner's discretion, be processed onboard in terms of the corresponding 75%.

The aforementioned classification of tonnage is a somewhat arbitrary line. Boats close to the 80 GRT level can be equipped to conduct fisheries over considerable distances and at the same time with efficiency in trawling comparable to the larger boats.

The history of Greenland's large-scale industrial fisheries has been intimately connected to Denmark. This is due not only to the role of KGH (Kongelige Grønlandske Handel), or former state-owned trade conglomerate, as trade monopoly and a main producer, but also because the pioneers in modern fisheries were two private companies based in Esbjerg, Denmark, which commenced their activities in 1948. The industrialization of fisheries also influenced the structure of the fleet, although small boats remained pervasive. The massive investments led to overcapacity: the fleet could, at the time, catch more fish than the Greenlandic seas could provide. The surplus investment was due to resource management in which the distribution of total allowable catch (TAC) based on the principle of first come, first served.

With the introduction of other approaches – a capacity quota for the coastal, or inshore, fleet and an individual transferable quota (ITQ) system for the offshore shrimp fishery, the relative imbalance between fleet and resources became indisputably obvious. Consequently, the fleet was restructured during the 1990s though 'strukturtilpasningsinitiativer', or structural optimization initiatives, in order to consolidate the fleet into a more manageable number of very large vessels. Despite the well-intended approach, the anticipated reduction in fishing capacity did not transpire.

Foreign fleets around Greenland have continually played and remain a significant contributor to Greenland's fisheries development as well. Norwegian and Faeroese fisheries began in the 1920s, which typically ranged in size from 100-300 and occasionally 500 GRT with a number of smaller dories using handlines and longlines, which have subsequently been replaced by jigging wheel equipment. On average, 40 Faeroese and Norwegian ships participated in the Greenlandic fisheries through the period of 1950-1977. In addition to the Norwegian and Faeroese fleets, an amalgamation of fleets from Portugal, France, Iceland, the United Kingdom, Russia and Germany also invested efforts in this international fishery from 1950 onwards. With the introduction of the 200 nautical mile EEZ in 1977, the foreign fleets were drastically reduced. Their remaining presence was negotiated partly through bi- and multinational agreements, in which fractions of the Greenland have been sold and/or exchanged (e.g., the existing Protocol IV agreement with the European Union). The following table expounds on the classification of different vessel configurations throughout the 20th century and initial stages of the 21st century with excruciating attention paid to vessel setups and their variances based on their origins from northern Europe and/or Greenland.

Table 4. Overview of 20th and 21st Century Fishing Technologies Used in Greenland's Waters

Fleet	Origin	Technology	1900-1910	1910-1920	1920-1930	1930-1940	1940-1950	1950-1960	1960-1970	1970-1980	1980-1990	1990-2000	2000-present
Offshore													
	Foreign	Longline						X	X				
		Trawl						X	X	X	X	X	X
	Denmark	Longline						X	X				
		Trawl						X	X	X	X	X	X
	Greenland	Longline						X	X				
		Trawl						X	X	X	X	X	X
Mixed													
	Foreign	Dory/Jig		X	X	X	X	X					
		Longline		X	X	X							
		Trawl			X	X	X	X	X				
	Denmark	Dory/Jig		X	X								
		Longline			X	X							
		Trawl				X	X	X					
	Greenland	Dory/Jig	X	X	X	X							
		Longline		X	X	X							
		Trawl			X	X	X	X	X	X	X	X	X
Local													
	Denmark	Jig											
		Longline				X	X						
		Bottom traps					X	X					
		Gill net							X				
		Trawl					X	X	X				
	Greenland	Jig	X	X	X	X	X	X	X	X	X	X	X
		Longline		X	X	X	X	X	X	X	X	X	X
		Bottom traps					X	X	X	X	X	X	X
		Gill net							X	X			
		Trawl				X	X	X	X	X	X	X	X

The fishing fleet has undergone elaborate adjustments with large investments during the 1980s in order to adjust to the circumstances. The offshore fleet is consequently exceptionally modern and well-consolidated with 2 major companies controlling the lion's share of the market and 4 additional companies maintaining sizable quota shares with consolidated gross revenues of these six operations in 2002 amassing a total of DKK 717.7 million (EUR 96.5 million) and consolidated net revenues of DKK 19.3 million (EUR 2.6 million) with an average of 5 267 tons of shrimp catch volume per trawler (12 trawler vessels in total). The total equity share amounts to DKK 422.4

For additional analytical, business and investment opportunities information,
please contact Global Investment & Business Center, USA
at (703) 370-8082. Fax: (703) 370-8083. E-mail: ibpusa3@gmail.com
Global Business and Investment Info Databank - www.ibpus.com

million (EUR 56.8 million) invested by these six operations as of December 31, 2002. Return on investment in 2002 averaged 4.9% according to the published annual reports based on financial figures released by the solely privately-held operations. Total seafood exports – amounting to nearly DKK 1.9 million (EUR 252.1 million) in 2002 – were accounted for on a revenue basis principally by the offshore shrimp vessel operations (38.3%) and likewise for total shrimp exports (60.2%).

In sheer contrast, the coastal fleet is quite antiquated and will require substantial investments within the next ten to twenty years to ensure liquidity and profitability going forward. The coastal shrimp fisheries managed a gross income level on a consolidated basis of DKK 155.7 million (EUR 20.9 million) and post-tax net revenues of DKK 7.5 million (EUR 1 million) in 2003, which is accounted for by 33 active vessels ranging between 16.2 and 810 BRT. The cumulative profitability margin amounted to a meager 2.3% in 2003, which further substantiates in economic turns the imminent need for additional consolidation of non-profitable ventures. The coastal shrimp fishery accounted for nearly 39.8% of total shrimp exports in 2002 – predominantly C&P shrimp (cooked and peeled, or Pandalus Borealis), which account for roughly 36 000 tons per year delivered to shrimp processing plants and an additional 10 000 tons processed onboard the 5 coastal vessels with production capacity (on average vessels with 79 BRT and approval from the government as a portion of their license to process 75% onboard and deliver the remaining 25% to onshore processing facilities). Meanwhile, in very similar fashion, the

Greenland halibut coastal fisheries has been mired by overcapacity in the vessel fleet with 25% of the fishing operations (97 boats as of December 31, 2002) accounting for 80% of the catch volume. Approximately 50% of the nearly 390 boats in the Greenland halibut coastal fisheries sector have other occupations concurrent with their fishing interests in order to maintain income and subsistence levels. Income levels on average between 2001 and 2003 have barely surpassed DKK 0.25 million (EUR 0.03 million) per year per fishermen prior to depreciation, amortization and B-income tax deductions.

The offshore fleet alone has invested DKK 570 million (EUR 76.6 million) in purchasing quota from the Home Rule Government since establishment of the ITQ system in the early 1990s. These quota shares are provided by the Home Rule Government on a 5-year basis, which requires notification prior to expiry of the 5-year time limitation regarding the impending allotments. Given the exorbitant investments required to procure a trawler vessel for the offshore fleet – typically upwards of DKK 150 million (EUR 20.2 million), the investment return levels are generally expected to be upwards of 6-8%. The increasing TAC levels – 57% of total shrimp TAC is allocated to offshore trawlers – have been very beneficial to these operations. Yet, despite this positive development, the investment returns commanded by their financiers have been exceptionally scrutinized given continued market volatility.

Roughly 75% of total shrimp catches in Greenland are processed on board the offshore trawlers, and the remaining catch volumes are processed in factories managed by Royal Greenland in towns and settlements. Many towns and settlements have their own processing facility and although these typically are not profitable, they are maintained in order to solidify the economic centers of these towns and settlements. This policy of ensuring maintenance of towns and settlements has shifted periodically through changes in administration, and by no means is seen as the carte blanche in Greenland's political sphere. Management of processing facilities has continually engulfed the political system with questions and debates of how best to ensure sustainable economic development, optimization of fleet capacity with production capacity, and deliberate engagement with maintaining socioeconomic conditions in both cities and settlements. Therefore, the question of managing productivity and employment factors is widely incorporated into structural policy considerations managed by the government, and done in strict congruence with the key enterprises with major investment stakes in these operations – both onshore and offshore.

TECHNICAL MEASURES TO MAINTAIN FISH STOCKS PRODUCTIVITY

25. Fisheries Management in Greenland: The ITQ System – The first law on fisheries dates back to 1984. The present law governing commercial fisheries dates back to 1990 with several amendments thereafter. The basic principles are the following:

Regulation by means of preservation and technical conservation measures. The Government is authorized to create limitations on time periods, in areas, and in use, types and characteristics of equipment.

Regulation of access to commercial fisheries. The quotas are reserved for vessels and owners of vessels from Greenland recognized as Greenlanders. The Home Rule administration has the possibility to make exceptions to this condition, as necessary.

Regulation by setting of TAC and limitations on access to resources. The decision is indisputably political, which is reached once a year by the Home Rule Government based on recommendations by biologists domestically and internationally.

Regulation is based on four different types of licenses: time-limited licenses with and without quotas and time-unlimited licenses with and without licenses. The Government decides what kind of license is mandated with the exception of those for shrimp (already pre-determined as both time-unlimited – quota allocations for offshore shrimp trawlers are renewed each 5-year period -- and transferable quota required) and salmon fisheries, which according to the Fisheries Act, require licenses. For fisheries where licenses are not required, the fisheries are open to all Greenlandic vessels, as long as the overall quota has not been utilized to its full extent. For species where no quota has been established, there are no limitations according to the Fisheries Act.

To maintain stocks' productive and reproductive capacity, Total Allowable Catch (TAC) represents the cornerstone of Greenland's fisheries management system. Currently, 11 species in the offshore sector, including shrimp, Greenlandic halibut, snow crab, grenadiers, redfish, Atlantic halibut, catfish, capelin, Blue Whiting, cod, and bottomfish (and 2 sub-stocks, including Arctic char and octopus/ squid, as well as by-catch), are subject to Total Allowable Catch (TAC). Individual quota agreements are established with Russia pertaining to haddock in Russian waters; Norway regarding haddock and saithe in Norwegian waters; the Faroe Islands in terms of herring; and, under 'International' agreements additional herring quota – these individual agreements establish quota limits for Greenlandic vessels fishing in the respective partners' fishing territories. These species account for over 96,6% (the remainder applies to catch where TAC does not apply) of the value of harvest taken within the EEZ with shrimp accounting for the most significant portion, 65% of the value of harvest subject to TAC in 2003. As pertains to the application of TAC limitations in the coastal fishery, only shrimp, crab and scallop are regulated.

The first regulation of foreign fisheries occurred with the EEZ expansion from 3 to 12 nautical miles in 1963. This mainly affected Portuguese fishermen, but a 10-year allowance of fisheries up to 6 nautical miles was established for France, Iceland, Norway, Portugal, Spain, the United Kingdom and Germany. The large international fishery – primarily cod at the time – was reduced following Greenland's assertion of a 200-mile EEZ in 1977. But since Greenland (together with Denmark) was a joint member of the European Community, EC rules had to govern its fisheries. Danish participation in Greenland fishing continued, with some limitations, until the Home Rule took effect in 1979. It had been required since the 1960s that all Danes involved in fisheries in specific areas within the 12-mile EEZ should have an address and live at least half the year in Greenland.

The basis for the present legal organization was the creation of the Home Rule in 1979. The Greenlandic government did not take over all activities immediately, but a process was instigated aiming at a total takeover by January 1st, 1985. Following a proper referendum, the Home Rule Government withdrew from the European Union in 1985, thereby allowing Greenlanders to take charge of fishery regulation. The first law concerning fisheries was passed in 1984. The present conglomeration of legal arrangements governing commercial fisheries is based on the Landstingslov (Greenland's parliament) nr. 17 of October 22, 1990. Several major amendments have since been added, including those of significant substantive amendments and ratifications of November 1991, October 1992 and May 1993.

The Greenland Home Rule Government carries out its administrative responsibilities through conveyance of quotas, licenses, and other rights and restrictions. First and foremost in importance, Greenland uses a quota system in the utilization of fish stocks, which has reaped manifold benefits for the government, industry and Greenland's ecosystem. The Ministry's Departments of Fisheries and Fisheries License Control maintain detailed and accurate information pertinent to quota utilization and license management.

With regards to Greenland's quota system, the Ministry of Fisheries and Hunting would like to mention that we introduced the ITQ system in 1990 for offshore shrimp fisheries and subsequently on January 1st, 1997 for coastal shrimp fisheries. From our perspective, this system sufficiently regulates

fishing capacity according to the available resources. Quota owners do not have any economic incentives to invest more than their respective quota share can support. For all commercially viable species, the Home Rule Government determines the TAC (Total Allowable Catch) each year and apportions quotas in accordance with quota ownership governances to the individual operations. The respective annual TAC is usually established in accordance with advice from international research institutions, such as ICES and NAFO, in which Greenlandic biologists are also represented.

In this connection, it is worth mentioning in that the Home Rule Government has taken preliminary, substantive steps towards a more ecosystem-based approach in order to be more aligned with external advisory from international research institutions. For instance, based on guidance and advice for the period 2003-2008, the Home Rule has contemplated TAC with an additional variable – the proportionate amount of shrimp consumed by cod. Accounting for such consultancy and ecosystem variables is by no means placed on the periphery when TAC figures are established. Shrimp biologists consider cod as one of the most prominent shrimp predators, and, consequently, developed a model that allows NAFO to extrapolate five years into the future when advising on TAC computations. This ecosystem-based approach is unequivocally useful in the management of marine resources in Greenland and elsewhere. It is also indisputably useful for the industry since, for example, quota owners can more easily regulate their catch capacity in accordance with necessary levels projected over a five-year period.

When the Greenlandic Government envisages TAC, the Ministry does not only seek scientific advice, but also significant input from the Greenlandic fishing industry. The Ministry makes every conceivable effort to establish TAC according to biological advice; however, biological guidelines on certain species are often exceptionally scarce or insufficient in terms of data validity. For instance, managing crab stocks is undeniably one area in the Greenlandic fishing industry that requires more support from biologists to more clearly elucidate and mitigate potential overfishing of certain stocks.

In this regard, another reverberating issue is management of stocks we share with adjacent coastal states. Despite a bevy of activity and efforts to develop further collaboration with these states, we have not succeeded agreeing upon how we divide the TAC between us and neighboring states. What transpires is virtually inevitable given constraints on information and insufficient international cooperation

- each state sets their own TAC individually. We are fully cognizant of and even more increasingly aware as time passes that this development is resulting in unfortunate implications and misappropriated usage of fish resources. Needless to say, the long-term solution is an irrepressible and well-construed agreement with the relevant coastal states to cooperate more closely.

CONTROL AND SURVEILLANCE

Management and control has been maintained through two different ways: inspection and license control and management of fish processing plants.

The control and compliance with quota and license regulations is the responsibility of the Greenland Fisheries License Control (GFLK), established in 1985. It employs on average 50 fisheries license controllers. Due to problems of discard, the Government introduced an amendment to the law in 1989 requiring government inspectors stationed onboard the vessels. Two inspectors are now installed onboard all high sea vessels fishing in Greenlandic waters, both domestic and foreign. Daily reports in form of written electronic messages and written logbooks have to be handed in by all large vessels. A satellite system monitors all trawler movements and activities in Greenlandic waters. Weekly reports on the fisheries as a whole are distributed to the relevant organizations and authorities. GFLK is also responsible for monitoring the observation of Greenlandic fisheries regulations by Greenlandic vessels fishing outside Greenlandic waters, in NAFO, NEAFC, Norwegian and Russian regulated waters.

Fisheries inspections regulating fishing vessels at sea (catches and equipment) is, in conjunction with GFLK, the responsibility of the Greenland Command (DK defense vessels). The management of fish processing plants, on the other hand, is a more political means of controlling fisheries, as the plants are the only places where fish can be sold. Restrictions on fisheries can therefore be implemented by limiting the time periods of purchase with very short notice and can therefore be used as a means of resource management.

CATCH REGULATION

37. The main structure of the regulation includes a number of basic principles and tenants, including the following key elements:

a) One element in the fisheries management system is the regulation by means of preservation and technical conservation measures, where the Government is authorized to create limitations in time periods, in areas, and in use, types and characteristics of equipment.

b) A fundamental principle is the regulation of access to commercial fisheries. Basically the quotas are reserved for vessels and owners of vessels from Greenland recognized as Greenlanders. But it is feasible for the Home Rule administration (Landsstyre) to make exceptions.

c) Another main principle of resource management in Greenland is regulation by establishing TAC annually and limitations on access to resources. It is a political decision usually taken by the government, but based highly on scientific recommendations from biologists.

d) The regulation is based on four different types of licenses: time-limited licenses with and without quotas and time-unlimited licenses with and without quotas. It is at the Home Rule government's discretion to determine what type of license (if any) should apply to a given fishery, except for the shrimp and salmon fisheries, which both, according to the law, require licenses. In the case of shrimp, the law requires time-unlimited and transferable quotas which can be transferred contingent upon market-driven values.

e) For fisheries where licenses are not required, the fisheries are open to all Greenlandic vessels as long as the overall quota has not been used to its limit. And for species where no quota has been established, there are no limitations on fishing.

The Home Rule Government has also asserted itself in protecting ecosystem interests. On that note, we have been very diligent in protecting spawning and juvenile fish areas. One exemplary example is on Greenland's east coast where we solidified a "Redfish protection area", wherein fisheries with bottom trawl were completely banned. Since the year 2001, the Ministry imposed the usage of sorting-grids as a mandatory requirement for shrimp fishing operations. This technical conservation step has been evaluated as being remarkably sufficient for protection of particularly juvenile redfish and halibut. As a result of the introduction of sorting-grids, we have among other things been able to effectively alleviate the "Redfish protection area", which was the ostensibly the world's largest fish stock protection area.

The Ministry would also like to mention the efforts of the Greenland Institute of Natural Resources, the institute that advises the Greenland Home Rule Government, which has undertaken a program envisioned to run for five years in order to establish a concentrated scientific background for long-term ecosystem-based management of natural resources in Western Greenland. The Ministry presumes that this program will allow us to ascertain very useful knowledge applicable to our daily management. Provided agreement between biologists, the Home Rule Government's Ministry of Fisheries and Hunting, Royal Greenland, and the offshore fisheries' interest group, APK, agreement was reached in late 2003 to implement conversion factors for the offshore shrimp fishery, which effectively minimize and

attempt to alleviate overpacking. The results of this well-construed effort have led to inclusion of conversion factors being integrated with computations of TAC for the offshore shrimp fishery.

LIMITATIONS ON FISHING PER SPECIES

Cod: In 1968, the first international rules appeared, a technical regulation of fairly significant stature. In 1974, international regulation of cod fishing was introduced and carried far-reaching consequences for coastal states. A yearly quota was determined by the Northwest Atlantic Fisheries Organization (NAFO), which encompassed a portion allocated to Greenland. The TAC was based on a biological evaluation of the resource. Following the 1977 expansion of the EEZ, virtually all of the cod was reserved for Greenland. A limited bi-catch of cod was permitted for German trawlers catching redfish (Sebastes sp.) and certain other fisheries.

Salmon: Political pressure from European and North American recreational fishermen drove regulation of the salmon fisheries. The expansion of Greenlanders' salmon fishing in the mid-1960s led to calls for international intervention – an attempt to totally ban fisheries for salmon was presented in 1969. But not until 1971 did regulation take effect (Nørrevang et al.). ICNAF established a yearly limit of 1,200 tons in 1972 based on the average of the previous three years' catch. At the present time, Greenland continues to be precluded from any commercial salmon fisheries given prevailing limitations on catch.

For additional analytical, business and investment opportunities information, please contact Global Investment & Business Center, USA at (703) 370-8082. Fax: (703) 370-8083. E-mail: ibpusa3@gmail.com Global Business and Investment Info Databank - www.ibpus.com

Shrimp: Until the 1950s, shrimp were predominantly pursued by inshore, or coastal, vessels, and therefore of interest mostly to Greenlanders. But with the inevitable expansion of shrimp fishing to the outer parts of banks, broader regulation became necessary. The introduction of TAC was the first overall regulation of the shrimp fishery. But in Greenland, it also created incentives for surplus investment and overcapacity, because the fishery was open to everyone until the TAC level was reached. To reduce the capacity and determine more efficient means for regulating the fishery, two types of quota arrangements were created:

Government Order 6 of April 8, 1991 determines the regulation of vessels above 75 GRT under the basic tenants of Greenland's ITQ system. The total TAC was divided amongst the shipping companies engaged in shrimp fisheries at that time in proportion to their respective catches during the last 3-year period. They received a certain percentage of the yearly TAC. The government order allowed for the companies to sell the whole share of portions of it with prices determined by the free market. The Home Rule has a precedent for buying the TAC share in order to reduce the fishing activity or to redistribute the share – a policy that is maintained even in 2004 through the administration of a quota bank.

Government Order 32 of November 21, 1991 determines the regulation of vessels below 75 GRT in a Capacity Quota System. The regulation method is through a number of points given to each fisherman involved in the fisheries based on the individual's activities in the previous years and determined according to their respective technical capacity – i.e., vessel size, gear type, etc. The points are fully transferable, and it is feasible to upgrade the fishing capacity by buying a certain number of points and upgrading gear. The government can reduce the "quality" of the points in connection with transfer of points from one fisherman to another. It is also permissible for the government to buy out points in order to reduce the catch capacity. At the time of introduction of this government order, given a license to fish, it is possible to do as much fishing as time enables with the specific equipment available; however, given the subsequent addendum to Greenland's Fisheries Law No. 18 of August 22, 1996, which converted the system regulating vessels under 75 GRT to be in compliance with Greenland's ITQ system applicable to both offshore and coastal fisheries following the revision to the Fisheries Law, the regulations became more stringent.

Snow Crab: Effective January 1, 2005, Regulation nr. 8 of June 7th, 2004, establishes six (6) specific management areas for snow crab (Chionoecetes opilio) fisheries and, furthermore, TAC quotas per each of the aforementioned management area in the following regions: Upernavik, Disko Bay-Uummannaq, Sisimiut, Maniitsoq-Kangaamiut, Nuuk-Paamiut and Narsaq-Qaqortoq. The regulation applies to crab vessels under 75 BRT/ 120 BT. Given more extensive scientific advisory concerning the ramifications for continuing crab fisheries at levels prior to 2004, this regulatory order contemplates specific TAC allocations based on more easily dissectable biological data.

SUMMARY OF MARKET-LIKE INSTRUMENTS TO REGULATE ACCESS: ITQ SYSTEM

Exclusivity: For those licenses combined with a maximum allowable catch, the Landsstyre shall publish information about the size of the annual quota every year. Each operator knows the quantity that other right holders are entitled to fish. This provides a high level of exclusivity. In addition, a quota share allocated to one fleet unit shall not be fished by any other fleet unit, and an annual quota allocated to one fleet unit shall not be fished by any other fleet unit. This provides a high level of exclusivity among groups.

Duration: Quota share are possessed by ship owners. [+Quota shares shall be transferable by inheritance]. The level of the characteristic is high.

For additional analytical, business and investment opportunities information,
please contact Global Investment & Business Center, USA
at (703) 370-8082. Fax: (703) 370-8083. E-mail: ibpusa3@gmail.com
Global Business and Investment Info Databank - www.ibpus.com

Quality of the title: The Cabinet may issue notices about time-limited changes of the conditions for fishing activities (which entails fairly significant sovereign risk).

Transferability: A ship owner may, without effect for the operation's license and quota shares, sell its annual quota or part of this quota, if damage or long-term repair at a shipyard transpires; natural obstructions such as ice or similar circumstances prevent the ship owner from exhausting the operation's annual quota. Transfer of an annual quota may moreover take place in special cases warranted by economic or administrative conditions. Enterprises owned by the Home Rule Government may irrespective of the provisions of subsections (1)-(3) in the Fisheries Act sell and buy annual quotas. It shall be a condition for transfer according to subsection (1) that the transfer [of both quota share and annual quota] is approved by the Landsstyre.

No company or individual may by purchase of quota shares attain a total quota share which exceeds 33.3% in the regulated area for the offshore fleet unit.

a) No companies or individuals may through purchases of quota shares acquire a quota share in the regulation area for the coastal fleet component which exceeds 10 percent.

b) An annual quota allocated to one fleet unit shall not be fished by any other fleet unit.

Divisibility: Fully divisible (idem Iceland).

Flexibility: The Cabinet may issue notices setting out when fishing activities may be commenced and when fishing activities must be stopped. For Greenland fisheries according to section 6 of the Fisheries Law, it may be required as a condition for acquiring a license (1) that the catch shall be delivered in full or in part to one or more specified processing plants in Greenland, possibly for definite periods and with respect to certain quantities, qualities and compositions of the catch (specified delivery), and (2) that a certain part of the crew shall be persons with a permanent connection with the Greenlandic society and/or community (crew share). The Cabinet may issue rules according to which a shipping company, which has exhausted its annual quota, may continue its fishing activities provided that the quantities fished in excess of the annual quota quantities are deducted from the shipping company's annual quota for the subsequent year. Further, the Cabinet may issue rules according to which a shipping company, which has not

exhausted its annual quota, may have its annual quota for the coming year increased by a quantity corresponding to the unused portion from the preceding year.

NATIONAL AQUACULTURE LEGISLATION OVERVIEW - DENMARK

BASIC LEGISLATION

The **Fisheries act (2004, as amended)** regulates the management, control and development of fisheries and aquatic resources in Denmark. Chapter 13 addresses ocean farming and establishes a licensing system governing the establishment and operation of mariculture facilities. The Act grants the Minister of Food, Agriculture and Fisheries general power to make regulations with regard to the issuing of licences for the establishment and operation of ocean farms. The Regulation on the establishment and operation of ocean farms (1991)[+] sets forth more detailed rules on the licensing system of mariculture facilities. The issuing of licences has been delegated to the Danish Directorate of Fisheries.

For aquaculture facilities taking in fresh water, facilities that are placed on land taking in marine water, and for the fish farming of mussels, oysters etc., no regulations have been issued pursuant to the Fisheries act (2004) concerning licensing. For fish farming that requires feed, however, an approval according to the **Environment protection act (2001)** is required. For the fish farming of mussels, oysters etc., an application for a licence shall be filed with the Directorate of Fisheries in accordance with the Instruction on Applications for Bivalve Aquaculture in the Limfjord (2003).

LEGAL DEFINITION

There is no general definition of aquaculture in the Fisheries Act (2004). The Regulation relative to the establishment and operation of ocean farms (1991), adopted under the Act, has, however, the following definition of ocean farming: "With ocean farming is understood fish farms consisting of cages and the like, placed in marine waters which requires the use of feed for its operation".

Concerning aquaculture facilities placed on land taking in marine water, the following definition appears in the Regulation relative to marine water aquaculture (1990)[+] , adopted under the Environment protection act (2001): "Fish farm placed on land that has an intake of marine water, including cooling water from power plants or the like, which requires the use of feed for its operation. Concerning aquaculture facilities taking in fresh water, the Regulation relative to fresh water fish farms (1998)[+] , adopted under the Environment protection act (2001), states that it is applicable for fish farms that exclusively takes in fresh water and has a water outlet to water ways, lakes or the ocean.

INTERNATIONAL ARRANGEMENTS

Denmark is a member of the following international arrangements:

World Trade Organization (WTO).

The European Union (EU).

North Atlantic Salmon Conservation Organization (NASCO).

World Organisation for Animal Health (OIE).

Denmark is party to the Convention on Biological Diversity (CBD). It ratified the Biosafety Protocol on 27 August 2002 and became a party on 11 September 2003.

AUTHORIZATION SYSTEM

According to the **Fisheries act (2004)**, fish farming in Danish fisheries territories (ocean farming) can only take place if a licence has been granted by the Ministry of Food, Agriculture and Fisheries, a power that has been delegated to the Directorate of Fisheries. The Directorate determines the conditions, including possible time limits, for the licence. The application for an ocean farming licence is considered to be an application for permits after all other relevant legislation. A licence can not be granted for the establishment of new fish farms in fjords. The durability of the licence will be settled in the conditions for the licence.

According to the Regulation relative to the establishment and operation of ocean farms (1991)[+], adopted under the Act, a licence is needed both for the setting up and for the operation of an ocean farm. An application for a new licence, for the expansion of an existing mariculture facility, or for the extension of a licence, is to be filed with the County Council. When processing the application, the following authorities will be heard by the Ministry: The Danish Forest and Nature Agency, the Royal Danish Administration of Navigation and Hydrography, the Coast Directory, the Fisheries and Ocean Surveys of Denmark, the local Fisheries Inspector, the Danish Fishery Organisation and The Danish Ocean Fishery Organisation.

A licence to establish and operate an ocean farm can be withdrawn by the Ministry upon the breach of determined conditions. If an ocean farm is to be established further ashore and outside the County Council planning area (see section 5), the power, according to the Act relative to coastal protection (1994)[+], lies with the Ministry of Transport, now delegated to the Coastal Directorate, as to granting a licence.

The Fisheries act (2004) applies to all kinds of fish farming, hence also for the fish farming of mussels, oysters etc., the setting up of aquaculture facilities placed on land using marine water, as well as for facilities using fresh water. The Regulation relative to the establishment and operation of ocean farms, does however not apply to these kinds of aquaculture facilities.

For the fish farming of mussels, oysters etc., an application for a licence shall be filed with the Directorate of Fisheries in accordance with the Instruction on Applications for Bivalve Aquaculture in the Limfjord (2003). For the setting up of aquaculture facilities, either placed on land using marine water or fish farms taking in fresh water, an approval according to the **Environment protection act (2001)**, can be required. This also applies in case of an expansion or change in the facility that will increase the pollution from such a facility. According to the Approval regulation (2004)[+], adopted under the Environment protection act, such an approval is needed unless the aquaculture facility has full recirculation or is without direct water outlet to water ways, lakes or the ocean. The application has to be filed with the municipality, which will forward it to the County Council. The approval is normally valid for eight years. The approval can however, be reconsidered by the authorities if the pollution from the facility exceeds permitted levels or there are other fundamental changes arising.

Access to land and water

According to the Act relative to planning (2002)[+], every county is obliged to have a Regional Plan. This is to be prepared by the County Council and shall cover a period of 12 years. The plan shall include guidelines for, inter alia, the use of water ways, lakes and waters, and accordingly establish aquaculture zones. Furthermore, the Act states that larger plants that are likely to have a considerable impact on the environment, must not be set up before the Regional Plan includes guidelines on the placement and the design of the plant, as well as an account including an Environmental Impact Assessment (EIA). The Regulations on supplementary rules (1999)[+] , adopted under the Act, provides rules on what aquaculture facilities that are included in the term larger plants (see section 6).

Pursuant to a the **Environment protection act (2001)**, a circular has been made, providing that the Regional Plan shall include quality goals for shore waters, dividing the areas into three categories, with either a general, reduced or high level quality goal. According to the Regulation relative to marine aquaculture (1990)[+] , adopted under the Act, a licence, pursuant to the Fisheries act, for operating a mariculture farm in an area with a high level quality goal, can be given when there is reason to believe that the influence on the environment will occur outside this area.

EIA

As stated in section 6, the Act relative to planning (2002)[+] , provides that larger plants that are likely to have a considerable impact on the environment, must not be set up before the Regional Plan includes an Environmental Impact Assessment (EIA) regarding the plant in question. The Regulation on supplementary rules (1999)[+] , adopted under the Act, provides rules on when an EIA shall be carried out, as well as requirements regarding the contents of the EIA. The Regulation provide that when establishing a new marine water fish farm outside a zone designated for aquaculture in the Regional Plan, or when changing such a facility considerably, an EIA shall be worked out. If the aquaculture facility in question is designated for intensive fish farming or has an intake of fresh water, an EIA shall be worked out as far as the facility it is likely to have a considerable impact on the environment, even when it is to be established in an aquaculture zone.

The Regulation lists the different criteria that shall be used when considering whether a facility is likely to have such an impact, i.e. the size of the facility, waste production, the vulnerability of the surrounding environment etc. When it comes to the contents of the EIA, the Regulation states that the EIA shall, inter alia, include a description of the planned facility, a summary of the most important alternative sites that has been examined, the reasons for the choice of alternatives, a description of the environment that can be considerably influenced by facility, as well as an account of the short term and long term influence on the environment. As to ocean farms outside the County Council planning area, the Coastal Directorate decides whether an EIA shall be carried out in relation with an application for the setting up of a facility, see the Regulation relative to EIA regarding plants on the ocean territory (1999)[+] , adopted under the Act relative to coastal protection (1994).

WATER AND WASTEWATER

According to the **Environment protection act (2001)**, the discharge or disposal of waste water into waterways, lakes or the ocean is prohibited unless a permit is granted by, depending on the capacity of the facility, the municipality or County Council. The Waste water permit regulation (1999)[+] , adopted under the Act, provides rules on, inter alia, the processing of applications, requirements that has to be met regarding the cleansing of the waste water, as well as other conditions that can be attached to a permit.

The Regulation relative to fresh water fish farms (1998)[+] , also adopted under the Environment protection act, determines provisions regarding, inter alia, maximum levels of wastewater, permitted levels of chemicals in outlet water from the farm, and requirements regarding the installation and design of cleansing systems. The Regulation Relative to marine water aquaculture (1990)[+] , also adopted under the Environment protection act, determines provisions regarding, inter alia, maximum use of feed, feed ratio, emission limits on nitrogen and phosphorus, the contents of nitrogen and phosphorus in the feed, as well as the carrying out of self monitoring. For on shore marine fish farms there are provisions on the design of the outlet and intake water system, as well as on the quality of the outlet and intake water.

FISH MOVEMENT

According to the **Fisheries act (2004)**, the introduction and the moving of fish, egg and fry is not permitted, unless: a) it is in accordance with a plan prepared by or approved by the Minister of Food, Agriculture and Fisheries, b) an approval is granted by the Minister or c) it is according to a verdict.

According to the Act relative to animal keeping (2004)[+] , the Minister of Family and Consumer Affairs can issue regulations on the export and import of animals, including fish, from which disease and zoonotic transmissible infectious agents can be spread. Furthermore, it can issue regulations regarding the introduction, use, trade, import and export of farmed animals that are genetically modified, including fish, as well as the prior notification or approval of this.

Pursuant to the Act, the Regulation relative to the sale of aquaculture animals and products within the European Union as well as import of this from countries outside the EU (1999)[+] has been adopted[+] .

Several provisions must be observed when placing on the market aquaculture animals, eggs and gametes within the EU; the animals must not show signs of clinical disease the day they are shipped; the animals must not be intended for destruction or slaughter under a scheme for the eradication of a disease as listed; the animals must not come from or have been in contact with animals from aquaculture facilities where, either there has been imposed a prohibition against sales due to animal health reasons, or that is being kept under the supervision of the Danish Veterinary and Food Administration due to proven disease or suspicion of disease.

A system of approved zones and farms, where specific health requirements are fulfilled, is established. When live fish, egg and gametes belonging to the susceptible species as referred to, as well as mollusc as referred to, are introduced into an approved zone, they must be accompanied by a movement document certifying that they come from an approved zone or an approved farm. When they are to be introduced into an approved farm they must be accompanied by a movement document certifying that they come respectively from an approved zone or from a farm of the same health status as the farm of destination.

The Veterinary and Food Administration can permit the movement of live fish, egg and semen from farms struck by disease to farms that are struck by the same disease, or when being slaughtered for the purpose of consumption.

Shipment within the EU of live, farmed fish, as well as their eggs and gametes between non-approved zones regarding infectious haematopoietic necrosis (IHN) and viral haemorrhagic septicaemia (VHS), as well as the shipment between two farms infected by IHN and VHS, shall be accompanied by a certificate as appropriate.

Susceptible fish shall be slaughtered and cleansed prior to shipment from a non approved zone to an approved one.

Live susceptible fish being shipped from a non-approved zone to an approved one for human consumption, must be delivered either for direct consumption or to the preserving industry, unless they originate in an approved farm, or they are temporarily immersed in specially approved storage ponds.

When live farmed fish or molluscs not belonging to the susceptible species as referred to, as well as their eggs and gametes are to be introduced into an approved zone they must be accompanied by a movement document certifying that they come from a zone of the same health status, from an approved farm in a non-approved zone or from a farm which may be situated in a non-approved zone on condition that such a farm contains no fish belonging to the listed susceptible species referred to and that is not connected with a watercourse or with coastal or estuarial waters.

When wild fish, molluscs and crustaceans, are to be introduced into an approved zone, they must be accompanied by a movement document certifying that they come from a zone of the same health status. When they are to be introduced into an approved farm situated in a non-approved zone, they must be accompanied by a movement document certifying that they come from an approved zone.

Wild fish being caught on the ocean and designated for reproduction in approved zones or approved farms, shall when they require so, be put in quarantine under the supervision of the Veterinary and Food Administration. Furthermore, the Regulation sets forth that the aquatic animals shall be transported to their destination as fast as possible with a means of transportation that has been cleaned and disinfected if necessary.

Regarding import of aquatic animals and products from outside the EC, the Regulation provide that this must only occur on conditions that are in accordance with EC legislation. A shipment from outside the EC must be accompanied by a certificate issued and signed by the authorities of the country of export.

The **Act on the environment and genetic engineering (1991)** applies to the production and use of genetically modified organisms. According to the Act, genetically modified organisms shall not be imported, introduced, transported or sold without the approval of the Minister for the Environment. Such approval can be given when the release serves for any purpose other than marketing, or serves for the marketing of products, that either consist of, or include GMO's. However, such an approval is not required when the GMO is approved for marketing in another state member of the European Union in accordance with Directive 2001/18/EC on the deliberate release into the environment of genetically modified organisms. Pursuant to the Act, the Regulation on the approval of the release to the environment of genetically modified organisms (2002)【+】 has been adopted. The Regulation implements the Directive 2001/18/EC, determining rules regarding, inter alia, procedures for application and processing, consultative rounds, as well as supervision.

According to the Regulation relative to the combating of infectious disease with fresh water fish (1984)【+】 , adopted under the Act relative to animal keeping (2004)【+】 , live fresh water fish and egg must only be exported when it is accompanied by a written health certificate provided by a veterinarian in accordance with instructions provided by the Veterinary and Food Administration.

DISEASE CONTROL

According to the Act relative to animal keeping (2004), the Minister of Family and Consumer Affairs can issue regulations on the examination of live fish for zoonotic transmissible infectious agents. The Act sets forth that anybody keeping fish being infected by ISA, or any other of the listed diseases, or when suspecting that so is the case, shall send for a veterinarian. Furthermore, the Regulation provides provisions on the examination that is to be conducted by the veterinarian, as well as his duty to notify the authorities in case of, or upon suspicion of diseases as listed. The Minister can issue regulations on the killing of animals for examination purposes, as well as regulations on procedures related to the taking of samples. For the purpose

For additional analytical, business and investment opportunities information,
please contact Global Investment & Business Center, USA
at (703) 370-8082. Fax: (703) 370-8083. E-mail: ibpusa3@gmail.com
Global Business and Investment Info Databank - www.ibpus.com

of eradicating, preventing, limiting, as well as countering the risk of the widespread of zoonotic transmissible infectious agents and other listed diseases, the Minister can issue regulations and order the carrying out of special measures. For live fish, this includes the examination, supervision, marking, treatment, vaccination, isolation, killing, destruction as well as imposing special conditions for the delivery of animals. For fish products, including feed, these measures can, in addition to the ones already listed, be the ordering of special use, disinfection, storing and withdrawal.

For the fish farms and processing plants these measures can be to impose special requirements related to operations, cleaning and disinfection, withdrawal of authorization, supervision, blocking, the drying out as well as prohibiting the water inlet and outlet. Furthermore, the Minister can also prohibit the use of fish, egg, feed etc. as well as other products and objects from where disease and zoonotic transmissible infectious agents can spread. The Minister can also issue regulations regarding the health status of animals whose semen and eggs are being transferred to other animals.

Concerning control measures, the Act relative to animal keeping (2004), regulates that the Minister can determine regulations or provisions on control measures that can be carried through in order to ensure compliance with the Act. The Minister can in this respect make decisions on orders and prohibitions, hereupon that foodstuffs that do not comply with the Act, regulations or provisions, shall be marked, confiscated, destroyed, withdrawn from the market or that the enterprise shall suspend production. The Act also provides for the legal admittance to processing plants etc. when necessary for the carrying out of control measures. In addition it provides for that persons in charge of a processing plant etc. has the duty to give necessary information to the authorities in case of control.

The Regulation relative to the combating of certain fish diseases (2001)[+] , adopted under the Act, sets forth provisions on how to combat infectious salmon anaemia, infectious haematopoietic necrosis and viral haemorrhagic septicaemia (ISA, IHN and VHS), and includes provisions implementing Council Directive 93/53/EEC of 24 June 1993 introducing minimum Community measures for the control of certain fish diseases. The Regulation sets forth that the owner or the responsible of an aquaculture facility shall keep a register over the live fish, semen and egg entering or departing the facility, as well as dead fish. Furthermore, it sets forth a duty to notify the Veterinary and Food Administration upon a suspicion of the occurrence of ISA, IHN and VHS. In case of suspicion of the occurrence of ISA, the Regulation also set forth provisions regarding the supervision of the facility by the Administration. In case of suspicion of the occurrence of ISA, as well as IHN and VHS, the Regulation provides for the ordering of examinations.

The Regulation relative to the combating of infectious disease with fresh water fish (1984)[+] , adopted under the Act relative to animal keeping (2004), sets forth provisions on the combating of IPN and VHS through the implementing of combat plans and keeping of a register by the Veterinary and Food Administration, as well as cleansing and disinfection provisions regarding premises and gear, packing and transport. The Regulation sets forth that newly established or re-established fish farms shall be registered with the Administration. They must not start operating before the outlet system has been approved and the Administration has decided whether the fish farm in question shall be included in a combat plan. Furthermore, the owner shall keep a record on the amount of live fresh fish, fry and egg being purchased and sold from fish farms, as well as the name of buyer and seller, and the date of the transaction. In case that disease included in a combat plan is proven in a fish farm included in a combat plan, the Administration can order the removal or destruction of the fish stock and eggs. This also applies to contagious diseases not earlier been diagnosed, representing a danger for the fish farm industry. Furthermore, the Administration can prohibit or limit the trade in fish, egg, semen from a fish farm if the stock is attacked by a contagious disease, as well as when there is suspicion that the stock has been infected.

Furthermore there are restrictions on the supplies of water, fish and eggs to fish farms that are included in a combat plan and that are VHS and/or IPN free. When there are indications of VHS and/or IPN in such a fish farm, the owner shall promptly notify the Administration.

The Regulation does also set forth that slaughtering houses and processing premises must not be established in connection with fish farms and water ways. Upon the establishment of such plants, they must not have neither direct nor indirect outlet through a sewerage to a water way.

Pursuant to the Act relative to animal keeping (2004), the Regulation relative to control with contagious diseases with bivalve mollusc (1997)[+] has been adopted. Firstly, aquaculture facilities farming bivalve mollusc shall be registered with the Veterinary and Food Administration. Furthermore, the Regulation sets forth provisions regarding the keeping of a journal, where a record of the origin of the stocks, the species that leaves the facility for reproduction, as well as the mortality rate is included. The person in charge of the facility shall promptly send for a veterinarian upon suspicion of the occurrence of one of the listed diseases. Furthermore, there are provisions on, inter alia, the veterinarian's obligations to notify the Administration in case of suspicion of disease, as well as the keeping of the facility under surveillance of the Administration due to this, as well as the owner's duty to give information to the Administration.

DRUGS

The Act relative to animal keeping (2004), states that the Minister of Family and Consumer Affairs can issue regulations on the use of veterinarian vaccinations, drugs etc. Pursuant to this, the Regulation relative to veterinary drugs (2003)[+] has been issued[+] . The Regulation provides that when treating animals, including fish, veterinary drugs that has obtained a marketing permit from the Danish Medicines Agency or been approved for marketing by the EU Council, shall be used. Veterinary drugs can however, be used pursuant to a distribution permit. In case there is no applicable veterinary drug that has been permitted, a veterinarian can in exceptional cases, particularly for preventing unacceptable suffering for animals use, distribute or prescribe the veterinary drugs listed, for the treatment of a single or a few animals.

The Regulation also provides rules that prohibit or impose limitations on the use of certain hormones, as well as restrictions on the use of therapeutic and zoo technical treatment of animals. Inter alia, it is prohibited to use veterinary drugs being growth-promoting. The Veterinary and Food Administration can, however, upon an application, permit a veterinarian to prescribe veterinary drugs with an androgenic effect for the treatment of fry, provided certain provisions are observed. Furthermore, the Regulation provides a list of veterinary drugs that can only be used by a veterinarian. There are also provisions on the keeping of journals and storing of documentation of both the veterinarian and the person in charge of the animals, as well as on the storing of veterinarian drugs in the enterprise, ordering, inter alia, that such drugs must be kept and used in accordance with the veterinarian's instructions. As to the treatment of animals with antibiotics, the Regulation determines that this can only take place if the treatment is aimed at specific diagnosed infections and at healing the animals, provided that the animals are clinically sick or are in the incubation period of a well defined disease. Moreover, there are provisions regarding the handing out and the prescription of antibiotics and other animal drugs aiming at infections, including rules on the permitted duration of the treatment. The Regulation also imposes restrictions on the trade in animals that have been treated with veterinary drugs, as well as rules on the carrying out of quarantines due to such treatment. Furthermore, the Regulation adopts provisions regarding the purchasing, storing, use, handing over and the prescription of veterinary drugs.

As to control measures, the Regulation provides for the adoption of Council Regulation (EEC) No 2377/90 of 26 June 1990 laying down a Community procedure for the establishment of maximum residue limits of veterinary medicinal products in foodstuffs of animal origin. Upon the occurrence of illegal drugs or residues exceeding the legal limits, the drugs in question shall be confiscated. Animals that have been treated with these drugs shall be submitted to public supervision, together with animal products that contains illegal residues/ drugs. Furthermore, there are provisions on the killing of animals in case of illegal treatment with drugs. The Regulation also provides for that animal products, including fish, must not be handed over, sold, preserved or used for human consumption if they contain levels of residues from veterinary drugs that are above the permitted levels, or contain residues that originate from illegal treatment. Furthermore, the undertaking of random samples is also addressed.

The Regulation relative to certain residues in foodstuffs (2004)[*] , adopted under the Foodstuffs Act (1998, as amended)[*] , provides that it is prohibited to use products that contain residue levels that exceed permitted levels, when producing foodstuffs, or to combine such products with products that comply with the permitted levels. The Regulation includes maximum permitted levels for, inter alia lead, tin, cadmium, mercury and mycotoxicants. Furthermore, it regulates that foodstuffs must not be sold if they contain residue levels of lead, cadmium, mercury, tin and mycotoxicants that exceed the permitted levels. Concerning levels of dioxins and 3-MCPD, the Regulation refers to the permitted levels settled by EU regulations. To control that the maximum permitted levels in animal foodstuffs, including fish, are being complied with, the Veterinary and Food Administration can decide that random samples of the levels in foodstuffs shall be taken according to a settled random samples schedule.

The Regulations relative to microbiological limits for foodstuffs (2004)[*] , adopted under the Foodstuffs Act (1998), determines such limits for live bivalve molluscs, echinoderms, crustaceans and ocean snails produced for consumption. Limits are also determined for these species when boiled, then also including crawfish.

The Regulation relative to the combating of certain fish diseases (2001), adopted under the Act relative to animal keeping (2004), sets forth that it is prohibited to vaccinate against ISA, unless permitted by the Veterinary and Food Administration. Vaccination against IHN and VHS is not permitted in approved zones or farms (see 8), as well as for zones and farms that will be approved.

The Regulation relative to the combating of infectious disease with fresh water fish (1984), also adopted under the Act relative to animal keeping (2004), sets forth that vaccination of fresh water fish can only take place when permitted by the Veterinary and Food Administration.

The Regulation relative to pesticide residues in foodstuffs and feed (2004)[*] , adopted under the Foodstuffs Act (1998), sets forth maximum residue levels of the listed pesticides in feed. The Regulation provides that it is prohibited to sell products that contain residue levels that exceed the maximal levels set forth. Furthermore, provisions regarding control are adopted, providing that this control should be in line with Council Directive 2000/63/EEC.

Concerning the use of different hazardous substances (antibiotics, copper etc.) the statutory order 921/1996, implementing Council Directive 76/464/EEC on pollution caused by certain dangerous substances discharged into the aquatic environment of the Community, is relevant. It states that certain quality standards should be carried out for all surface water and that all discharge permits should contain limits for the discharge of the substances listed in the directive.

The Regulation on health related conditions of fishing, treatment, processing and trade of living bivalve molluscs (1993)[*] , adopted under the Foodstuffs Act (1998), prescribes, inter alia, microbiological quality standards and certain production areas for bivalves[*] . Production areas are to be determined by the Danish Veterinary and Food Administration, who monitors for algal toxins, micro-organisms and polluting chemicals.

FEED

The **Act relative to feeding stuffs (2000)** enables the Minister of Food, Agriculture and Fisheries to issue regulations on, inter alia, production, storing, the trade in and the use of feed for animals, including fish, as well as the authorization of producers and importers, and permitted levels of residues. The Act states that when imported or sold, the feed shall be healthy and sound and of a normal quality. When sold or being used in an appropriate manner, the feed shall not represent any threat to human or animal health or to the environment. Furthermore it shall not be sold in a manner that can be misleading. Feed that do not comply with regulations pursuant to the Act, must not be used for feeding. Upon a justified suspicion that a quantity of feed will pose a health risk to humans or animals, or to the environment, the Minister can prohibit the sale or the use of the feed until the result of an examination is available. The Minister can order that feed not complying with regulations, shall be used for other purposes than feeding, destroyed or, if imported, return the shipment. The Act also provides for the legal admittance of the authorities to processing plants etc. when necessary for the carrying out of control measures. In addition it provides that the person in charge of a processing plant etc. has the duty to give necessary information to the authorities in case of control.

The Regulation relative to feed (2004)[*] , adopted under the Act, addresses the production, transport, trade, import, export and use of feed for animals, including fish. The Regulation lists substances that are illegal to use in feed and includes provisions on the labelling and packing of feed, as well as provisions regarding the chemical and biological purity of feed and maximum permitted residue levels.

The Regulation relative to pesticide residues in feed (2004)[*] , adopted under the Act, sets forth maximum residues levels of the listed pesticides in feed. The Regulation provides that it is prohibited to sell products that contain residue levels that exceed the maximal levels set forth. Furthermore, provisions regarding control are adopted, providing that this control should be in line with Council Directive 2000/63/EEC.

The Regulations relative to fresh water fish farms (1998)[*] , adopted under the Environment protection act (2001), determines provisions regarding feeding quotas and its composition. The Regulation sets forth that the County Council will determine the annual feed quota for fresh water fish farms. Furthermore, provisions are set forth regarding the use and composition of the feed, determining maximum levels of nitrogen, phosphorus etc. in the feed. The Regulation relative to marine water aquaculture (1990)[*] , also adopted under the Act, determines similar requirements as to aquaculture facilities that are placed on land taking in marine water, as well as ocean farms.

According to the Regulation relative to the combating of infectious disease with fresh water fish (1984)[*] , adopted under the Act relative to animal keeping (2004), fresh water fish, as well as fish waste from slaughtering houses and processing premises, must not be used as feed in fish farms.

According to the Regulation on organic aquaculture (2004)[*] , pursuant to the Act on Organic Farming (1999, as amended in 2001) [*] and the Foodstuffs Act (1998, as amended in 2001) and the Regulation on feed for organic aquaculture (2004, as amended same year)[*] , certain restrictions on the use of fish feed came into force for a voluntary red Danish "Organic" label (see below). Among other measures, there is a ban on adding colour to the feed, and no kind of GMO feed is allowed. Control and inspection regarding feed are covered by the Danish Plant Directorate, and for organic feed also by the Danish Veterinary and Food Administration.

FOOD SAFETY

The Foodstuffs act (1998)[+] is addressing the processing, storing, transport, sale and distribution of foodstuffs, including farmed fish, for human consumption. The Act states that the production of foodstuffs intended for sale must not be started before an authorization is issued by the Minister of Family and Consumer Affairs.

Furthermore, the Act states that foodstuffs being processed and sold shall be healthy and of good quality and have a reasonable durability when being sold. Foodstuffs shall not be sold or distributed if they upon regular use presumably can transmit or cause disease or cause poisoning, or because of depravation etc. is unsuitable for human consumption. The Act also states that the processing of foodstuffs shall be conducted in a hygienically secure way, ensuring that the foodstuffs are not exposed to fouling etc. Persons that have, or that are presumed to have a disease, infections etc. that can make the foodstuffs unsuitable for human consumption, must not be employed for processing, selling and controlling foodstuffs.

Furthermore, the Act regulates that the Minister can determine regulations or provisions on control measures that can be carried out in order to ensure compliance with the Act. The Minister can in this respect make decisions on orders and prohibitions, hereupon that foodstuffs that do not comply with the Act, regulations or provisions, shall be marked, confiscated, destroyed or withdrawn from the market. The suspension of the operations in an enterprise can also be ordered. The Act also provides for the legal admittance to processing plants etc. when necessary for the carrying out of control measures. In addition, it provides that a person in charge of a processing plant etc. has the duty to give necessary information to the authorities in case of control.

Pursuant to the Act, the Regulations on trade, production etc. of fish and fish products ashore (1997)[+] , has been adopted[+] . According to the Regulation, an authorization from the Veterinary and Food Administration is required in order to produce and store fish and fish products, cleanse mollusc and repack fish products for commercial production. In order to get an authorization, the processing plant needs to comply with several provisions stated in the Regulation, related to, inter alia, location, premises, water supply and installation, storing, furniture, operation, cleaning and disinfection measures, maintenance and hygiene provisions for staff. In addition, the plant needs to establish a product quality control system (HACCP), a system that is to be approved by the Administration. Furthermore, there are special provisions on the handling, use, production, packing and storing of fresh, conserved, salted fish and fish products, as well as on snails. The authorization can be withdrawn by the Administration upon an infringement of provisions set forth in the Act or conditions set forth in the authorization.

Pursuant to the Foodstuffs act, the Regulation relative to fish farming and hygiene conditions for the production of roe for consumption (1999)[+] has been adopted. Concerning the production of roe, the Regulation sets forth hygiene requirements regarding premises, equipment, staff, packing, as well as the fish from which the roe is taken. Furthermore, there are requirement to the keeping of separate pools for the storing of fish designated for consumption in fresh water fish farms.

The Regulation on HACCP in foodstuff enterprises (2004)[+] , adopted under The Foodstuffs act (1998), sets forth provisions on HACCP related to bivalve mollusc, echinoderms etc.

The Regulation relative to labelling of foodstuffs (2004)[+] , adopted under the Foodstuffs act (1998), also applying to aquaculture products, impose requirements to labelling of foodstuffs that are being traded. Foodstuffs are to be labelled with, inter alia, information on name of product, ingredients, content, expiry date, storage, name of producer and country of origin[+] .

For additional analytical, business and investment opportunities information, please contact Global Investment & Business Center, USA at (703) 370-8082. Fax: (703) 370-8083. E-mail: ibpusa3@gmail.com Global Business and Investment Info Databank - www.ibpus.com

Pursuant to the Foodstuffs act (1998) and the Act relative to organic farming (1999), the Regulation relative to organic aquaculture (2004)◀+] has been adopted, establishing a voluntary red Danish "Organic" label for both fresh water and marine aquaculture. The Regulation sets forth that farmed fish for labelling may be treated with antibiotics only once. Furthermore, it prohibits the adding of colour to the feed, as well as banning GMO feed, GM fish or biologically treated fish from entering the farm. Apart form feed matters, the control and inspection is administrated by the Danish Veterinary and Food Administration.

AQUACULTURE INVESTMENT

Pursuant to the Act relative to The Fisheries Bank of Denmark (2001)◀+] , the Fisheries Bank is a state credit bank granting long-term debenture loans to Danish fisheries and aquaculture. In accordance with the Regulation on Statutes of the Fisheries Bank of Denmark (1999)◀+] , loans are granted on mortgage, guarantee or other security, and by debenture loan, bond or cash credit. Loans for aquaculture are granted for real property investments (up to 60 percent of the mortgage value, repayment time up to 20 years) or other investments (up to 60 percent of the investment amount, repayment time up to 10 years).

Development/restoration fund
Danish aquaculture is eligible to funding from FIFG (the Financial Instrument for Fisheries Guidance) in accordance with Act on structural Assistance in the Fisheries Sector (2001, as amended in 2002)◀+] . The conditions for aquaculture grants are laid down in Regulation on Funding for establishing and modernizing Aquaculture Facilities (2001). Grants should be given for the purpose of contributing to environmentally and economically sustainable development of the sector, and to promote the possibilities for producing fish and fish products of high quality. Eligible costs should be at a minimum of 200 000 Danish kroner, and the grant may equal 20 percent thereof (15 percent from EU and 5 percent from the Danish state).

IMPORTANT REGULATIONS

Title of text	Date of text	Consolidated date	Entry into force	Countries
Act amending the Act on the administration of EU regulated organization of agricultural markets and the Fisheries and Aquaculture Act (No. 1513 of 2009).	2009-12-27		This Act enters into force on 1 January 2010.	Denmark
Act on Green Development and Demonstration Program (No. 1502 of 2009).	2009-12-27		The Minister for Food, Agriculture and Fisheries determines date of entry of the Act.	Denmark
Act on structural methods in the fishing sector (No. 316 of 2001).		2001-05-03		Denmark
Act on the Kingdom of Denmark Fishing Bank (No. 92 of 2001).		2001-02-08		Denmark
Act relative to structural measures in the fisheries		2001-05-13		Denmark

Title of text	Date of text	Consolidated date	Entry into force	Countries
sector.				
Fisheries Act (No. 281 of 1999).	1999-05-12		Entry into force shall be decided by the Minister of Food, Agriculture and Fisheries.	Denmark
Fisheries Act (No. 828 of 2004).		2004-07-31	Entry into force shall be decided by the Minister for Food, Agriculture and Fisheries.	Denmark
Fisheries Act (No. 978 of 2008).		2008-09-26	The Minister of Food, Agriculture and Fisheries will determine entry into force of this Act.	Denmark
Fisheries Act.		2017-01-04		Denmark
Fishery development and aquaculture Act (No. 1552 of 2006).	2006-12-20		Entry into force of the Law shall be determined by the Minister for Food, Agriculture and Fisheries. The Minister shall determine the date of repeal of the Act No. 316 of 3 May 2001, or parts thereof.	Denmark
Guidelines for applications for subsidy for innovative projects related to the processing and marketing of fish, fishery and aquaculture products (No. 9041 of 2014).	2014-01-29			Denmark
Guidelines for the approval of aquaculture water supply in connection to IPN and BKD health status as Category I or II.	2014-05-01			Denmark
Guidelines No. 9582 on subsidy to promote fisheries through projects on traceability.	2014-08-07			Denmark
Maritime and Fisheries Fund Act (No. 19 of 2017).		2017-01-04	1 February 2017.	Denmark
Notification No. 104 relative to the control of oysters.	1984-03-22			Denmark
Notification No. 22 on the control of infectious diseases in freshwater fish.	1970-01-28			Denmark
Order No. 1013 on mussels.	2011-10-19		This Order enters into force on 6 November	Denmark

Title of text	Date of text	Consolidated date		Entry into force	Countries
				2011.	
Order No. 1019 on subsidies for municipal projects regarding watercourse restoration.	2012-10-29			1 November 2012.	Denmark
Order No. 1022 on assessment criteria for municipal projects regarding watercourse restauration.	2012-10-30			1 November 2012.	Denmark
Order no. 105 on subsidy for investment in aquaculture.	2015-01-29			4 February 2015.	Denmark
Order No. 1086 on subsidy for innovative projects for the processing and marketing of fish, fishery and aquaculture products.	2015-09-15			17 September 2015. Provisions under section 2 shall be valid for agreements and applications thereof yet not completed by 16 September 2015.	Denmark
Order No. 1116 on financial subsidy to initiatives in fishery and aquaculture sectors.	2015-09-21			23 September 2015.	Denmark
Order No. 1203 on Food Administration Authority's functions and powers.	2012-12-13			Entry into force on 1 January 2013.	Denmark
Order No. 1219 on subsidy for joint efforts in aquaculture.	2015-10-29			1 November 2015.	Denmark
Order No. 1261 on Green Development and Demonstration Programme (GDDP).	2014-11-24			1 January 2015.	Denmark
Order No. 1300 on reporting information on Danish aquaculture.	2012-12-17			Entry into force on 1 January 2013.	Denmark
Order No. 1317 on subsidy for innovative projects for the processing and marketing of fish, fishery and aquaculture products.	2009-12-16			21 December 2009.	Denmark
Order No. 1324 on monitoring and controlling certain infectious diseases in aquatic organisms.	2015-11-26			1 December 2015.	Denmark
Order No. 140 on subsidies for certain protection measures to develop aquatic fauna and flora.	2013-02-12			Entry into force on 14 February 2013.	Denmark
Order No. 1451 on the use of mariculture feed types.	2015-12-07			31 December 2015.	Denmark
Order No. 1588 the use of feed types by mariculture.	2007-12-11			The Order enters into force on 3 September	Denmark

For additional analytical, business and investment opportunities information, please contact Global Investment & Business Center, USA at (703) 370-8082. Fax: (703) 370-8083. E-mail: ibpusa3@gmail.com Global Business and Investment Info Databank - www.ibpus.com

Title of text	Date of text	Consolidated date	Entry into force	Countries
			2007.	
Order No. 164 on veterinary controls on import of animal-originating food and on penalties for infringement of related EU legislation.	2015-02-19		23 February 2015.	Denmark
Order No. 176 on subsidies for conversion to organic aquaculture production and their animal health measures.	2012-02-28		The Order enters into force on 1 March 2012.	Denmark
Order No. 1788 repealing certain regulations in The Danish Agrifish Agency sector.	2015-12-16		Entry into force on 1 January 2016.	Denmark
Order No. 205 on access to fishing in Danish waters up to 12 nautical miles from the baseline.	2015-02-25		1 March 2015.	Denmark
Order no. 212 on subsidy for the establishment and modernization of aquaculture.	2010-03-09		Entry into force on 12 March 2010.	Denmark
Order No. 220 on veterinary controls on import of animal-originating food and on penalties for infringement of related EU legislation.	2014-03-10		15 March 2014. Regulations regarding colostrum and colostrum-based products (Appendices 3-4, 15) enter into force 26 March 2014.	Denmark
Order No. 25 on veterinary controls on import of animal-originating food and on penalties for infringement of related EU legislation.	2014-01-13		20 January 2014.	Denmark
Order No. 260 on financial subsidy to initiatives in fishery and aquaculture sectors.	2010-03-24		27 March 2010.	Denmark
Order No. 299 on the health advisory agreements for aquaculture facilities.	2004-04-29		The Order enters into force on 10 May 2004.	Denmark
Order No. 306 on administrative operation of Local Action Groups pursuing the fisheries development programme for 2007-2013, and delegation of certain land district administrative powers in adherence to the fishery and aquaculture development Act.	2012-03-29		Entry into force on 2 April 2012.	Denmark
Order No. 308 on subsidy for projects of fisheries development and delegation of certain ministerial	2012-03-29		Entry into force on 2 April 2012.	Denmark

Title of text	Date of text	Consolidated date		Entry into force	Countries
administrative tasks in adherence to the development of fishery and aquaculture.					
Order No. 308 on the functions and powers of the Ministry of Food, Agriculture and Fisheries.	2013-03-20			1 April 2013.	Denmark
Order No. 35 on repealing the Order on subsidies to promote energy efficiency in commercial fisheries and aquaculture sector.	2011-01-19				Denmark
Order No. 396 on import of food with special restrictions and penalties for violation of various acts of the EU legislation.	2012-04-26			Entry into force on 10 May 2012.	Denmark
Order No. 508 on the control of transmissible diseases in freshwater fish.	1984-10-02				Denmark
Order No. 511 on the functions and powers of the Ministry of Food, Agriculture and Fisheries.	2015-04-23			1 May 2015.	Denmark
Order No. 558 on the functions and powers of the Ministry of Food, Agriculture and Fisheries.	2014-05-28			15 June 2014.	Denmark
Order No. 670 on Food Administration Authority's functions and powers.	2012-06-25			Entry into force on 1 July 2012.	Denmark
Order No. 715 on veterinary controls on import of animal-originating food and on penalties for infringement of related EU legislation.	2012-06-27			Entry into force on 1 July 2012.	Denmark
Order No. 91 on investment subsidy for aquaculture, fishing vessels and processing of commercial fishery activities.	2017-01-25			1 February 2017.	Denmark
Order No. 910 on subsidy to promote fisheries through projects on traceability.	2014-08-05			12 August 2014.	Denmark
Order No. 965 on authorization and operation of farms and on the turnover of aquatic organisms and products.	2013-07-18			1 August 2013. The provisions regarding the requirements for obtaining the approval of aquaculture farming (art. 5) shall enter into force on 31 December	Denmark

For additional analytical, business and investment opportunities information, please contact Global Investment & Business Center, USA at (703) 370-8082. Fax: (703) 370-8083. E-mail: ibpusa3@gmail.com Global Business and Investment Info Databank - www.ibpus.com

Title of text	Date of text	Consolidated date	Entry into force	Countries
			2013.	
Order No. 967 on the monitoring and recording of Infectious pancreatic necrosis (IPN) and Bacterial Kidney Disease (BKD).	2013-07-18		1 August 2013.	Denmark
Order No. 968 on monitoring and controlling certain infectious diseases in aquatic organisms.	2013-07-18		1 August 2013.	Denmark
Order No. 973 on CHR registration of herds.	2011-09-28		This Order enters into force on 1 October 2011.	Denmark

IMPORTANT LAWS AND REGULATIONS AFFECTING FISHING AND AQUACULTURE

FISHERIES ACT

CHAPTER 1 PURPOSE, AREA AND DEFINITIONS OF THE ACT

§ 1. The purpose of the Act is through a management to ensure the protection and remediation of living resources in salt and freshwater and the protection of other animal and plant life, to ensure a sustainable basis for commercial fishing and related industries and the possibility of recreational fishing.

§ 2 This Act applies to fishery in saline and freshwater, cf. section 3, 3 and 4 for fish farming and for sales of fish and for areas covered by EU legislation in the area of fisheries. The Minister for the Environment and Food [2)] may decide that the law or parts thereof shall also apply to algae.

PCS. 2. The Minister may decide that the law and rules laid down by law shall also apply to fish landed here in the country, even if the fisheries are not covered by subsection (1). First

PCS. 3. Rules laid down by law may be issued for the whole country or for specified local areas. The rules may include all or some types of fishing, cf. Chapter 4.

§ 3. For the purpose of this Act:

1) Fish: Any species of fish, echinoderms, crustaceans and molluscs and their constituents, products and parts thereof, including farmed species.

2) Pool fishing: Fishing jointly carried out between self-employed or commercial fishing vessels by vessels to which they are owners or co-owners, so that a participant with his vessel may use catch rights attached to another vessel's vessel.

3) Saltwater: Danish Fisheries Territory and fishing with Danish registered vessel outside this area.

4) Freshwater: Lakes, streams, streams and other similar natural fresh waters, as well as canals, ditches and similar artificially produced waters that form part or substitute for parts of a natural water system or which have drains to saline and, Where this is particularly determined, cf. Section 41, flooded areas and artificially produced fresh waters that are not part of or substitute for parts of a natural water system or have drains to saline.

5) Turnover, etc.: Negotiation, storage, transportation, processing, acquisition, reception, transfer and import of fish in Denmark and trade in and export of fish from Denmark.

6) EU acts: European Union regulations, directives and decisions, cf. Section 10.

7) International nature conservation area and species for which an area is designated: Area and associated species to be protected according to rules laid down by the Minister for the Environment and Food, pursuant to Council Directive 92/43 / EEC of 21 May 1992 on conservation of natural habitats and of wild fauna and flora (EC Habitats Directive) and

Council Directive 79/409 / EEC of 2 April 1979 on the conservation of wild birds (EC Birds Directive).

CHAPTER 2 ADVISORY COMMITTEE

Section 4. For advice on the implementation of the provisions of the Act, the Minister for the Environment and Food shall set up the following committees:

1) EU Fisheries Committee, cf. Section 5.

2) The Committee for Business Fishing, cf. Section 6.

3) The Committee for Recreational Fisheries, Freshwater Fisheries and Fisheries, cf. Section 7.

4) The Mussel Committee, cf. section 6 a.

PCS. 2. The Minister may also set up committees for local areas, cf. section 8.

Section 5. The EU Fisheries Committee advises the Minister for the Environment and Food on the positioning of the European Union Fisheries Policy and on the preparation of the rules necessary to implement the EU legislation in the field of fisheries referred to in Section 10.

PCS. 2. (Repeated)

§ 6. The Committee for Business Fisheries advises the Minister for the Environment and Food on the planning and preparation of rules on the exercise and regulation of commercial fishing, as well as on the fishing capacity, utilization of gear, etc. and on the establishment of rules concerning the first-time turnover of fish.

PCS. 2. (Repeated)
PCS. 3. (Repeated)

Section 6a. The Mussel Committee advises the Minister for the Environment and Food on initiatives to promote sustainable business development of fishing and breeding of mussels, oysters and other bivalve molluscs, including the establishment of rules on fisheries and breeding. The Committee also advises other authorities that issue and administer rules that affect the commercial exploitation of mussels, oysters and other bivalve molluscs.

PCS. 2. (Repeated)

§ 7. The Committee for Recreational Fisheries, Freshwater Fisheries and Fisheries Care advises the Minister for the Environment and Food on the establishment of rules applicable to recreational fishing and freshwater fishing and fish care.

PCS. 2. (Repeated)

Section 8. The Minister for the Environment and Food may set up committees to advise with a view to drawing up rules for fisheries for a defined local area.

PCS. 2. (Repeated)

§ 9. The Minister for the Environment and Food shall establish the rules of procedure of the committees referred to in Sections 5-8 and appoint the chairmen of the committees.

PCS. 2. The rules of procedure shall define the composition of the committees, including the organizations to be represented in each committee and the number of representatives of the individual organizations or groups of organizations.

PCS. 3. The Minister may decide that, for a period or for discussion of individual questions, the committees shall be extended to persons with special expertise or representatives of authorities or organizations other than those included in the composition of the Committee. In addition, the Minister may set up subcommittees.

CHAPTER 3 ADMINISTRATION OF EUROPEAN COMMUNITY ACTS AND INTERNATIONAL AGREEMENTS IN FISHERIES AND FISH FARMING

Section 10. The Minister for the Environment and Food may lay down rules or make provisions for compliance with the European Union directives and decisions in the fisheries and fisheries sectors. The Minister may also lay down the rules and implement the measures necessary to comply with the regulations of the European Union in fisheries and fish farming.

PCS. 2. The Minister may lay down rules or make provision for a derogation from the rules in the cases referred to in subsection 1, to the extent that they provide access thereto.

PCS. 3. The Minister may also lay down rules necessary for the fulfillment of international treaties and conventions concerning fisheries and fish farming conditions concluded prior to accession to the European Union, and which continue to apply.

PCS. 4. In the case of EU fishing and fisheries legislation falling within the jurisdiction of other ministries, the powers referred to in paragraph 1 shall be exercised. 1 and 2 of the Minister concerned.

CHAPTER 3 A ENVIRONMENTAL DAMAGE TO PROTECTED SPECIES OR INTERNATIONAL NATURE CONSERVATION AREAS

Section 10a. An environmental damage or an imminent threat of environmental damage is understood in accordance with sections 7, 10 and 11 of the Environmental Damage Act.

Section 10b. The person responsible for the operation is the person who controls or controls the business activity.

PCS. 2. The person responsible for an environmental damage or an imminent danger of environmental damage shall be understood to be the person responsible for the operation if the damage or imminent threat of injury is caused by unreasonable conduct by the person concerned.

Section 10c. The Minister for the Environment and Food shall lay down rules for the prevention and notification of environmental damage or an imminent threat of environmental damage to protected species and international nature conservation areas in connection with the pursuit of commercial fishing activities for the implementation of the Environmental Liability Directive as regards prevention and remediation of environmental damage, including about

1) Notification and disclosure obligation for the person responsible for operation in case of environmental damage or an imminent danger of environmental damage,

2) notification of an injunction to the person responsible for the operation of the submission of information that is relevant for the assessment of environmental damage or imminent danger of environmental damage, including injunctions to conduct investigations, drug analyzes and the like. in order to clarify the cause and effects of an environmental damage or an imminent threat of environmental damage, and

3) Appeals against decisions, including those entitled to appeal.

CHAPTER 3B CONSERVATION AND PROTECTION, ETC., OF CERTAIN HABITATS, WILDLIFE AND PLANTS

Section 10 d. The Minister for the Environment and Food shall lay down rules for fisheries and fish farming activities covered by this Act in order to avoid deterioration of habitats and habitats of species in international protection areas and disturbance of the species to which the areas are designated if these disturbances have significant consequences for the objectives of Council Directive 92/43 / EEC of 21 May 1992 on the conservation of natural habitats and of wild fauna and flora.

PCS. 2. For the purpose of carrying out the duties referred to in paragraph 1, 1, the Minister for the Environment and Food shall also take appropriate measures for fishing and fishing activities covered by this Act, including the issuance of terms or notice of prohibition or injunction.

Section 10 e. Authorization for fishing and fish farming activities covered by this Act or rules laid down pursuant to this Act, which may be assumed in itself or in conjunction with other activities, may significantly affect an international nature conservation area shall be assessed for the impact of the activity on the site, taking into account to the conservation objectives for this (environmental impact assessment).

PCS. 2. The environmental impact assessment may be carried out by the Minister for the Environment and Food or by the applicant for authorization to carry out the activity. However, the Minister may refuse to make an assessment if it is assessed in advance that the requested activity will be incompatible with the conservation objectives of the site or if the scope of the requested project is deemed to be disproportionate to the cost of an environmental impact assessment. If the assessment is not made by the Minister, any assessment that may be provided by the applicant will form the basis for the Minister's decision as to whether permission may be granted for the requested activity.

PCS. 3. If the Minister for the Environment and Food considers it necessary, the environmental impact assessment shall be subject to consultation with the public, authorities and organizations before deciding whether permission may be granted.

PCS. 4. Authorization for fishing and fish farming activities covered by this Act or rules laid down pursuant to this Act may be notified only if

1) the activity does not harm the integrity of an international nature conservation area or

2) significant social interests, including social or economic nature, make it imperative to carry out the activity and no alternative solution exists, cf. section 10f.

§ 10 f. If an activity covered by Section 10, itself or in conjunction with other activities, is considered to be capable of harming a particular conservation area with a priority nature or priority species, the Minister for the Environment and Food may only authorize the activity if

1) this is necessary for human health, public safety or the achievement of significant beneficial effects on the environment or

2) Other important social interests make implementation imperative.

PCS. 2. Permission pursuant to subsection 1, No 2, can only be notified after obtaining the opinion of the European Commission.

§ 10 g. When an authorization is granted pursuant to section 10 e, subsection 4, No. 2, or Section 10f, paragraph. 1, the Minister for the Environment and Food shall lay down conditions for appropriate compensation measures. The Minister shall inform the European Commission of the compensatory measures taken.

Section 10 h. The Minister for the Environment and Food may lay down further rules on

1) notification and permission for fishing and fish farming activities covered by this Act, including the content and extent of the environmental impact assessment,

2) notification and consultation of the affected public and the relevant authorities and organizations regarding environmental impact assessments carried out pursuant to section 10e 2

3) terms and compensation measures that may be attached to an authorization, and

4) notification of injunctions in order to avoid significant disturbance or deterioration of a conservation area and the associated species.

Section 10 i. The Minister for the Environment and Food may stipulate that before a decision is taken pursuant to sections 10d-10f, an opinion shall be obtained from the Minister for the Environment [3] or a board authorized by the Minister for the Environment and Food, regarding environmental or nature conservation

§ 10 j. The Minister for the Environment and Food shall lay down the rules or implement those measures which, in view of the conservation and conservation of wildlife conservation status of the Minister for the Environment and Food, mentioned in Annex 2, are deemed necessary to ensure that the collection of the wild animals in question and its utilization is consistent with the maintenance of a satisfactory conservation status of these species.

PCS. 2. The Minister may make a decision with a view to derogating from rules laid down in paragraph 1 in order to

1) protect wildlife and conserve natural habitats,

2) prevent serious damage in particular to crops, herds, forests, fisheries, water and other forms of property,

3) ensure public health and safety considerations or other imperative considerations of essential social interests, including social and economic considerations, and considerably beneficial effects on the environment,

4) promote research and education and

5) restore a stock and resuscitate or breed species, including artificially propagating plants.

PCS. 3. Exception according to paragraph. 2 shall not prevent maintaining the conservation status of that stock in its natural range.

CHAPTER 4 FISHING PERMITS AND FISHERMEN

A. General provisions

Section 11. Self-employed fishing in saltwater may only be operated by

1) fishermen with A-status registered in accordance with section 14 1, according to rules laid down pursuant to section 14 4, or after permission pursuant to section 21 1

2) Beef fishermen registered pursuant to section 17 1, according to rules laid down pursuant to section 17 2 or 3, or after permission pursuant to section 21, paragraph 2. 1

3) companies registered pursuant to section 16,

4) Party companies that fulfill the conditions for ownership of a fishing vessel, cf. section 39 (1). 1, and

5) self-employed educational establishments which train professional fishermen and which have been approved by the Minister for the Environment and Food pursuant to section 16a.

PCS. 2. Self-employed fishing in saline must also be carried out

1) in connection with yard rights and other special fishing rights, cf. section 24, and

2) by certain farmers, cf. section 25.

PCS. 3. Recreational fishing must be exercised by

1) anglers, cf. section 26, and

2) recreational fishermen, cf. section 27.

PCS. 4. For fishery rights in freshwater, the rules in section 28 apply.

§ 12. Only persons or companies registered as eligible for self-employed fishing, cf. section 11 (1). 1 and 2 may, for consideration, transfer catches from their fishing activities. However, the Minister for the Environment and Food may allow institutions, etc. with a social or educational purpose for consideration, to transfer catches from fisheries operated with more permissible gear.

PCS. 2. The Minister may, in addition to documented commercial conditions, allow for catches derived from fresh waters to be transferred for consideration. Landowners wishing to obtain a permit to sell catches that originate from the waters encountered may obtain permission without providing the said documentation.

Section 13. Fish may only be transhipped following permission from the Minister for the Environment and Food.

B. Fishing in saltwater

Commercial fishermen

Section 14. Persons are entitled to be registered as fishermen with A status when it is documented that

1) they have Danish citizenship or have been resident in Norway for an uninterrupted period of at least 2 years immediately before registration,

2) they have been engaged in commercial fishing for the preceding 12 months, cf. 2, and

3) At least 60 per cent. of their gross income from personal activities in the previous 12 months derives from commercial fishing, cf. Third

PCS. 2. Persons employed on board a Danish registered fishing vessel shall, as proof of compliance with the requirement in subsection 1, No. 2, is pre-notified to the Minister for the Environment and Food. The person is then registered as commercial fisherman with B status. The Minister may lay down rules on this, including rules on requirements for documentation of prior employment as mentioned in subsection (1). 1, No. 2, in cases where employment has not taken place in a Danish registered fishing vessel.

PCS. 3. For the calculation of gross income for personal activities, cf. 1, No. 3, except income from civilian representative. In addition, income from retirement pensions is excluded from persons who, before obtaining the right to old-age pension, were registered as commercial fishermen. Income from trust posts in fisheries organizations, from recruitment at rescue stations and public offices, is equal to gross income from commercial fishing for persons previously employed in commercial fishing.

PCS. 4. For persons who do not meet the requirements of paragraph 1, No. 1 on Danish citizenship or residence, but subject to the European Union and EEA rules on establishment, freedom of movement for workers and the provision of services, the Minister shall determine the conditions for registration and maintenance thereof, that the fishing activity is carried out in connection with activities in the Danish fishing industry.

§ 15. Persons who can prove that they have fulfilled the conditions for registration pursuant to section 14 (1) within the last 5 years before the application. 1, can register on this basis.

PCS. 2. Registration pursuant to subsection 1 lapses if the person concerned does not document the conditions in section 14 (1) within 14 months after registration to the Minister for the Environment and Food. 1, No. 3, has been met for a period of 12 months after registration. If the registration is lost, the person concerned can not be registered again for 5 years from registration. First

Commercial fishing companies and certain independent educational institutions.

Section 16. Private and public limited companies may be registered as eligible for commercial fishing when

1) at least 2/3 of the share capital or capital is owned by persons registered as professional fishermen pursuant to section 14 1, according to rules laid down pursuant to section 14 4, or after permission pursuant to section 21 1, or

2) the company for 2/3 is owned by one or more companies in which the entire share capital or capital is owned by persons registered as professional fishermen pursuant to section 14 1, according to rules laid down pursuant to section 14 4, or after permission pursuant to section 21 First

PCS. 2. Registration may only be made when the Articles of Association provide that

1) Shares and shares corresponding to 2/3 of the Company's capital may only be issued or transferred to ownership or mortgages to persons and companies registered by the Minister for the Environment and Food, who are entitled to engage in commercial fishing pursuant to section 14 1, according to rules laid down pursuant to section 14 4, or after permission pursuant to section 21 1

2) 2/3 of the issued shares in joint-stock companies are listed with the restriction on transferability as specified in No. 1, and that the shareholder's register for limited liability companies is endorsed by this limitation in the transferability,

3) The transfer of the quoted shares and shares requires the consent of the Board of Directors or, for a limited company, by the supreme governing body,

4) the quoted shares and voting rights or similar shares have an effect that is at least equal to the equity, and

5) The listed shares and shares shall be attributed to a particular share or class of shares.

PCS. 3. The Minister may lay down rules that the registration of shares or part-time companies pursuant to subsections 1 and 4 shall lapse if notification of transfer of quoted shares or shares has not been notified to the control authority within 30 days of the transfer.

PCS. 4. Companies registered with the right to pursue commercial fishing after 1 July 1986 shall retain this right, without prejudice to section 39 (1). 1 and 2, cf. 4 on the possibilities of these companies to obtain permission for a vessel to be used for commercial fishing.

Section 16a. The Minister for the Environment and Food may approve self-governing educational institutions that train professional fishermen pursuant to the Act on Maritime Education, entitled to engage in commercial fishing.

PCS. 2. Educational institutions approved under subsection 1 may only engage in independent commercial fishing as part of the internship and with at least one student on board.

Sideline Fishermen

For additional analytical, business and investment opportunities information, please contact Global Investment & Business Center, USA at (703) 370-8082. Fax: (703) 370-8083. E-mail: ibpusa3@gmail.com
Global Business and Investment Info Databank - www.ibpus.com

Section 17. Entitled to registration as hive fishermen are persons who have Danish citizenship or have been resident in Norway for an uninterrupted period of at least 2 years immediately prior to registration if they

1) were registered as herd fishermen by the end of 1983 and the registration has been maintained,

2) are registered as commercial fishermen,

3) is authorized by decision of the board referred to in section 19 to engage in commercial fishing in a specified area or

4) can demonstrate that for a period of 12 consecutive months during the period 1 January 1996 to 1 October 1998 they had a income of DKK 10,000 or more from the turnover of catches obtained by recreational fishing.

PCS. 2. The Minister for the Environment and Food may lay down rules that, on application, authorization may be granted to persons who do not fulfill the conditions set out in subsection 1, may be registered as herd fishermen if they can document otherwise acquire knowledge of commercial fishing.

PCS. 3. For persons who do not meet the requirements of paragraph 1, 1 concerning Danish citizenship or residence, but subject to the European Union and EEA rules on establishment, freedom of movement for workers and the provision of services, the Minister shall determine the conditions for registration and maintenance thereof, including the requirement that fishing activities be carried out in connection with for activities in the Danish fishing industry.

PCS. 4. Beef fishermen who are registered in accordance with paragraph 1. 1, No. 2, 3 or 4, or in accordance with permission pursuant to paragraph 1. 2, in order to maintain this right, must prove that at least 5 per cent. of the gross income of personal business in the previous 12 months derives from hive fishing. In calculating gross income for personal activities, except for income from retirement pensions for persons who, before obtaining the right to old-age pension, were registered as herd or fishermen.

PCS. 5. The Minister may authorize registered registered fishermen who do not comply with the requirement in paragraph 1. 4 may maintain registration as a professional fisherman if they can prove that they have fulfilled the income requirement in paragraph 12 for a period of 12 consecutive months within the last 5 years where they have been registered as business or business fishermen. 4th

PCS. 6. Enforcement of registration pursuant to subsection 5 is conditional upon the person concerned not later than 14 months after the authorization has been issued for maintaining registration pursuant to subsection 5, document that the income requirement in paragraph 4 has been met for a period of 12 months after the issue of the license. If the registration is lost, the person concerned for 5 years from the issuing of licenses can not again obtain permission pursuant to paragraph. 5th

Section 18. Bierhvervsfiskeri may only be operated personally and without the use of both paid and unpaid help.

Section 19. For final administrative decision of applications for a license to engage in commercial fishing, cf. section 17 1, No. 3, the Minister for the Environment and Foodstuffs will appoint a board.

PCS. 2. The Board consists of 2 representatives of the Ministry of Environment and Food, 2 representatives of the Danish Fisheries Association, and a representative of the Danish Coastal Fisheries Association, the Danish Federation of Fish Marketers, the Danish Fisheries Association, the Danish Fisheries Association for Denmark, the Danish Amatørfiskerforening and the Danish Recreational Fisheries Association. The Minister shall determine the rules of procedure of the board and appoint the chairman of the board.

PCS. 3. Permission may be granted to persons who can prove to have been fishing anglers for 5 years. In its decisions, the Board shall pay particular attention to whether an acceptance of the application will be essential for the maintenance of fishing in that area and for the possibility of a versatile harbor environment, which also includes commercial fishing and related activities. In connection with this, account must be taken of commercial fishing that is already taking place in the local area. The board must also emphasize whether the applicant has gained knowledge of the type of fishing that he wishes to pursue during his recreational fishing. The board may lay down restrictions on the nature and number of tools that may be used in the field of hunting.

Common provisions for the right to commercial and commercial fishing in saline

Section 20. The Minister for the Environment and Food may lay down further rules on the approval and maintenance of the right to engage in business and occupational fishing for persons and companies as well as evidence that the conditions for registration and maintenance are met.

Section 21. The Minister for the Environment and Food may, even if the conditions set out in Sections 14 and 17 or in rules laid down thereunder are not fulfilled, authorize persons to be registered as business or occupational fishermen when special social or health considerations speak therefor.

PCS. 2. The Minister may lay down rules for the involvement of expert assistance for the purpose of determining whether permission may be obtained pursuant to paragraph. First

§ 22. The Minister for the Environment and Food may authorize persons to take over an ongoing fishing company or a share of it by inheritance or taking over unchanged living may continue fishing, irrespective of whether the conditions in sections 14 and 17 or in rules laid down in accordance with of which are not met.

Section 23. The Minister for the Environment and Food may derogate from the provisions of sections 14 and 16 when deemed relevant for the development of fisheries.

C. Special fishing rights in saline

Repeated Oath Rights and similar special rights

Section 24. Fishing carried out pursuant to decisions pursuant to section 13a and section 13b of Law No 178 of 23 June 1956 on the redemption and the state's acquisition of the right to fishing with eagles and other special rights for fishing in saltwater areas , may continue until the rights to their content expire. The details of the right of the right holders are laid down in the individual orders. In addition, the special rules in section 74 must be observed.

farmers

§ 25. Persons who, according to previously applicable legislation, are registered with the Ministry of Environment and Food as farmers entitled to fish in connection with agriculture, retain this right.

D. Recreational fishing

Anglers

§ 26. Anyone may engage angling with pole, pilk or similar light hand tools when the rules of section 54 on angling are observed.

Recreational Fishermen

§ 27. In addition to the fishing referred to in section 26, persons who are not registered as business or occupational fishermen or who are not particularly entitled to fishing pursuant to sections 24 and 25 may engage in recreational fishing. The Minister for the Environment and Food may lay down rules on the conditions for the pursuit of recreational fishing, including the tools that may be used for recreational fishing.

PCS. 2. Fishing in fresh waters not angling is subject to the rules for recreational fishing unless the Minister for Environment and Food, taking into account documented business conditions, allows the catch to be transferred for consideration, cf. section 12 2nd

E. Fisheries in freshwater

Section 28. The right to fish in freshwater shall be due to the owner for the reason that is adjacent to the fishing waters, unless others have acquired a special right to fish in the fishing waters.

PCS. 2. The right to engage in fishing may not be transferred to anyone other than the landowner, the state or municipalities. Furthermore, fishing rights can be hired, but not more than 25 years at a time.

PCS. 3. Fishing in Gudenåen on the line between Randers Bro and Frisenvold Fiskegård can be exercised by anyone.

Section 29. Anyone who has acquired the right to fishing shall be entitled to move along the width of the water in question to the extent necessary for the purpose of fishing.

PCS. 2. The fishery owner shall be able to prove his right to fishing at the landowner's request.

PCS. 3. During the exercise of the fishing effort, the fishery owner shall be entitled, if necessary, to temporarily land his boats and gear on the adjacent property.

PCS. 4. Landowners may at any time prohibit traffic in the garden and in the courtyard.

PCS. 5. In the event of damage caused by road and landing rights, the amount of compensation shall be determined in the absence of agreement between the parties to the valuers appointed under the Act on Land and Road Peace.

For additional analytical, business and investment opportunities information,
please contact Global Investment & Business Center, USA
at (703) 370-8082. Fax: (703) 370-8083. E-mail: ibpusa3@gmail.com
Global Business and Investment Info Databank - www.ibpus.com

CHAPTER 5 REMEDIATION, PROTECTION AND CONSERVATION OF FISH STOCKS

Section 30. The Minister for the Environment and Food may lay down rules

1) Full or partial conservation of specified stocks and waters,

2) Minimum allowance for fish and fish

3) Total allowable catches of specified stocks.

PCS. 2. The Minister may lay down rules that, irrespective of a conservation under subsection 1, No. 1, may permit fishing and landing of a certain number of salmon in specified water systems. The Minister may, inter alia, decide that such authorization may only be granted to an open association of fishermen in the water system or, if appropriate, to several associations thereof, each comprising at least one third of the part of the water system in which salmon is to be landed. The Minister may also lay down rules on the application, permission and conditions for the pursuit of the fisheries.

§ 31. In order to secure the fishing pass, the Minister for the Environment and Food may lay down rules on protection belts where fishing or special fishing is prohibited in whole or in part by and by

1) watercourse outlet in larger streams and in lakes

2) watercourse estuary in saline,

3) the estuaries of the fjords and other waters of the sea and

4) Other places where fishing conditions make it difficult.

CHAPTER 6 FISHING GEAR

Section 32. The Minister for the Environment and Food may lay down rules concerning the use, design, mesh size, location and number of authorized fishing gear, marking and marking of fishing gear and poles, including rules on the location and distance between these and the registration of seats for permanent fishing gear.

PCS. 2. Rules on the marking and placement of fishing gear in saline shall be determined after consultation with the Minister of Defense and the Minister for Economic and Business Affairs.

PCS. 3. The Minister for the Environment and Food may lay down rules as to whether new fishing gear and aids, whose structure differs significantly from previously known methods, may be used and the use of such tools. The Minister may also lay down rules on the measurement of mesh sizes.

PCS. 4. Along all coastlines, the entire year is forbidden at a distance of 100 m from the shallow line to use the downwind. The Minister may set rules on deviations in the distance from the coast and the prohibition period.

§ 33. All fishing gear shall, as the weather conditions permit, be smoked regularly and so often that the living conditions of the fish caught do not unduly deteriorate.

PCS. 2. The Minister for the Environment and Food may lay down rules for fishing gear not to be smoked at certain times of the day.

CHAPTER 7 REGULATION OF COMMERCIAL FISHING IN SALINE

A. Regulatory measures

Section 34. The Minister for the Environment and Food may lay down rules on the commercial exploitation of resources, including

1) the allocation of available catches on time and on waters,

(2) the complete or partial suspension of fishing and landing of specified species or conditions thereof, when the catch level for the fishery concerned, relative to the available catches,

3) allocation of available catches with specified quotas for groups of vessels, individual fishing vessels or gear types,

4) distribution of available catches for their use, including for consumer and industrial purposes, respectively;

5) the maximum fishing time, the number of landings and the allowable catches per landing and

6) Special quotas within the available catches for by-catches.

PCS. 2. In establishing rules as mentioned in subsection 1, in addition to the conservation and reproduction of resources, focuses on the rational, including seasonal best practices, utilization, the relationship between available resources and fishing capacity in fisheries as well as economic and employment considerations in the fishing industry, processing industry and other related industries both for the country as a whole and individual lands of the country.

PCS. 3. Rules on the stopping of fishing and changing the conditions for the exercise of fishing activities issued pursuant to this Act shall not be introduced in the Official Gazette.

PCS. 4. The items mentioned in subsection 3 mentioned rules are published in accordance with rules laid down by the Minister for the Environment and Food.

§ 35. Rules pursuant to section 34 may be issued for a year or for a period of several years. The rules issued may be amended in light of the development of fisheries, cf. section 34 (1). 2nd

B. Fishing permits and pool fishing

Section 36. The Minister for the Environment and Food may lay down rules requiring authorization to carry out commercial fishing on fishery resources available to Danish fishermen and on the issue of a permit. In this connection, the Minister may lay down rules for the licensing of a vessel owner's fishing rights in a pool fishing, cf. section 3, no. 2, including which fishing rights may be subject to a pool fishing, a pool fishing, reporting to the Environment- and the Ministry of Food and the number of participants in a pool fishing.

PCS. 2. Permission may be made on a time-limited basis subject to compliance with specified conditions.

Section 36 a. Permission for pool fishing, cf. section 3, no. 2, according to rules issued pursuant to section 36 1, presupposes

1) that the pool fishing is organized as a public limited company, a public limited company, a partnership or an association,

2) a pooled fishery organized as an association provides collateral of DKK 125,000 in the form of a bank guarantee or other secure collateral for claims arising from violations of fishing legislation in connection with fishing for pool fishing unless the participants personally hold such requirements, as the pool fishing might incur, and

3) Participants in pool fishing commit themselves to allowing 2-year assignments of catch rights to be included in pool fishing.

PCS. 2. A license for pool fishing may only be granted for a period of 13 months from 1 January for one year to 1 February of the following year. If the pool fishing within the 13-month period has applied for a license for pool fishing for the following 13-month period to count on 1 January, a permit will apply, however, from 1 January. A pool fishing may not be dissolved during the period for which the permit is granted, cf. section 36d. Catches that are part of a pool fishing shall remain in the pool fishing during the 13-month period, cf. 4th

PCS. 3. Upon expiry of the license for a pool fishing, the party responsible for pool fishing or all the vessel owners whose vessels are subject to the relevant pool fishing shall inform the Minister for the Environment and Food of how the fishing rights covered by pool fishing are then distributed among the participants. If the Minister has not received notification of the distribution 14 days after the expiry of the permit, the Minister allocates the catches between the participants. However, this does not apply if an application for a license for pool fishing with the same participants for the following 13-month period to count from 1 January has been met or if permission has been granted pursuant to section 36c 1, for a pool participant to enter a new pool fishing.

PCS. 4. The Minister may lay down rules on

1) that no matter what paragraph 2 may be granted permission for fishing rights that form part of a pool fishing, upon application, to be removed from the pool fishing before the expiry of the quota referred to in subsection 2 stipulated 13-month period, including in connection with swapping of fishing rights, vessel replacement etc.,

2) that an authorization pursuant to rules established under paragraph 1 can only be notified if security is provided in the form of a bank guarantee or other secure collateral for claims arising from a decision in a pending, pending criminal case for violations of pool fishing,

3) submission of an application for authorization after No. 1 and

4) Documentation for compliance with the conditions in paragraphs 2 and 3. 1, No. 1-3.

§ 36b . If fishing in a pool fishing has resulted in the overrun of catches subject to the relevant pool fishing, the Minister for the Environment and Food may decide to reduce fishing rights that are subject to pool fishing or catch rights as in the following year is part of the pool fishing. A reduction in fishing rights may exceed the observed exceedance of fishing rights.

PCS. 2. If a decision to reduce fishing rights pursuant to subsection 1 has particularly important economic importance for the participants in the pool fishing, pool fishing may demand the decision brought before the courts. Requests must be made to the Minister within 4 weeks after the decision has been given to the pool fishery. The Minister institutes proceedings against pool fishing in the forms of civil procedure. Requests for action have no suspensory effect.

PCS. 3. A decision pursuant to subsection 1, which has particularly important economic significance for the participants in pool fishing, shall provide information on access to justice pursuant to paragraph 1. 2 and the deadline for this.

Section 36c. The Minister for the Environment and Food may allow a participant in pool fishing upon application to withdraw from the pool fishing after the expiration of the 13-month period for which the permit has been granted, cf. section 36a 2 and then before 1 March, entered into a new pool fishing with effect from the preceding 1 January and until 1 February of the following year on condition that,

1) the pool fishing from which the applicant withdraws has made a calculation and allocation of catch rights pursuant to section 36a, subsection 3, 1st paragraph,

2) Reduction of fishing rights in the pool fishing from which the applicant withdraws, if a decision has been taken pursuant to section 36b, and

3) that the fishing rights have been calculated in the new pool fishing.

PCS. 2. As a condition for permission pursuant to subsection 1, the Minister may require collateral in the form of a bank guarantee or other assurable collateral for claims resulting from a decision in a pending, final criminal case of infringement in the pool fishing from which the applicant resigns.

PCS. 3. The Minister may lay down rules for supporting the fulfillment of the conditions set out in paragraph 1. 1 and 2 and for submission of application for permission pursuant to subsections First

§ 36d. Notwithstanding section 36a, subsection 2, the Minister may allow a participant in a pool fishing upon application to withdraw from pool fishing before the expiration of the 13-month period for which the permit is granted, if

1) the vessel of the person concerned has been taken over by a deceased or a bankruptcy estate,

2) the person concerned due to illness is unable to fish or

3) There are other special circumstances.

PCS. 2. Permission pursuant to subsection 1 can only be announced if

1) the other participants in the pool fishery consent to the requested withdrawal and

2) pool fishing makes an inventory and allocation among participants of rights and obligations per. The date of expiry, which may be approved by the Minister. The calculation and distribution must include any requirements for reduction of fishing rights according to the decision pursuant to section 36b (1). 1. As a condition of approval, the Minister may require collateral in the form of a bank guarantee or other satisfactory collateral for claims arising from a decision in a pending, fined criminal case for infringement in pool fishing.

PCS. 3. The Minister may lay down rules for supporting the fulfillment of the conditions set out in paragraph 1. 1 and 2 and for submission of application for permission pursuant to subsections First

§ 36e. By way of derogation from section 36a, subsection 2, the Minister for the Environment and Food may lay down rules that a vessel owner with his fishing rights may enter a pool fishing after the commencement of the 13-month period for which the license for pool fishing has been granted, including if

1) the person initially established according to rules issued by the Minister has been authorized to acquire quota shares from other vessels or to receive quota shares on a loan basis or

2) the vessel owner concerned has taken over his vessel from a current or former participant in the pool fishing concerned.

PCS. 2. Permission pursuant to subsection 1 can only be announced if

1) all participants in the pool fishing license applied for will consent to the requested entry and

2) a statement of catch rights and obligations per. the date of entry into the pool fishing license applied for, which may be approved by the Minister.

PCS. 3. The Minister may lay down rules for the submission of an application for entry into pool fishing, including documentation for compliance with the conditions in paragraph. 1 and 2.

§ 37. A permit pursuant to section 36, subsection 1, can not be transferred without approval from the Minister for the Environment and Food. The Minister may lay down rules on conditions and conditions for approval of transfer of catch rights according to a permit.

PCS. 2. The Minister may revoke an authorization granted pursuant to section 36 (2). 1, and a right that has been approved to be transferred pursuant to paragraph 1. 1 if the holder has been guilty of gross or repeated breach of the terms set out in the license. If a license to operate a pool fishing is revoked, the rules in section 36a, paragraph 1, shall apply. 3, use.

PCS. 3. In the case of revocation of a license, the holder may be informed that it can not be granted permission for a period of up to 1 year. In case of revocation of a license, the right to capture the amount of catches allocated for the period in question will be void, and this right can not be transferred by the holder. This provision applies regardless of whether the fishing permit attached to the permit is part of a pool fishing, cf. section 3, no. 2.

PCS. 4. If an infringement which causes revocation of a license pursuant to subsection 1 is committed to a vessel subject to a pool fishing, the Minister may notify the holder that he may not be allowed to participate in a pool fishing in the following year.

PCS. 5. A decision pursuant to subsection 2 to 4 shall contain information on the right to appeal and the time limit for such proceedings.

PCS. 6. A decision pursuant to subsection 2 to 4 may be required by the license holder to be brought before the courts. Requests must be made to the Minister within four weeks after the withdrawal has been notified to the holder. The Minister appeals against the proprietor in the forms of civil procedure. Requests for action have no suspensory effect.

CHAPTER 8 VESSELS WITH FISHING LICENSE

§ 38. It is not permitted to use a vessel for commercial fishing in saline unless the vessel is registered with the fishing license of the Ministry of Environment and Food, and it is also registered with the Ministry of Business [4].

PCS. 2. The Minister for the Environment and Food may, with a view to adapting the fishing fleet capacity to the fishing opportunities available, lay down rules for the issue and maintenance of fishing licenses and the conditions attached thereto and the registration of the vessel's fishing license in the Environment and Food Ministry of Foods' Register of Vessels. The Minister may stipulate that the fishing license and registration may expire if the conditions for issuing the fishing license and registration are no longer met or if the fishing license is suspended or permanently suspended, cf. section 39 a.

PCS. 3. The Minister shall lay down rules that the issuance and maintenance of the fishing license pursuant to subsection 2 is conditional on the fishery being operated so that there is real connection to the Danish fishing port.

PCS. 4. The Minister may also lay down rules under which shipbuilding, which increases fishing capacity, is subject to a special fishing license.

Section 39. Fishing license issued pursuant to rules laid down pursuant to section 38 (1). 2 may only be issued for vessels owned for 2/3 by persons who are registered as eligible for commercial or commercial fishing pursuant to sections 14 or 17 or according to rules laid down pursuant thereto or pursuant to the fishing license pursuant to section 21 1. The fishing license may also be issued to companies approved pursuant to section 16 (1). 1 and 2, and to independent education institutions approved in accordance with section 16a.

PCS. 2. If a vessel changes owner, the fishing license lapses to use the vessel for commercial fishing if the new owners do not meet the requirements of paragraph. 1. The fishing license shall also lapse if the persons or companies that own the vessel no longer meet the conditions of paragraph 1. 1. The Minister for the Environment and Food may furthermore, cf. section 38 2, stipulates that the fishing license for the use of a commercial fishing vessel lapses if the vessel is transferred or if the owner of the vessel ceases to use this for commercial fishing.

PCS. 3. The Minister for the Environment and Food may grant an exception to paragraph 1. 1 and 2 for a defined period if a vessel is taken over as part of a debt settlement or in conjunction with commercial trade in vessels. The Minister may also grant an exception if the change of ownership takes place by inheritance or the transfer of unchanged residence.

PCS. 4. The Minister may grant exemption from subsection 1 and 2, so as to permit a company pursuant to section 16 (1). 4, to acquire a vessel to replace a diversified vessel. The newly acquired vessel must have at most the same catch capacity as it lost.

PCS. 5. The Minister may lay down rules that the fishing license for the commercial fishing vessel shall lapse if notification of change of ownership has not been received by the Ministry of the Environment and Foodstuffs within 30 days of the change of ownership.

Section 39a. The Minister for the Environment and Food may lay down rules for the allocation of points, for temporary suspension and for permanent withdrawal of the fishing license in accordance with the serious breach points system covered by the EU Regulations referred to in Section 10 to prevent, ward off and stop illegal, unreported and unregulated fishing (IUU fishing).

PCS. 2. Decisions taken in accordance with rules established pursuant to subsections 1 regarding permanent withdrawal of the fishing license may be required by the fishing license holder to be brought before the courts. Requests must be made to the Minister within 4 weeks after the involvement has been notified to the holder. The Minister appeals against the proprietor in the forms of civil procedure. Requests for action have no suspensory effect.

Section 39b. The Minister for the Environment and Food may lay down rules for the allocation of points to a master of the vessel who, as a responsible leader of a fishing vessel with a fishing license, has committed serious infringements for which the holder of the fishing license has also been awarded points pursuant to the points system for serious violations covered by the EU Regulations referred to in Article 10, which shall prevent, deter and stop illegal, unreported and unregulated fishing (IUU fishing).

*PCS. 2nd*The Minister may temporarily or permanently prohibit a master of a vessel from having a fishing license with a fishing license. The prohibition is announced when the person concerned has been responsible leader during fishing trips on a fishing license with a fishing license, in which the holder of the fishing license has also been awarded a certain number of points for serious offenses, cf. 1. The length of the period during which the master of the vessel is unable to carry a fishing vessel on the basis of a certain number of points shall be the same as the length of the period during which the fishing license is withdrawn in accordance with the serious infringements system covered by the Section 10 EU Regulations to Prevent, Prevent and Stop Illegal, Unreported and Unregulated Fisheries (IUU Fisheries), where the holder of the fishing license has also been awarded a certain number of points for serious infringements, cf. First

PCS. 3. Decisions on permanent prohibition of fishing vessels with a fishing license, cf. 2 may be brought before the courts by the vessel master concerned. Requests must be made to the Minister within 4 weeks after the prohibition has been notified to the master. The Minister appeals to the master of the Civil Procedure. Requests for action have no suspensory effect.

CHAPTER 9 REGULATION OF RECREATIONAL FISHING

Section 40. When setting rules for the pursuit of recreational fishing, the Minister for the Environment and Food shall emphasize that fishing and recreational fishing is exercised in such a way that consideration is given to the protection of fish stocks and plans, cf. 62nd

CHAPTER 10 SPECIAL RULES FOR FRESHWATER

A. Special validity rules for freshwater areas

Section 41. For flooded areas and artificially produced fresh waters which do not form part of or substitute for parts of a natural watercourse system or have drains for saline, only Articles 30, 32, 109, 117-123 and 130 apply. -134.

PCS. 2. The Minister for the Environment and Food may, however, lay down rules that the other provisions of the Act shall also apply to those referred to in subsection 1, if required to ensure the stock of fish or otherwise has a fishing significance.

Section 42. In addition to food channels, sections 32, 33, 48 and 63-65 do not apply to that part of an artificially landscaped and legally existing fish farm, duly deposited against other waters.

PCS. 2. Sections 32, 33, 48, 50-52 and 63-65 shall not apply to waters which have only one owner or are owned by public authorities, companies or the like and which do not have any drainage at sea, river or beach, or whose drain is of such a nature that fish can not pass it. However, the Minister for the Environment and Food may stipulate that the provisions of section 1 mentioned provisions shall apply.

B. Fishing passages for barriers and drainage of water, etc. in freshwater

Section 43. The watercourse authority may, according to law on watercourses, instruct the owner of voting, milling, milling, irrigation plants, industrial plants or similar facilities to establish and maintain fishing passages at the plant and lay down conditions for the design and operation of the fishing passage. The provision in the 1st paragraph. applies mutatis mutandis to the owner of a plant installed turbine. The rules on injunctions, complaints and penalties in the Act on Watercourses apply correspondingly to the decision of the watercourse authority in accordance with paragraphs 1 and 2.

PCS. 2. Are they in paragraph 1 plant or a turbine installed after 19 July 1898, the cost of establishing and maintaining the fishing passages shall be borne by the owner. The same applies if the plant is installed or the turbine has been installed before 19 July 1898, but after that time changes or changes have been made to the installation or use of the plant or turbine.

PCS. 3. It is not possible for the owner to establish a fishing pass if the costs and disadvantages of the establishment are not proportionate to the intended purpose.

Section 44. The owner of the facilities mentioned in section 43 shall at his own expense place and maintain one or more eel passes at the plant.

PCS. 2. The Minister for the Environment and Food may lay down rules on the layout, maintenance and maintenance of eel passes as well as rules for the period during which eels shall work.

Section 45. The Minister for the Environment and Food may lay down rules that the owner of the plant referred to in section 43 shall at his own expense place and maintain a passenger facility for migratory fish at the plant as well as rules on the design and operation of the passage.

Section 46. The Minister for the Environment and Food may lay down rules for the installation of a grid in the plants referred to in section 43, so that all the water to and from the turbine passes the grid.

Section 47. (Repeated)

Section 48. In connection with permission pursuant to the Act on Water Supply for Discharge of Water for Irrigation, etc., the local council may require grids arranged to prevent fishing passages.

For additional analytical, business and investment opportunities information,
please contact Global Investment & Business Center, USA
at (703) 370-8082. Fax: (703) 370-8083. E-mail: ibpusa3@gmail.com
Global Business and Investment Info Databank - www.ibpus.com

Section 49. The Minister for the Environment and Food may lay down rules on the placement, design and approval of the grid referred to in section 46.

C. Blocking catch devices in fresh water

Section 50. Blocking fishing gear and other types of fishing gear of any kind shall not be used in fresh water unless they were notified and registered before the 1st of January 1995 at the Ministry of Agriculture and Fisheries.

PCS. 2. The Minister for the Environment and Food may lay down rules on the use of catching catch devices which do not comply with rules laid down in section 32 (1). 1, but legally established and maintained in accordance with paragraph 1. First

Section 51. If , pursuant to section 50, fishing with catching fishing gear is carried out, the fishermen entitled to fishing for the entire fishing water may, in respect of such voyage, demand that this fishery be terminated against full compensation.

PCS. 2. The Minister for the Environment and Food shall define the length of fishing waters and decide whether the request is to be met, taking into account whether the termination of fishing will significantly promote the possibilities of migratory fish to exploit spawning and rearing areas throughout the river basin system or a significant part thereof.

PCS. 3. Fishing rights pursuant to subsection 1 are landowners or tenants of fishing rights that can prove that their tenant lasts at least 10 years after the claim has arisen.

Section 52. (Repeated)

D. The central flow line

Section 53. The watercourse authority according to the law on watercourses determines where the central flow line in freshwater is, as the authority determines the boundary between sea and river.

PCS. 2. The Minister for the Environment and Food or a fisherman in the water area concerned may request the river authority to take a decision pursuant to paragraph. First

PCS. 3. The decision of the river authority may not be brought before another administrative authority.

CHAPTER 11 FISHING CHARTERS AND RECREATIONAL FISHING CHARACTERS

Section 54. All fishing anglers, cf. section 26, must have a valid fishing license. Except from this, persons under the age of 18 and persons entitled to receive retirement pension.

PCS. 2. All persons engaged in recreational fishing, cf. section 27, must have a valid fishing license.

PCS. 3. Persons who have a valid recreational fishing license may engage in angling without having a fishing license.

Section 55. By way of derogation from section 54, no fishery and recreational fishing license shall be required for fishing in waters owned by individuals, public bodies, companies or the like and which do not have any drainage to the sea, river or beach, or whose drainage is of such a nature, that fish does not pass it.

PCS. 2. In freshwater, the landowner and his household are exempted from the requirement for angling and recreational fishing vessels when fishing is carried out in the fishing waters adjacent to the ground.

PCS. 3. In saline, the landowner and his household are exempted from the requirement for angling when fishing takes place during the stay at the beach breeding covered by the land.

Section 56. The Minister for the Environment and Food issues fishing vessels and recreational fishing vessels.

PCS. 2. Fishing certificates may be issued for a period of 1 day, 1 week or 12 months. Recreational fishing licenses may be issued for a period of 12 months.

PCS. 3. The price for the fishing license for 12 months is 185 kr., For 1 week 130 kr. And for 1 day 40 kr.

PCS. 4. The price for the recreational fishing license is 300 kr.

PCS. 5. The Minister for the Environment and Food may, in the light of price and wage developments, lay down rules for changing the price of angling and recreational fishing vessels.

PCS. 6. The Minister may lay down rules on the payment of angling and recreational fishing licenses, including requirements for proof of payment and administration.

Section 57. (Repeated)

§ 58. Proof of payment for angling, recreational fishing license and identification must be carried out during fishing.

PCS. 2. Fishing license and recreational fishing license and proof of payment thereof are personal and may not be transferred to others.

§ 59. (Repeated)

§ 59 a. Anyone who engages in fishing or recreational fishing may, in the event of a criminal offense in the event of a serious or repeated violation of the rules applicable to fishing or recreational fishing, be denied the right to exercise this fishing for a period of up to 1 year .

PCS. 2. Instead of ruling by judgment pursuant to subsection 1, the Minister for the Environment and Food may state that the case can be settled without legal prosecution if the person who committed the violation acknowledges the offense and declares himself ready within a specified time limit that may be extended upon request a fine declared in the declaration and a prohibition on the pursuit of leisure and recreational fishing for a specified period of up to 1 year.

For additional analytical, business and investment opportunities information,
please contact Global Investment & Business Center, USA
at (703) 370-8082. Fax: (703) 370-8083. E-mail: ibpusa3@gmail.com
Global Business and Investment Info Databank - www.ibpus.com

PCS. 3. For the purposes of paragraph 1, The declaration referred to in paragraph 2 finds the provision in section 831 (1) of the Code of Civil Procedure. 1, No. 2 and 3, if the contents of a statement of objection apply mutatis mutandis.

PCS. 4. A decision pursuant to subsection 1 or an adoption after paragraph. 2, according to which fishing and leisure fishing can not be exercised for a period of time does not entitle to full or partial repayment of paid fishing signs.

Section 60. Persons engaged in fishing or recreational fishing and who do not provide proof of payment and identification at the request of the inspection authority shall pay an amount equal to four times the price of a fishing license for 12 months, within 14 days of collection. cf. section 56 (1). 3, and for recreational fishermen an amount equal to four times the price of a recreational fishing license, cf. section 56 (1). 4, cf. 2nd

PCS. 2. If the fishing and recreational fishing license was paid when the fishing took place and proof thereof is submitted within 14 days of the claim, an amount equal to half the price of a fishing license for 12 months shall be paid, cf. section 56 . 3. For recreational fishermen, an amount equal to half the price of a recreational fishing license shall be paid, cf. section 56 (1). 4th

§ 61. The resources of angling and recreational fishing vessels are used for

1) fish care, including for the release of fry and herring fish, as well as measures and research that also affect reproduction, growth, etc. of fish stocks, and

2) administration and information on fish care and on angler and recreational fishing license schemes.

PCS. 2. The means may also be used to monitor compliance with the rules for fishing and recreational fishing vessels.

CHAPTER 12 FISHING AND LAUNCHES ETC.

A. Fish care

§ 62. The Minister for the Environment and Food shall, for a period of one or more years, draw up a plan for fisheries care and the use of revenues from angler and recreational fishing license. The Minister shall endeavor to ensure that the overall fishing effort takes into account all waters and a wide range of species.

B. Exposures, etc.

§ 63. The placing or transplantation of fish and eggs and fry thereof shall not be permitted unless

1) it is made in accordance with a plan prepared or approved by the Minister for the Environment and Food,

2) The Minister's special permission is available or

3) a ruling has been issued by a National Service Tribunal.

PCS. 2. The Minister may lay down rules for the deliberate release of fish, fry and eggs for release.

Section 64. The Minister for the Environment and Food may lay down rules for companies, associations and persons to be authorized to carry out expulsions and other activities for the purpose of carrying out fishing activities.

PCS. 2. The authorized persons have the right to pass due diligence across land and private roads adjacent to the waters in which release must take place.

Section 65. The Minister for the Environment and Food may, taking into account delays, make special provisions for the fishing activities, including, in whole or in part, prohibiting fishing for a specified period.

CHAPTER 13 BREED IN SALINE

Section 66. Breeding of fish in the Danish Fisheries Territory may only take place after permission from the Minister for the Environment and Food.

PCS. 2. An application for permission under the law shall simultaneously apply for an application for permission under other legislation. The Minister may lay down conditions for a permit, including time limit, sampling and documentation of collateral in the form of either insurance or bank guarantee to cover expenses at the end of the facility. The Minister also determines terms under other legislation as determined by the competent authority.

Section 67. The Minister for the Environment and Food may lay down rules for permission for the establishment, utilization and operation of breeding facilities and that an authorization requires that the applicant meets the requirements for practical and theoretical education. The Minister may also provide for the transfer of rights under a permit for the establishment, utilization and operation of breeding facilities.

§ 68. (Repeated)

Section 69. No obstacles may be placed in the way of legal breeding.

§ 70. The Minister for the Environment and Food may issue rules on the total or partial prohibition of fishing in the breeding area and at a specified distance from breeding facilities.

PCS. 2. The Minister may allow the owner of a breeding facility and the person responsible for the operation of the plant to catch escaped fish from the plant with specified fishing gear.

CHAPTER 14 RULES OF MUTUAL ORDER BETWEEN FISHERMEN

A. Distance rules, etc.

Section 71. In order to avoid genes for other fisheries, the Minister for the Environment and Food may, in order to avoid any other fishing effort, lay down rules for the exercise of fishing activities or other rules for fishing, including the obligation to take special measures so that fishing gear, etc., is not inconvenient to others.

Section 72. Anyone who has begun the establishment of legal tools has priority over other fishermen and no obstacles may be placed in this way as long as the construction of gear or fishing is exercised.

B. Privileges in saline

Section 73. The Minister for the Environment and Food may lay down rules for persons or companies entitled to engage in commercial fishing pursuant to section 11 1, No. 1-4, may acquire and maintain the right to fish in certain places for up to 6 years with specified types of fixed gear.

PCS. 2. The Minister may lay down rules for the registration of preferential rights, cf. 1 and that the allocation of the rights is made by drawing lots of commercial fishermen, commercial fishing companies and fishermen. It may, inter alia, provide that fishing fishermen can only participate in the draw on an equal footing with commercial fishermen if they have previously fished from the places concerned and that the period of priority acquired may be shorter for beet fishermen than for business fishermen.

PCS. 3. The Minister may lay down rules on the preservation of a right of priority for persons who inherit or sit in the unchanged residence after the holder of a pre-emptive right.

§ 74. Fishing may not be exercised in such a manner that interference with the reckless and other special rights mentioned in section 24 occurs. The protection of the right applies while the fishing gear is exposed and no longer than 30 November of the year in question.

PCS. 2. It is a condition for the continued exercise of the obligation referred to in subsection 1 mentioned right that

1) the outermost main pole of the tool and one of the tool's inner posts, indicating the direction of the tool together with the main pointer, will be postponed before 1 August of the year in question,

2) rows and yarns in a viable condition shall be postponed before 10 September of the year in question; and

3) The entered toolbox with the exact location of the place before 1 August of the year in question has been notified to the Ministry of Environment and Food.

PCS. 3. The main pole must be marked and marked in accordance with section 32 (3). 1, laid down rules.

PCS. 4. Fishermen who want to put their gear at or beyond the designated or caught fishing grounds of the rightholder must clearly mark the place where they will put their fishing gear before 1 September of the year in question.

C. Replacement

Section 75. During fishing, damage to legally exposed and properly marked fishing gear or breeding facilities, without the condition covered by section 83, shall be replaced by the fisher or exercised unless the offender proves that the damage could not be deterred by usual caution.

CHAPTER 15 FISHERIES RELATIONSHIP WITH OTHER ACTIVITIES

A. Provisions for the protection of fisheries

General provision

§ 76. No obstacles may be placed in the way of legally practiced fishing.

Measures etc. in saline areas

§ 77. Measures or interventions that may cause inconvenience or prevent fishing in saline waters, make landing conditions unsuitable for fishing or otherwise affecting the fauna and flora of the fisheries territorial area, may only be carried out after permission.

PCS. 2. If measures or interventions on the fishing rights criterion, cf. 1, does not require permission from another authority under the law or state sovereignty of the territorial sea, measures may only be carried out with the permission of the Minister for the Environment and Food.

PCS. 3. In cases where authorization is issued by another authority, this will be done after consultation with the Minister for the Environment and Food.

Section 78. Authorization may only be granted for measures or interventions that may be given in section 77 (1). 1, mentioned effect when

1) a final decision has been made on the issue of compensation for fishermen who normally carry on-site commercial fishing and whose earnings will be affected by the measure or intervention,

2) negotiations have been initiated for possible compensation between the person carrying out the measure or intervention and the fishermen who normally carry on-site commercial fishing and whose earnings will be affected by the measure or the operation; or

3) The question of possible compensation to the affected fishermen has been referred to a decision by a board, cf. sections 79 and 80.

PCS. 2. In the case of permission for mineral extraction pursuant to the Act on Raw Materials, paragraphs 1 and 2 shall apply. 1 only when the permit concerns raw material recovery for large single construction works and the permit is issued to the developer.

Section 79. Minister for the Environment and Food, or other Minister for Authorization, cf. section 77 2 shall, at the request of the fishermen concerned or the person implementing the measure or intervention, refer questions concerning possible compensation for final administrative decision by a board. The request can be made both before and after the issuance of an authorization pursuant to section 77 (1). 1. The minister concerned hereby provides for the establishment of a board, cf. section 80.

PCS. 2. The Minister who may set up the panel may require that the party requesting the panel be reduced to provide security for the costs.

§ 80. The board referred to in section 79 consists of three members.

PCS. 2. The Minister for the Environment and Food shall appoint two members. However, if permission pursuant to section 77 is issued by another authority, one member of the responsible minister shall be appointed. The two members appoint in agreement a third member who is chairman of the board. If there is no agreement on the election of the chairman, the president shall be appointed by the President for the relevant national court.

PCS. 3. The board shall decide on the procedure itself and may, for guidance, call upon expert assessors who are particularly aware of the fisheries affected by the measure in question.

PCS. 4. The board shall decide definitively who will pay the costs and the amount of the case.

PCS. 5. Any compensation payable shall be paid within 15 days of the decision being served to the party liable for damages, unless otherwise decided by the board.

PCS. 6. Compliance with the decision of the board is a condition for the notification or maintenance of the license in question.

PCS. 7. The compensation may be granted in whole or in part to the local fisheries association for use in accordance with the provisions of the Association to cover losses incurred.

Measures in freshwater areas

§ 81. Prior to issuing permits or decisions regarding changes to polls, industrial facilities and turbines in watercourses or permits or measures that may affect fishing passages, fisheries and fish fauna, plans shall be submitted before freshwater areas of authorities. for the Environment and Food Minister.

B. Relationship to sailing and shipping

Section 82. The Minister for the Environment and Food may lay down rules to ensure that fishing does not prevent or impede safe navigation, including rules on the marking, placement and removal of gear, piles, etc., as well as how the costs of removal of poles placed in Contravention of the rules must be held.

PCS. 2. Rules issued pursuant to subsections 1, applicable to saline shall be determined after consultation with the Minister for Economic and Business Affairs and the Minister of Defense.

Section 83. If a vessel is injured on legally exposed and properly marked gear, the shipowner is obliged to replace the damage unless it is proved that the damage could not be avoided by usual caution.

C. Rights in relation to coasters in saltwater areas

Section 84. One or more commercial or commercial fishermen may request a committee to decide whether a landowner must accept that a more delimited space on the beach or nearest location may be used for

1) collection of boats,

2) Layout and preparation of tools and

3) Drying area for tools with necessary yarn shelters.

PCS. 2. In connection with a decision pursuant to subsection 1, the board also considers the compensation payable by the fisherman or the fishermen to the landowner for the use of the land. Decisions on the amount of compensation are taken for 5 years at a time. The compensation is paid annually before the seat is taken into service.

PCS. 3. The board shall be reduced and 3 members shall be appointed by the municipality. One of the members is appointed taking into account his expertise in fisheries. The board finally makes an administrative decision.

PCS. 4. In determining whether the space may be used, it is assessed whether it is necessary for the pursuit of profitable fishing that the request is met, in comparison with the genes it would mean for the owner to be given access to the space.

PCS. 5. The board shall decide which of the parties shall pay the costs and the amount of the proceedings. The costs must be paid within 15 days after the decision is served.

PCS. 6. The provisions of subsection Question 1 can be filed by fishermen or the landowner not later than five years after the decision.

D. Replacement rules in freshwater areas

§ 85. Anyone who has unlawfully fished in a fishing lake or in areas where another is entitled either to the whole fishing or to fishing for that species in fresh water shall replace the fishery loss.

PCS. 2. Anyone who contravenes any prohibitions in the law or other legislation and rules laid down thereunder shall replace the damage sustained by the fishery and the public. The same applies to violations of regulations, decisions, orders, agreements, etc. entered into under the law or earlier laws, cf. sections 139 and 140.

PCS. 3. Claims for compensation to the public can be made by the Minister for the Environment and Food, the local council concerned and the Danish Sports Fisheries Association, the Freshwater Fisheries Association for Denmark and the Danish Fisheries Association.

CHAPTER 16 FIRST-TIME SALES OF FISH

A. Appropriation for first-time sales and for public fish auction

§ 86. Only persons, companies and companies that have a license issued by the Minister for the Environment and Food must conduct self-employment with first-time sales of fish, which means turnover etc., cf. Section 3, No. 5, of first-class fish by

1) public fish auction,

2) reception or purchase of fish without a public fish auction,

3) receipt of fish in commission as an agent or the like;

4) collection center and fish sorting,

5) Other forms of reception and storage of fish and fish

6) import of fish.

PCS. 2. The obligation to provide for subsection 1 can for the same party fish comprise more persons and companies.

PCS. 3. Persons and companies carrying fish after landing are not subject to the requirement for first-time fish allocation. However, for the sake of control, the Minister may lay down rules and issue orders for such carriers to have a grant.

PCS. 4. The Minister may decide that the rules for first-time conversion of fish shall also include the sale of own catch or breeding directly to the consumer for export or trade.

PCS. 5. The Minister may lay down rules under which specified fish, including imported fish, are exempted from the provisions of this chapter.

Section 87. It is not permitted to sell or deliver fish to persons liable for payment, companies or companies not authorized.

B. Issuing of appropriations

Section 88. First-time conversion of fish may be communicated to persons who meet the requirements of subsection (1). 2. In addition, grants may be granted to companies in accordance with the rules in paragraph. 3 and 4.

PCS. 2. Persons may obtain a grant under paragraph. 1 when they

1) has Danish citizenship, is a citizen of one of the other EU or EEA member states or has a residence and work permit in this country,

2) Have a residence in this country or in one of the other EU or EEA member states and

3) are legitimate and not under guardianship or intergovernmental agreement according to the law of guardianship.

PCS. 3. In partnerships and partnerships, all personally responsible participants shall comply with the requirements set forth in subsections 2 mentioned conditions.

PCS. 4. Grants may be granted to equity and limited liability companies and other limited liability companies registered or reported under the Companies Act as being registered or founding in the Ministry of Economic and Business Affairs when the directors and the majority of directors and holders of a controlling share or share fulfills the conditions in subsection 2nd

§ 89. In connection with the granting of a public fish auction, in addition to the requirements referred to in section 88, persons are required that they are not under reconstruction or bankruptcy proceedings and do not have significant overdue debts to the public, which means amounts in the order of DKK 50,000 and above .

PCS. 2. In partnerships and limited partnerships, the personally responsible participants shall meet the conditions set out in subsections First

PCS. 3. The holder of an appropriation pursuant to subsection 1 may only engage in other business activities related to the fishing industry, with permission from the Minister for the Environment and Food.

Section 90. The Minister for the Environment and Food may allow the granting of a grant, even if the conditions set out in sections 88 and 89 are not met.

Section 91. The Minister for the Environment and Food shall lay down the detailed rules for the issue and maintenance of the grant, including that the authorization is conditional on the law and rules, terms and conditions laid down by law and other legislation that are of importance to the undertaking liable to pay, Keep.

PCS. 2. The Minister may for the purpose of checking compliance with the conditions for granting stipulation pursuant to subsection 1 obtaining information from other public authorities, including information on offenses, income and property, VAT settlement etc.

§ 92. Appropriation for persons may be denied if

1) The applicant within the previous 5 years has been found guilty of a criminal offense that may give grounds for believing that he or she will not conduct the business properly,

2) The applicant's first-time revenue within the previous 5 years has been revoked and there is reason to believe that the person concerned will not conduct the business properly, or

3) In addition, information about the person who has reason to believe that he or she will not conduct the business properly.

PCS. 2. In partnerships and limited partnerships, a grant may be denied if there is information available to one of the participants as referred to in subsection 1 may justify refusal of authorization.

PCS. 3. If the applicant is a limited liability company or other limited liability company, a grant may be denied if there is information about a member of the company's management or board of directors or the holder of a controlling shareholding, share or similar information as provided for in subsection 1 may justify refusal of authorization.

PCS. 4. In the case of refusal of appropriation pursuant to subsection 1, a renewed application for a grant may be submitted at the earliest one year after the decision.

C. Cancellation or revocation of authorization

Section 93. The grant lapses if it has not been used for 12 consecutive months or when the holder of the license dies, cf. section 94. The same shall apply where the holder no longer meets the conditions in sections 88 and 89 in order to obtain a grant .

PCS. 2. If there are new members of a partnership or partnership, or in a limited liability company, new members of the Executive Board or the Board of Directors, or in the event of a transfer, a controlling stake, share or similar, within 14 days, notification shall be made to the Ministry of Environment and Food, which determines whether the authorization can be maintained or if the appropriation based on the changes will expire, cf. section 92.

PCS. 3. The Minister for the Environment and Food may derogate from the provisions of paragraph 1. First

PCS. 4. The Minister may lay down special rules for the granting of appropriations when granting a public fish auction.

Section 94. Upon application to the Minister for the Environment and Food, a death-living, a spouse who is in an unchanged residence, a bankruptcy estate or a guardian of a person under guardianship may be allowed to continue to be expelled, the case-mate or person under guardian's business for settlement , disposal or similar of the company. The operation will in all cases be carried out by a person approved under section 97.

PCS. 2. An authorization to carry on a public fish auction may only be maintained if the beneficiary of the grant meets the conditions set out in sections 88 and 89.

Section 95. The Minister for the Environment and Food may revoke the authorization if the Holder has committed a gross or repeated breach of the terms attached to the grant. The decision must contain information about access to justice under Section 96 and the deadline for this.

PCS. 2. In case of revocation of a grant, the holder of the license will be notified that it will be able to apply for a grant at the earliest 2 years.

Section 96. A decision pursuant to section 95 may be requested by the licensee before the courts. Requests must be submitted to the Minister for the Environment and Food within 4 weeks after the withdrawal has been notified to the holder of the authorization. The Minister appeals against the grant holder in the forms of civil procedure.

PCS. 2. Request for action does not have suspensory effect. However, the court may decide that during the proceedings the person concerned must be allowed to perform business on specified terms.

D. Rules for the operation of a statutory undertaking

§ 97. The day-to-day operation of the undertaking subject to the license must be carried out by the licensee himself or by a manager approved by the Ministry of Environment and Food.

PCS. 2. If the business is operated from several business locations, only one of these may be carried out by the licensee. The operation of the other business premises must be carried out by authorized directors.

PCS. 3. If the holder of the grant is a company or the like, the operation must be carried out by an approved director.

PCS. 4. The provisions of sections 88, 92, 93, 95 and 96 shall apply mutatis mutandis with regard to the approval of directors and refusal, cancellation and revocation of directors' approval. For managers of public fish auctions, section 89 also applies.

Section 98. The Minister for the Environment and Food may prohibit a licensee from leaving his business to anyone who does not meet the conditions for obtaining a grant, conducting a receipt of fish or finishing a purchase and sale or other similar business.

Section 99. The Minister for the Environment and Food may lay down further rules on which obligations under the Act and the EU Acts referred to in Section 10 may be imposed on a licensee in connection with the exercise of mandatory activities, including rules on

1) Obligation to require suppliers and their representatives identification and documentation regarding purchased or received fish,

2) preparation of bills, notes, bills, etc. and

3) reporting to the Ministry of Environment and Food of purchased, sold or received fish.

PCS. 2. The Minister may, among other things, lay down rules that information and written documentation regarding the operation etc. may be submitted to the Ministry of Environment and Food, upon request or on a continuous basis. In addition, the Minister may set rules governing the weighing of fish covered by the activity of the company, either by the use of authorized or accredited weighing and measuring or using approved and controlled weights.

E. Especially regarding public fish auctions

§ 100. Until 1 January 2002, no additional appropriations may be issued for public fish auction in a port where an authorization for public fish auction has been issued before 1 January 2000.

PCS. 2. Notwithstanding the provision in subsection 1, after the application, additional appropriations may be issued from the date on which the original grantor waives the grant or the auction for other reasons is not continued by the licensee.

§ 101. The Minister for the Environment and Food may lay down detailed rules for the operation of public fish auctions, including new auction methods.

CHAPTER 17 ADMINISTRATION OF PRODUCTION TAXES

§ 102. The Minister for the Environment and Food may lay down rules for the reduction of one or more production levy funds which shall administer the provisions of subsection 2 mentioned charges.

PCS. 2. The Minister may, on the recommendation of the parties referred to in section 104 (1) establish rules on the payment of taxes on fish landed, reared, produced or marketed in the country or on similar products imported into the country and on the extent to which such taxes are to be reimbursed for fish when these included as material in industrially manufactured goods. The charges are included in a production tax fund for each sector, cf. 1, where charging takes place.

PCS. 3. The Minister shall lay down rules for the payment of the fees referred to in subsection 2 mentioned public funds.

PCS. 4. The Minister may allow a Production Tax Fund, cf. 1, receive income other than those referred to in subsection 2 stated.

§ 103. Funds from the Funds referred to in section 102 shall be used for measures and subsidies for fisheries care, improvement and adaptation of fisheries and aquaculture structures, counseling, education, disease prevention, disease control and control measures, including business promotion measures, research projects and trials in the interests of the fishing industry, as well as measures approved by the Minister for the Environment and Food. The Minister may also allow the Funds to pay expenses to members of the Funds Board. The funds are also used to cover the costs of checking the correct use of the funds. The funds must be used in the part of the fishing industry where they are collected.

§ 104. Each fund is managed by a board appointed by the Minister for the Environment and Food. The Articles of Association of the Funds must be approved by the Minister. Each board is composed of representatives of both producer and industry interests and representatives of public interests. Representative producer and trade organizations make an agreement on 2/3 of each board member. The Consumer Council, the Labor Movement's Business Council and the Danish Free Research Foundation jointly declare one third of each board member. The boards are appointed for a period of 4 years.

PCS. 2. The Board shall ensure that the management of the funds takes place in accordance with the law, rules laid down thereunder and the legislation in general. The Minister may appoint a member of the Board who has contributed to decisions contrary to these provisions.

PCS. 3. The Minister may notify the Board of Directors of bringing into conflict with the law against rules laid down thereunder and against the law in general, in accordance with the provision.

Section 105. Budgets and accounts for individual funds shall be approved by the Minister for the Environment and Food, on the recommendation of the board concerned.

PCS. 2. The Minister may lay down rules for the Funds on the preparation of budgets and accounts, as well as on administration and auditing. The funds' accounts must be audited by state-authorized or registered auditors.

PCS. 3. Each fund creates an independent website on the internet. The Minister shall lay down the detailed rules for the publication of budgets and accounts by the Funds, as well as deadlines for applications, application procedures, etc.

PCS. 4. The Minister shall lay down the detailed rules for the evaluation of the funds by the Funds on the effect of the measures that have been granted, cf. Section 103.

PCS. 5. The Minister shall lay down the detailed rules for the granting of compensation for fish diseases by the Funds.

Section 106. Everyone shall, at the request of the Minister for the Environment and Food, communicate the information deemed necessary for the collection and use of the information referred to in section 102 1 mentioned means.

PCS. 2. The Minister may lay down rules for the control of this information, including accounting etc., cf. Chapter 22.

§ 107. Members of a board of directors who, in the performance of their duties intentionally or negligently, have incurred a fund damage are obliged to replace this.

PCS. 2. The provision in subsection 1 also applies to auditors. If an audit firm is elected to the auditor, both the audit firm and the auditor to whom the audit is assigned, is responsible.

For additional analytical, business and investment opportunities information,
please contact Global Investment & Business Center, USA
at (703) 370-8082. Fax: (703) 370-8083. E-mail: ibpusa3@gmail.com
Global Business and Investment Info Databank - www.ibpus.com

PCS. 3. The compensation may be reduced when this is reasonable considering the level of debt, the size of the damage and the circumstances in general.

PCS. 4. Decisions to bring actions against directors, audit firms or auditors may be taken by members of the board or by the Minister for the Environment and Food.

Section 108. At the end of each financial year, the Minister for the Environment and Food shall announce a committee appointed by the Folketing, which funds have been entered into in the funds and how the funds have been used.

CHAPTER 18 SCIENTIFIC STUDIES, ETC.

Section 109. Notwithstanding the provisions of this Act or rules laid down by law, the Minister for the Environment and Food may implement the measures or provide for measures necessary for the initiation of studies, projects etc. by public measure or with the permission of the State. for scientific, environmental and fishing purposes. The Minister may lay down rules for fishing and sampling of landings of fish in this connection.

PCS. 2. The Minister may lay down rules requiring a shipowner under professional fishing to include an observer on board for the purpose of collecting data for scientific use.

PCS. 3. Persons who carry out fishery surveys in freshwater at the state's request shall be entitled to pass the identification of appropriate identification documents over the land and private roads adjacent to the waters where the fisheries investigation is to take place.

CHAPTER 19 DELEGATION AND APPEAL

§ 110. The Minister for the Environment and Food may lay down rules according to which certain decisions or dispositions may be made by producer organizations or trade associations or associations thereof pursuant to the EU acts referred to in section 10. These decisions may be brought before the Environment and Food Complaints Board within 4 weeks after the decision has been notified to the complainant. The decision must contain information about appeal and appeal deadline. The Minister may amend the decision without a complaint.

PCS. 2. The Minister may refuse to take certain decisions pursuant to rules laid down in section 34 (2). 1, No. 3, concerning the interchange of vessel owners with the fishing rights allocated to their vessels to producer organizations, interbranch organizations or associations thereof. These decisions may be brought before the Environment and Food Complaints Board within 4 weeks after the decision has been notified to the complainant. The decision must contain information about appeal and appeal deadline. The Minister may change a decision without a complaint. The Minister may lay down additional rules on the right to appeal against the decisions of the organizations. An organization is subject to the ministry's instruction and supervision in the cases assigned to the organization pursuant to this provision.

PCS. 3. The Minister may relinquish his powers under the law of an institution under the ministry or other public institution. The Minister may, in this connection, lay down rules on the right to appeal against the decisions of these authorities, including whether a complaint may not be brought before another administrative authority and the authority's access to resume a case after a complaint has been lodged.

Section 110a. Decisions taken pursuant to this Act or rules issued pursuant thereto may, unless otherwise provided by the Act or in accordance with rules issued thereunder, be appealed to the Environment and Food Appeals Board which will handle the matter in one of the boards sections, cf. section 3 1, No. 5 and 6, in the Act on the Environment and Food Appeals Board, and can not therefore be brought to another administrative authority.

PCS. 2. Appeals to the Environment and Food Appeals Board shall be submitted in writing to the authority that has made the decision, using digital self-service, cf. section 21 (1). 2-4, in the Act on the Environment and Food Appeals Board. If it wishes to maintain the decision, the Authority must forward the complaint to the appeal body as soon as possible and not later than 3 weeks after receipt of the complaint. The appeal must be accompanied by the contested decision, the documents obtained in the assessment of the case and an opinion from the Authority with its observations on the case and the complaints made in the complaint.

Section 111. Decisions taken by the board of a fund, cf. section 104, may be referred to the Minister for the Environment and Food within 4 weeks after the decision has been notified to the complainant. The Minister may amend the Board's decisions without a complaint.

CHAPTER 20 RELEASE AND PROCESSING OF INFORMATION

Section 112. The Minister for the Environment and Food may, for the purposes of administration of the law, including for statistical use and for control purposes, lay down rules for the delivery and processing of information on

1) vessels, gear and other equipment,

2) fishing, catching, turnover, etc. and rearing of fish, including from whom they are acquired, and

3) Information of technical, economic and operational nature regarding fishery and fish farming.

PCS. 2. The Minister may also lay down rules for issuing and processing accounting and economic data for statistical purposes.

Section 112a. The Minister for the Environment and Food shall keep the computer register of transferable quota shares, cf. section 37 1. The register is publicly available.

PCS. 2. The Minister shall lay down rules for notification and registration of transferable shares, cf. 1. The Minister may, among other things, lay down rules for the parties to report the selling price of a transferred quota share.

PCS. 3. The Minister may lay down rules that the exchange of documents in connection with notification and registration may take place electronically and that they must be submitted to the National Agency for Economic Affairs [5)] in a standardized form prescribed by the Board.

Section 112b. The Minister for the Environment and Food may lay down rules on public access to specified parts of the Ministry of Environment and Food Ministries in the fisheries sector.

Section 112c. The Minister for the Environment and Food may lay down rules that communication under the provisions of the European Union Regulations on a Community system for preventing, preventing and halting illegal, unreported and unregulated fishing shall take place digitally between the Minister and companies.

PCS. 2. The Minister may lay down rules on digital communication, cf. 1, including the use of particular IT systems, special digital formats, digital signatures or the like.

PCS. 3. The Minister may lay down rules that the Minister or the Minister authorized to do so may issue decisions and other documents, cf. 1, without signature, by machine or equivalent signature or using a technique that ensures clear identification of the person who issued or attested the decision or document. Such decisions and documents are resembled decisions and documents with personal signature.

PCS. 4. The Minister may lay down rules that decisions and other documents made or issued solely on the basis of electronic data processing may be issued solely with a statement by the Ministry of the Environment and Foodstuffs or the Minister which authorizes it as consignor.

PCS. 5. A digital message is considered to be available when it is available to the addressee of the message.

CHAPTER 20A MEASURES IN THE EVENT OF ACCIDENTS AND DISASTERS, INCLUDING ACTS OF WAR, ETC.

Section 112d. The Minister for the Environment and Food may, in the event of accidents and disasters, including acts of war and other extraordinary circumstances, lay down the rules and make the decisions necessary to ensure the supply of fish and fish products by the population, including laying down detailed rules for fishing activities and for the disposal of the catches. The Minister may, inter alia, lay down rules and make provision for a derogation from the rules laid down by law.

PCS. 2. The Committee for Business Fisheries, set up pursuant to section 6 and supplemented by 1 member appointed by the Minister for Defense, advises the Minister in preparation for the matters referred to in subsection 1, rules and regulations.

PCS. 3. Before issuing rules or decisions or provisions pursuant to subsections 1, as far as possible, be negotiated with the persons or companies concerned or with their organizations regarding the scope and implementation of the rules, decisions or provisions, including possible compensation from the state, cf. 4th

PCS. 4. Includes a rule, decision or provision issued pursuant to paragraph. 1 financial loss for a person or company, the state is liable for damages under the general rules of the legislation. Compensation can not be claimed if the costs associated with the implementation of the rule or decision can be covered by calculation in the price or service price concerned. The persons or companies concerned may not therefore be placed less favorably than others in the same industry.

PCS. 5. Compensation shall be determined in the absence of a memorandum of understanding in accordance with rules laid down by the Minister.

CHAPTER 21 FEES, ETC.

§ 113. The Minister for the Environment and Food may lay down rules for full or partial payment for special services provided by the controlling authorities upon request.

§ 114. The Minister for the Environment and Food may lay down rules on payment of fees as a condition for the issue and maintenance of permits for participation in certain, particularly limited fisheries requiring special biological studies.

PCS. 2. The fee shall be paid to the Minister for the Environment and Food. The Minister may lay down rules for the payment.

PCS. 3. The funds shall be used to cover all or part of the costs of scientific work in connection with the fisheries concerned.

Section 114a. The Minister for the Environment and Food may lay down rules governing the costs of the inspection or supervision of compliance with the provisions of the regulations of the European Union on a Community scheme to prevent, ward off and stop illegal, unreported and unregulated fishing in connection with the following:

1) Imports of fish and fishery products landed by a fishing vessel registered in a country outside the European Union, except where the fish or fishery is landed directly in Denmark from a vessel which has not previously been in port with that fish or fish product (direct landing).

2) Re-export to countries outside the European Union of fish and fishery products previously imported into the European Union, including by direct landing, cf. No 1, which are not further processed in the European Union.

3) Exports to countries outside the European Union of fish and fishery products landed by Danish fishing vessels.

PCS. 2. The Minister may lay down rules for the collection of the fees referred to in paragraph 1. 1, including the term for collection.

Section 115. Amounts determined pursuant to this Act or pursuant to the EU acts referred to in Section 10, which shall be paid to the Minister for the Environment and Food, or other authority, and which are not paid in due time, shall be paid unless otherwise stipulated in the EU acts referred to in section 10, an annual interest rate equal to the interest rate stipulated in section 5 of the Interest Act, from the due date, to be calculated. The paid interest, however, amounts to at least DKK 50. For a letter of remuneration, a fee of DKK 100 is paid, which is adjusted with the adjustment rate in the Act on a rate adjustment percentage. The amount will be rounded to the nearest with 10 divisible krona amounts.

PCS. 2. Unless otherwise provided for in the EU acts referred to in Article 10, unduly received amounts shall not be recovered before the expiry of a time limit set by the paying authority, the amount referred to in paragraph 1. 1 mentioned interest from the expiry of the deadline. However, this applies only if the authority, while requiring repayment, provides notification of the obligation to pay interest.

§ 116. (Repeated)

CHAPTER 22 CONTROL AND SUPERVISION

A. General provisions

Section 117. The control of compliance with the law, rules laid down by law and the EU acts referred to in section 10 shall be the responsibility of the Minister for the Environment and Food.

PCS. 2. If deemed necessary, the inspection authority shall at all times be duly authorized and without a court order

1) the right to travel across land and private roads adjacent to freshwater or saline, including the right to travel by motor vehicle,

(2) access to fishing vessels, fishing vessels and vessels from which recreational fishing is carried out;

3) access to businesses and, moreover, everywhere where fish are traded etc., reared and hatched, including companies which form part of the chain of sales in the past or later, and companies which are obliged to pay taxes under section 102,

4) The right to open shipments containing fish in order to monitor compliance with the Act,

5) access to control installation, operation and maintenance of equipment on board fishing vessels and

6) The right to use motorized vessels in freshwater.

PCS. 3. The inspection authority shall, among other things, be entitled to conduct investigations and to take samples without sampling or to take samples and to carry out checks, to the extent necessary to examine the nature of the tests.

PCS. 4. The inspection authority is also entitled to duly verify and without a court order to inspect the documents referred to in subsection 2 logs, inventories, business books, other accounting documents, accompanying documents, prescriptions, analytical material, correspondence and other documentation, etc., including material stored in electronic form.

PCS. 5. The police shall, if necessary, provide assistance for the implementation of the checks. The Minister for the Environment and Food may, in agreement with the Minister for Justice, lay down further rules.

PCS. 6. In agreement with the Minister for the Environment and Food, it may be stipulated that the Ministry of Environment and Food Affairs participates in the monitoring of compliance with such rules as part of rules on fishing restrictions issued under other legislation.

Section 117a. By way of derogation from section 9 of the Act on legal certainty in the administration of enforcement and disclosure obligations, the control authority may carry out checks on seagoing vessels when the master, vessel owner or employee on board is reasonably suspected of committing a criminal offense of fishing legislation. The inspection authority may, inter alia, check catches, fishing gear and documents on board the vessel.

Section 117b. The Minister for the Environment and Food may lay down rules that a person must declare his cpr number in connection with the acquisition of fishing signs.

Section 118. The inspection authority may obtain the information from other public authorities necessary to verify compliance with the law, inter alia for the purpose of registering and compiling the information for purposes of control, including information on income and property, VAT settlement etc.

§ 119. Vessels, business owners and employed persons shall provide, in the context of the verification of section 117, at the request of the supervisory authority, all information, including financial and accounting matters relevant to the performance of the inspection, and free of charge, provide the supervisory authority with the necessary assistance in checking, sampling, copying and disclosure of written material and printing of electronic data. Vessels, business owners or their representatives have the right to attend to the inspection authority's collection of tests etc. pursuant to section 117.

§ 120. The inspection authority may issue injunctions and prohibitions, as necessary

1) for the exercise of the inspection, including landings, landing times and the presence of the inspection authority on landing or

2) to ensure the presence of a fishing vessel, fishing vessel, motor vehicle transporting fish and fishing gear and catching until the police can attend and make the necessary enforcement efforts in accordance with the Code of Criminal Procedure for Criminal Procedure.

PCS. 2. In the context of the control of persons and companies converting etc., the control authority may, in exceptional cases, designate a state-authorized or registered accountant for the account of the person making turnover, etc., for review of the material subject to control.

§ 121. Turnover etc. of fish is not allowed if

1) there is fishing in violation of the rules governing fishing activities,

2) the content is not in accordance with the rules on the composition of the catch or

3) The content is not registered, logged in or reported in accordance with the law, rules laid down by law or the EU acts referred to in Section 10.

PCS. 2. The Minister for the Environment and Food may lay down rules on documentation, etc., for example, that the person who translates etc. fish meets the requirements of paragraph 1. First

PCS. 3. In addition, as part of the control of companies covered by Chapter 16 of the Act, which do not have a permanent place of business in the country, the Minister may lay down special rules regarding documentation, etc., for the conversion of etc. first-class fish, cf. Section 86 fulfills the requirements of paragraph. First

PCS. 4. Fish covered by paragraph 1, shall be resettled as far as possible in the living state immediately after catch.

Section 122. The person who translates etc. fish covered by section 121 (1). 1, may be released from liability pursuant to section 130 (1). 1, No. 1, cf. section 121, paragraph 1. 1, immediately upon receipt of the fish, report to the inspection authority indicating the approximate size and composition of the lot and the sender's name and address.

PCS. 2. Fish declared pursuant to paragraph 1, must be kept in such a way that control can be exercised and may not be carried out without the consent of the inspection authority.

PCS. 3. In a lot of fish where part of the content is covered by section 121 (1). 1, the whole party is illegal unless the illegal parting of the illegal part takes place under the control of the inspection authority or sampling is carried out to determine the extent of the illegal act.

PCS. 4. The Minister for the Environment and Food may lay down rules on turnover, etc., of fish during periods of conservation and other periods when fishing for one or more species of fish is not permitted.

Section 122a. The inspection authority may cause or prohibit the disposal of catches caught in violation of the rules governing fishing activities or whose content is not in accordance with the rules on the composition of the catch.

§ 123. In the event of violation of provisions of the Act, rules issued pursuant to the Act and the EU Acts on the use, design, location, marking and marking of fishing gear and on mesh size, the regulatory authority may make the necessary, including the removal of tools and poles.

PCS. 2. If a gear is removed at the request of a fisherman and the violation concerns the distance rules between gear set in accordance with section 32 1, any costs incurred by the person who made the request shall be borne in so far as the violation of the rule is subject to a private prosecution, cf. section 136. The inspection authority may require collateral for such costs. The person who has made a notification and incurred expenses is entitled to cover the costs of the person who placed the tool illegally.

Section 124. The Minister for the Environment and Food may lay down detailed rules for landing fish, fitting and operation of fishing vessels and means of transport where deemed necessary for the purpose of the inspection.

PCS. 2. The Minister may lay down rules on the control of the information to be used for the payment of benefits or the collection of taxes under the Act and the EU acts referred to in Section 10.

PCS. 3. The person who receives benefits or who is liable to pay taxes under the Act and the EU acts referred to in Section 10 shall keep it in section 117 (3). 4, including material in electronic form, for at least 5 years from the end of the year in which the benefit is received or the tax is paid.

§ 125. The Minister for the Environment and Food may lay down rules for the payment of amounts and grants under the Act and the EU Acts mentioned in Section 10, including from the Funds referred to in Section 102, that the beneficiary indicates An account in a bank on which the amount can be deposited.

PCS. 2. The Minister may lay down rules on the accounting etc. to be carried out by companies in connection with the payment of benefits or the collection of taxes.

B. Specific control provisions for EU legislation in the field of fisheries

Section 126. The National Audit Office may, together with the European Court of Auditors, on the same terms as mentioned in section 117 (1). 2, check the inventories of the companies concerned and the section 117 (1). 4, which is relevant to the audit control of the administration of the EU acts referred to in section 10.

§ 127. (Repeated)

C. Special inspection regulations for fresh water

§ 128. The Minister for the Environment and Food may lay down rules on the involvement of municipal councils in the inspection of freshwater.

§ 129. Fishery rights that are fishery in freshwater may hire one or more observers to be approved by the Minister for the Environment and Food.

PCS. 2. The Minister shall provide the Supervisor with special identification and an instruction approved by the Minister.

PCS. 3. The Minister may revoke it in subsection 1, if the supervisor fails to comply with the duties imposed upon him if the supervisor abuses the authority transferred to him or if the supervisor otherwise acts improperly.

PCS. 4. The supervisor supervises that the law, rules laid down pursuant to the Act and decisions or with the Ministry of the Environment and Food Administration, shall be complied with, etc., with the fishery water which they have in paragraph 1. 1 mentioned fishery resources may be disposed of.

PCS. 5. Detention officers have the right to cross the land and private roads that are adjacent to those mentioned in subsections 4 mentioned fishing waters.

CHAPTER 23 PUNISHMENT, PROSECUTION AND CONFISCATION

§ 130. Unless higher punishment is implied by other legislation, fines shall be fined by the person who

1) violates or attempts to violate section 11 1, section 12 1, § 13, § 18, § 28, subsection 2, § 32, paragraph 1. 4, § 33, subsection Article 38 (1). 1, section 44 Section 1, section 50 1, § 58, paragraph 1. 2, a waiver by judgment pursuant to section 59 a, subsection 1, an adopted ban pursuant to section 59a, subsection 2, § 63, para. Article 66 (1). 1, § 69, § 72, § 74, paragraph 1. 1, § 76, § 77, paragraph 1. Article 86 (1). 1, section 87, section 97, section 98, section 119, section 121, paragraph 1. Article 122 (1). 2, § 124, para. 3, those pursuant to section 10 1, provisions and the regulations and decisions referred to in section 10,

2) overrides or attempts to override terms relating to an authorization or grant issued under the law or rules laid down pursuant to the Act;

3) violates, attempts to violate or fail to comply with an injunction or prohibition issued under the law or rules laid down by law,

4) delivers or tries to provide false or misleading information or deserves or tries to declare information required by law, rules laid down by law or the regulations and decisions referred to in section 10,

For additional analytical, business and investment opportunities information,
please contact Global Investment & Business Center, USA
at (703) 370-8082. Fax: (703) 370-8083. E-mail: ibpusa3@gmail.com
Global Business and Investment Info Databank - www.ibpus.com

5) Fails to provide the documentation and information required to deliver or as required by law, rules laid down by law or the regulations and decisions referred to in section 10,

6) intentionally or grossly negligently violates its obligations under section 104 2, or

7) unlawfully conducts fishing in a freshwater area, cf. section 28 First

PCS. 2. In rules issued pursuant to the Act, penalties may be imposed on fines for violation or attempted violation of the provisions of the rules.

PCS. 3. The person who commits a relationship as mentioned in subsection 1, No. 2, 4 or 5, or as mentioned in the provisions of paragraph 1. 2 rules with the intention of evading or other payment of taxes in accordance with the regulations referred to in section 10 or in accordance with rules determined pursuant to section 102 or intentionally to obtain unjustified payment or reimbursement of benefits to themselves or others pursuant to the regulations referred to in section 10 or pursuant to section 103 or rules laid down pursuant to section 102, be fined or imprisoned for up to 1 year and 6 months unless higher punishment is implied by section 289 of the Penal Code.

PCS. 4. Companies etc. (legal persons) may be subject to criminal liability in accordance with the provisions of Chapter 5 of the Criminal Code.

PCS. 5. If an offense has been committed with one or more vessels subject to a pool fishing, an increased fine may be imposed.

PCS. 6. The limitation period for criminal liability is in no case less than 5 years for violations that cause or are likely to result in unauthorized persons being exempt from payment of taxes under the EU acts referred to in section 10, pursuant to this Act or rules laid down by law, or that anyone receives unwarranted payments under the aforesaid provisions.

PCS. 7. For violations of section 11, subsection 1, section 12 Article 38 (1). Article 86 (1). 1, section 87, section 119, section 121, paragraph 1. 1, and those pursuant to section 10 1, regulations and the regulations and decisions referred to in section 10 and violations covered by subsections 1, No. 2-5, and paragraph. 2, the limitation period for criminal liability is in no case less than 5 years if the violation concerns fishing that can only be exercised as commercial fishing, cf. section 11 1, No. 1, or turnover etc. of the fish, cf. Section 3, No. 5.

PCS. 8. Infringement of provisions laid down in the EU Regulations referred to in Section 10, to prevent, deter and stop illegal, unreported and unregulated fishing (IUU fishing), is under Danish jurisdiction (jurisdiction) regardless of whether the offense has been committed outside Denmark if the violation has been committed by a person who, at the time of the act, had Danish citizenship and was not domiciled or otherwise resident in the Faroe Islands or in Greenland. Similarly, the violation is under Danish criminal authority if it has been committed in favor of a legal person with its registered office in Denmark. This applies irrespective of whether the conditions in section 6 to 9 of the Criminal Code are met and even if the offense is not punishable under the legislation of the state concerned.

§ 131. Investigation in cases of breach of the provisions of this Act or rules laid down pursuant to this Act may be in accordance with the provisions of the Code of Judicial Procedure for Search in Cases which, pursuant to the Act, may lead to imprisonment.

PCS. 2. The inspection authority may, in accordance with the provisions of Chapter 74 of the Code of Civil Procedure, seize the equipment and catches of violations of provisions of this Act or rules laid down pursuant to this Act.

§ 132. Fish caught in violation of the law or rules laid down pursuant to the Act or the value thereof may be confiscated, although it can not be conclusively established that the catch as a whole is derived from an illegal relationship. Insofar as such fish are in viable condition, they shall be immediately returned by the inspection authority or by the supervisors approved under section 129.

PCS. 2. Fishing gear found in the water can be confiscated, although it can not be disclosed who it belongs to when the gear

1) are not legally designed, marked, marked, used or placed under the law, rules laid down by law or the EU acts referred to in section 10;

2) has not been smoked in accordance with section 33 or

3) has been placed or left in places in freshwater, where another is entitled to fishing or to the species concerned.

§ 133. If an offense is deemed not to result in higher punishment than fines, the Minister for the Environment and Food may declare that the case can be settled without legal prosecution if the person who committed the offense declares himself guilty of the violation and declares himself ready before the specified time limit which may be extended upon request to pay a fine specified in the notice. Likewise, confiscation requirements, including value-added tax, may be adopted without legal prosecution.

PCS. 2. For the purposes of paragraph 1, The first sentence mentioned in paragraph 1 finds the provision in section 832 (1) of the Code of Civil Procedure. 2, corresponding application.

PCS. 3. If the fine is paid in due time, or if it is received after the date of adoption or withdrawal, further proceedings will be canceled.

§ 134. In cases dealt with administratively, cf. section 133 (1). 1, section 752 (2) of the Code of Judicial Procedure. 1, corresponding application.

§ 135. Foreign ships that have been used for fishing activities contrary to the EU acts referred to in section 10 against this Act or against rules laid down pursuant to this Act may be detained by the inspection authority. The enforcement of detention by the inspection authority takes place in accordance with Chapter 74 of the Code of Conduct on Seizure.

PCS. 2. Retention pursuant to subsection 1 can only happen if required

1) to secure evidence,

2) to ensure the public's claim for costs, confiscation and fines,

3) to ensure the injured party's claim for return or replacement or

4) for the purpose of control and prosecution.

PCS. 3. There may be no detention pursuant to paragraph. 1, if security has been provided for the payment of the items referred to in subsection 2, No. 2 and 3, or the person who had available the vessel during the fishing activity was unjustified in possession of it.

PCS. 4. Paid in paragraph 2, no. 2 and 3, or if no such security is lodged within two months after the final decision of the case, a claim may be made on the ship.

§ 136. Violations of the rules in sections 69, 72 and 76 are subject to private prosecution. The same applies in case of violation of the fishing right pursuant to section 28 1, and in violation of rules on distance between fixed fishing gear determined pursuant to section 32, unless public interest is required by public interest.

CHAPTER 24 ENTRY INTO FORCE AND TRANSITIONAL PROVISIONS ETC.

A. Entry into force

§ 137. The date of the law or parts of the Act's entry into force shall be determined by the Minister for Food, Agriculture and Fisheries. [6)]

PCS. 2. In this connection, the Minister may stipulate that the following legal provisions are repealed in full or in part:

1) Act on saltwater fishing, cf. Laws No 803 of 11 November 1998.

2) Act on regulation of fisheries, cf. Decree No 802 of 11 November 1998.

3) Law No 285 of 27 April 1994 on first-time sales of fish.

4) Law No 482 of 12 June 1996 on the administration of the European Union's regulations in the field of fisheries and administration of production taxes, etc.

5) Act on freshwater fishing, cf. Decree No 495 of 16 June 1997.

6) Act No. 227 of 8 April 1992 on fishing signs, etc.

7) Act No. 101 of 27 March 1933 on the rules of conservation and order for fisheries in the waters of the United Kingdom Denmark and Sweden.

8) Act No. 67 of 23 March 1965 on fishing in Randers Fjord and Gudenå, etc.

9) Act No. 42 of 13 February 1959 on fishing in Flensburg Inderfjord.

PCS. 3. Rules laid down pursuant to the provisions of subsections The laws mentioned above shall remain in force until they are replaced by rules laid down pursuant to this or other laws. Violations of the rules are punished by the rules in force until now.

B. Transitional provisions for statutes in saline and regulations in freshwater

§ 138. Statutory provisions established pursuant to previous legislation on saltwater fishing continue to apply unless the Minister for Food, Agriculture and Fisheries has laid down rules that completely or partially repeal the statute. Violation of articles of association is punishable by fine until the statutes cease to apply.

§ 139. Regulations laid down in accordance with previous legislation on fresh water shall apply until 1 July 2010 unless the Minister for Food, Agriculture and Fisheries determines rules that completely or partially repeal the regulation. Violation of regulations will be fined until the regulations cease to apply.

PCS. 2. The Board of Regulators shall hold at least one annual meeting with at least 14 days' notice and shall, in addition, hold together when two members of the Board so require. The Board convenes the Annual General Meeting once a year.

PCS. 3. The annual general meeting determines the economic exploitation of the fishing waters covered by the Regulation, whether or not membership fees and their amount are to be collected and how any profits may be distributed.

C. Specific transitional provisions in fresh water

Section 140. Orders, decisions and agreements, etc. made or concluded pursuant to previous legislation on freshwater fishing, are valid until they are repealed or, according to their content, are no longer valid. Violations of the orders etc. are punished with a fine.

D. Transitional provisions on fines

Section 141. Penalties pursuant to the Act shall accrue to the Treasury. However, until the end of 2002, the Minister for Food, Agriculture and Fisheries will allocate up to DKK 200,000 annually from the fines paid by the Danish Fisheries Cultural Fund, the Danish Fisheries Association's Aid Fund - East and Denmark's Fisheries Association's Aid Fund - West, respectively, 1/2, 1/3 and 1/6 to each.

PCS. 2. If, in paragraph 1, the Minister determines how the fines allocated to the Funds are applied.

E. Transitional provisions concerning appropriations, authorizations and production levy funds

Section 142. Appropriations and licenses issued under previous applicable legislation remain in force until replaced by appropriations and licenses issued pursuant to this Act or rules laid down pursuant to the Act.

PCS. 2. Production tax funds reduced according to previously applicable legislation are maintained.

F. Faroe Islands and Greenland

§ 143. The law does not apply to the Faroe Islands and Greenland, cf. 2nd

PCS. 2. However, the law shall apply to breach of provisions laid down in the EU Regulations referred to in section 10, to prevent, deter and stop illegal, unreported and unregulated fishing (IUU fishing) committed in the Faroe Islands or Greenland by Danish nationals who do not have a residence or are otherwise resident in the Faroe Islands or in Greenland, cf. section 130 (1). 8th

Law No. 1336 of 19 December 2008 (Consequences Changes Due to Government Debt Settlement Act) [7] contains the following entry into force:

§ 167

PCS. 1. The Act shall enter into force on 1 January 2009, cf. 2. Section 11 applies solely to decisions on pay retention taken after the entry into force of the Act.

PCS. 2. (undivided)

Act No. 1513 of 27 December 2009 (Authorization for the introduction of voluntary schemes, changed transfer of pesticide tax proceeds from the Ministry of Taxation to the Ministry of Foods following the Green Growth Agreement, etc.) [8] contains the following entry into force:

§ 3

The act enters into force on 1 January 2010.

Law No. 718 of 25 June 2010 (Reconstruction, etc.) [9] contains the following entry into force and transitional provisions:

§ 55

PCS. 1. The Minister of Justice shall determine the date of entry into force of this Act. [10]

PCS. 2 - 10. (Undivided)

Law No. 604 of 14 June 2011 (Control campaigns, dietary supplements, organizational structure of the Food Authority, fee-financed controls, digital communications, etc.) [11] contains the following entry into force:

§ 4

The law enters into force on 1 July 2011.

Law No. 388 of 2 May 2012 (Advisory Committee, Fisheries of Salmon in Certain Water Systems, EU Points System for Serious Violations, Seizure of Fishing Tackle, etc. and Penalties for Certain Extra-territorial Offenses) [12] Contains Effective and Transitional Provisions:

§ 2

PCS. 1. The Act enters into force on 1 June 2012.

PCS. 2. Rules issued pursuant to section 127 of the Fisheries Act as repealed by section 1, no. 19, shall remain in effect until further notice.

Law No. 446 of 23 May 2012 (Implementation of the Industrial Emissions, Digital Authorization, Authorization and Surveillance Systems Directive, Release of Freshwater Dams, and Regulation of Inorganic Fertilizer, etc.) [13] contains the following entry into force:

§ 7

PCS. 1. The Act shall enter into force on 7 January 2013, cf. 2 and 3.

PCS. 2. Section 1, No. 4, 8-10 and 12-14, and Section 6 shall enter into force on 1 July 2012.

PCS. 3. (undivided)

Act No. 1148 of 11 December 2012 (Fishing License for Certain Educational Institutions) [14] contains the following entry into force:

§ 2

The law enters into force on 15 December 2012.

Act No. 310 of 29 March 2014 (Amendments pursuant to the Danish Innovation Fund Act) [15] contain the following entry into force and transitional provisions:

§ 12

PCS. 1. The Act enters into force on April 1, 2014.

PCS. 2. (undivided)

PCS. 3. Danmarks Innovationsfond will come into force on the entry into force of the Act in the rights and obligations that have so far been granted to the Danish Council for Strategic Research and the High Technology Foundation.

PCS. 4. (undivided)

PCS. 5. Authorizations issued to the Strategic Research Council's program committees or to the Secretariat of the Strategic Research Council pursuant to the Act on Research Advice, etc., as well as authorizations issued to the High Technology Foundation's Secretariat pursuant to the Act on the High Technology Foundation remain in force until amended pursuant to the Danish Innovation Funds Act.

PCS. 6. (undivided)

Act No 1715 of 27 December 2016 on the Environment and Food Appeals Board [16] contains the following entry into force and transitional provisions:

Section 24. The Act shall enter into force on 1 February 2017.

PCS. 2. (undivided)

PCS. 3. The Minister of Business [17] may, after consulting the Minister for the Environment and Food, lay down transitional rules.

PCS. 4. (undivided)

PCS. 5. Rules set in accordance with previously applicable rules shall remain in force until terminated or replaced by rules established pursuant to this Act. Violations of the rules are punished by the rules in force until now.

PCS. 6. Pending complaints in the Nature and Environmental Appeals Board or Appeals Center for Food, Agriculture and Fisheries, which have not been finalized by the entry into force of this Act, shall be finalized and decided by the Environment and Food Appeals Board in accordance with the provisions of this Act. This does not apply, however, to pending complaints by the Nature and Environmental Complaints Board, which by the Act's entry into force must be finalized and decided by the Board of Appeals Board, cf. Section 1 of the Act on the Board of Appeals.

PCS. 7. (undivided)

Act No. 384 of 26 April 2017 on the Danish Research and Innovation Policy Council and the Danish Research Fund for Research [18] contain the following entry into force and transitional provisions:

§ 36. The Act enters into force on 1 July 2017.

PCS. 2. Law on research advice etc., cf. Public Order No. 365 of 10 April 2014, is repealed.

PCS. 3. Order No. 322 of 30 March 2014 on the grant function etc. under the Free Research Council remains in force until amended or repealed.

PCS. 4. Authorizations issued to academic research councils under the Free Research Council or the secretariat of the Free Research Council pursuant to the Law on Research Advice, etc. shall remain in force until amended or repealed.

PCS. 5. (undivided)

PCS. 6. Members of the Board of the Free Research Council continue as members of the board of the Danish Free Research Fund until the end of their current period with the possibility of re-appointment if re-appointment can be made according to the new rules.

PCS. 7. The Academic Research Council of the Free Research Council shall continue as standing committee pursuant to this Act until the Governing Board of the Danish Free Research Fund decides otherwise.

PCS. 8. Members of academic research councils under the Free Research Council continue as members of the standing committees under the Danish Free Research Fund, with the possibility of re-appointment if re-appointment can be made according to the new rules.

PCS. 9. Complaints concerning decisions taken by academic research councils under the Free Research Council, which were submitted prior to the entry into force of the Act, shall be settled in accordance with the rules currently in force.

Agriculture and Fisheries Agency, 19 June 2017

Jette Petersen

/ Dorthe Nielsen

Annex 1

Table of Contents

E. Transitional provisions concerning appropriations, authorizations and production levy funds	Section 142
F. Faroe Islands and Greenland	§ 143

Appendix 2

Animal species of common importance whose collection in nature and exploitation may be subject to management measures

Only species relevant to the law are incorporated	Salmoniformes
	Salmonidae
The species listed in this Annex are listed	Thymallus thymallus
either by	Salmo salar (fresh water only)
1) the name of the particular species or subspecies; or	Cyprinidae
	Barbus spp. (The abbreviation "spp." Refers to
2) all species belonging to a higher one	all species belonging to this family or
systematic unit (taxon) or a closer	genus.)
specified part of this.	CLUPEIFORMES
Petromyzoniformes	clupeidae
Petromyzonidae	Alosa spp.
Lampetra fluviatilis	Arthropoda
ACIPENSERIFORMES	CRUSTACEA - DECAPODA
Acipenseridae	Astacidae
- all species not listed in Annex IV of	Astacus astacus
The habitats Directive	

Official notes

[1] The Act contains provisions implementing parts of Directive 2004/35 / EC of the European Parliament and of the Council of 21 April 2004 on environmental liability with regard to the prevention and remedying of environmental damage, Official Journal 2004, No L 143, page 56 , parts of Council Directive 79/409 / EEC of 2 April 1979 on the conservation of wild birds (EC Birds Directive), Official Journal 1979, No L 103, page 1, as last amended by Council Directive

2006/105 / EC of 20 November 2006, Official Journal 2006, No L 363, page 368 and Council Directive 92/43 / EEC of 21 May 1992 on the conservation of natural habitats and of wild fauna and flora (EC Habitats Directive), EU Temporary 1992, No. L 206, page 7, as last amended by Council Directive 2006/105 / EC of 20 November 2006, Official Journal 2006, No L 363, page 368.

[2] By Royal Decree of 28 June 2015, the Ministry of the Environment and the Ministry of Food, Agriculture and Fisheries were convened for an Environment and Food Ministry, cf. Executive Order No. 1229 of 3 November 2015, amending the distribution of shops between the ministers.

[3] By Royal Decree of 28 June 2015, the Ministry of the Environment and the Ministry of Food, Agriculture and Fisheries were convened for a Ministry of Environment and Food, cf. Executive Order No. 1229 of 3 November 2015, amending the distribution of shops between the ministers.

[4] The Ministry of Economic and Business Affairs was transformed into the Ministry of Business and Growth in October 2011. By Royal Decree of 28 November 2016, the name of the Ministry of Business and Growth was changed to the Ministry of Business, cf. Executive Order No. 1777 of 23 December 2016.

[5] The Nature Agency was formed in October 2011 by a merger of the Food Industry, the Directorate of Fisheries and the majority of the Plant Directorate.

[6] §§ 4-9 and 17-20 of the Act, § 110, subsection 2, section 116, paragraph 9, sections 117-129, section 130, paragraph 1. 1, No. 1-5 and. 2-5, and sections 131-134 have entered into force on 3 July 1999, cf. Order No. 520 of 24 June 1999 and Chapter 1, Section 10, subsection 1, section 30, chapter 7 and section 137 entered into force on 7 December 1999, cf. Order No. 864 of 2 December 1999. The remaining parts of Act No. 281 of 12 May 1999 entered into force on 1 January 2000, see Order No. 864 of 2 December 1999.

[7] The amendment of the Act concerns the repeal of section 116.

[8] The amendment of the Act concerns the insertion of new paragraph. 3 and 4 of section 105, according to which paragraph 3 has become a paragraph. 5th

[9] The amendment of the Act concerns amendment of section 89 (1). First

[10] The act has come into force on April 1, 2011, cf. Executive Order No. 208 of 15 March 2011.

[11] The amendment of the act relates to a change in the law of the European Community to the European Union and the European Community is changed to the European Union's amendment of Chapter 20a and the insertion of sections 112c, 114a and 115d. 1, 3 pct.

[12] The amendment of the Act refers to the amendment of the Act of Community Acts to EU Acts, Section 9, Chapter 7, Section B, Section 36, subsection. 1, 1st sentence, the title of chapter 8, section 38, section 39, paragraph 1. 1-2 and 5, section 56 3 and 4, section 60, section 117 2, No. 5, § 130, paragraph 1. 1, No. 1, and Section 143, repeal of section 5, subsection 2, § 6, subsection 2 and 3, § 6 a, subsection 2, § 7, subsection Section 2, Section 8 2 and 127 and insertion of section 30 2, sections 39 a - 39 b, section 130 paragraph 8 oh § 131, paragraph. 2nd

[13] The amendment of the Act concerns the repeal of section 47 and amendment of sections 49 and 130 1, No. 1.

14) The amendment of the amendment relates to the amendment of section 11, paragraph 1. 1, No. 3 and 4, the title before § 16 and section 39, paragraph 1. 1, 2nd paragraph and insertion of section 11 1, No. 5 and § 16 a.

15) The amendment of the Act refers to the amendment of section 104 (1). 1, 5th paragraph

16) The amendment of the Act concerns amendment of section 110 (1). 1 and 2, and insertion of section 110a.

17) By Royal Decree of 28 November 2016, the name of the Ministry of Business and Growth was changed to the Ministry of Business, cf. Executive Order No. 1777 of 23 December 2016.

18) The amendment to the amendment relates to a change of 104. First

REGULATION OF FISHERIES IN 2014-2020

Pursuant to section 10 1 and 2, sections 10d-10j, § 22, section 30, sections 34-36, section 37 Article 38 (1). 2, § 110, paragraph 1. 2, § 112a, § 112b, § 121, subsection Article 122 (2). 4, § 124, para. Paragraphs 1 and 130 2 of the Act on Fisheries and Fisheries (Fisheries Act), cf. Laws No 978 of 26 September 2008, as amended by Law No. 604 of 14 June 2011 and Law No. 388 of 2 May 2012, shall be determined by authorization :

CHAPTER 1 GENERAL REGULATION

Field of application

§ 1 The Order includes activities related to commercial fishing, as well as the commercial exploitation of fish in all waters by Danish fishermen and Danish registered fishing vessels. The order also includes landings, turnover, etc. in Denmark, originating from foreign registered fishing vessels.

PCS. 2. No matter where fishing has taken place, the master of a vessel registered in a Member State of the European Union shall, on landing in Danish port, comply with the provisions for the catch composition of percentages of target species and other species for the fishing gear and ranges used of mesh sizes in the individual regions or geographical areas set out in the European Union's Fisheries Conservation Regulations through technical measures for the protection of marine resources.

Change of conditions for fisheries

§ 2. The Nature Agency may, in accordance with Annex 6, issue notification of rules for fisheries, including setting and changing conditions for specified fisheries. The date of entry into force is stated in the notice.

§ 3. When the total allowable catches of a species or fishing effort, etc. allocated to Denmark under the regulations of the European Union or allocated for a specified period, vessel category, etc. have been upgraded or exhausted, or this is considered to be imminent , the NatureEconomy will set the fishing in question. Notice of this is issued in accordance with Appendix 6.

PCS. 2. The notice may stipulate special conditions for fishing after the date of dispatch of the notice, including that only vessels that have commenced a fishing trip may fish after the message has been read over Lyngby Radio.

PCS. 3. Prohibition of bringing fish from the fishery concerned shall enter into force two days after the date of entry into force of the Fisheries Invitation, unless otherwise stated in the notice.

Section 4. The Nature Agency may, after consultation of the Business Fisheries Committee, and in the light of the quantities available, the catch, supply and sales situation of the quantities landed in a given period and the consumption of fishing effort, determine amended rules for fisheries. Notice of the terms shall be issued in accordance with Annex 6.

PCS. 2. Among other things, changes may be made regarding the following:

1) The available quantities for certain periods.

2) Rations or number of days of sea, kW days, etc. in certain specified fisheries.

3) Transition to requirements for special authorization in certain fisheries.

4) Requirement for fishing for specified types or groups of vessels.

5) Requirements for fishing and landing to take place on special terms, including in specified geographical areas.

6) Use of the catch.

7) Setting of specified fisheries.

8) The requirement that landing for a period be limited as part of a fishing plan that will enable the landed quantities to be disposed of continuously.

9) Changed terms for already issued permits.

10) Terms for allocating fishing opportunities for the Fisheries Fund and the kW Fund for single vessels.

General provisions

Section 5. The National Environmental Protection Agency may, upon application, grant a derogation and make decisions regarding fishing opportunities, etc. for groups of vessels or individual vessels, taking account of particular circumstances.

PCS. 2. A decision pursuant to this Executive Order may be subject to compliance with conditions, including the extent of fishing activity, personal participation in fishing, limitation of the possibilities for transferring quota shares to other vessels and participation in pool fishing. If a condition that is set as a condition for allocation of quota shares, kW units or annual quantities is not observed, the Nature Agency may transfer the allocated quota shares to the Fisheries Fund or the kW Fund.

For additional analytical, business and investment opportunities information,
please contact Global Investment & Business Center, USA
at (703) 370-8082. Fax: (703) 370-8083. E-mail: ibpusa3@gmail.com
Global Business and Investment Info Databank - www.ibpus.com

Section 6. To the extent that the basis for calculating entitlement to landings from a vessel is deducted, landings attributable to illegal fishing ascertained by:

1) Finally judgment.

2) Adopted fines.

3) Adoption of confiscation orders.

4) Final decision on administrative revocation of fishing permit pursuant to section 37 2 and 3 of the Fisheries Act.

PCS. 2. The Nature Agency may subsequently deduct deductions from FKA and IOK granted to the extent that landings that form part of the basis of calculation after the allocation are found to be attributable to illegal fishing according to decisions, including fines and confiscation proceedings referred to in subsection First

PCS. 3. To the extent that deductions are made in quota shares, simultaneous deductions shall be made in the amounts declared.

PCS. 4. Deduction according to subsection 1-3 may be made, regardless of whether the vessel has changed owner, quota shares have been transferred or the vessel has been expelled as a registered fishing vessel after the illegal fishing has taken place.

PCS. 5. Deduced quota shares and annual volumes are included in the Fisheries Fund.

PCS. 6. To the extent that the calculation basis for granting rights attaches importance to action in the form of seasons using certain tools, deducted days are not legally used if this is determined by the provisions of paragraph 1. 1, No. 1-3.

PCS. 7. The Nature Agency may later deduct deductions from assigned rights to the extent that the days of seas that are included in the calculation basis after the allocation are found to be not legally used, cf. First

PCS. 8. To the extent that pursuant to subsection 7, deductions are made in kW units, at the same time, corresponding deductions are made in declared annual quantities of kW days.

PCS. 9. Deductions according to subsection 6-8 can be made, regardless of whether the vessel has changed ownership, the rights have been transferred or the vessel has been expelled as a registered fishing vessel after the illegal fishing has taken place.

PCS. 10. Deduced kW units and annual volumes are included in the kW Fund.

Section 7. A vessel's owner may dispose of the vessel's quota shares and kW units and the associated annual volumes according to the rules applicable to FKA, IOK and kW units.

PCS. 2. Quotas and kW shares and associated annual quantities may be used only by vessels registered in the Norwegian Commerce Register Register and owned by persons or companies entitled to pursue commercial fishing, cf. Section 39 of the Fisheries Act. Quotas and kW shares may only be transferred to persons or companies entitled to pursue commercial fishing, cf. section 16 of the Fisheries Act.

PCS. 3. If there is more than one owner of a vessel, the owner assigns and notifies the NaturErhvervstyrelsen a proxy who is authorized to give and receive binding messages in relation to the board on behalf of the whole owner.

PCS. 4. If changes occur in the owner's circle, it must be reported to the Swedish Agency for the Protection of the Environment if a new proxy has been appointed. Until the Nature Agency has received a notice from the owner about the replacement of the proxy, the person appointed as a proxy is still legitimized to provide and receive communications relative to the board.

§ 8. For the power of attorney in connection with pool fishing, the rules of the Order on Pool Fishing shall apply.

§ 9. The waters of the North Sea, English Channel, Skagerrak, Kattegat and the Baltic Sea and the Belts with ICES sub-areas are defined in Appendix 1.

Section 10. Regardless of the types of regulation used, all specified amounts of fish in this notice are in messages in accordance with Annex 6 and in licenses issued in accordance with the Order, expressed in live weight. However, for salmon, quantities are calculated in pieces (number of salmon).

PCS. 2. If the fish are landed with a different treatment than live weight, the conversion factors listed in Annex 4 shall be used for conversion to live weight. Landing of fish in a degree of treatment not listed in Annex 4 may only be carried out with the prior permission of the Danish Nature Agency.

PCS. 3. For salmon caught in the Baltic Sea and the Belts, the catch must be entered in the vessel's logbook, both in pieces (number of salmon) and in live weight. Licenses for fishing may also be required for the division and indication of catches in size categories.

§ 11. The right to dispose of FKA and IOK may be terminated with 8-year notice. Termination will be determined by notice and notified to the owners of the vessels for which it is listed in the Nature Agency that the vessel has disposed of quota shares.

PCS. 2. Disposals of allotted FKA and IOK, fishing activities and allocations of fishing rights in each year shall be in accordance with the rules currently in force issued in the period of the European Union and by Danish authorities.

PCS. 3. For the provisions and dispositions of kW units, the rules in paragraph 1 apply. 1 and 2 to the extent that the European Union's rules on effort regulation for the use of certain types of gear in the affected waters, cf. Section 156, continue to apply.

Publicly available information about FKA and IOK

§ 12. The National Energy Agency keeps the computerized register of transferable quota shares (FKA and IOK), cf. section 37, paragraph 1. 1, in the Fisheries Act. The register is publicly available, cf. section 112 a, subsection 1, in the Fisheries Act.

PCS. 2. Information in the Nature Agency's registers of holders of rights to kW units, indicating the associated kW shares and annual quantities, as well as the current consumption of annual quantities are publicly available.

PCS. 3. Information in the Nature Agency's registers of vessels' annual quantities of sea days in the Baltic Sea, as well as the current consumption for these annual quantities, are publicly available.

Section 13. At the same time as information about the transfer of quota shares, the vessel owner or contact person must report the selling price of the IOC units transferred, cf. Appendix 8. The selling price is included in the publicly available registers, cf. Section 12.

definitions

Section 14. This Executive Order means:

1) Species covered by multiannual plans: Cod in ICES divisions III, IV, VIa, VIIa and VIId, hake in ICES zones IIIa, IV, Vb, VIa, VII and VIIIa, b, d and e, Zone IV, sole in ICES zones IV and VIIe and salmon in ICES subareas 22-32.

2) Atlantic cod herring: Herring in ICES subareas I, II, V and XIV.

3) Calculation basis: Landings in specific parts of the reference period, attributed to a specific vessel and the amounts which it is otherwise decided to include in the calculation basis by the allocation of shares of each quota or catch effort.

4) Gross turnover: The value of landings for a vessel registered in the National Agency for Records.

5) Disposable capacity: Gross tonnage measured in BT and engine power measured in kW which can be attributed to a particular vessel deleted in the registers of the Danish Maritime Authority and in the Norwegian Maritime Administration's vessel register and which may be reused in whole or in part for the deployment of a registered fishing vessel or capacity-expanding modernization .

6) Ownership: The total shares in per capita of the shares allocated for distribution as FKA or IOK, which a person possesses through wholly or partly ownership of fishing vessels, is wholly or partly owned by companies that own fishing vessels, or through wholly or partly Ownership of companies that own companies that own fishing vessels.

7) Half a calendar month: The period from 1st to the 15th of a month or from the 16th to the end of the month.

8) EU waters: The areas covered by the EU Member States' fisheries territories.

9) Fisheries Committee: The Committee for Business Fishing, cf. Section 6 of the Fisheries Act.

10) Catching: A fishing trip duration is calculated from the time the vessel leaves port until the time of the vessel arriving at port.

11) Capture per. Unit of action: The amount of cod, expressed in live weight, caught per year per fishing effort expressed in kW days.

12) Vessel owner: A vessel's total ownership, as stated in the registers of the Danish Maritime Authority and the Vessel Register of the Danish Nature Agency.

13) Vessel categories: FKA vessel, MAF vessel or Other Vessel.

14) Vessel Quotas (FKA): Quotas shares that can be fished, carried and landed by a specific vessel and, as a whole, a vessel's entire ownership can transfer completely or partially to other vessels.

15) Length of vessel: Length of vessel throughout, and for vessels where the length of the vessel has not been calculated, the vessel's length of notice. The length or the length of the license must be in accordance with the registration in the National Agency of Commerce's vessel register.

16) Fisheries Fund: Reserve shares of quotas, permanently or in individual years, are excluded from the allocation, such as FKA or IOK.

17) Fishing, carrying and landing: Any fishing activity from fishing gear is exposed to the water until the fish is landed.

18) Fishing effort: A vessel's fishing, sailing and other fishing related activities under specified conditions.

19) FKA vessel: A vessel which, in 2006, was appointed by the Ministry of Food, Agriculture and Fisheries as a FKA vessel entitled to fish certain quotas with FKA or which has been transferred to FKA and where the Nature Authority has confirmed the transfer.

20) FKA-FE vessel: A vessel which, having regard to the fact that one or more first-time crew is the owner or co-owner of the vessel, has obtained the approval of the Authority for a period of status as a FKA vessel on special terms.

21) Management period: Period of one year in EU kW-day regulation. The period runs from 1 February to 31 January in the following calendar year.

22) Sea days: Number of days when a vessel using certain types of gear must be at sea in certain waters according to rules laid down by the European Union.

23) Individual quota exchanges: Transfer of the right to use annual quantities for vessels from other EU countries against the transmission of catches made available to certain Danish registered single vessels.

24) Individual Transferable Shares (IOC): Quota shares that can be fished, carried and landed by a specific vessel and, as a whole of the vessel's ownership, may transfer wholly or partly to one or more vessels.

25) Industrial fish: Fish landed for purposes other than human consumption.

26) Industrial fisheries: Fishing where a vessel fishes, brings or lands fish for purposes other than human consumption.

27) Calendar week: One week starting midnight night between Sunday and Monday.

28) Calendar Month: Period from 1st to Month Expiry.

29) Quota: The amount of a stock in a specified watershed, which is available for Danish fishing in a calendar year.

30) Quota shares: The shares in bulk, to which a vessel is assigned or has been transferred by that part of a given Danish quota, allocated for distribution as FKA or IOK. Quotas share the basis for the allocation of annual quantities of parts of the quotas in each year.

31) Coastal fishing vessel: A vessel that meets the requirements of this Executive Order for inclusion in the Coastal Fisheries Scheme, which is included in the Scheme.

32) KW Shares: The shares of the kW days to which a vessel is assigned or has been transferred from another vessel by the amount of kW days allocated for distribution in each gear category in the individual waters.

33) KW days: The number of days a vessel must be at sea multiplied by the power in kW, which is registered in the shipowner's vessel register of the Nature Authority.

34) The KW Fund: Reserves of kW days, permanently or in each year, are excluded from the allocation of annual quantities on the basis of kW shares.

35) Landings underlying the allocation of fishing rights: Quantities of fish of the different live weight ratios for salmon died in pieces, which have been reported to the Swedish National Agency for Nature and Fisheries as the land of the individual vessel and registered in the National Agency for Records.

36) MAF vessel: A vessel designated by the Ministry of Food, Agriculture and Fisheries in 2006 as a Small Active Vessel or having obtained approval as a MAF vessel later because it replaces a MAF vessel.

37) MAF extra vessel: A MAF vessel, which in 2012 through the transmission of annual volume from one or more FKA vessels, has access to additional catches.

38) MAF capacity: Disposable capacity attributable to MAF vessel.

39) Co-owner: Person who owns a share of a vessel or is a shareholder, partner or similar in a company that owns a vessel, cf. Section 16 of the Fisheries Act.

40) Engine power: The engine power specified by the Danish Maritime Authority in the vessel's permit or inspection book, and which has not subsequently been amended.

41) Transhipment: Wholly or partly delivery of the catch from a fishing vessel or its fishing gear to another vessel. Transhipment shall not take place when catching between two vessels engaged in pairing or if a catch is delivered directly from a fishing gear to another Danish vessel which may also legally participate in the fishery concerned.

42) Parfishing: Fishing carried out by two vessels which, in connection with this, uses and traps the same fishing gear.

43) Pool fishing: Fishing jointly carried out between self-employed or commercial fishing vessels by vessels to which they are owners or co-owners, so that a participant with his vessel can use the fishing rights associated with another vessel's vessel.

44) Ration fisheries: Fishing on a fixed common amount to which several vessels have access for a specified period on the basis of the individual vessel's classification or authorization.

45) Reference year: Fishing with a vessel in a previous year, which forms the basis for allocating fishing rights or fishing effort.

46) Regulated species: Species where a maximum allowable catch amount is determined for each vessel for a given period.

47) Registers of the Danish Maritime Authority: The Register of Special Ship Registers of the Ship Register and the Register of Shipowners' Register of the Ship.

48) Tonnage: Gross tonnage associated with a vessel registered as a fishing vessel or linked to available capacity.

49) Vestkvoten: Quotas of certain species in the Baltic Sea and Belts, ICES subdivisions 22-24.

50) East Quotas: Quotas of certain species in the Baltic Sea, ICES subdivisions 25-32 (EU waters).

51) Other Vessel: A vessel designated by the Ministry of Food, Agriculture and Fisheries in 2006 as an Other Vessel or a vessel being registered as a registered fishing vessel later without the FKA status or MAF status. In addition, a FKA or MAF vessel may, by decision of the Nature Agency, or regulations change the status to Other Vessel.

52) Annual amount: Quantity for a calendar year of the individual quotas that may be fished, carried and landed by a specific vessel.

53) Quantity of kW days: Quantity of kW days which may be used by a specific vessel during a management period, where rules apply for issuing annual quantities on the basis of kW shares that are applicable in accordance with EU rules thereof.

permissions

§ 15. Fishing may be subject to a license. Permits issued by the Nature Agency in accordance with Appendix 3. Information about which licenses issued to a vessel are publicly available.

PCS. 2. A permit for a vessel may include more detailed conditions for the pursuit of fishing, cf. Appendix 3.

PCS. 3. Irrespective of the type of regulation in which a fishing activity is carried out, fishing may be canceled, cf. section 3 1, increase or reduction in assigned catches or maximum permitted effort and change of conditions for the permit, include fishing according to already granted permits.

PCS. 4. By decision on the issuance and content of permits, including the number of permits in each fishery, the NatureEuropean Agency emphasizes the considerations mentioned in section 34 (1). 2 of the Fisheries Act, including the supply situation and the rational utilization of the quantities available at a given time. In cases where selection must be made among applicants, the NaturErhvervstyrelsen can prioritize where account can be taken of the dependence of the applicants on the fishery concerned and the possibility of disposing of the catch for human

For additional analytical, business and investment opportunities information,
please contact Global Investment & Business Center, USA
at (703) 370-8082. Fax: (703) 370-8083. E-mail: ibpusa3@gmail.com
Global Business and Investment Info Databank - www.ibpus.com

consumption. In addition, emphasis can be placed on advice from organizations represented in the Business Fisheries Committee.

Section 16. The National Economic Authority may, cf. section 37 (1). 2 of the Fisheries Act, revoke a license if the holder has committed a gross or repeated breach of the terms laid down in the license.

PCS. 2. It shall be included in the terms of an authorization that the permit may be withdrawn when the terms of another permit for the same vessel are violated in a way that interferes with the stock of the species to which the permit relates.

Section 17. Authorization shall be issued upon application by the vessel owner in accordance with Appendix 2 to eligible vessels. However, at the beginning of a calendar year, no fishing license shall be allowed to fish, carry and land annual volumes on the basis of the FKA shares and IOC shares that are affiliated to a vessel and which can be allocated at the time and kW-day permit valid from 1 February for vessels that have associated kW shares.

Section 18. Permissions must always be kept on board, cf. 2, section 19 2 and 49 2nd

PCS. 2. The Nature Authority may, by notice issued in accordance with Annex 6, stipulate that fishing subject to a permit until a specified date may be exercised without the license being issued and on board the vessel. Any quantity caught and landed with the vessel after 1 January in a given year will depart from the quantities that can be caught and landed with the vessel during the license period under the permit issued later.

Section 19. Regardless of the regulatory form of fishing, it is a condition for fishing, bringing and landing in the following fisheries that the owner of the vessel has special permission to do so with the vessel:

1) Cod in the Baltic Sea and the Belts.

2) Herring in the Baltic Sea and Belts.

3) Splashing in the Baltic Sea and the Belts.

4) Salmon in the Baltic Sea and the Belts.

5) Industrial fishing in all waters.

6) Sprinkling in the Limfjord.

PCS. 2. However, during the period from 1 January to 18 January in a given year, fishing in the Baltic Sea and industrial fisheries may be exercised even if no permit has been granted under paragraph 1. 1 if the vessel was authorized for the fishery concerned on 10 December of the previous year or the vessel owner has applied for the authorization to be granted for that year.

Section 20. Permissions in section 19, subsection 1, apply throughout the calendar year unless they are involved or the vessel owner delivers them. Permits in section 19 1, No. 1-4, shall be temporarily derecognised during the year before commencing fishing in other waters with the vessel. If a license has been unsubscribed, new registration must be made before fishing with the Baltic vessel.

PCS. 2. Registration and unsubscribe after subsection 1 must be done no later than 16.00 the day before, fishing in or outside the Baltic Sea can begin from midnight. Registration and cancellation is given in accordance with the rules in Appendix 2.

reports

§ 21. All vessels irrespective of the length of the logbook shall indicate arrival at port when the vessel carries more than 300 kg on board of a species covered by a multi-annual plan, but for salmon the requirement applies when the vessel carries 10 pieces. or more. The same applies to vessels carrying industrial fish, herring, mackerel or horse mackerel. For eels, message must be entered when landing 100 kg or more per calendar days.

PCS. 2. In case of a notification of arrival at port or landing, this must be in accordance with Appendix 5a or the terms of the permit. In fisheries where there are no rules of unloading obligation in connection with arrival at the port, any arrival must be reported, regardless of whether it is intended to be unloaded or not. The message must indicate the time of release, if this differs from the time of arrival.

PCS. 3. The rules in subsection 2 applies to both Danish and foreign registered fishing vessels arriving at Danish port. Unless, in accordance with European Union legal acts, longer deadlines for notification of arrival than specified in the Annexes are laid down, the deadlines set out in Annex 5a shall be complied with by Danish registered fishing vessels.

PCS. 4. The amount of fish expressed in live weight per Species reported by the message must correspond to the quantities registered in the logbook upon arrival at the port.

PCS. 5. Companies shall not receive industrial duty from Danish and foreign registered vessels if no notification has been made before arrival and unloading, cf. Appendix 5a.

PCS. 6. The master is exempted from the obligation to report to the National Agency for Immigration, whose landing and unloading takes place directly to a company which makes the prior notification of landing and unloading on behalf of the master in accordance with Annex 5a.

PCS. 7. In all cases where there is a duty of arrival and unloading prior to arrival, the logbook shall affix the receipt number shown in Annex 5a. Arrival and unloading must not take place before the notified date.

Section 22. The Nature Agency may, in accordance with Annex 6 or under conditions in permits for specified fisheries, stipulate that prior to entry into the waters where fishing takes place and prior to the departure from this waters, notification must be made in accordance with Annex 5b.

PCS. 2. On any departure from a watershed to another watershed, the electronic logbook shall be updated and sent to the NaturErhvervsstyrelsen before leaving the watershed when the vessel leaves a waters where it has fished, cf. Third

PCS. 3. On departure from areas a, b or c of the Baltic Sea, the change of waters shall be as indicated in the vessel's permit for fishing for cod in the Baltic Sea.

transhipment

Section 23. Transhipment may only take place after prior permission from the NaturErhvervstyrelsen.

PCS. 2. The transhipment application shall contain the following information:

1) Position and time of transhipment or delivery of the fish.

2) Species and quantity covered.

3) Vessel name.

4) Harbor identification number.

5) Radio call signal and nationality of the dispatching and receiving vessel.

6) Reply Address (E-mail or Phone Number).

PCS. 3. In addition to those referred to in subsection 2, the NaturErhvervstyrelsen may require further information when necessary to assess the actual circumstances surrounding the transhipment and to lay down conditions for permission to do so.

PCS. 4. If transhipment takes place following direct injunctions from the Norwegian Coast Guard, the information in paragraph 2 sent per. fax or e-mail at fmc@naturerhverv.dk to the NaturErhvervstyrelsen before transhipment is made.

CHAPTER 2 GENERAL LIMITATIONS

Fishing and landing restrictions

Section 24. If a vessel owner is the owner or co-owner of several vessels entitled to participate in the fishing of regulated species, logs shall be kept for all of these vessels irrespective of the length of the vessels unless the vessels are used for bottom fishing and in the NatureEconomy Board are registered in same bottom nets company. The obligation to keep a logbook applies even if the vessels to which he or she owns or is co-owner is classified in different vessel categories.

Section 25. The Nature Agency may order a vessel which is the basis for a permit or used for fishing to be displayed at a specified landing point at a specified time before the vessel is again used to fish, bring and land fish.

§ 26. In all cases when a vessel is assigned a yearly quantity, the total landed quantity shall not exceed the amount allocated after the last fishing trip. This applies to both the individual vessel and the total landings in the pair and pool fishing in which the vessel participates. This applies, despite the fact that according to the rules for logbooking a tolerance for the estimation of the quantities on board is allowed.

PCS. 2ndIf, however, last fishing on a fishing trip is fished more than the amount remaining under the permit, the master must immediately report to the NaturErhvervstyrelsen, immediately after the catch. Notification must be given by telephone at 7218 5609 or by e-mail at fmc@naturerhverv.dk. The notification shall contain information on the vessel's port of call letters and numbers, the species and quantity of fish on board, the amount taken over the catch quoted in the permit and the waters where the fishing has taken place. Upon notification, the master receives a registration number which must be entered immediately in the logbook. In addition, the master or his / her proxy must submit documentation to the NaturErhvervstyrelsen for as soon as possible and no later than 5 days after landing.

paired

§ 27. In the case of pairing, both vessels are responsible for ensuring that the entire fishing activity is legal, ie that fishing, transport and landing are in accordance with the fisheries legislation.

§ 28. In the case of pairing, the total amount of fish caught, carried and landed shall not exceed the sum of what is allowed to fish, bring and land with both the vessels participating in the parfishing.

PCS. 2. Par fishing may only be carried out by vessels classified in the same vessel category. NaturErhverhyrelsen has the opportunity to grant exemption to vessels wishing to practice par fishing with a vessel registered in another EU country. Vessels forming part of a pool may not engage in fishing by vessels outside the pool of quotas included in the pool. However, the Nature Authority may grant permission for a vessel to fish parcels with a vessel outside the pool fishing on the quotas provided for in section 89 (1). Third

Prohibition against discarding fish

§ 29. All species listed in Annex 7 which can be landed in accordance with the applicable rules for fisheries, including minimum size, composition of catches and allowable catches, must be landed and must not be revoked.

Vessel and gear restrictions and rules for fishing and landing of cod mm

§ 30. It is prohibited to use a commercial fishing vessel in ICES sub-area 22 of the Baltic Sea and the Belts if the vessel's engine power exceeds 221 kW / 300 HP. It is also forbidden that the vessel has a length of 17 meters or more and at the same time the length expressed in meters times the width expressed in meters must not exceed 100.

PCS. 2. Vessels for which in 2007 on the basis of section 29 2 of Executive Order No. 1535 of 18 December 2006 was authorized for use in Sub-area 22, even if the vessel is greater than the limits specified in paragraph. 1, 2nd paragraph

PCS. 3. Permission, cf. 2, is issued solely to the vessels identified by the EU identification number meeting the conditions. No other vessels may be authorized, eg. due to vessel replacement.

§ 31. Fishing permits for herring and sprat in the Baltic Sea and the Belts may be prohibited from using vessels whose power exceeds 588 kW / 800 HP when fishing takes place within 12 nautical miles of the German baseline.

§ 32. In ICES sub-area 22 of the Baltic Sea and the Belts, par fishing is prohibited.

PCS. 2. Vessels fished for herring and whiting or industrial fish shall be exempted from the provisions of paragraph 1. 1 mentioned prohibition.

PCS. 3. In ICES sub-area 22 of the Baltic Sea and the Belts, it is prohibited to fish with trawls and seines from Friday, 18:00 to sunday at 18.00.

§ 33. In ICES sub-area 23 of the Baltic Sea and the Belts it is prohibited to fish with Danish seine. However, except for angling in the area, more than 3 miles of land is bounded and bounded to the north by the line from Gilbjerg Head to the Hill Lighthouse and to the south of the line from Ellekilde Garden to Lerberget.

§ 34. Only vessels whose owners have a license issued pursuant to section 15 may fish, carry and land fish when the vessel on board has automatic classification equipment for sorting fish and can freeze fish on board.

§ 35. It is not permitted to fish with notes in the Kattegat, the Baltic Sea and the Belts.

PCS. 2. In the case of fishing with trawls and / or other trawling gear in the Kattegat, which shall be carried out with mesh sizes of 90 mm or more, the gear of vessels of 10 meters or more in length shall be fitted with a selective catch of one of the three types , described in Appendix 14.

PCS. 3. From 1 October to 31 December, instead of the catches described in paragraph 1, 2, cf. Annex 14, the sorting panel described in Annex 13, as well as in Annex 15, paragraph 3, is the period for vessels fishing for seines, from 1 August to 31 October.

PCS. 4. Instead of the catches described in Annex 14, the selective gear described in Order No. 391 of 16 April 2010 prohibiting certain types of fishing in defined areas in the Kattegat and northern parts of Øresund, Annex 4.

PCS. 5. For vessels carrying a paper logbook or e-logbook, the logbook shall indicate which of the tools listed in Annex 14 are used. The tools are referred to as 1, 2 or 3 respectively in the tool size section regarding paper logbook and in the panel panel as regards the e-logbook.

Section 36. When fishing in Skagerrak with trawls, seagulls and / or other towed gear, the gear shall be designed in accordance with the provisions of paragraph. 2-6.

PCS. 2. For targeted fishing of deepwater rays shall

1) Diagonal mask with minimum mesh size of 35 mm,

2) a rectangular sorting grid with a maximum distance between the bars of 19 mm is used, where the grate bars are parallel to the longitudinal axis of the grate, and

3) The trawl's upper panel contains a fish spill in front of the upper edge of the screening grid.

PCS. 3. Vessels fishing in accordance with paragraph 2 and having appropriate quotas of the species that the gear can be expected to capture, a fish / tunnel can be installed in a tunnel / collection bag, as described in Appendix 15, in order to withstand larger fish.

PCS. 4. For targeted fishing of Norway lobster, a sorting screen and gear shall be used, as described in Annex 15, No. 2.

PCS. 5. For mixed demersal fishing, use a diagonal mask of at least 120 mm on the catch and extension piece, but at least 8 meters of the fishing gear.

For additional analytical, business and investment opportunities information, please contact Global Investment & Business Center, USA at (703) 370-8082. Fax: (703) 370-8083. E-mail: ibpusa3@gmail.com Global Business and Investment Info Databank - www.ibpus.com

PCS. 6. Notwithstanding paragraph 5, trawls or other towing gear with a mesh size of 90 mm may be fished if one of the panels described in Annex 15 is used.

PCS. 7. For vessels carrying a paper logbook or e-logbook, the logbook shall indicate which of the tools referred to in Annex 15, point 3 are used. The tools are named 7, 8 and 9, respectively, in the tool size heading regarding paper logbook and in the panel panel as regards e-logbook.

§ 37. Landings of more than 2,000 kg of cod and / or 2,000 kg of hake (live weight) from the North Sea, Skagerrak and Kattegat may only be made in the ports listed in Appendix 10. The same applies to landings exceeding 10,000 kg of herring, mackerel and horse mackerel or a combination thereof caught in ICES zones I, II, IIIa, IV, Vb, VI and VII, in the case of mackerel, are caught in ICES zones IIa, IIIa, IV, Vb, VI , VII, VIII, IX, X, XII and XIV and for horse mackerel are caught in ICES zones IIa, IV, Vb, VI, VII, VIII, IX, X, XII and XIV.

CHAPTER 3 VESSEL CATEGORIES AND DIFFERENT TYPES OF REGULATION VESSEL CATEGORIES

§ 38. In relation to the regulation, vessels registered in the Norwegian Maritime Authority's vessel register are classified in the following vessel categories:

1) FKA vessels.

2) MAF vessels.

3) Other Vessels.

PCS. 2. A vessel registered in the Norwegian Maritime Authority's vessel register shall be classified as Other Vessel. This applies regardless of whether the vessel as identified by the EU identification number has previously been registered in the National Agency's vessel register with the status of FKA or MAF vessel.

PCS. 3. An Other Vessel Can Get Status As

1) FKA vessel if FKA shares are transferred to the vessel, cf. section 39 (1). 2

2) MAF vessel if it replaces another MAF vessel and is introduced with MAF capacity with permission from the Nature Authority pursuant to sections 41 and 42, or

3) FKA-FE vessel, cf. section 70.

FKA vessels

Section 39. An FKA vessel retains its status as a FKA vessel, regardless of ownership, and regardless of whether all FKA shares are transferred to other vessels until the vessel is deleted in the Nature Registration Authority's vessel register.

PCS. 2. A vessel can only obtain the status of FKA vessel if FKA shares are transferred to the vessel and the Nature Authority confirms the transfer. A vessel does not become an FKA vessel, even if it is introduced with available capacity from an FKA vessel, unless FKA shares are transferred to the vessel.

MAF vessels

Section 40. An MAF shall change the status of Other Vessel if the vessel is acquired by persons or companies who in 2006 or later have been owners or co-owners of vessels classified as FKA vessels. However, the Nature Authority may allow a first-time owner who has been the owner or co-owner of an FKA-FE vessel to acquire a MAF vessel without this changing status to Other Vessel

PCS. 2. If modernization or other modification of a MAF vessel is made without the requirements of section 43 being fulfilled, the vessel changes status to Other Vessel.

Section 41. Upon application, the NatureEconomy Authority may allow a MAF vessel to be replaced, cf. section 42, or modernized, cf. Section 43. Only permission to increase gross tonnage and engine power may be granted if the entire increase originates from expired MAF vessels .

PCS. 2. Only vessel replacement or modernization or other modification may be granted in accordance with the provisions of subsections 1, if the owner of the MAF does not include a person or company which in 2006 or later has been the owner or co-owner of a vessel designated as an FKA vessel.

§ 42. In order for a vessel to obtain MAF status in connection with vessel replacement, the following conditions must be fulfilled:

1) An MAF vessel shall be deleted from which the gross tonnage and engine power of the new MAF shall originate.

2) The MAF vessel must, as a result of the replacement, have a maximum length which places the vessel in the same rational length category as the vessel it replaces.

PCS. 2. In order for a vessel to be classified as a MAF vessel on the basis of purchased available MAF capacity, the vessel owner shall acquire all available capacity from the expired MAF vessel.

Section 43. In order for a MAF vessel to continue to maintain its MAF status in connection with modernization or other change for which permission is required under the current regulations of vessels used for commercial fishing in saline, The following conditions are met:

1) The gross tonnage and engine power used in connection with the permit for modernization or other modification shall be derived from MAF vessels.

2) The MAF vessel must, as a result of the modernization or alteration, have a maximum of length that places the vessel in the same rational length category as it had before the modernization.

Overview of quotas by regulation

Section 44. The following quotas are regulated either with FKA or Ration fisheries:

1) Cod in the North Sea.

2) Cod in the Kattegat.

For additional analytical, business and investment opportunities information,
please contact Global Investment & Business Center, USA
at (703) 370-8082. Fax: (703) 370-8083. E-mail: ibpusa3@gmail.com
Global Business and Investment Info Databank - www.ibpus.com

3) Cod in the Skagerrak

4) Cod in the Baltic Sea and Belts, ICES subdivisions 22-24.

5) Cod in the Baltic Sea, ICES subdivisions 25-32 (EU waters).

6) Tongues in the Skagerrak, Kattegat and the Baltic Sea and the Belts.

7) Heavy in the North Sea (EU waters).

8) Plaice in the North Sea.

9) Plaice in the Kattegat.

10) Plaice in the Skagerrak.

11) Sprouts in the Baltic Sea and the Belts.

12) Norway lobster in the Skagerrak, Kattegat and the Baltic Sea and the Belts.

13) Norway lobster in the North Sea (EU waters).

14) Norway lobster in Norway (Norwegian zone).

15) Mørksej in the North Sea, Skagerrak, Kattegat and the Baltic Sea and the Belts.

16) Kuller in Skagerrak, Kattegat and the Baltic Sea and Belts.

17) Hills in the North Sea.

18) Deepwater rains in Skagerrak and Kattegat.

19) Deepwater rains in the North Sea (EU waters).

20) Deepwater rains in the North Sea (Norwegian zone).

21) Mule in the North Sea (EU waters).

22) Atlantic marshes and marshes in the North Sea (EU waters).

23) Havtaske in the North Sea (Norwegian zone).

24) Salmon in the Baltic Sea and Belts (EU waters).

PCS. 2. The following quotas are regulated by IOC or ration fisheries:

1) Herring in the North Sea.

2) Herring in the Skagerrak and Kattegat.

3) Herring in the Baltic Sea and Belts (EU waters).

4) Sprat in Skagerrak and Kattegat.

5) Splashing in the North Sea (EU waters).

6) Splashing in the Baltic Sea and Belts (EU waters).

7) Mackerel in all waters.

8) Tobias in the North Sea (EU waters and Norwegian zone) and Skagerrak and Kattegat (EU waters).

9) Blue whiting in EU waters and international waters.

10) Sperling in the North Sea (EU waters) as well as the Skagerrak and Kattegat.

PCS. 3. The following quotas are regulated by IOC:

1) Atlantic cod herring (north of 62o N)

2) Horse mackerel in ICES zones IIa, IVa, Vb, VI, VIIa-c and ek, VIIIa, b, d and e, XII and XIV.

3) Blue whiting in Faroese zone.

4) Sea trout in EU and international waters of ICES divisions VI, VII and VIII.

PCS. 4. Other fisheries available to Danish vessels, including fisheries in third-country fishing zones and in international waters, shall be regulated by rationing fishery.

CHAPTER 4 GENERAL RULES FOR ALLOCATION ON THE BASIS OF QUOTA SHARES (FKA AND IOK) AND TRANSMISSION OF ANNUAL QUANTITIES

Breakdown of quotas

§ 45. For the quotas covered by FKA, cf. section 44, subsection 1, as well as for quotas for herring and sprat in the Baltic Sea and sprat in Skagerrak and Kattegat and sprat in the North Sea, are earmarked prior to the allocation of annual volumes on the basis of vessel shares per. January 1 in a given year:

1) Shares to the Fisheries Fund.

2) Proportion of the quotas where the quota has not been upgraded so far, cf. section 59.

3) Shares for rationing for MAF vessels, cf. 2nd

4) Extra quantity of cod and sole for coastal fishing vessels, cf. section 61.

5) Shares for landing inevitable by-catches for vessels not having FKA on these species, cf. section 47 2nd

6) Shares of sprat in the North Sea.

7) Shares of cod and herring in the Baltic Sea for fishing under ration conditions for vessels fishing exclusively for bottom nets throughout the year. 1.3% of the initial quota is allocated for the total quota of cod in the Baltic Sea (East and West Quota) and 2.5% of the total quotas of herring in the Baltic Sea and the Belts (East and West Quota).

PCS. 2. For MAF vessels, cf. 1, point 3, the shares of the quotas, which, in the classification of vessels in 2006, are calculated as the total shares of the MAF vessels of the quotas referred to in section 44 (1). First

Section 46. Before allocating annual quantities, Danish quotas shall be reduced by the quantities that may be expected to be deducted from the Danish quota in the year in question as a result of any overfishing of a quota in the previous year.

PCS. 2. Reduction in individual annual quantities allocated on the basis of IOC may occur in connection with a vessel's overrun of its annual volume, cf. section 49 (1). 5th

Section 47. With the allocation of quota shares in volume, it is rounded to 2 decimal places.

PCS. 2. The share of the shares resulting from the rounding down under subsection 1, not assigned to specific vessels shall be made available for fishing for inevitable by-catches for vessels not entitled to fish on these species in view of the catch and quota situation. Rules on this can be issued in accordance with Appendix 6, in light of the catch and quota situation.

Section 48. If the Danish quotas are increased or reduced during the year, the changes are distributed in proportion to the different forms of regulation. However, this does not apply if changes occur as a result of individual quota exchanges with other countries.

Annual fishing on the basis of quota shares

Section 49. Vessels allocated to quota shares may fish, carry and land the annual amount as stated in the permit issued by the Swedish Nature Agency. The Nature Authority authorizes the vessel to fish, carry and land the annual quantities of the quotas relative to the quota shares available to the vessel at the time of the notification. If, from the start of the year on the basis of EU rules, the Member States have allocated available quantities of individual quotas that do not cover the whole year, quantities are issued in proportion to the quantities available to Denmark at any time.

PCS. 2. In the period from 1 January to 18 January in a given year, vessels holding quota shares may, by way of derogation from paragraph 1, 1, carry out fishing on the quotas in question, even though the vessel owner has not yet received authorization with annual quantities from the NaturErhvervstyrelsen. Fishing must take place within the quantities of quotas for which quota shares allow. If special circumstances apply, it may be notified in accordance with Annex 6 that fishing is continued on the basis of the authorization for the previous year, also after 18 January of the following year.

PCS. 3. In the allocation of annual quantities, the NaturErhvervstyrelsen will be able to reserve shares of the quotas as a reserve, among other things. taking account of possible adjustments to the quotas. The reserved shares are distributed as a supplement to the annual quantities, if the quotas are not reduced.

PCS. 4. To the extent that, under EU legislation, the possibility of continuing unfinished quantities of individual quotas from the year in question to the following year may be issued by notice issued in accordance with Annex 6, which allows Unfinished quantities, distributed on the basis of quota shares held by a vessel at the end of the year in question, shall be continued so that the quantity can be fished by the same vessel in the following year.

PCS. 5. To the extent that, under EU legislation, the possibility of fishing for parts of the annual quantities for the following year already in the year concerned may be issued by notice issued in accordance with Annex 6, which allows vessels after prior approval in the Nature Agency, their annual amount will be overwritten in the year in question. This amount is set off against the vessel's quantity for the following year, regardless of whether the vessel has changed its owner.

§ 50. If the Danish quota is reduced following the issuance of a license to fish annual quantities or if a fishery is canceled before the allocated annual quantities have been fished, the Nature Agency may issue adjusted permits where the annual quantities are reduced to such an extent that overfishing of the Danish quota is counteracted as much as possible. Unfinished quantities are involved in proportion to the quota shares available to each vessel or pool at the time when the quota is reduced. Vessels which do not have the opportunity to land a quantity of the final quota corresponding to the vessel's quota share can be allocated a yearly amount in the following year.

PCS. 2. Following the possible increase in the Danish quota, new licenses may also be issued for fishing, bringing and landing volumes.

PCS. 3. A temporary ban may be introduced in the fisheries for the purpose of issuing new annual permits, cf. 1 and 2. Prohibition of fishing for the quota concerned shall be communicated in accordance with Annex 6.

Transfer of annual quantities to other vessels

Section 51. For the annual quantities distributed on the basis of FKA, a vessel's total owner of the vessel may transfer the right to fish up to 25% of the value of the vessel's total annual quantity of these quotas to other vessels, cf. 2. For the quotas covered by section 44 1, there may only be transfers of annual quantities to vessels classified as FKA vessels or to MAF vessels in accordance with section 134.

PCS. 2. The estimate of the amount of the maximum amount of transfer, cf. (1) shall be made in proportion to the annual quantity available to the issuing vessel by the quotas concerned at the time of the transfer. The value of the transferred volumes is calculated in accordance with section 83 (1). 3. The annual quantities of IOC for herring and sprat in the Baltic Sea, sprat in Skagerrak and Kattegat, and sprat in the North Sea, available to a vessel, may be included in the calculation.

PCS. 3. Notwithstanding paragraph 1, the Nature Agency may authorize a vessel to transfer in excess of the amount mentioned in paragraph 1 in case of accident or illness. 1 in the year in question.

PCS. 4. For a vessel with a coastal fisherman's status, the additional amount of water allocated to the vessel, cf. section 65, may only be transferred to a vessel with a coastal fisherman status.

Section 52. For the annual quantities distributed on the basis of IOC, a vessel's total owner of the vessel may transfer the right to fish up to 25% of the vessel's total annual quantities on these quotas to other vessels.

PCS. 2. The amount of the maximum annual quantities may be calculated in proportion to the annual quantity available to the dispatching vessel at the time of transfer.

PCS. 3. Notwithstanding paragraph 1, the Nature Agency may authorize a vessel to transfer in excess of 25% a quantity corresponding to a quantity greater than 25% and to transfer the remaining part of the vessel's annual amount of herring allocated from the generation shift pool of the year in question.

PCS. 4. Notwithstanding paragraph 1, when a vessel's replacement license has been applied for, a vessel's total ownership may transfer the right to fish the vessel's total annual quantities to another vessel during the period from the vessel being deleted by the Norwegian Maritime Authority's vessel register until replaced by another vessel, but not exceeding 18 months.

CHAPTER 5 PURPOSE AND SHARE OF THE FISHERIES FUND AND RATIONING FOR FKA SPECIES FOR FKA VESSELS

Quotas shares sold for other purposes prior to the allocation of annual quantities of FKA and IOK

Section 53. The Fisheries Fund may take the following purposes:

1) Implementation of quota swap with other countries.

2) Development of fisheries.

3) Promotion of first-time and younger fishermen's participation in fisheries, cf. Chapter 7.

4) Coverage of inevitable by-catches to the extent that rules are laid down.

5) Coverage of possible overfishing.

6) Other purposes for which rules are laid down, including increased fishing opportunities for smaller island communities, cf. section 60.

PCS. 2. Rules for allocating fishing opportunities pursuant to subsections 1 shall be determined after consultation of the Business Fisheries Committee, insofar as the rules are not laid down in the Executive Order. The rules are published in accordance with Appendix 6.

PCS. 3. Of the quota shares allocated to the Fisheries Fund, annual volumes are issued in relation to increases in quota shares allocated in previous years to vessels on the basis of the Fisheries Fund, which continue to apply, cf. Section 55.

Section 54. Prior to the allocation of quota shares, the following shares and amounts of Danish quotas are allocated to the Fisheries Fund:

1) 45 ‰ cod in the North Sea.

2) 55 ‰ of cod in the Kattegat.

3) 55 ‰ of cod in the Skagerrak.

4) 30 ‰ of cod in the Baltic Sea and Belts, ICES subdivisions 22-24.

5) 353 ‰ of cod in the Baltic Sea, ICES subdivisions 25-32 (EU waters).

6) 80 ‰ of tongue in Skagerrak, Kattegat and the Baltic Sea and Belts.

7) 35 ‰ of tongue in the North Sea (EU waters).

8) 40 ‰ of plaice in the North Sea.

9) 85 ‰ of plaice in Kattegat.

10) 65 ‰ of plaice in Skagerrak.

11) 55 ‰ of plaice in the Baltic Sea and the Belts.

12) 100 ‰ of Norway lobster in Skagerrak, Kattegat and the Baltic Sea and the Belts + 50 tons.

13) 60 ‰ of Norway lobster in the North Sea (EU waters).

14) 90 ‰ of Norway lobster in the North Sea (Norwegian zone).

15) 70 ‰) of dark ice in the North Sea, Skagerrak, Kattegat and the Baltic Sea and the Belts.

16) 80 ‰) of hills in the Skagerrak, Kattegat and the Baltic Sea and the Belts.

17) 460 ‰) of hills in the North Sea.

18) 70 ‰) of deep-water prawns in the Skagerrak and Kattegat.

19) 50 ‰) of deep sea rains in the North Sea (EU waters).

20) 50 ‰) of deep sea rains in the North Sea (Norwegian zone).

21) 55 ‰) of hake in the North Sea (EU waters).

22) 40 ‰) of turbot and bristle in the North Sea + 100 tons.

23) 25 ‰) of sea bag in the North Sea (Norwegian zone).

24) 120 ‰) of sprat in the North Sea (EU waters).

25) 70 ‰) of sprat in Skagerrak and Kattegat.

26) 70 ‰) of sprat in the Baltic Sea and the Belts.

27) 70 ‰) of herring in the Baltic Sea and the Belts.

28) 100 ‰) of salmon in the Baltic Sea and the Belts.

PCS. 2. Unallocated annual volumes, which are based on the quota shares in the Fisheries Fund, may during the quota year be allocated proportionately to vessels with quota shares or for the other purposes mentioned in section 53.

Section 55. From the total shares allocated to the Fisheries Fund, which is set aside in Section 54, from the beginning of the year, the following prominent shares will be used in connection with the issuance of annual quantities to the vessels that have increased quota shares in previous years on the basis of the Fisheries Fund, cf. Section 53 , PCS. 3. These shares represent:

1) 21.3 ‰ cod in the North Sea

2) 32.2 ‰ of cod in the Kattegat.

3) 30.6 ‰ of cod in the Skagerrak.

4) 23.1 ‰ of cod in the Baltic Sea and Belts, ICES subdivisions 25-32 (EU waters).

5) 58.7 ‰ of tongue in the Skagerrak, Kattegat and the Baltic Sea and the Belts.

6) 10.8 ‰ of tongue in the North Sea (EU waters).

7) 10.8 ‰ of plaice in the North Sea.

8) 32.3 ‰ of plaice in Kattegat.

9) 12.7 ‰ of plaice in the Skagerrak.

10) 45.4 ‰ of Norway lobster in Skagerrak, Kattegat and the Baltic Sea and the Belts.

11) 8.1 µm of Norway lobster in the North Sea (EU waters).

12) 37.8 ‰ of Norway lobster in Norway (Norwegian zone).

13) 47.0 ‰ of dark ice in the North Sea, Skagerrak, Kattegat and the Baltic Sea and the Belts.

14) 26.2 ‰ of hills in the Skagerrak, Kattegat and the Baltic Sea and the Belts.

15) 8.2 ‰ of hills in the North Sea.

16) 4.4 ‰ of hake in the North Sea (EU waters).

17) 18.9 ‰ of turbot and bristle in the North Sea.

18) 4.9 ‰ of sea bag in the North Sea (Norwegian zone).

19) 50.0 ‰ of sprat in the North Sea (EU waters).

Section 56. In addition to the shares allocated pursuant to section 54, inter alia, Considering the uncertainty about the final Danish quotas, shares of each quota are sold as a reserve for the distribution of annual volumes per. January 1 in a given year.

PCS. 2. Amendments to the shares of the quotas provided for in section 54 may be notified in accordance with Annex 6.

PCS. 3. At least once a quarter, after consultation of the Business Fisheries Committee, a decision is taken on whether to release quantities from the Fisheries Fund.

PCS. 4. Years that the vessel owners notify the NatureEconomy that they do not wish to fish that year are included in the Fisheries Fund.

Section 57. The quantities reserved for the reserve of herring and mackerel and other quotas covered by the IOC may be used for disposal within the purposes mentioned in section 53.

§ 58. Of the promulgated promille for the Fisheries Fund of Cod in the Eastern Baltic Sea of 353 ‰, cf. section 54 1, No. 5, 303 ‰, for flexibility and exchange years and 50 ‰ for other purposes in the Fisheries Fund, cf. section 53 First

Shares of quotas that have not been fished up or otherwise reserved.

§ 59. Of the following allowances covered by section 44 1, which has not been upgraded so far, in addition to reserve shares for the Fisheries Fund, etc., the following percentages of Danish quotas are excluded from allocations of annual volumes to vessels with quota shares. The shares are used as specified in subsection 2:

1) 200 ‰ of plaice in the Baltic Sea.

2) 100 ‰ of plaice in Kattegat.

3) 100 ‰ of plaice in Skagerrak.

4) 500 ‰ of hills in Skagerrak.

5) 750 ‰ of deep sea rains in the North Sea (EU waters).

6) 300 ‰ of salmon in the Baltic Sea.

7) 50 ‰ of tongue in the North Sea (EU waters).

8) 100 ‰ of hake in the North Sea (EU waters).

9) 100 ‰ of turbot and bristle in the North Sea.

PCS. 2. The shares of the individual quotas marketed pursuant to paragraph 1. 1, may be made available for ration fishing or included in the Fisheries Fund. The conditions for ration fishing shall be determined by notification in accordance with Annex 6, cf. Chapter 16, including which categories of vessels may participate in the fisheries.

Other purposes

For additional analytical, business and investment opportunities information,
please contact Global Investment & Business Center, USA
at (703) 370-8082. Fax: (703) 370-8083. E-mail: ibpusa3@gmail.com
Global Business and Investment Info Databank - www.ibpus.com

Section 60. The Fisheries Fund may, to a limited extent, provide for the possibility for vessel owners authorized to pursue fishing activities under section 19 of the Fisheries Act to participate in rationing fishery.

PCS. 2. The Nature Agency may allocate additional catches of cod and brisling to vessels with a base at Agersø, Fejø, Sejerø, Omø and Årø, which have been in operation since 1 January 2005. However, it is permissible to carry out a vessel replacement without losing the opportunity for the allocation of additional catches. Vessels must comply with the conditions set out in subsection 2-7. Additional catches can be allocated within a total of 60 tonnes of cod and 100 tonnes of sprat.

PCS. 3. Vessels, cf. 1, according to the National Agency's catch recordings in each of the years from 2005 onward, the country has a catch corresponding to at least 80% of the value of the vessel's total consumption landings on the island where the vessel is based. Vessels must have a quota share of either cod in subareas 22-24 or sprat in subdivisions 22-32 in the Baltic Sea and the Belts.

PCS. 4. If for a legitimate vessel, cf. 2 and 3, according to the Nature Registration Authority's catch registers, less than 500 kg of the assigned annual quantity of the vessel is allocated to one of the above quotas, the Danish Nature Agency may, upon application, first allocate additional quantities of cod or sprat, respectively, from 1 March until 22 July of the same year. Dividends are made during the grant period as long as there are quantities available. However, in the light of the number of applications received, the National Agency may decide that the allocations are made together. A vessel may be applied for again if the assigned amount of additional aid has been fished before 15 July.

PCS. 5. In the period as a rule, the same vessel may at most be allocated 4 tonnes of cod and 30 tonnes of sprat in accordance with paragraph. 2. However, to the extent that quantities still available at the end of the application deadline on 22 July, there is no upper limit for the quantities to be allocated to the same vessel. If a vessel is part of a pool, the amount of additional allowance may only be granted if, for each vessel in the pool, 500 kg of the amount of the annual quantity applied for is not more than 500 kg.

PCS. 6. If there are unallocated quantities after 22 July, these are included in the Fisheries Fund for the other purposes.

PCS. 7. Additional quantities of cod, cf. 2, shall be landed on the island where the vessel has its base port. The additional quantity may only be fished, carried and landed with the vessel to which the quantity is allocated.

PCS. 8. If the vessel owner, cf. 2, estimates that an additional quantity can not be fished, this must be notified to the Danish Nature Agency and the amount returned to the Fisheries Fund. If this does not happen so early that the quantity may be made available to other vessels in that year, the vessel will not be entitled to receive additional quantities in the following years, irrespective of whether the vessel meets the conditions laid down for each year.

CHAPTER 6 SPECIAL ARRANGEMENTS FOR COASTAL FISHING

§ 61. The following quota shares are allocated to the coastal fisheries scheme for the Danish quotas for fishing in the aforementioned waters:

1) 22.4 ‰ of cod in the North Sea.

2) 30.8 ‰ of cod in the Kattegat.

3) 47.7 ‰ of cod in the Skagerrak.

4) 58.1 ‰ of cod in the Baltic Sea and the Belts.

5) 44.0 ‰ of tongue in Skagerrak and Kattegat.

6) 21.3 ‰ of tongue in the North Sea (EU waters).

7) 40.0 ‰ of plaice in the Baltic Sea.

8) 25.9 ‰ of plaice in Kattegat.

9) 22.0 ‰ of plaice in the Skagerrak.

§ 62. At the request of the vessel owner concerned, the Nature Authority may permit a vessel designated as FKA vessel and having a maximum length of 17 meters in total to fish under the conditions applicable to coastal fishing vessels. The vessel owner can choose which of the vessel's quotas of cod, sole and plaice, which are desired to be registered with the scheme. An application for this must be received by the Danish Environmental Protection Agency no later than 31 January of the year in question.

PCS. 2. If, pursuant to Sections 82 and 83, the owner of a fishing vessel transfers FKA to one or more vessels of a maximum length of 17 m which he owns, the vessel or vessels shall be included in the seabed instead of the original vessel.

§ 63. A vessel which has been authorized pursuant to section 62 will be subject to the terms of use for coastal fishing vessels, cf. sections 64-66, until 31 December 2016.

PCS. 2. By way of derogation from subsection 1, the vessel owner may file the vessel from the coastal fishing scheme until 1 May 2014 if the vessel has not fished more than the annual quantities corresponding to the FKA of the vessel without the allocation of additional quantity as a result of the vessel's status as a coastal fishing vessel.

Section 64. Coasters with a coastal fishery status may only transfer the FKA shares to which the coastal fishing vessel is disposed of to other coastal fishing vessels, cf. sections 82 and 83.

PCS. 2. For each individual vessel with a coastal fishery status for which a logbook is kept, 80% of the fishing trips in a calendar year, the first time in 2014, shall be 2 days or less.

PCS. 3. Vessels for which the condition in subsection 2, if the length of the voyages has not been met in the previous year, can not be part of the additional annual quantities in the following year.

Section 65. Vessels with a coastal fishing license shall be allocated an additional annual amount each year on the basis of the shares of cod, sole and plaice, as provided for in section 61.

PCS. 2. Quantities according to paragraph 1 is distributed proportionally in relation to the individual vessels quota shares of cod, sole and plaice of the individual quotas.

PCS. 3. When allocating additional annual quantities, the size of the supplement is differentiated according to the type of gear to which the vessel is fishing. Vessels fishing exclusively with the gear listed in Annex 18 shall be awarded a 50% higher surcharge per vessel. quota share than vessels not fishing with these gear.

PCS. 4. The additional annual quantities are allocated by the Swedish National Agency for Nature and Fisheries during the first quarter to individual coastal fishing vessels. From 2014, the allocations will only be made if the terms of section 64 2-3 and 66 1-2, have been met for the vessel in the previous year.

Section 66. A vessel with a coastal fishing permit may be allocated the additional annual quantities if at least 50% of the vessel's total annual quantity in the previous year has been fished with the vessel concerned.

PCS. 2. If a vessel with a coastal fishing permit owned by a pool company or pool does not comply with paragraph 1. 1, the additional amounts of cod, sole and plaice may be allocated if at least 50% of the vessel's total annual quantity for all species in the previous year has been fished by other coastal fishing vessels in the pool company or pool.

PCS. 3. It is a condition for granting a coastal fishing allowance that vessels with a coastal fishing license do not transfer annual quantities of the quotas to which they have registered the scheme to vessels not registered with the coastal fisheries scheme.

PCS. 4. Estimation of the vessel's total annual quantity for all species according to paragraph 1 and 2 may also be made on the basis of the value of the vessel's total annual quantities for all species calculated in accordance with section 83 (1). 3-4.

CHAPTER 7 FIRST-TIME ESTABLISHMENT WITH FKA VESSELS OR IOC INDUSTRIAL SPECIES

Approval of FKA vessel for first-time established (FKA-FE vessels) or approval of vessel initially established with IOC industrial types (IOKINDUSTRI-FE)

§ 67. On application by younger vessel owners established with a vessel after 30 March 2007, the Nature Agency may approve the vessel's status as FKA vessel for first-time established (FKA-FE vessel) or status as a vessel initially established with IOC Industrial Species (IOKINDUSTRI-FE).

PCS. 2. Applications that are requested to be processed during the year in question must reach the NaturErhvervstyrelsen no later than 1 November of the year in question.

PCS. 3. A vessel may be approved as a IOKINDUSTRI-FE vessel, even if it is already approved as a FKA-FE vessel, or vice versa if the first-time manufacturer meets the specified requirements for both schemes.

§ 68. A vessel may obtain the status of FKA-FE vessel or IOKINDUSTRI-FE vessel if the following is fulfilled:

1) The applicant must be fishermen with A status and must not be over 40 years at the time of application. If the ownership is established before the application is submitted, approval may be given if the applicant was not over 40 years at the time of establishment, cf. No. 2.

2) After 30 March 2007, the applicant has established itself as owner or co-owner of the vessel applied for FKA-FE or IOKINDUSTRI-FE status with a minimum ownership interest of 10%.

3) The applicant must not already be or have been the owner or co-owner of a vessel in which the owner's ownership interest has exceeded DKK 1,000,000 of the insurance value.

4) The vessel is listed in the Norwegian Commerce Agency's vessel register with a length of 7.5m or more overall if FKA-FE status is requested. If the IOKINDUSTRI-FE status is searched, the vessel must be noted at a length of 17 m and above.

5) The applicant must not previously own or be a co-owner of a vessel that has been in the status of FKA-FE vessel if FKA-FE status is sought. If IOKINDUSTRI-FE status is being searched, the applicant must not previously own a vessel that has been in the status of IOKINDUSTRI-FE status.

PCS. 2. If the applicant has established himself as sole owner, the insurance value of the vessel sought FKA-FE status shall be at least DKK 250,000 and for applications for the status of the IOKINDUSTRI-FE vessel shall be at least 500,000 kr.

PCS. 3. If the applicant has established himself as a co-owner of a vessel also owned by persons or companies that do not fulfill the conditions of paragraph 1, the newly established applicant shall own at least a portion of the vessel seeking FKA-FE or IOKINDUSTRI-FE status equal to at least DKK 1,000,000 of the vessel's insurance value.

PCS. 4. If more applicants, all of whom fulfill the requirements of paragraph 1, together as the owner of a vessel, the insurance value of the vessel sought FKA-FE status shall be at least DKK 250,000 and for applications for the status of the IOKINDUSTRI-FE vessel shall be at least DKK 500,000. Applicants establish themselves as co-owners of a vessel also owned by persons or companies that do not meet the requirements of paragraph. 1, each of the newly established shall establish an ownership interest equivalent to at least DKK 1,000,000 of the vessel's insurance value.

Section 69. Applicants who have not yet acquired a vessel may apply for the vessel that the person or persons intends to acquire, pre-approved as FKA-FE or IOKINDUSTRI-FE vessel. The application must state that the conditions in section 68 will be met in connection with the planned establishment.

PCS. 2. The Nature Agency may grant final approval to the applications when the applicant's acquisition is registered in the Danish Maritime Authority's ship register and the Norwegian Maritime Authority's vessel register. The owner's ownership must be registered no later than 6 months after the Agency's prior approval. Failure to do so will void prior approval and all rights attached thereto.

§ 70. A vessel may be approved as FKA-FE or IOKINDUSTRI-FE vessel regardless of which vessel category the vessel is assigned. From the time when a MAF vessel is given the status of FKA-FE vessel, the vessel can not be used for rationing on the shares of quotas allocated to MAF vessels. An FKA vessel, which is given the status of FKA-FE vessel, may continue to dispose of the FKA Shares and IOK Shares attached to the vessel on a regular basis. A vessel that is given the status of IOKINDUSTRI-FE vessel may continue to dispose of the FKA Shares and IOK Shares attached to the vessel on its terms.

PCS. 2. After final approval or prior approval as FKA-FE or IOKINDUSTRI-FE vessel, the owners of the vessel may apply for the loan FKA if the vessel has the status of FKA-FE vessel,

PCS. 3. An FKA-FE or IOKINDUSTRI-FE vessel may participate in pool fishing according to the current rules for pool fishing with the FKA or IOK fishing rights attached to the vessel, including the loan FKA or loan IOK, which stands available to the vessel.

§ 71. Vessels receive status as FKA-FE or IOKINDUSTRI-FE vessels from the final approval.

PCS. 2. For vessels approved with FKA-FE or IOKINDUSTRI-FE status, this status will end after 8 years. Vessels with FKA-FE status are subsequently classified as FKA vessels with disposition of the FKA shares attached to the vessel, except for the loan FKA. Vessels with IOKINDUSTRI-FE status are subsequently classified as FKA vessels if they are affiliated with FKA Shares or as an Other Ships if they do not have any FKA Shares. The right to fish on allotted loan-FKA or loan-IOK is also permanently terminated for both FKA-FE and IOKINDUSTRI-FE vessels.

PCS. 3. If the first-time established, cf. section 68, subsection 1, cease to be owners or co-owners of the vessel within 8 years, the vessel's status as FKA-FE or IOKINDUSTRI-FE vessel from the change of ownership ends, and assigned annual amounts on the basis of the loan FKA or loan IOK shall lapse at the end of the year.

PCS. 4. If the ownership or ownership of the vessel's first-time establishment becomes less than at the time of approval, the allocation of the loan FKA or the loan IOK is reduced accordingly. If the ownership of the vessel or the newly established ownership of the vessel is reduced to an ownership share of less than 10%, the vessel's status as FKA-FE or IOKINDUSTRI-FE vessel ends.

PCS. 5. It is a condition for maintaining the approval as FKA-FE or IOKINDUSTRI-FE vessel that the vessel and the newly established participant actively engage in fishing. During the course of each calendar year, the person concerned shall participate in fishing for at least half of the days at which the vessel is at sea.

Loan-FKA to FKA-FE vessel and loan-IOK to IOKINDUSTRI-FE vessel

§ 72. First-time established, owners or co-owners of vessels approved as FKA-FE or IOKINDUSTRI-FE vessels, or which are pre-approved may apply for loan shares (loan-FKA or loan-IOK) by 31 March at the latest. from the proportions of quotas allocated for this purpose. Allotment of loan-FKA and loan-IOK is only made once a year on the basis of applications received on time.

PCS. 2. It is possible to apply for both loan-FKA and loan-IOK if the first-time established is approved or pre-approved as both the FKA-FE vessel and the IOKINDUSTRI-FE vessel, cf. section 67 Third

PCS. 3. In section 74, the shares of the quotas so far devoted to the applicants who will be entitled to the loan FKA and the shares of the quotas so far allocated to the applicants who will be entitled to borrow -IOK. Loan-FKA and Loan-IOK are allocated for a period of 8 years, but after 4 years a reduction in the allocation will begin. The reduction is made by 25% per year.

PCS. 4. For each approved FKA-FE vessel, the loan FKA shall be allocated on the basis of a calculation basis determined on the basis of FKA vessels' average gross turnover of FKA quotas in the previous year. For each approved IOKINDUSTRI-FE vessel, loan-IOK is allocated on the basis of a calculation basis determined on the basis of IOK vessels' average landing value in the previous year of industrial types covered by IOC. The turnover figures to be used per. vessels in the specified length categories will be published on the NaturErhverststyrelsens website during the first quarter of a given year.

PCS. 5. For vessels in which one or more first-time established cf. section 68 1, owns 100% of the vessel, the calculation basis is 20% of the turnover figures cf. 4th

PCS. 6. If one or more first-time establishments have established themselves as co-owners of a vessel which is also owned by other fishermen, the calculation basis shall be reduced, cf. 5, in relation to the owner's share of the vessel or its first-time establishment.

PCS. 7. In the period when a vessel has FKA-FE or IOKINDUSTRI-FE status, the loan FKA or loan IOK may be granted at most 20% of the turnover figures per. vessel, cf. 4, no matter how many first-time, who are co-owners.

PCS. 8. The amount of loan-FKA or loan IOK allocated may be increased by acquiring a larger ownership of the FKA-FE or the IOKINDUSTRI-FE vessel by the first-time establishment. However, this does not extend the period for which the original loan-FKA or loan-IOK was awarded.

§ 73. On the basis of the basis of calculation, the first-time established FKA-FE vessel is entitled to the vessel in question pursuant to section 72 4-6, is granted to loan FKA, which is composed of whether the vessel is to be used for yarn or trawl fishing and the vessel's port of origin. On the basis of the basis of calculation of the first-time established as IOKINDUSTRI-FE vessel, the loan IOK is eligible for that vessel pursuant to section 72, paragraphs 4 to 6.

PCS. 2. In Annex 12, for FKA-FE vessels, the percentages of the individual allowances allocated to yarn or trawlers are determined depending on whether the vessel's home port is located to the North Sea, Skagerrak, Kattegat, Baltic Sea (area 22-24) or the Baltic Sea (range 25-32). For vessels with a home port in Hanstholm or Skagen, separate percentages of quotas are stated. Irrespective of the port of origin of the vessel, the applicant may apply for the allocation to be made on the basis of one of the other waters listed in Annex 12, or on the basis of the percentages of quotas applicable to vessels with a home port in Hanstholm or Skagen.

PCS. 3. For FKA-FE and IOKINDUSTRI-FE vessels, quota shares shall be allocated corresponding to the basis of calculation converted into shares of the allowances to which the vessel is entitled, cf. 1 and 2. The allocation takes place on the basis of the average settlement prices the previous year, cf. notice issued according to the rules in Appendix 6 and the Danish quotas per. 1 January of the year in question.

PCS. 4. Applicants for the loan FKA may apply for the allocation with a different percentage of the individual quotas than indicated in Annex 12. However, for cod and sole, no higher aggregate shares of these species may be applied for in all waters specified in Annex.

PCS. 5. Loans of IOK equivalent to a value of 200 tonnes of herring in the North Sea may be granted at most. The calculation is based on the average settlement prices in the year prior to the allocation of loan IOK.

PCS. 6. Applications for loan-FKA or loan-IOK may be granted to the extent that sufficient quota shares are available for each quota, otherwise the allocations are made pursuant to section 75.

PCS. 7. The Swedish National Agency for Economic Affairs may, under special circumstances and upon application from the first-time establishment, authorize the allocation of the loan-FKA or loan-IOK by a different percentage of the allocation of the individual shares than originally allocated. Permission for change in loan-FKA or loan-IOK will only come into effect the year after the license is granted.

Section 74. For the purposes of the shares of the quotas allocated to the Fisheries Fund, cf. section 54, the following shares of the Danish quotas for the loan FKA to FKA-FE vessels are so far allocated:

1) 20 ‰ cod in the North Sea.

2) 20 ‰ of cod in the Kattegat.

3) 20 ‰ of cod in the Skagerrak.

4) 20 ‰ of cod in the Baltic Sea and Belts, ICES subdivisions 22-24.

5) 20 ‰ of cod in the Baltic Sea, ICES subdivisions 25-32 (EU waters).

6) 20 ‰ of tongue in the Skagerrak, Kattegat and the Baltic Sea and the Belts.

7) 20 ‰ of tongue in the North Sea (EU waters).

8) 20 ‰ of plaice in the North Sea.

9) 50 ‰ of plaice in Kattegat.

10) 50 ‰ of plaice in Skagerrak.

11) 50 ‰ of plaice in the Baltic Sea and the Belts.

12) 50 ‰ of Norway lobster in Skagerrak, Kattegat and the Baltic Sea and the Belts.

13) 50 ‰ of Norway lobster in the North Sea (EU waters).

14) 50 ‰ of Norway lobster in the North Sea (Norwegian zone).

15) 20 ‰ of dark ice in the North Sea, Skagerrak, Kattegat and the Baltic Sea and the Belts.

16) 50 ‰ of hills in Skagerrak, Kattegat and the Baltic Sea and the Belts.

17) 50 ‰ of hills in the North Sea.

18) 50 ‰ of deep-water rains in Skagerrak and Kattegat.

19) 50 ‰ of deep sea rains in the North Sea (EU waters).

20) 50 ‰ of deepwater rains in the North Sea (Norwegian zone).

21) 50 ‰ of hake in the North Sea (EU waters).

22) 20 ‰ of turbot and bristle in the North Sea.

23) 20 ‰ of sea bag in the North Sea (Norwegian zone).

24) 50 ‰ of sprat in the North Sea (EU waters).

25) 50 ‰ of sprat in Skagerrak and Kattegat.

26) 50 ‰ of sprat in the Baltic Sea and the Belts.

27) 50 ‰ of herring in the Baltic Sea and the Belts.

28) 50 ‰ of salmon in the Baltic Sea and the Belts.

PCS. 2. The shares of the quotas allocated to the fishery fund, cf. section 54, and the shares of the quotas reserved for reserve, cf. section 118 (3), shall be allocated as follows the following prominent shares of the Danish allowances for loan-IOK to IOKINDUSTRI-FE vessels:

1) 10 ‰ of sandeel in the North Sea (EU waters and Norwegian zone) and Skagerrak and Kattegat.

2) 10 ‰ of sperling in the North Sea (EU waters) as well as the Skagerrak and Kattegat.

3) 10 ‰ of sprat in the North Sea (EU waters).

PCS. 3. In the application for loan-IOK, the applicant must indicate the distribution of the quotas requested.

§ 75. To the extent that, within the proportions of the individual quotas for the various watershed areas provided for in section 74, there are insufficient quantities to meet all applications, the allocations for each quota are reduced proportionally. To the extent that there are still shares of other quotas available, these may be assigned instead of.

Section 76. Loans-FKA and Loan-IOK include, during the period they are available to the vessel, in the total annual quantities that can be fished by the vessel. Up to 25% of the vessel's total annual amount including the amounts allocated on the basis of the loan FKA may be transferred to other FKA vessels, cf. Section 51.

PCS. 2. Loan-FKA and Loan-IOK can not be transferred to other vessels pursuant to sections 82-83. However, the NatureEurope Agency may allow the newly established person to make a vessel replacement during the period, cf. section 71, where the loan FKA or loan IOK is available to the newly established person. The right to the loan FKA can only be continued if the newly established owner has at least the same ownership interest in the changed vessel as in the replaced vessel. In addition, it is a condition for approval that the vessel to be changed is in at least the same length category, cf. section 72 (1). 4th

CHAPTER 8 REPLACEMENT OF ANNUAL QUANTITIES OF ALLOWANCES COVERED BY IOC AND FKA

Swap between Danish registered vessels

§ 77. Vessel owners may, upon application, exchange annual quantities within the individual quota year.

PCS. 2. The Nature Agency may authorize the transfer of annual quantity from a vessel (the shipping vessel) to another vessel (the recipient vessel), while moving the amount of the year from the recipient vessel to the delivery vessel. The switches must take place within a frame relative to the value of the quantities exchanged, cf. 4th

PCS. 3. After the Nature Authority has granted permission pursuant to subsection 2, the Board registers the changes made by annual amount.

PCS. 4. The Nature Agency may only authorize and register the switch according to paragraph 1, if there is a maximum of 10% difference between the value of the quantities exchanged. The value is calculated in relation to the average settlement prices for the previous year for the quotas for which quantities are exchanged. The average settlement prices for the previous year will be shown in a table published in accordance with Appendix 6.

PCS. 5. An application must be submitted as a joint application by the owners of the vessels concerned.

Replacement of the right to use annual quantities for vessels from other EU countries (individual quota switches)

§ 78. From the Fisheries Fund 303 ‰ of the provisions of Section 54 1, No. 5, allocated 353 ‰ such that these promulgers are distributed as an annual amount to all vessels that possess FKA on the west quota. The distribution is made in relation to the FKA, which vessels have disposed of on the west quota. Vessels can fish the annual amount in the eastern Baltic Sea or notify the Nature Agency that the amount is available for exchange with other countries that Denmark makes of cod between the two quotas in the Baltic Sea. If Denmark completes the exchange of cod from the East Quota to the West Quotas, the vessel is available for quantities on the west quota proportional to the amount of cod from the East quota provided by the vessel owner for quota swap. If the ratio in the swap between countries is different from 1: 1, the amount of west cod that the vessel may have available, correspondingly reduced or increased. If no change is made for the entire quantity provided by the vessel owners for exchange, the NaturErhvervstyrelsen shall proportionately exchange the quantities exchanged for the vessels that have made quantities available for exchange.

PCS. 2. Vessels holding quota shares of cod in the Baltic Sea from the western quota and having maximum quota shares equal to 500 kilograms of cod per year. waters in waters other than the western Baltic Sea and which inform the Nature Agency that there are volumes available for exchange before 1 February in a given year, have priority to cod that becomes available on the west quota through exchange. For quantities made available for exchanges after 1 February in a given year, the western cod which is received by swapping shall be distributed to all vessels.

PCS. 3. The terms of exchange pursuant to subsections 1 and 2 may be determined by notification in accordance with Annex 6. In addition, it may be stipulated that

1) The vessel owners can make a larger proportion of the vessel's annual quantity of cod from the East Quake available for exchange than the part of the annual amount distributed as flexibility and exchange year, and

2) Vessel owners disposing of the annual amount of cod on the west quota may make available to the NaturErhvervstyrelsen quantities that they may be included in exchanges made by cod between Denmark between the two quotas in the Baltic Sea.

§ 79. Vessel owners may, in the same way as stated for cod, cf. section 78, notify the NatureEconomy that quantities available to the East quota of herring on herring are available for exchange of herring on the west quota. Detailed rules may be issued in accordance with Annex 6.

PCS. 2. The Nature Agency may issue Appendix 6 notice of the possibility that vessel owners can make annual amounts of a certain quota available for exchange.

§ 80. A vessel's total owner may transfer the right to fish part of the vessel's total annual amount of herring and mackerel covered by IOC and industrial species covered by IOC to a specified Community vessel against the transfer of quantities, including in other waters, of Other allowances from the Community vessel concerned, which may be fished in the same year or the following calendar year.

PCS. 2. Individual quota swap after paragraph. 1-3 are carried out between the fisheries authorities in Denmark and the Member State concerned in accordance with the applicable rules. The Nature Agency may refuse to implement the exchange on the basis of an assessment that this does not contribute to the overall opportunities for the fishing industry in Denmark. Owners of a Danish registered vessel wishing to have an individual quota swap must submit an application to the Danish Environmental Protection Agency with the following information:

1) Date of conclusion of individual quota swap agreement.

2) Vessels name and port number and the nationality of the foreign vessel or name and address of foreign producer organization with which an individual quota swap agreement has been reached if the foreign vessel is not known.

3) The size of the quotas of the species concerned and the waters in which the quotas are allocated.

4) Declaration that the parties commit to the transaction.

PCS. 3. If the Nature Agency may approve the application for quota exchanges and when the quota has been completed with the fisheries authorities of the Member State concerned and notified to the European Commission, the NatureEconomy Registers the transferred quantities for the Danish vessel concerned and authorizes the amount of the quota allocated can be fished with this vessel.

CHAPTER 9 TRANSFER OF FKA

§ 81. If a vessel changes owner, the FKA, which is attached to the vessel at the time of ownership change, remains attached to the vessel after ownership.

Transfer of FKA

§ 82. The owner of a vessel may transfer the vessel's total FKA to up to 10 other vessels. The transfer must be made at one time, so that the shipping vessel after the transfer has no disposal over FKA. Notification of transfer shall be given to the Swedish Environmental Protection Agency.

PCS. 2. After the transfer, the owner must not use the delivery vessel identified by the EU ID. No. for rationing fishery.

PCS. 3. The Nature Agency may allow the shipping vessel identified by the EU ID. No. After replacing the entire owner circle, can be used for rationing.

PCS. 4 pcs. 3 also applies to FKA vessels from which FKA shares have been transferred, cf. 1. Vessels may be used for ranching if the owner has been replaced by the owner who transferred the vessel's total FKA shares.

Section 83. By way of derogation from section 82, the Nature Agency may allow a given year to be transferred up to 25% of the FKA shares held by the delivery vessel at the time of transfer to other vessels. An estimate of the size of the vessel shares that the shipping vessel can transmit at most may be made on the basis of the value of the FKA shares held by the dispatching vessel at the time when the first transfer takes place, cf. 2. If, after the first transfer, the vessel receives quota shares, up to 25% of these shares may be transferred.

PCS. 2. The Nature Agency may allow a vessel's quota share of deepwater rains in the North Sea (Norwegian zone) to be transferred, regardless of whether it represents more than 25% of the vessel's total FKA.

PCS. 3. Calculation of the value of the FKA shares transferred from the individual vessel, cf. 1, on the basis of the Danish quotas per. On 1 January of the year in which the transfer takes place, the quantities deducted for the individual quota in the year in question are for fishing for schemes other than FKA. These figures for the individual quota are published in a table. In addition, according to Annex 6, a table of average settlement prices for the previous year is published.

PCS. 4. The shares of the individual allowances transferred by the individual vessel are converted into volumes. The value of the transferred quota share is calculated on this basis in relation to the average settlement prices for the previous year.

§ 84. During the period from 15 November to 31 December, the NaturErhvervsstyrelsen will not receive a transfer of FKA to other vessels pursuant to sections 82-83. Transfer and exchange of annual volume pursuant to sections 51, 52 and 77 may continue during this period.

§ 85. If a vessel to which FKA is affixed is registered as a registered fishing vessel without the vessel owner having notified the Nature Authority of the vessel to which the FKA shares are to be transferred, the right to the FKA shares shall expire and shall be transferred to the Fisheries Fund.

PCS. 2. By way of derogation from subsection 1, however, the right to FKA may be retained after application within one calendar year after a vessel has been deleted in the Swedish National Agency for Nature Registration. The National Agency may also, upon application, allow the FKA shares to be retained for a longer period but for a maximum of 18 months if the vessel owner before the vessel has been deleted has applied for the FKA shares to be transferred to another vessel which the owners have entered into binding contract to acquire.

§ 86. It is a condition for the transfer of FKA from a vessel and its registration in the NaturErhvervstyrelsen that no owners or co-owners of the vessel received are persons who, upon transfer of FKA, will exceed one or more of the maximum rates of ownership as set out in Appendix 17. Furthermore, it is a condition that the receiving vessel will not exceed one or more of the maximum rates for quota shares set out in Appendix 17, as well as the conditions set out in paragraph. 3-4.

PCS. 2. It is also a prerequisite for registration of a change of ownership of a vessel in the National Agency for Records that no owners or co-owners are persons who, upon registration of the change of ownership, will exceed one or more of the maximum rates for ownership, as stated of Annex 17, as well as the conditions set out in subsection 4th

PCS. 3. It is a prerequisite for the transfer of FKA from a vessel and its registration in the NaturErhvervstyrelsen that there are neither persons nor co-owners of the receiving vessel persons who own shares in a vessel with IOC shares and which owns at yearly level of IOC shares corresponding to more than 2% of the total Danish IOC quotas, which will exceed 25% of the stated rates for maximum ownership shares for FKA quotas, as shown in Appendix 17. The calculation is based on Denmark's initial quota per On January 1, however, an average of the previous 3-year quotas is used if the quota is not fixed per. 1st of January.

PCS. 4. There is also a condition for registering a change of ownership of a vessel in the National Agency for Nature Registration, that there are no owners or co-owners who own shares in a vessel with IOC shares and which owns annual amounts of IOC shares corresponding to more than 2% of the total Danish IOC allowances, which upon registration of the ownership change will exceed 25% of the stated rates for maximum ownership shares for FKA quotas, as shown in Appendix 17. The calculation is based on Denmark's initial quota per On January 1, however, an average of the previous 3-year quotas is used if the quota is not fixed per. 1st of January.

PCS. 5. If the available Danish quotas are changed from one catch to another, and the total annual amount of IOC allowances of a person exceeds the 2% as set out in paragraph. 3-4, the owner must in each case, where this is the case, not purchase additional quota shares for the vessel for the FKA quotas, where they exceed 25% of the maximum rates, cf. 3-4.

PCS. 6. If the conditions in subsection 1-5 is not complied with, the Nature Agency will impose on the persons who fail to meet the conditions at the latest after 3 months. This applies regardless of whether the Danish Agency for Nature Ownership has granted a license to fish with the shares.

PCS. 7. Are the conditions mentioned in subsection 1-2 not met no later than 3 months, cf. 6, the right to the quota shares on the vessel, as in the case of the transfer of FKA, cf. 1, or upon registration of ownership change, cf. 2 exceeds the maximum rates as set out in Appendix 17, and these quota shares are transferred to the Fisheries Fund. Are the conditions mentioned in paragraph 3-5 not met no later than 3 months, cf. 6, the Nature Agency will reduce the FKA shares of the vessel in question, which exceeds the conditions, so that the person after the reduction owns 25% of the maximum rates for ownership shares of FKA quotas, as set out in Appendix 17, cf. 3-4, and the withdrawn quota shares are transferred to the Fisheries Fund.

PCS. 8. Persons or vessels who, as of April 23, 2012, exceeded the maximum rates for ownership interests or quota shares as set out in Appendix 17, cf. 1-2, or persons who did not meet the conditions in paragraph. 3-4, are exempt from paragraph. 6-7. It is not allowed for these persons or vessels to increase their ownership interests or quota shares for the quotas where they exceed the maximum rates, cf. Appendix 17, and cf. 3-4.

Transfer of FKA in special situations

§ 87. If a vessel is taken over by a bankruptcy auction by a financial institution, the Danish Financial Supervisory Authority (formerly the Danish Fisheries Bank), Denmark's Ship Finance Fund or mortgage-creditors, mortgage holders may sell the vessel with its FKA to a person or company complying with the terms of the Fisheries Act in order to engage in commercial fishing.

PCS. 2. The National Agency may, upon application, allow a surviving spouse or other heirs who possess the vessel to sell the vessel with an associated FKA to a person or company entitled to engage in commercial fishing.

PCS. 3. When the vessel has been sold, cf. 1 and 2, the new owner may dispose of the vessel and the associated FKA in accordance with the rules in sections 82-86.

Section 88. In the event that a vessel is taken over by a bankruptcy auction, the National Agency for Economic Affairs (formerly the Danish Fisheries Bank), Denmark's Ship Finance Fund or to mortgage-creditors, and the NaturErhvervsstyrelsen may, in accordance with the regulations in the Decree on vessels used for commercial fishing in saline, permits the vessel to be leased while permitting the vessel to engage in fishing in accordance with the license to fish an annual amount during the period during which the vessel is leased.

PCS. 2. If a vessel is taken over by a surviving spouse or other heirs in accordance with the rules of the Executive Order on vessels used for commercial fishing in saline, the vessel's FKA shall be taken over at the same time. After the acquisition, the NatureEconomy Board may authorize the vessel to fish under license to fish an annual amount during the period during which the vessel is leased.

CHAPTER 10 POOL FISHING

§ 89. A vessel owner's fishing rights may only be included in a pool fishing if the NaturErhvervstyrelsen has granted permission pursuant to the regulations in the executive order on pool fishing. A pool fishing must be exercised in accordance with the terms and conditions.

PCS. 2. In a pool fishing, annual quantities received on the basis of FKA shall be taken to vessels connected to the pool fishing during the period for which the license for pool fishing is granted.

PCS. 3. For vessels enrolled in a pool, the annual quantities available to the vessels of the following quotas in pool fishing shall also be included:

1) Annual quantities allocated on the basis of IOC for sprat in the North Sea.

2) Annual quantities allocated on the basis of IOC for herring and sprat in the Baltic Sea.

3) Annual quantities allocated on the basis of IOC on sprat in Skagerrak and Kattegat.

4) Annual volumes awarded on the basis of IOC on Northern Southeast Atlantic Ocean (EU waters and Norwegian zone) and Skagerrak and Kattegat (EU waters), Blue whiting in EU waters and international waters, North Sea sparring (EU waters) as well as Skagerrak and Kattegat, and blue whiting in the Faroese zone.

5) Years allocated on the basis of IAC on horse mackerel in ICES zones IIa, IVa, Vb, VI, VIIa-c and Ic, VIIIa, b, d and e, XII and XIV.

PCS. 4. A vessel owner shall, by 1 March of a given year, notify the NaturErhvervstyrelsen if one or more of the items mentioned in subsection 3, no. 1-5, shall not be included in the pool fishing on which one vessel is affiliated. The notification must be signed by the pool manager or his deputy, cf. the order for pool fishing.

PCS. 5. If a pool fishing at the end of a year has exceeded the annual quantities available for pool fishing, until 6 January of the following year, pool fishing has the opportunity to purchase quota shares or annual quantities of other vessels or pool fisheries to cover the exceedance. If the pool fishing after 6 January has still landed more than the annual quantities available for pool fishing, the Nature Agency regards it as an overfishing.

CHAPTER 11 COMMON PROVISIONS FOR FISHERIES WITH IOC

Ownership and maximum quota concentration

§ 90. It is a condition for the transfer of IOC from a vessel and its registration in the NaturErhvervstyrelsen that there are no persons among the owners or co-owners of the receiving vessel who, upon the transfer of IOC, will exceed one or more of the maximum rates for ownership as set out in Annex 17. It is also a condition that the receiving vessel does not exceed one or more of the maximum rates for quota shares as set out in Appendix 17 and the conditions set out in subsection (1). 3-5.

PCS. 2. It is also a prerequisite for registration of a change of ownership of a vessel in the National Agency for Records that no owners or co-owners are persons who, upon registration of the change of ownership, will exceed one or more of the maximum rates for ownership, as stated of Annex 17, as well as the conditions set out in subsection 5th

PCS. 3. A total of a vessel and a person's annual quantities of IOC shares may not exceed 10% of the total Danish IOC quota. The calculation is based on Denmark's initial quota per. On January 1, however, an average of the previous 3-year quotas is used if the quota is not fixed per. 1st of January.

PCS. 4. It is a prerequisite for the transfer of IOC from a vessel and its registration in the Nature Agency that no ownership of the vessel to which the quota shares are transferred are among the owners or co-owners of shares in a FKA vessel and as on Personnel level owns more than 25% of one or more of the maximum shareholding ratios for FKA quotas, as set out in Appendix 17, which upon the transfer of IOC will hold annual amounts of IOC shares equal to 2% or more of the total Danish IOC quotas. The calculation is based on Denmark's initial quota per. On January 1, however, an average of the previous 3-year quotas is used if the quota is not fixed per. 1st of January.

PCS. 5. It is also a prerequisite for registration of a change of ownership of a vessel in the National Agency for Records that no owners or co-owners are persons who own shares in a FKA vessel and which owns more than 25% of one or more Several of the rates for maximum shareholdings for FKA quotas, as set out in Appendix 17, which, when registering the ownership change, will hold annual amounts of IOC quotas corresponding to 2% or more of the total Danish IOC quotas. The calculation is based on Denmark's initial quota per. On January 1, however, an average of the previous 3-year quotas is used if the quota is not fixed per. 1st of January.

PCS. 6. A person who owns IOC allowances shall not own vessels which together represent more than 6000 GT. If this condition is not complied with, the Nature Authority may require a person to sell one or more vessels.

PCS. 7. If the available Danish quotas are changed from one catch to another, and the total annual amount of IOC allowances of one vessel or a person, for this reason, exceeds the 10% as set out in paragraph. 3, or a person's total annual amounts of IOC allowances for this reason exceeds the 2% as stated in paragraph. 4-5, the owner must in each case, where this is the case, not purchase additional IOK quota shares for the vessel.

PCS. 8. If the conditions in subsection 1-5 and pcs. 7 is not complied with, the Nature Agency may impose on persons who do not comply with the conditions not later than 3 months. This applies regardless of whether the Danish Agency for Nature Ownership has granted a license to fish with the shares.

PCS. 9. Are the conditions mentioned in subsection 1-3 not fulfilled no later than 3 months, cf. 8, the right to the quota shares on the vessel lapses as in the transfer of the IOC, cf. 1, or upon registration of ownership change, cf. 2 exceeds the maximum rates as set out in Appendix 17, and these quota shares are transferred to the Fisheries Fund. Are the conditions mentioned in paragraph 4-5 and pcs. 7 not fulfilled no later than 3 months, cf. 8, the Nature Agency will reduce all of the IOCs of the relevant person on the vessel proportionately, so that the person after the reduction will own the maximum amount of annual IOC allowances corresponding to 2% of the total Danish IOC quotas and the transferred quota shares will be transferred to the Fisheries Fund.

PCS. 10. Persons or vessels who, as of April 23, 2012, exceeded the maximum rates for ownership interests or quota shares as set out in Appendix 17, cf. 1-2, or persons who, as of April 23, 2012, did not meet the conditions in paragraph. 3-6, will be exempt from paragraph. 8 and 9. It is not allowed for these persons or vessels to increase their ownership or quota shares for the quotas where they exceed the maximum rates, cf. Appendix 17, and cf. 4-5.

Registration of quota shares and annual quantities

§ 91. If a vessel changes owner, the IOK, which at the time of ownership change is attached to the vessel after ownership change, remains attached to the vessel.

PCS. 2. A vessel's total owner may transfer the share of the vessel (the delivery vessel) to wholly or partly to owners of other vessels (recipient vessels) meeting the requirements of sections 7 and 90.

PCS. 3. Transfer quota shares to a vessel or owner who does not meet the requirements, cf. 1, the Nature Agency does not issue a revised permit for fishing with the recipient vessel.

PCS. 4. The vessel owner who has acquired quota shares or annual quantities must document in writing to the Nature Agency that transfer has taken place.

PCS. 5. Notice of change of ownership is registered in the National Agency for Economic Affairs.

PCS. 6. In the case of transfer of quota shares, the information listed in Annex 8, including the selling price, shall be given to the NaturErhvervstyrelsen.

§ 92. The Nature Agency shall calculate the revised quota shares and the corresponding annual quantities for the vessels concerned.

For additional analytical, business and investment opportunities information,
please contact Global Investment & Business Center, USA
at (703) 370-8082. Fax: (703) 370-8083. E-mail: ibpusa3@gmail.com
Global Business and Investment Info Databank - www.ibpus.com

PCS. 2. The NatureEconomy Board hereby authorizes the recipient vessel to fish the total annual amount. The amount already fished in the catches concerned is deducted before the license is issued.

PCS. 3. If a vessel has only transferred a portion of its quota share, the NatureEconomy Board authorizes fishing for the remaining annual quantity in the fishery in question.

PCS. 4. The plenipotentiary, cf. section 7, shall in connection with the transfer of shares inform that the requirements for the vessel and its owners, cf. sections 7 and 90, and its influence on the utilization of quota shares, cf. section 90, have been complied with . If these requirements are not complied with, the right to exercise the quota share will expire immediately and the right to the quota share will lapse if the share is not transferred to a person or company complying with the requirements of sections 7 and 90 within 3 months. This applies, regardless of whether the Danish Agency for Nature and Fisheries has granted permission for fishing with the share. Delayed quota shares accrue to the reserve pool for the relevant quotas or the Fisheries Fund for the quotas covered by section 54.

PCS. 5. The Nature Agency does not issue a revised permit for fishing with the recipient vessel if the IOC has been transferred to a vessel or owner who does not comply with the requirements of sections 7 and 90. The NatureEconomy Board may revoke an authorization for fishing if it subsequently appears that the conditions of sections 7 and 90 for transfer of IOC were not fulfilled at the time of issue of the license.

§ 93. If a vessel with IOC and / or a yearly amount of herring from the generation shift pool is deleted by the National Agency of Commerce's vessel register without the quota shares previously being transferred to one or more vessels, the right to the quota shares and / or the amount of the year from the generation change pool shall lapse.

PCS. 2. Quotas and annual quantities may, however, be maintained for up to 18 months if permission has been sought for replacement of another vessel. During the period until the new vessel is loaded into the fleet, the owner of the outgoing vessel may transfer the vessel's quota shares and annual volumes.

Transfer and use of quota shares in special situations

Section 94. If a vessel is taken over by a forced sale by a bank, the Danish Financial Supervisory Authority (formerly the Danish Fisheries Bank), Denmark's Ship Finance Fund or mortgage-backed creditors, mortgages may transfer the vessel's quota share to owners of vessels complying with the terms of the Fisheries Act to engage in commercial fishing .

PCS. 2. The National Economic Authority may, upon application, allow a surviving spouse or other heirs disposing of the vessel to transfer the vessel's quota shares to owners of vessels that fulfill the conditions.

Section 95. In the event that a vessel is transferred by a forced sale to a bank, the Danish Agency for Economic Affairs (formerly the Danish Fisheries Bank), Denmark's Ship Finance Fund or to mortgage-creditors, and the NaturErhvervstyrelsen may, in accordance with the regulations in the Decree on vessels used for commercial fishing permits the vessel to be leased while allowing the vessel to fish in accordance with its quota share during the period during which the vessel is leased.

PCS. 2. If a vessel of a surviving spouse or other heirs is taken in accordance with the rules of the Decree on vessels used for commercial fishing, the vessel's quota share shall be taken over at the same time. After the acquisition, the NatureEconomy Board may issue a permit for fishing according to the vessel's quota share and transfer of quota share.

CHAPTER 12 MACKEREL IN THE NORTH SEA, SKAGERRAK, KATTEGAT, THE BALTIC SEA AND IN THE NORWEGIAN FISHING ZONE NORTH OF 62° N

General provisions

§ 96. Only vessels whose owners have a license issued pursuant to sections 17-18 must fish, bring and land mackerel.

PCS. 2. Exempt from the requirement in subsection 1 is landing of mackerel with up to 400 kg from one fishing trip per day-to-day fishing as well as fishing carried out by fishermen who exclusively engage in fishing with bundle yarn and other pole gear throughout the year.

PCS. 3. It is not permitted to fish, bring and land mackerel for purposes other than human consumption. Except here are permitted by-catches of mackerel in industrial fisheries.

§ 97. The Nature Authority issues permission to fish an annual amount of mackerel to owners of vessels that have disposed of IOC, which are allocated per. January 1, 2006 or acquired later in accordance with the rules.

PCS. 2. The Nature Agency may authorize fishing with hooks for vessels not in possession of IOC. The fishery takes place on the amount allocated pursuant to section 98 (1). First

Section 98. Prior to the calculation of annual quantities, the Danish quota of mackerel in the North Sea, Skagerrak and Kattegat and in the Norwegian fishing zone is north of 62°N 500 tonnes for fishing with vessels authorized to fish with hooks, cf. section 97 , PCS. 2. However, from this amount an amount equal to 2,65 ‰ shall be deducted, corresponding to the IOC shares allocated to vessels engaged exclusively in fishing with hooks.

PCS. 2. The balance is distributed for the following purposes:

1) 10 ‰ for fishing in accordance with section 96 (1). 2nd

2) 30 ‰ to a reserve pool.

3) The remaining amount for fishing with IOC.

§ 99. If, on September 1, a portion of the amount devoted to hooked fishing or a quantity that the vessel owners have notified to the Swedish Agency for the Environment that they do not wish to refine that year, the Danish Agency for Nature and Fisheries may, after consultation, from the Business Fisheries Committee decide when to allocate this balance to vessels with mackerel license.

PCS. 2. The quantities are distributed in relation to the individual vessels' IOC. NaturErhvervstyrelsen may also not allocate used reserve quantities, cf. section 98 (1). 2, No. 2, and annual quantities that have been withdrawn on the basis of permission withdrawal. Quantities that are not fished in a given year will be included in the reserve pool.

Conditions for fishing for vessels authorized to fish mackerel

§ 100. Vessels fishing for mackerel shall fish, carry and land the catches taken on each fishing trip.

PCS. 2. Fishing can not be fished, but fishing can take place as a pair of fishery, each bringing and landing the amount assigned to each vessel. Par fishing must be carried out according to the applicable rules, including that the vessels must be on the same license list.

Particularly about transfer

§ 101. After all or part of the transfer of a vessel's quota share of mackerel, the dispatching vessel shall not fish mackerel without permission or with hooks.

PCS. 2. If quota share has been transferred from a vessel carrying bottom nets fishing, the limitation in paragraph 1 shall apply. 1 for all the vessels in which the vessel owner is the owner or co-owner of the vessel.

§ 102. By way of derogation from the rule in section 52, the NatureEconomy Board may authorize a vessel to hand over an amount corresponding to more than 25% of the vessel's total annual amount in case of accident.

PCS. 2. The Nature Authority may, irrespective of the rule in section 52, grant permission that a vessel's entire owner group may, when applying for a vessel replacement, transfer the right to fish all the yearly amount during the period from a vessel being deleted by the Norwegian Maritime Authority's vessel register to the replaced by another vessel, but not exceeding 18 months.

Mackerel in Faroese and Norwegian fishing zone

§ 103. Mackerel in Faroese fishing zone is allocated vessels with access license to Faroese zone in proportion to the quota shares that vessels have in Faroese zone.

PCS. 2. Access licenses available to Denmark in the Norwegian zone are allocated among the vessels with the largest share of mackerel per. January 1 in a given year. The permits may add conditions for the licenses to be returned when the quantities have been upgraded to allow access licenses to be made available to other vessels.

CHAPTER 13 HERRING IN THE NORTH SEA, SKAGERRAK AND KATTEGAT, AS WELL AS ATLANTIC HERRING

General provisions

§ 104. Only vessels whose owners have a permit issued pursuant to sections 17-18 must fish, bring and land herring in the North Sea, Skagerrak and Kattegat, as well as Atlantic salmon.

PCS. 2. By way of derogation from subsection 1, vessels not authorized for herring in accordance with sections 17-18 must fish, bring and land herring if

1) landing up to 400 kg from one fishing trip per day or night

2) The vessel fishing, bringing and landing herring throughout the year is only used for fishing with bottom yarn and other pole gear.

§ 105. The Nature Authority shall issue permission, cf. section 104 (1). 2, to fish an annual amount of herring to owners of vessels allocated to IOC of herring per. 1 January 2003 and which have not transferred quota shares to other vessels. In addition, permission is granted to owners who subsequently have documented against the Danish Nature Agency that a right to herring fishing with quota shares has been acquired with the vessel concerned.

PCS. 2. Fisheries with annual quantities allocated from the generation and reserve pool for herring shall also be authorized.

§ 106. The National Energy Authority calculates the annual quantities for a given year on the basis of the quota shares available to each vessel. 31 December of the previous year.

PCS. 2. Prior to the calculation of annual quantities, the following shares of the Danish quota are sold for the following purposes:

1) 11.0 ‰ for the North Sea and 10.032 ‰ for Skagerrak / Kattegat for herring fishing.

2) 50.0 ‰ in North Sea, Skagerrak and Kattegat, respectively, and Atlantic Herring for the Herring Generation and Reserve Pool, including at least 12.5 ‰ to reserve and a maximum of 37.5 ‰ for a Generation Change Pool.

3) 9.43 ‰ for the North Sea and 20,314 ‰ for Skagerrak / Kattegat, for the generation and reserve pool, corresponding to the quota shares that were allocated to the reserve pool in 2003 as a result of the withdrawal of allocated quota shares.

4) Quota shares that may expire and then access the generational and reserve pool because the quota shares have been transferred in violation of the rules.

PCS. 3. Where the quantities disposed of pursuant to paragraph 1 1 and 2, or when the total allowable catches of herring allocated to Denmark pursuant to the regulations of the European Union have been upgraded, or opacity is deemed to be imminent, the Nature Agency shall suspend the fishery concerned. Notice of this is issued in accordance with Appendix 6.

§ 107. Vessels fishing herring shall fish, carry and land the catches taken on each fishing trip.

PCS. 2. Fishing can not be fished, but fishing can take place as a pair of fishery, each bringing and landing the amount assigned to each vessel. Par fishing must be carried out according to the applicable rules, including that the vessels must be on the same license list.

Section 108. It is not allowed to store herring in the same space as fish that has not been treated for consumption. Except here are permitted by-catches of herring in industrial fisheries.

Reserve pool and (generational change)

Section 109. In the reserve pool, in addition to amounts allocated pursuant to section 106, subsection 2, No. 2, also amounts that vessel owners notify to the Danish Eco-nomic Agency that they do not wish to fish for the year in question, as well as the amount of annual quantities involved.

For additional analytical, business and investment opportunities information,
please contact Global Investment & Business Center, USA
at (703) 370-8082. Fax: (703) 370-8083. E-mail: ibpusa3@gmail.com
Global Business and Investment Info Databank - www.ibpus.com

PCS. 2. NaturErhvervstyrelsen has the disposal of the reserve pool, including any quota exchanges with other countries and possibly overfishing, and possibly increase of the amount for bottom nets, etc. If the pool or parts thereof are not disposed of for other purposes, the NaturErhvervstyrelsen for the year in question may hand over the quantities to the vessels, There are allocated quota shares of herring or amounts of herring from the generation and reserve pool. Allotments are made in proportion to the quantities distributed.

§ 110. The Nature Agency shall annually allocate the quantities in the generational shift pool to younger fishermen who have submitted an application for this and fulfill the conditions set out in section 111. For applicants who have received a previous amount of age, section 112 also applies.

PCS. 2. Each fisherman can, as a rule, be allocated an annual amount from the pool for up to a total of 3 years.

PCS. 3. In the application, the applicant must indicate the amount of quantity, cf. section 112, from which waters are applied for.

PCS. 4. If, at the expiration of the application deadline, the NatureEconomy Agency has not received applications for the allocation of Atlantic herring from the pool, the NatureEconomy Board allocates the amount of Atlantic herring to the Atlantic, cf. section 106 (1). 2, No. 2, to eligible vessels as soon as possible.

PCS. 5. Applications from fishermen who wish for herring from the pool in a given year must be received by the NaturErhvervstyret by 18 January of the year in question.

PCS. 6. Newly established fishermen established after the deadline may also submit applications until November 1 of the year in question. Herring can be awarded if there is still herring in the pot.

§ 111. Ready for herring from the generation shift pool are fishermen with A status which, in the first year of allocation of the annual amount, meet the following conditions:

1) The applicant must not be over 45 years at the time of submission of the application.

2) The applicant must establish himself as owner or co-owner of a vessel in the year in which the herring may be fished, cf. section 112 (1). 2, 3rd paragraph and paragraphs. 4. The applicant shall not have an ownership interest in the vessel in advance. The ownership must be at least DKK 500,000 and at least 10% in relation to the vessel's insurance value.

3) The applicant must not already have established himself as an owner or co-owner of a vessel in which the ownership interest in question has exceeded the insurance value of more than DKK 1,000,000.

PCS. 2. It is a prerequisite for the allocation of a quantity in each catch state and the maintenance of the permit for that applicant to participate actively in the fisheries. The person concerned shall participate in the fishing for at least 1/3 of the days when the vessel is at sea after the establishment has taken place. The NatureEuropean Agency may, upon application, approve that participation in teaching at the skipper and navigation schools equals active participation in the fisheries.

§ 112. Each applicant may be allocated a total of 200 tonnes in total for establishment with a vessel.

PCS. 2. In allocating the volumes, NaturErhvervstyrelsen takes the starting point of the number of eligible applicants, as applicants who have previously been allocated an annual amount from the generation change pool have priority to a quantity from the pool. If an application can not be fully met in the requested waters, the applicant is offered allocation in other waters to the extent available. For later years, including applicants who will be established after 1 November, a quantity may be allocated to the extent that amounts are available.

PCS. 3. It is a condition for issuing a license to fish the amount allocated in that year that the establishment is completed by 1 November.

PCS. 4. If there are insufficient quantities of herring available to new applicants in a given year, these applicants will have priority over the following years in relation to new applicants in the year in question.

§ 113. It is a prerequisite for the allocation that the fisherman has fulfilled the condition of active participation in the fishing year of the previous year, cf. section 111 (1). 2, and continue to be part of the owners with at least the same ownership interest as at the time of establishment.

PCS. 2. Notwithstanding the provision in subsection 1, deductions may be made in the amount allocated to each vessel from the pool in a given year if

1) the amount of the year allocated to the vessel from the pool in the previous year was not renewed; or

2) Less than 90% of the vessel's total registered landings of herring in the previous year were disposed of for consumption. The percentage is calculated on the basis of the registered landings from the relevant waters, during the period from the fishing permit, issued in the preceding year to the end of the year.

PCS. 3. Deductions in accordance with subsections 2 may be made with a proportion corresponding to the difference between the amount allocated and the amount of the fish caught, cf. 2, No. 1, and the difference between the share disposed of for consumption from the vessel and 90% of the total landed quantities of herring from the waters during the period, cf. 2, No. 2.

§ 114. If a vessel is wholly or partly owned by a younger fisherman who has been allocated an annual amount of herring from the generation change pool, the NatureEconomy Authority may grant permission for the annual quantity to be maintained for fishing purposes.

PCS. 2. Permission is granted only if the requirements of section 111 1, No. 2, for the younger fisher's share of ownership is also met for the new vessel and the new vessel has been placed in the Danish fishing fleet by 1 November in a given year.

Particularly about transfer etc.

Section 115. Annual quantities allocated from the generation shift pool may not be transferred, cf. section 52 (1). 3 on accident and disease and section 93 2, regarding vessel replacement.

§ 116. The IOC shares allocated on the basis of fishing in the Limfjord may only be fished in the Limfjord. This applies regardless of whether the quota shares have been transferred to one or more other vessels.

PCS. 2. The vessel's total ownership can transfer up to 25% of the vessel's annual volume in the Limfjord for fishing in the North Sea outside the Limfjord. For vessels where a fisherman is the owner or co-owner of both the delivery and the receiving vessel, up to 75% of the annual quantities for fishing in the North Sea outside Limfjorden can be transferred. Vessels which transfer up to 75% of the annual quantities of herring in the Limfjord for fishing in the North Sea may transfer quantities exceeding 25% stated in section 52 First

PCS. 3. The possibility of transferring up to 75% of the annual quantities for fishing in the North Sea outside Limfjorden pursuant to subsections 2 ends if the owner of the delivery vessel is changed after 25 August 2011.

PCS. 4. No quantities of annual quantities or quota shares allocated on the basis of fishing outside Limfjorden may be transferred to fishing in the Limfjord. Furthermore, herring can not be awarded from the reserve pool, cf. section 106 (1). 2, No. 3 for fishing in the Limfjord

Access licenses to other countries' fishing zones

Section 117. Access licenses available to Denmark for the fishing of Atlantic herring in the Faroese zone, the Norwegian zone around Jan Mayen and the Norwegian fishing zone are distributed among the vessels with the largest annual amount of Atlantic herring. The available quantities of herring in the zones concerned are distributed proportionally to the vessels' total annual amount of Atlantic herring per January 1 for vessels with access licenses. Changes in the vessels' total annual volume after transfer of quota shares will only affect the entry licenses from 1 January in the subsequent fishing years.

PCS. 2. Access licenses can not be transferred.

CHAPTER 14 TOBIS IN EU WATERS OF THE NORTH SEA, SKAGERRAK AND KATTEGAT AS WELL AS NORWEGIAN NORTH SEA ZONE, BLUE WHITING IN EU WATERS AND INTERNATIONAL WATERS, BLUE WHITING IN FAROESE ZONE, HORSE MACKEREL IN ICES AREAS IIA, IVA, VB, VI, VIIA-C AND EK, VIIIA , B, D AND E, XII AND XIV, SEA-GULLED IN EU WATERS AND INTERNATIONAL WATERS OF ICES DIVISIONS VI, VII AND VIII, AND NORTH SEA (EU) WATERSPIKES, SKAGERRAK AND KATTEGAT

General provisions

Section 118. The Nature Authority authorizes fishing for an annual amount of the above quotas to owners of vessels that have over the IOC of the quotas concerned. If Denmark receives a sperm quota for a given year, the Nature Agency will decide whether the size of the quota provides grounds for issuing a license to fish an annual amount of owners of vessels that have disposal over the IOC of Sperling in the North Sea and Skagerrak and Kattegat.

PCS. 2. For the above quotas, allocate before allocation of annual quantities on the basis of IOC for each vessel per. January 1 in a given year for rationing fishery:

1) 5% of the quota of sandeel in EU waters in the North Sea, Skagerrak and Kattegat, as well as in the Norwegian zone in the North Sea, at least 15,000 tonnes.

2) 15% of a possible Danish quota for spatling in EU waters in the North Sea, as well as Skagerrak and Kattegat, with a maximum of 10,000 tonnes. To the extent that, on 15 October each year, unfinished quantities of the portion of the quota quota allocated for rationing fish will

be assessed as to whether the residual amount can be distributed to vessels that have disposal over the IOC for spatling.

PCS. 3. In addition to those referred to in subsection 2 mentioned shares and volumes are allocated before allocation of annual volumes the following percentages of the individual quotas to reserves:

1) 50 ‰ of sandeel in EU waters in the North Sea, Skagerrak and Kattegat, as well as in the Norwegian zone in the North Sea.

2) 50 ‰ of a possible sperling quota in EU waters in the North Sea, as well as the Skagerrak and Kattegat.

PCS. 4. The reserves may be used for the purposes specified in Section 53, including participation of first-time and younger fishermen in the fisheries.

PCS. 5. Before the end of the first quarter, after consulting the Business Fisheries Committee, decide what percentage of the reserves, cf. 3, which may be released and distributed proportionally to vessels with quota shares. In this connection, Consider which projects for the development of fisheries towards the consumption of industrial fish, cf. section 53 1, No. 2), which can be expected during the year.

Section 119. The IOC, available to the individual vessel for fishing at the Tobacco quota in EU waters of the North Sea, Skagerrak and Kattegat, also includes a possible quota of sandeel in the Norwegian North Sea North Sea.

PCS. 2. To the extent that the The quota referred to in paragraph 1 is divided into several administrative areas, before 1 April, the conditions for vessels' participation in fisheries in the individual areas shall be determined. The terms are published by notice issued in accordance with Appendix 6.

§ 120. If IOC has been allocated to an industrial quota for a vessel, the vessel as identified by the EU identification number after 1 January 2008 must not be used for rationing fishing on that quota.

PCS. 2. The limitations in subsection 1 also applies to recycled tonnage from vessels applied and allocated to the IOC for the industrial quota concerned on the basis of.

Sperling in the North Sea, Skagerrak and Kattegat

§ 121. Targeted shredding fishing may only be carried out if a sorting grate is used which uses a fixed grid in steel, plastic or fiberglass / nylon with a maximum 35 mm braking distance. The grate must be mounted in a grid section in front of the bag covering the entire section of the section and with an opening that allows the discharge of all the fish that does not pass through the grid.

PCS. 2. Changes to the design of the sorting grid, including requirements for grid spacing, assembly, etc. will be published by notice issued in accordance with Annex 6.

PCS. 3. It is forbidden to pursue targeted fishing for sperling in the Norwegian zone in the North Sea.

Tobis in EU waters in the North Sea, Skagerrak and Kattegat, as well as the Norwegian zone in the North Sea

Section 122. No sandeel may be fished before 1 April in a given year.

§ 123. To the extent that the Tobacco Fisheries is commenced without establishing a final quota, the quantities of each vessel landed in the total annual quantities to which the vessel is subsequently allocated. The annual quantities are distributed in proportion to the quota shares each vessel has disposed of. To the extent that some vessels have landed larger volumes than the vessel's quota share justifies, the annual quantities the other vessels can be allocated proportionately.

PCS. 2. Of the total quota shall be reserved from the date the amount of the quota has been definitively determined for the amount of rationing fishery, cf. section 118, which may be fished by vessels not having quota shares. The proportion of rationing fishery can be reduced in view of the size of the total landed quantities for vessels not in possession of IOC until the date of the quota determination, cf. First

PCS. 3. Among others In view of the quota sizes, fishing conditions, etc., established by rules issued by the European Union for the practice of poultry fishing, the terms and conditions for the pursuit of fishing activities and the quantities sold shall be determined by notice issued in accordance with Annex 6.

CHAPTER 15 INDUSTRIAL FISHING

General rules

§ 124. Only vessels whose owners have a license issued pursuant to section 15 may engage in industrial fishing. Applications for a license that apply throughout the year may be applied under the terms that will apply to industrial fishing at any time. For vessels whose owners are authorized for industrial fishing on 10 December of the previous year, without the prior application, permission shall be issued for the year in question under the terms of the license.

PCS. 2. In addition to the license for industrial fishing pursuant to subsections 1 Requests for individual industrial fisheries are required to the extent that this is stated in the provisions.

PCS. 3. Vessels for which an industrial fishing permit has been issued pursuant to paragraph 1. 1, may pursue other fisheries according to the rules applicable to these fisheries.

PCS. 4. In case of industrial fishing, a notice of arrival and unloading shall be given in accordance with Annex 5a.

PCS. 5. The industrial fishing permit is subject to the requirement that only industrial fishing vessels in ports shall be permitted where the vessel may use a semi-automatic sampling approved by the National Agency for the purpose of obtaining representative samples for inspection.

§ 125. Prior to commencement of fishing under a private agreement outside the Danish fisheries area and outside the European Union fisheries agreements, the license for industrial fisheries must be reported to the NaturErhvervstyrelsen, cf. § 131.

Section 126. In accordance with Annex 6, the NatureEconomy Board may announce that the fishery is set in a specified watershed. This may depend on the species composition of industrial fisheries in this area and the utilization of the total available quantity of by-catches.

PCS. 2. The Nature Agency may, in accordance with Annex 6, declare that industrial fisheries for a specified period must be made in accordance with a special fishing plan.

PCS. 3. The provisions in subsection The mentioned waters shall be mentioned in the notice.

Section 127. For fishing and landing of industrial fish from the North Sea, Skagerrak and Kattegat, the proportion of fish that can not be sorted for species determination may not exceed 25% of the total amount of fish on board.

PCS. 2. The Nature Authority may, when special weather conditions occur, allow a larger proportion of indelible fish on board than 25%.

PCS. 3. If a shipowner considers that a situation has occurred that causes the proportion of unsorted fish in the cargo to become too high, this must be notified to the NaturErhvervstyret as soon as possible and prior to arrival at the port. Inquiry can be made by telephone on +47 72 18 56 09. In connection with this, the master must provide information about the species composition of the cargo.

Provisions for certain industrial fisheries exercised under ration conditions

Sprinkling in the English Channel

§ 128. Only vessels whose owners have a license issued pursuant to section 15 may fish, bring and land sprat from the English Channel.

CHAPTER 16 RATION

General rules for rationing fishery

§ 129. In fisheries regulated as ration fishing, a fisherman may, for a period of irrespective of the length of the period, only participate in fishing as a vessel operator on one vessel:

1) A master of a MAF shall not in the same ration period be a master of a FKA vessel or an additional vessel fishing for regulated species.

2) A vessel master may be a leader in several FKA vessels on the condition that none of the vessels participate in ration fishing.

PCS. 2. The Nature Agency may, regardless of paragraph 1 grant permission for a master of a vessel to change a vessel during a regulatory period.

PCS. 3. By decision on the issuance and content of licenses in the fisheries regulated under conditions of ration, including the number of licenses and the amount of effort in each fishery, the Nature Agency shall emphasize the considerations referred to in section 34 2, the Fisheries Act, including the supply situation and the rational utilization of the quantities available at a given time. In cases where selection must be made among applicants, the NaturErhvervstyrelsen can prioritize where account can be taken of the dependence of the applicants on the fishery concerned and the possibility of disposing of the catch for human consumption. In addition, emphasis can be placed on advice from organizations represented in the Business Fisheries Committee.

General ration restrictions and volume statements

§ 130. Fish landed in a given ration period are amortized on the ration of this period.

PCS. 2. When a vessel's periodication of a species in a Regulatory Area has been reared, it is not permitted during the Ration Period to initiate fishing for that species upon release of fishing gear.

PCS. 3. Notwithstanding paragraph 2, for species regulated by calendar weather, it is permitted to commence fishing for the current calendar recovery from Friday on the preceding calendar week.

§ 131. For fisheries regulated under conditions of rationing, the withdrawal of authorization or change from one regulatory area to another may only occur if at the time of the shift the maximum amount of the authorized catches is proportional to the number of days in ration period in the fisheries left. However, this condition shall not apply to switching to unregulated fisheries or by switching to fisheries of the annual quantities that the vessel may fish, bring and land under the FKA and IOK rules.

PCS. 2. After switching, it is permitted to fish, bring and land a proportion of the amount of ration proportional to the number of days remaining during the ration period of the changed fishery.

PCS. 3. The shift time is considered to be the time when fishing in another regulatory area begins.

PCS. 4. Withdrawal must be made as specified in Appendix 2.

§ 132. Unless it is notified in accordance with Annex 6 that other rules apply, vessels which, according to the National Agency of Commerce's vessel register, are owned by one or more commercial fishermen, must fish, bring and land 1/3 of the ship's rations for all species. However, for cod fishing, unless otherwise stated in accordance with Annex 6, vessels shall be allowed to land half-ship riots. For fish plaice and salmon in the Baltic Sea, these vessels shall, unless otherwise notified in accordance with Annex 6, land the same rations as vessels owned by commercial fishermen.

Ration fishing on FKA quotas for MAF vessels

§ 133. For vessels designated as MAF vessels, in accordance with Annex 6, the quantities of the quotas referred to in section 44 (1) shall be notified. 1, and in section 44 2, No. 4 and 7, it is allowed to fish, bring and land per. Quarter for vessels of the following length:

1) Under 6 m.

2) At least 6 m and under 9 m.

3) 9 m and above.

PCS. 2. Depending on the evolution of fishing in relation to the available quantities, changes may be made to the fishing conditions for each quota. Any changes will be notified in accordance with Appendix 6.

PCS. 3. If, on the basis of the catch progression, following advice from the Business Fisheries Committee, it is estimated that the quantities available for MAF vessels are not perished, the quantities by rules notified in accordance with Annex 6 may be made available to other vessel categories.

Transfer of annual quantity from FKA vessel to MAF vessel

§ 134. Within the part of the annual volumes, the individual FKA vessel may transfer to another vessel, cf. section 51, in a given year, annual quantities may be transferred from one or more FKA vessels to a MAF vessel. The transfers may relate to annual quantities in several waters / regulatory areas.

PCS. 2. Fishing on the transferred annual quantities may not commence until the Nature Authorities have granted permission. It is a condition for the license that the MAF vessel rests and landes fish from a regulatory area during each ration period for the remainder of that year, only fishing.

PCS. 3. Following the issuance of an authorization pursuant to subsections 2, the vessel has the status of MAF extra vessel for the rest of the year in question. The vessel is allowed to fish, bring and land the rations that apply at any time to MAF vessels in the waters or waters where the vessel has received additional annual quantities. The additional annual quantities, cf. 1, can be fished at any time the rest of the year.

PCS. 4. No permission may be granted for a MAF vessel to forward them in paragraph 1. 1, unless it is a vessel replacement.

PCS. 5. Application for transfer of annual quantity to a MAF vessel may be submitted to the NaturErhvervstyrelsen on 1 February.

Ration fishery for bottom-nest fishermen who have chosen the right to fish on shares of cod and herring quotas in the Baltic Sea instead of FKA

§ 135. For a tedder company which does not use any gear other than bottom yarn during the year and where the main vessel is not classified as a FKA vessel, a license may be granted for ration fishing. Allocation is based on the longest vessel in the company. Only one permit for a vessel can be obtained from each bottom nets company during the year.

§ 136. Owners of vessels that have chosen in the course of 2006 to fish for shares of cod and herring quota in the Baltic Sea instead of FKA, and which are still exclusively used for fishing with bottom yarn and bundle-like gear, may obtain permission for cod and orchard fishery under ration conditions within the amount allocated pursuant to section 45 1, No. 7.

Ration fishing on FKA quotas for FKA vessels

§ 137. Only FKA vessels for which a license has been applied and obtained is allowed to participate in ration fishing on a quota covered by section 44 (1). 1. Authorization can not be obtained if, after 1 January 2014, quota shares of the quota concerned have been transferred from the vessel or if in that year the amount of the quota concerned has been transferred from the vessel.

PCS. 2. FKA vessels for which a license has been granted to participate in ration fishing may not fish outside the waters covered by the permit during the permit period.

PCS. 3. Regardless of the application for a FKA vessel and a license to participate in ration fishing, landed quantities of the quota concerned will at all times initially depart from the vessel's current annual amount, unless it has already been fished.

PCS. 4. Application for a license for ration fishing with a vessel participating in pool fishing shall contain the consent of the other participants in pool fishing. The consent can be given by the pool manager on behalf of the other pool participants or his deputy.

Ration fishing on FKA quotas for Other Vessels

Section 138. Unless otherwise stipulated by rules notified pursuant to Annex 6, vessels designated as Other Vessels may not participate in the rationalization of the quotas allocated to MAF vessels.

PCS. 2. By rules notified in accordance with Annex 6, it may be stipulated that owners of Other Vessels will be able to apply for rationing on FKA quotas on specified terms.

Ration fisheries for consumer quotas that are not FKA quotas

Cod by Svalbard and Bjørneø (ICES sub-areas II a and b)

§ 139. Only vessels whose owners have a permit issued by the Danish Nature Agency, cf. section 15, must fish, bring and land cod from the waters of Svalbard and Bjørneø.

PCS. 2. Application for permission must be received by NaturErhvervstyrelsen no later than 1 February.

Whiting in the North Sea and in Skagerrak / Kattegat

§ 140. It is not permitted to fish, bring and land whales for purposes other than human consumption. Except here are permitted by-catches in industrial fisheries.

weever

§ 141. Only vessels whose owners have a permit issued by the Swedish National Agency for the Environment, cf. section 15, must fish, bring and land fjäing.

PCS. 2. By way of derogation from subsection 1, it is permitted without special permission to fish, bring and land a feather if

1) No gear with mesh sizes of less than 90 mm shall be carried on the fishing trip concerned or

2) The feather brought and landed is the fish in the bottom yarn.

Special fisheries and fisheries in third country fishing zones and in international waters

For additional analytical, business and investment opportunities information,
please contact Global Investment & Business Center, USA
at (703) 370-8082. Fax: (703) 370-8083. E-mail: ibpusa3@gmail.com
Global Business and Investment Info Databank - www.ibpus.com

Fishing in international waters or activities related to fisheries regulated by regional fisheries organizations

§ 142. Only vessels whose owners are licensed pursuant to section 15 may fish, bring and land fish from international waters. An application must be submitted to the Nature Agency with details of which fishing plan is planned.

PCS. 2. Only vessels whose owners have a license issued pursuant to section 15 may fish, bring and land fish or participate in other activities in connection with the activity covered by rules set by regional fisheries organizations.

Fishing under effort regulation in the waters west and south of the British Isles

§ 143. Only vessels whose owners are licensed pursuant to section 15 may fish, bring and land fish from ICES areas VX as well as CECAF 34.1.1., 34.1.2. and 34.2.0.

PCS. 2. Authorization for fishing for demersal species in ICES zones VX and CECAF 34.1.1., 34.1.2. and 34.2.0 can include contain rules on the maximum allowed effort days in the individual action areas.

Deepwater rains in Greenland waters

§ 144. Only vessels whose owners are licensed pursuant to section 15 may fish, carry and land deepwater rains from ICES zones XIV and V, as well as NAFO areas 0 and 1.

Soldering in Greenland waters

§ 145. Only vessels whose owners are authorized pursuant to section 15 may fish, bring and land solder from ICES zones XIV and V and NAFO areas 0 and 1.

Blue whiting in Faroese and Greenland waters

§ 146. Only vessels whose owners have a license issued pursuant to section 15 may fish, bring and land blue whiting from Faroese and Greenland waters.

Shrimps in the North Atlantic NAFO area

§ 147. Only vessels whose owners are licensed pursuant to section 15 may fish, carry and land deepwater rains in the area regulated by NAFO.

Deep-sea species

Section 148. Only vessels authorized to do so under section 15 may fish, carry and land deep sea species. The list of deep sea species is set out in Appendix 11.

PCS. 2. The Nature Agency shall issue the permit within the European Union's rules for the operation of this fishery by Danish vessels. When issuing a permit, emphasis is placed on the vessels' prior dependence on this fishery.

Other species in Norwegian fishing zone

Section 149. For other species in the Norwegian fishing zone in the North Sea, this Order means all other species of fish, shellfish and molluscs other than cod, haddock, dark corn, whiting, plaice, mackerel, herring, sandeel, sperling, blue whiting, shrimps, long, brosme, sea bag and deepwater swamp.

Section 150. When the available amount of other species in the Norwegian fishing zone in the North Sea is increased by 50%, a decision is made as to whether a regulation should be introduced. Any conditions will be notified in accordance with Appendix 6.

PCS. 2. Vessels engaged in nesting and longline fishing shall be exempted from this fishing activity from paragraph 1. 1 mentioned regulation.

§ 151. Only vessels whose owners have a license issued by the Swedish National Agency for the Protection of Nature, pursuant to section 15, fish, bring and land horse mackerel, mackerel, stream, school eel and sprat from the Norwegian fishing zone in the North Sea.

Fish and crustaceans covered by Norwegian prohibition of discarding

Section 152. Catches subject to prohibition of discards in the Norwegian fishing zone shall be rescinded immediately after entry into EU waters if the fish can not be brought and landed in accordance with this notice or according to the following rules:

1) Minimum standards laid down in the Executive Order on minimum size for fish and crustaceans in saline and Council Regulation laying down technical measures for the conservation of fishery resources.

2) Rules for authorized by-catches and target species of the species concerned, cf. Council Regulation laying down technical measures for the conservation of fishery resources, Council Regulation fixing the total allowable catches for certain fish stocks and groups of fish stocks and certain conditions for fishing for these catches and Council Regulation laying down the conditions for landing herring for industry other than the food industry.

Herring in the English Channel (ICES subarea VII d)

§ 153. Only vessels whose owners have a license issued pursuant to sections 15 may fish, bring and land herring from the English Channel. Section 107 also applies to fishing for herring in the English Channel.

CHAPTER 17 EFFORT REGULATION IN GENERAL

Section 154. In fisheries where only limited effort in terms of time, use of power, etc. may be allowed, the permitted effort may be divided for use over the year. Rules may be laid down for the application of the efforts of individual vessels and groups of vessels, as may be required for a permit to participate in these fisheries.

PCS. 2. The Nature Agency may issue rules and requirements for permission pursuant to subsection (2). 1 in accordance with Annex 6.

CHAPTER 18 KW DAYS IN CONNECTION WITH THE RESTORATION OF CERTAIN STOCKS IN ICES ZONES III A, IC, VI A, VII A, VII IN EU WATERS WITHIN ZONES II A AND V B

Section 155. In accordance with the rules of the European Union, for each of the categories of tools in the 2 - 4 waters of Danish registered fishing vessels during the period 1 February in a given year to 31 January of the following year, a maximum amount of kW days may be used.

PCS. 2. In the North Sea / Skagerrak, the maximum permitted number of kW days is valid for the following categories of gear:

1) Bundtrawl and wodder 100 mm and above (3AN / 4, TR. 1).

2) Bundtrawl and vod 70-99 mm (3AN / 4, TR. 2).

3) Bundtrawl and vod 16-31 mm (3AN / 4, TR. 3).

4) Yarn, infiltration grid (3AN / 4, GN1).

5) Twisted yarn (3AN / 4, GT1).

6) Langliner (3AN / 4, LL1).

7) Bomb trawl 120 mm and above (3AN / 4, BT1).

8) Bomb trawl 80-119 mm (3AN / 4, BT2).

PCS. 3. For Kattegat the maximum permitted number of kW days for the following categories of tools applies:

1) Bundtrawl and wodder 100 mm and above (3AS, TR. 1).

2) Bundtrawl and vod 70-99 mm (3AS, TR. 2).

3) Bundtrawl and vod 16-31 mm (3AS, TR. 3).

4) Yarn, infiltration grid (3AS, GN1).

5) Twisted yarn (3AS, GT1).

6) Langliner (3AS, LL1).

PCS. 4. The items mentioned in subsection 2-3, no. 1-8 and in paragraph 4, Nos. 1-6, each constitute a segment with a certain number of kW days available.

Section 156. Fishing subject to the European Union's kW-day regulation may only take place if the NatureEconomy Board has granted kW-days permission to the vessel owner.

PCS. 2. The Nature Agency shall notify vessel owners of the management period 1 February for a given year until 31 January of the following year to vessels that have been allocated kW units pursuant to Order No. 541 of 15 June 2009 or which subsequently have acquired kW shares. The permit gives access to fishing in the gear segments where the vessel has kW shares.

PCS. 3. If, on application, kW-shares are allocated on the basis of fishing with a vessel which has been discontinued or not yet registered as a fishing vessel, the Nature Agency may issue a kW-day permit, cf. 1, to the vessel which the applicant places as registered Danish fishing vessel.

PCS. 4. KW shares provide for the allocation of annual quantities of kW days in later management periods. Rules for the pursuit of fishing for the vessels authorized to participate may be laid down, cf. section 159.

PCS. 5. Until processing of the allocation of kW units and not yet finalized complaints regarding the allocation of kW shares has been completed, the treatment of allocation of kW shares may lead to a downgrading or cancellation of allocated kW shares in view of the total distribution of the kW days available for distribution in each segment pursuant to the paragraph 2 mentioned executive order. If the downgrading results in no kW shares being allocated to a vessel, the NatureEconomy revokes the license issued to participate in the fisheries during the management period, cf. 1. Deduction and cancellation of authorization may take place regardless of whether the relevant kW shares or the associated annual quantities have been transferred to another vessel before the downgrading or cancellation takes place.

§ 157. In the light of the consumption of kW days available to Denmark, the NatureEconomy may set conditions that allow vessels with kW-days permission, cf. section 156, to participate in fishing in several gear segments and waters. The terms will then be notified in accordance with Appendix 6.

§ 158. The Nature Authority may, upon application, allow a vessel that has over kW units in gear segments BT1 and BT2 to switch to fishing in another gear segment. The Nature Agency may grant the permit if it is assessed at the time of the permit that during the management period the vessel's fishing may take place within the total utilization of the kW days in the gear segment to be replaced. It is a condition for the permit that the vessel permanently passes to the second gear segment.

PCS. 2. For vessels licensed under paragraph 1, in the coming management periods, where the kW shares allow for the allocation of annual quantities of kW days, it may be permitted for the vessel to use a number of kW days in the gear segment to be changed to the maximum equivalent to the number of kW days that the vessel would be entitled to in the boom trawl segments.

PCS. 3. The Nature Agency may not authorize other vessels to be equipped for beam trawling instead of vessels authorized pursuant to paragraph 1. First

PCS. 4. Permission to switch to other gear segment pursuant to subsections 1 can not be granted to vessels authorized for hunting fishing.

PCS. 5. In connection with permission pursuant to subsection 1, kW days are transferred from the boom trawl segments to the gear segment to which the vessel is transferred, cf. section 160 (1). 3, No. 5.

§ 159. In view of the total number of kW days available to Denmark in the individual segment, cf. section 155 (1). 2-3, and its utilization, the Nature Agency may lay down rules limiting the number of kW days that may be used by individual vessels for specified periods or ceasing fishing with the affected gear in the segment concerned. Limitations may also be introduced if this is necessary to comply with the maximum capacity measured in kW, which applies to Denmark, cf. Section 171. Notice is given of the terms in accordance with Appendix 6.

CHAPTER 19 KW FUND, ETC.

§ 160. The kW units available to Denmark in accordance with the European Union kW-day regulation, and which are not assigned by the National Energy Authority to individual vessels on the basis of kW, are included in the kW Fund. In addition, prior to the allocation of annual quantities of kW days in each individual year, the National Agency may decide that certain shares of Denmark's disposable quantities in the individual gear segments may be disposed of in the kW Fund.

PCS. 2. All kW days available to Denmark are included in the kW fund for a total regulation, cf. section 159, and the possibility of meeting the purposes mentioned in subsection (2). 3-5.

PCS. 3. The quantities sold each year in the kW Fund may be used for the following purposes:

1) Implementation of trade with other countries.

2) Development of fisheries.

3) Promotion of first-time young fishermen's participation in fisheries.

4) Coverage of possible overuse of Danish quantities of resources and for allocation in connection with handling of complaints.

5) Transfer of kW days to other segments for distribution for use in these tool categories.

6) Other purposes for which rules are laid down.

PCS. 4. Unallocated annual quantities in the kW Fund may be allocated proportionately to vessels with kW units or for the other purposes mentioned in paragraph 1 during the management period. Third

PCS. 5. Rules for allocating kW days from the kW Fund shall be determined after consulting the Business Fisheries Committee, insofar as the rules are not laid down in the Executive Order. The rules are published in accordance with Appendix 6.

CHAPTER 20 ALLOTMENT OF KW SHARES TO FIRST-TIME CREDITORS WHO HAVE BEEN GRANTED LOAN-FKA OR LOAN-IOK

§ 161. The Nature Agency may allow vessel owners who have obtained approval or prior approval as FKA-FE or IOKINDUSTRI-FE vessels after 1 January 2010 to apply for the allocation of kW shares that allow fishing with the relevant gear categories corresponding to to the FKA and IOK, which the vessel owner is made available as loan-FKA and loan-IOK. To the extent that the vessel already has the maximum number of kW days in the segment concerned, as set out in Appendix 16 of Order No. 541 of 15 June 2009, no additional allocation can be made. The application deadline is 1 June. Allotment of kW shares takes place only once a year on the basis of applications received on time.

PCS. 2. The Nature Agency shall carry out the calculation of the allocation in subsection 1 on the basis of an estimate of an average time spent in 2008 for fishing in the waters area of the quota concerned with the claimed gear category in relation to the quota share that the vessel has been made available as a loan FKA or loan IOK.

PCS. 3. Within the kW days allocated in the kW fund, see section 160, so far 2% of the Danish kW days in each of the segments listed in section 155 (3). 2-3 for the allocation of kW days cf. paragraph 1.

§ 162. To the extent that within the kW days allocated in the various segments pursuant to section 161, there are insufficient quantities to meet all applications, the allocations for the individual segments are reduced proportionately.

CHAPTER 21 TRANSFER OF KW SHARES TO OTHER VESSELS

§ 163. The kW shares allocated to a vessel are still linked to the vessel after ownership. Vessel owners may assign all the kW shares a vessel has disposed of to another vessel that meets the requirements of section 7.

PCS. 2. After transferring all kW units from one vessel to another, the Nature Agency may authorize the recipient vessel to participate in the fisheries in the segments for which the kW shares allow access to the vessel that has transferred the kW shares . As a rule, it is a prerequisite for the Naturhververstyrelsen to authorize the recipient vessel to participate in fishing instead of the ship delivered, that the receiving vessel does not have a registered engine power that is more than 20% larger relative to the engine of the vessel.

PCS. 3. After the transfer, the recipient vessel has access to fishing in the segments that the kW shares provide access to. The Nature Agency issues a license for kW days, cf. section 156 (1). 2, to the recipient vessel and at the same time withdraw permission of the vessel's kW-days.

PCS. 4. In connection with transfer to another vessel, the NaturErhvervsstyrelsen may, if there are special circumstances, including that the same owners have acquired another vessel in connection with vessel replacement, allow the vessel to which the kW shares are transferred to switch to other gear than the gear segments on which the vessel delivered has kW units. The receiver vessel can then fish during the management period in the gear segment (s) authorized to change instead of fishing in the gear segments that have been replaced.

PCS. 5. Replacement of gear segments may be permitted only if the NaturErhvervstyrelsen estimates that within the total number of kW days available to Denmark during the management period there is space in the gear segment that is replaced by the replacement of the vessel.

PCS. 6. If, in accordance with the rules for this, kW units have been allocated to a vessel which has been discontinued as a registered fishing vessel or a vessel has been discontinued after the grant, the kW may be transferred to another vessel in accordance with the same guidelines as for vessels, It is still registered as fishing vessels.

Transfer of kW shares to other vessels in later management periods, where the kW shares provide the basis for the allocation of annual volumes

Section 164. If in subsequent management periods it is decided that the kW shares will be the basis for the allocation of annual quantities, it will be possible to transfer allotments to other owners of vessels complying with the requirements of section 7 in whole or in part. The terms and

For additional analytical, business and investment opportunities information,
please contact Global Investment & Business Center, USA
at (703) 370-8082. Fax: (703) 370-8083. E-mail: ibpusa3@gmail.com
Global Business and Investment Info Databank - www.ibpus.com

conditions , and the time of transfer, shall be determined in a notice issued in accordance with Annex 6.

Generally about the transfer of kW units

Section 165. The vessel owner who has acquired the kW shares must document in writing to the NaturErhvervstyrelsen that the transfer has taken place.

PCS. 2. Notice of ownership of kW shares is registered in the National Agency for Economic Affairs.

PCS. 3. In the case of transfers of kW, the information referred to in Annex 16 shall be given to the Danish Environmental Protection Agency.

PCS. 4. Regardless of whether a kW has been transferred to a vessel, the Nature Authority may issue permission only to the recipient vessel for kW days if the vessel can obtain a permit within the maximum capacity, cf. sections 171-172.

Section 166. Nature Agency does not issue revised permit for fishing with the recipient vessel whose kW shares have been transferred to a vessel or owner who does not comply with the requirement in section 7. The Nature Authority may revoke an issued fishing license if it subsequently appears that The conditions in section 7 for the transfer of kW shares were not met at the time of issue of the license.

§ 167. If a vessel with kW units is erased by the National Agency of Commerce's vessel register without the kW shares previously being transferred to one or more vessels, the right to the kW shares will lapse and the kW shares will be transferred to the kW Fund.

PCS. 2. KW shares may, however, be maintained for up to 6 years if permission has been obtained for replacement of another vessel in the Norwegian Agency for Nature and Fisheries. In the period until the new vessel has been put into the fleet, the owner of the ship may transfer the vessel's kW shares.

§ 168. If a vessel ceases to be subject to European Union rules on the maximum permissible number of kW days, cf. Chapter 18, the right to the kW shares attached to the vessel shall lapse and the kW- The shares are transferred to the kW Fund. This applies regardless of whether the kW shares are transferred to another vessel.

Transfer and use of kW units in special situations

Section 169. If a vessel is taken over by a forced sale by a bank, the Danish Financial Supervisory Authority (formerly the Danish Fisheries Bank), Denmark's Ship Finance Fund or mortgage-creditors, mortgage holders may transfer the vessel's kW shares to owners of vessels that fulfill the requirements of the Fisheries Act to pursue business fishing.

PCS. 2. The National Economic Authority may, upon application, allow a surviving spouse or other heirs disposing of the vessel to transfer the vessel's kW shares to owners of vessels that fulfill the conditions.

§ 170. In cases where a vessel is transferred by a forced sale to a bank, the Danish Financial Supervisory Authority (formerly the Danish Fisheries Bank), the Danish Ship Finance Fund or to mortgage-creditors, and the NaturErhvervstyrelsen, in accordance with the regulations in the

Decree on vessels used for commercial fishing permits the vessel to be leased while allowing the vessel to fish according to its kW shares during the period during which the vessel is leased.

PCS. 2. If a vessel of a surviving spouse or other heirs is taken in accordance with the rules of the Executive Order on vessels used for commercial fishing, the vessel's kW shares shall be taken over at the same time. After the acquisition, the NatureEconomy Authority may authorize fishing according to the vessel's kW units and the transfer of kW units.

CHAPTER 22 MAXIMUM CAPACITY MEASURED IN KW FOR VESSELS AUTHORIZED TO FISH IN AN AREA OF ACTIVITY (KW-CEILING)

§ 171. The total capacity, expressed in kW, for vessels capable of obtaining kW-day permits shall not exceed the ceiling applicable to vessels for fishing in one of the North Sea / Skagerrak or Kattegat areas under the European Union rules.

PCS. 2. Before the issuance of kW days, the Nature Agency shall decide whether there is room for issue of the permit within the meaning of subsection 1 mentioned ceiling. At the same time as a kW-day permit is granted, the Nature Agency shall record the vessel on the list that the Member State shall establish and update in accordance with the rules of the European Union.

PCS. ThirdBy deciding which vessels can be admitted to and retaining space on the list, the NaturErhvervstyrelsen uses the priority specified in section 172. If a vessel can not be included on the list, the NatureEuropean Agency rejects the application for kW-day permission. This also applies even if the vessel owner has disposed of allocated kW units or has acquired these or annual quantities of kW days upon transfer. The right to entry on the list can not be transferred but is determined for the individual vessel which has at the time of application available over kW days solely in accordance with the rule in section 172. However, the right of entry on the list may be transferred to another vessel inserted in Danish fishing instead of a vessel which is being deleted at the same time. It is a prerequisite for this that the FKA or IOK associated with the replaced vessel,

Section 172. If there are several applications for admission to the list of vessels with kW-days permits than is permitted within the scope of the action ceiling, cf. section 171 (1), the Nature Agency shall prioritize the vessels referred to in subsection 2, Nos. 1-3, mentioned order. Vessels listed on the list retain the rights attached thereto, provided that the vessel continues to dispose of kW units or annual quantities. However, rules may be laid down that vessels not using the kW-day permit will be permanently or temporarily removed from the list.

PCS. 2. In relation to inclusion in the list of intervention ceilings, vessels are prioritized in the following order:

1) Vessels that have spent seaways in the area of action in 2008 or vessels included in a vessel replacement, cf. section 171 (1). 3, with such a vessel.

2) Vessels allocated to kW units pursuant to the rules in Chapter 21 of Order No. 541 of 15 June 2009 or vessels included in a vessel replacement with such a vessel.

3) Other vessels, which allocate over kW units or annual volumes, are included in the list to the extent available.

PCS. 3. Sealers or vessels filed as registered fishing vessels in the Nature Agency's vessel register with capacity in kW from launchers that have been granted rights to shares of kW days on the basis of calculation element 3, cf. section 186 of the section 156 . 2, mentioned order, is included in the priority set out in subsection 2 under No. 3.

CHAPTER 23 FISHING REGULATED BY CATCH QUOTAS

Section 173. To the extent that, in a given year after EU rules, Member States may allocate additional catches of cod for fishing by catch quotas to some vessels, vessels which have been granted a fishing quota for the previous year, and which has documented the fisheries and landed the catches in accordance with the terms. From 1 January, licenses shall be issued for these vessels to operate under the conditions applicable to catch quotas.

PCS. 2. Vessel owners who do not wish the vessel to continue as a catch quota may issue the license by 15 February of the year in question. It is a prerequisite for declaring the vessel that no additional amount has been used. It will be possible to divulge the license in part, so that it will only apply to Skagerrak and the North Sea or the Baltic Sea.

PCS. 3. The vessels shall be allocated additional quantities by 30% for annual quantities of cod up to 100 tonnes in the waters concerned and 20% for annual quantities exceeding 100 tonnes in the watershed in relation to the vessel's annual quantity based on the vessel's FKA on 1 January of that year.

PCS. 4. Depending on the final quotas and the associated conditions, etc. In the acts of the European Union, no matter what paragraph 3 sets other percentages and rules for the allocation of additional quantities as well as conditions for participation in fisheries. These shall be published in a notice issued in accordance with Annex 6.

PCS. 5. Vessels shall be so arranged that the master may establish and regularly apply the prescribed equipment for documentation of fishing, including documentation of total catches.

PCS. 6. The documentation must be carried out throughout the voyage, and the vessel owner and the master shall ensure that this is done and that all conditions imposed by the NaturErhvervstyrelsen in this respect are respected.

Section 174. Catch vessels shall, after the license has been issued for the remainder of the year in question

1) land all cod catches that comply with the minimum size of the waters in question for which the permit applies and

2) write off all catches of cod on the quantity of catch available to the vessel, corresponding to the amount of annual available to the vessel at any time including the additional amount of year allocated to the vessel as a fishing quota vessel.

PCS. 2. Catches of cod below the minimum target shall be depreciated on the amount of catch available to the vessel and resubmitted in accordance with applicable rules.

PCS. 3. Catch vessels which do not have cod available, cf. 1, shall not engage in fishing gear which, in the waters to which the permit applies, may be lawfully used for fishing with cod as a target species.

Section 175. To the extent that still available cod is available to Denmark for extra volumes in the individual catchment areas for catch quota vessels, the NaturErhvervstyrelsen may allocate additional extra volumes to vessels authorized as catch quotas.

PCS. 2. Additional additional quantities may be allocated to vessels that have increased their annual amount of cod by increasing FKA shares or after transfer of annual quantities since the vessel was allocated additional quantities during the year in question when issuing the permit as a catch quota.

PCS. 3. Additional additional quantities are allocated in relation to the vessel's increased annual quantity of cod in the individual watershed. 30% extra amount is granted in relation to increased annual quantities of up to 100 tonnes and 20% in relation to increased annual quantities exceeding 100 tonnes, cf. 4th

PCS. 4. Allotment of additional extra volumes will be based on application from the vessel owner. The National Environmental Protection Agency handles applications received once a month and makes allocation as long as there are quantities available, cf. section 177. Applications to be included in the allocation for the month in question must reach the NaturErhvervstyrelsen no later than the 1st of the month.

PCS. 5. For the first time on March 1, there will be the possibility of allocating additional extra volumes for vessels that acquire higher annual volumes over a given year.

Section 176. Owners of vessels not already authorized as catch quotas may apply for the vessel to be authorized as a fishing quota vessel for the remainder of a given year. Vessels authorized shall have the rest of the year in question comply with all conditions for fishing as catch quotas, cf. sections 174 and 179. It will be possible to register as catch quota vessels in both the Skagerrak and the North Sea and the Baltic Sea, or only to sign up such as catch quotas in the Skagerrak and the North Sea or in the Baltic Sea. Applications to be included in the prioritization of additional quantities during the month concerned must reach the Nature Agency by the 1st of the month in question.

PCS. 2. The allocation of additional quantities to vessel owners shall be in proportion to the unfinished amount of cod in the vessel in question at the time of issue of the permit. 30% extra amount shall be allocated in relation to an unfinished annual quantity of up to 100 tonnes and 20% in relation to an unfinished quantity of more than 100 tonnes, cf. 4th

Section 177. Applications for additional additional quantities or permission as catch quotas are only accepted if the vessel can be awarded with the percentages specified in section 175 (1). 3 and 176 (1). 2, cf. section 173 (1). 4th

PCS. 2. Applications submitted for a month shall be prioritized for vessels already authorized as catch quotas. Subsequently, allocation may be granted to vessels not already authorized as a catch quota if sufficient quantities are available. When prioritizing applications pursuant to sections 175 and 176 respectively, both groups apply that, if there are insufficient quantities available to meet all applications, priority vessels of lesser length are given priority over vessels with the largest length overall.

Section 178. To the extent that, under EU rules, additional catches may be allocated for fishing quotas other than cod for fishing with catch quotas, rules for participation shall be laid down. The rules shall be published in a notice issued in accordance with Annex 6. If fishing quotas are caught in the same fisheries as cod, it may be determined that catch quotas for Cod also includes the new catch quotas.

Section 179. The Nature Agency may lay down special conditions for catch quota vessels. This stipulates terms and conditions for the control and departure of the applicable control rules for fisheries. The terms will appear from the licenses.

PCS. 2. Catch vessels shall, from the issue of the permit and the rest of the year concerned, have installed and use the monitoring equipment required under the permit conditions.

PCS. 3. The allocation and the right to fish, bring and land the extra catches are subject to compliance with the terms. If the terms are not observed and therefore there has not been the required documentation of the fishing activity, the additional amount may expire or be reduced.

PCS. 4. The Nature Agency may grant refusal to apply for a license to participate in documented fishing if the vessel has participated in a fishing quota vessel in prior years without the fishing being documented in accordance with the terms.

PCS. 5. All costs for monitoring equipment and operation thereof and compliance with special inspection requirements shall be borne by the vessel owner.

PCS. 6. The Nature Agency may, on further terms, exclude catch quotas from effort regulation and certain control and conservation rules, etc.

CHAPTER 24 CONTROL, APPEAL, PUNISHMENT, ETC.

Verification provisions

Section 180. The master of a fishing vessel shall stop this when the Nature Authority makes an order and facilitate the access of the inspection authority to the vessel.

PCS. 2. The master of a fishing vessel shall also assist in the investigations of catches and gear and of ship documents deemed necessary by the Nature Agency.

PCS. 3. The Nature Agency is entitled to demand explanations, require printouts of ship documents and take photographs of vessels, gear and cargo.

Section 181. Within the framework of the organization of the control efforts, the Nature Agency may order that on arrival, unloading and change of waters in given fisheries, in given areas, within a given period or for individual vessels, a notification shall be given in accordance with Annexes 5a or 5b or that unloading may not take place without the prior permission of the Danish Agency for the Environment.

PCS. 2. The Nature Agency may dispense with the requirements of this Executive Order on Unloading.

PCS. 3. For the purposes of carrying out checks, rules may be issued for the pursuit of fishing activities covered by this Executive Order. The rules are published in accordance with Appendix 6.

Section 182. In waters and waters where fishing for a fish species is prohibited, the fish species concerned may not be transported and landed in ports located next to this water without the permission of the Nature Agency.

PCS. 2. In waters where fishing is regulated by more than one of the following forms of regulation: Rations, annual quantities or maximum allowable number of fishing days, vessels fishing under a particular form of regulation in this or in other waters may report a change of waters in accordance with the Annexes 5b.

Section 183. Anyone who sells a lot of herring for use other than human consumption shall

1) obtain information from the transferor to whom and when the party was sought to be disposed of for human consumption without being able to sell it; and

2) Record the information mentioned in number 1, sign and date the note and keep the note for one year so that it can be handed over to the NaturErhvervstyrelsen upon request.

Section 184. Recipients of fish resolved in boxes shall immediately place banknotes in all top boxes (boxes in the upper layer) indicating the port letter and number of the vessel with which the fish are caught.

Appeals

Section 185. Appeals against decisions made by the Nature Agency pursuant to this Executive Order shall be submitted to the Swedish Environmental Protection Agency and sent to the Danish Veterinary and Food Administration's complaints center within 4 weeks after the person concerned has received notification of the decision.

Penalties

§ 186. Penalties shall be punished by that person

1) violates or attempts to violate the provisions of this Executive Order and the provisions contained in notices of amended rules and terms issued in accordance with Section 2 in accordance with Annex 6,

2) overrides or attempts to override conditions relating to a license issued pursuant to the Order,

3) Try to violate or fail to comply with an injunction or prohibition issued pursuant to the Order, or

4) Provides or attempts to provide false or misleading information or deserves or tries to declare information required by the Order.

PCS. 2. Companies etc. (legal persons) may be subject to criminal liability in accordance with the provisions of Chapter 5 of the Criminal Code.

§ 187. The Order shall enter into force on 1 January 2014.

PCS. 2. At the same time, Order No 1405 of 19 December 2012 on the regulation of fisheries in 2013 and certain conditions for fisheries in the following year will be repealed.

NaturErhvervstyrelsen, December 12, 2013

Jette Petersen

ANNEX 1 WATERS OF THE NORTH SEA, ENGLISH CHANNEL, SKAGERRAK, KATTEGAT AND THE BALTIC SEA AND THE BELTS WITH ICES SUB-AREAS

Kattegat (ICES sub area III a, south) :

The waters are bounded to the south by lines between Hasenøre and Gniben's tip as well as Gilbjerg Hoved and Kullen, and to the north by a straight line from Skagen lighthouse to Tistlarne Fyr and then to the nearest point on the Swedish coast. The Isefjord and Roskilde Fjord are attributed to the Kattegat.

Skagerrak (ICES subarea III a, north) :

The waters bounded to the south and east of the Kattegat, cf. above, and to the west by a straight line between Hanstholm lighthouse and Lindesnes lighthouse.

North Sea (ICES Division IV and EU waters of ICES Sub-area II a) :

ICES Area IV bounded to the north by 62°00 'north latitude, west of 4°00' west longitude from 62°00 'north latitude to the Scottish coast, to the south of 51°00' north latitude and to the east of Skagerrak, cf. above.

ICES division IV is divided into :

ICES subarea IVa, comprising the North Sea between 62°00 'north latitude and 57°30' north latitude,

ICES subarea IVb, comprising the North Sea between 57°30 'north latitude and 53°30' north latitude, and

ICES subarea IV c, comprising the North Sea south of 53°30 'north latitude.

EU waters of ICES subarea IIa, located between 64°00 'north latitude and 62°00' north latitude.

Ringkøbing Fjord, Nissum Fjord and Limfjorden are allocated to ICES sub area IVb.

The English Channel (ICES Divisions VII d and VII e) :

The waters bounded to the east and north by 51°00 'north latitude and to the west by a line from the English coast west west along 50°00' north latitude to 7°00 'west longitude, thence due south to 49°30' north latitude, thence due east to 5°00 'west length, thence due south to 48°00 'north latitude and thence due east to the French coast.

The English Channel is divided into ICES subarea VII d, which comprises the English Channel east of 2°00 'west longitude and ICES subarea VII e, which comprises the English Channel west of 2°00' west longitude.

The Baltic Sea and the Belts (ICES subareas III b, c and d) are divided into the following ICES subdivisions :

Sub area 22

Northern border: A line from Hasenøre to Gniben's tip.
Eastern border: Faroe line and a line from Gedser right east to 12°00 'east longitude and south south along 12°00' east longitude.
Sub area 23
Northern border: A line from Gilbjerg Head to the Hill.
Southern border: A line from Stevns Red Lighthouse to Falsterbo Lighthouse.
Sub area 24
Western border: Corresponds to the eastern border of ICES sub-area 22 and the southern border of ICES sub-area 23.
Eastern border: A line from Sandhammaren Lighthouse to Hammerodde Lighthouse and a line from the south coast of Bornholm right south along 15°00 'east longitude.
Sub area 25
Northern boundary: 56°30 'north latitude.
Western border: Corresponds to the eastern border of ICES sub area 24.
Eastern border: 18°00 'east longitude.
Subarea 26
Northern boundary: 56°30 'north latitude.
Western border: 18°00 'east longitude.
Sub area 27
Eastern border: A line from 59°41 'north latitude to south along 19°00' east longitude to Gotland and a line from the south coast of Gotland right west along 57°00 'north latitude to 18°00' east longitude and thence due south.
South boundary: 56°30 'north latitude.
Subarea 28
North boundary: 58°30 'north latitude.
South boundary: 56°30 'north latitude.
Western border: north of Gotland: 19°00 'east longitude
South of Gotland: a line west west along 57°00 'north latitude until 18°00' east longitude and thence south.
Subarea 29
Northern boundary: 60°30 'north latitude.
South boundary: 58°30 'north latitude.
Western border: A line from 59°41 'north latitude south south along 19°00' east longitude.
Eastern border: A line south south along 23°00 'east longitude to 59°00' north latitude and thence due east.
Subarea 30
Northern boundary: 63°30 'north latitude.
South boundary: 60°30 'north latitude.
Subarea 31
South boundary: 63°30 'north latitude.
Sub area 32
Western border: Corresponds to the eastern border of ICES sub area 29.

ANNEX 2 APPLICATION FOR PERMISSION AND WITHDRAWAL OF AUTHORIZATION

1) Application for permission and withdrawal of permission is made by written request to the National Agency for Economic Affairs, Nyropsgade 30, 1780 Copenhagen V.

2) Application for permission must be submitted to the Nature Authority 3 working days prior to the beginning of the period for which the permit is to apply.

3) Unsubscribe of permission must reach the NaturErhvervstyret no later than 3 working days before the cancellation must be effective. When transferring from a fishing license to another, unsubscribe and apply for a new permit must be submitted together within 3 working days before the transition must be effective. At the same time, in connection with the cancellation, the amount of catch landed during the ration or license period to be abolished shall be indicated.

4) Certain permissions may be enrolled and unsubscribed by SMS. The National Agency's SMS numbers are: 2124 3319 or 2523 7390

List of permissions that can be enrolled and unsubscribed via SMS:

License 1200	Cod in the Baltic Sea and the Belts
License 1201	Splashing in the Baltic Sea and the Belts
License 1202	Herring in the Baltic Sea and Belts
License 1203	Salmon in the Baltic Sea and the Belts
License 1209	Ration permission after heavy in the North Sea
License 1211	Ration permission after plaice in Kattegat
License 1212	Ration permission after plaice in Skagerrak
License 1213	Ration permission for plaice in the Baltic Sea
License 1218	Ration permission after litters in the Skagerrak, Kattegat, Baltic Sea and Belts
License 1223	Ration permission after hake in the North Sea
License 1224	Ration permission after turbot and bristle in the North Sea
License 1232	Ration permission for salmon in the Baltic Sea

An application submitted via SMS must contain:			
Registration	Vessel president.	License.	Date of recording on license
LIT	Ex. : KE999	Ex. : 999	Mmdd Ex. : 0109

Withdrawal	Vessel president.	License.	Date of last day on license no.
LIF	Ex. : KE999	Ex. : 999	Mmdd Ex. : 0115

The Nature Authority automatically sends a receipt indicating whether the unsubscribe is correct (OK) or if there was an error.

After kl. 16.00 no cancellation can take place, which has effect for the current day, and no registration will take effect from the following day.

APPENDIX 3 PERMISSIONS

A. Special Terms.

A license may include be subject to compliance with the following conditions as well as terms of individual fishing:

1) Determination of a maximum allowable catch for a period.

2) Requirements for marketing or use of the catch and the processing of the catch.

3) Requirements for target species, by-catches, minimum size and the like.

4) Requirements for the use of the license within a specified time limit as a condition for maintaining the license.

5) Requirements for prior notification of arrival and unloading in accordance with Annex 5a or requirement for prior notification of entry and exit of waters in accordance with Annex 5b.

6) It is stated in the permit whether other fisheries are allowed to carry or bring along and land other species during the licensing period or in connection therewith.

B. General Terms.

A license is granted on the following terms and conditions:

1) The fishing must take place in accordance with applicable laws, regulations, etc. regarding fishing, including EU legislation.

2) The permit must always be kept on board.

3) The license can not be transferred or otherwise surrendered to others.

4) The license lapses in whole or in part change of ownership.

5) For all vessels not subject to logging requirements under national rules and EU rules, logbooks must always be kept irrespective of the species being fished. The logbook must be handed over to Denmark's local port of landing port, irrespective of whether there is a longer deadline for delivery, in accordance with the general rules for landing in Danish ports in immediate connection with landing and unloading. When landing in a foreign port, the logbook leaflets are sent to the local department of the Nature Agency, in whose area the home port of the vessel is located, cf. the Order of the National Agency for the Registration of Logbooks, etc.

6) Changed terms for the license, including its expiration as a whole, may be notified in accordance with Appendix 6.

7) Only vessels with the same license (same license list number) may engage in par fishing.

8) During the operation of fisheries subject to observer schemes, the master is obliged to take observers on board in accordance with detailed rules.

C. Failure to comply with conditions.

If the terms (both special and general) of the license are not observed, it may be withdrawn without notice, cf. section 37 2, in the Fisheries Act.

ANNEX 4 CONVERSION FACTORS WHEN CALCULATING QUANTITIES

Factors used by the National Agency for the conversion of fish caught in EU waters and landed with a degree of treatment other than "live fish" to "live fish" for the purpose of controlling quantitative restrictions, cf. section 10 . 2:

Nature	landing mode	Factor for conversion into living fish
Cod, Coal, Birkelange and Lyssej	Purified with head	1.17
hake	Purified with head	1.11
Long and Brosme	Purified with head	1.14
Whiting	Purified with head	1.18
Mørksej and Rødfisk	Purified with head	1.19
grenadier	Purified with head	1.11
Dogfish	Purified with head	1.35
Dogfish	Purified with head and skin	2.52
Tongue	Purified with head	1.04
Red pepper, Reddish and Helleflynder	Purified with head	1.05
Glashvarre and Cutting	Purified with head	1.06
Slethvar and Pighvar	Purified with head	1.09
Ising	Purified with head	1.11
Scrub	Purified with head	1.08
Skates	Purified with head	1.13
Skates	wings	2.09
Cod	Purified without head	1.70
Cod	Fillet with skin without bones	2.60
Cod	Fillet without skin and legs	2.60
Cod	Fillet without skin without bones without buglap	3.80
coalfish	Purified without head	1.60
coalfish	Fillet with skins and legs	2.55
coalfish	Fillet without skin with bones	2.80
coalfish	Fillet with skin and without legs	2.85
coalfish	Fillet without skin without bones	3.00
haddock	Purified without head	1.46
haddock	Fillet with skins and legs	2.65
haddock	Fillet without skin with bones	2.95
haddock	Fillet without skin and without	3.15

	bones	
haddock	Fillet without skin without bones and without buglap	3.70
Whiting	filet	2.80
Monkfish	Purified with head	1.22
Monkfish	Purified without head	3.00
Norway lobster	Tails	3.00
porbeagle	Purified with head	1.33
Salmon in ICES zone 14 or 5B	Purified with head	1.11
Salmon in ICES zones 1, 2A and 2B	Purified with head	1.16
Salmon in other waters	Purified with head	1.10
Deepwater rains in Greenland waters	Cooked Tunnel	1.05
Deepwater rains in Greenland waters	Frozen (raw tunnel frozen)	1.05
Other species	Lips and wings	1.70
For certain species, they are not traditionally landed in Denmark, conversion factors can be found in Commission Regulation (EC) No. 404/2011		

APPENDIX 5A NOTICE OF ARRIVAL AND UNLOADING TO NATURERVHERVSTYRELSEN

1) Arrival and unloading notice must contain the following information:

(a) the vessel's letter and number of the vessel;

b) Species and quantity of fish on board.

c) Arrival port, expected arrival time, and expected time of departure, if this is too bad from the time of arrival.

2) Notification must be given by the master no later than 2 hours before arrival to the port, unless longer deadlines are required in accordance with EU requirements.

3) Notification of arrival and unloading must be made once the fishing is completed. If fishing is not completed 2 hours before arrival at port, however, a message may be provided with information about it. on board catches and that fishing has not been completed. No later than 15 minutes before arrival at the port, the final report will be comprehensive throughout the fishing industry. The amount and species listed in the message must be in accordance with the record in the vessel's logbook.

4) Notification shall be made for vessels covered by the electronic reporting of logbook data via this system. For other vessels, messages must be submitted via mobile phone applications or the website of the Swedish Environmental Protection Agency. A notification must be made to the NaturErhvervstyrelsen, also if unloading takes place abroad. Message to the Nature Agency does not exempt the obligations that apply in the country where it is lost. Upon receipt, the master will receive a receipt number which must be entered in the logbook before arriving at the port.

5) Arrival and unloading must not take place before the stated date and before the above acknowledgment number is entered in the logbook. If unloading has not occurred within 2 hours

For additional analytical, business and investment opportunities information,
please contact Global Investment & Business Center, USA
at (703) 370-8082. Fax: (703) 370-8083. E-mail: ibpusa3@gmail.com
Global Business and Investment Info Databank - www.ibpus.com

after the notified date, a notice of change of time of delivery must be submitted. The master is responsible for not losing before the above acknowledgment number is entered in the logbook and before the notified date.

6) An undertaking receiving the fish may submit a message on behalf of the vessel operator. The master is responsible for the content of the message and for no loss before the receipt number is entered in the logbook and before the notified date.

7) Any doubt as to whether the message has been submitted correctly can be resolved by contacting the Nature Agency at phone number 7218 5609 before unloading, by the company or by the master.

APPENDIX 5B NOTIFICATION OF CHANGE OF WATERS TO THE NATURERHVERVSTYRELSEN

1) Notification of a change of waters for the purpose of fishing in other waters or landing at a port situated next to other waters shall contain the following information:

(a) the vessel's port of call letters and numbers;

b) Species and quantity of fish on board. For industrial fish, the most significant fish species is declared in the party.

c) Expected time and position for border crossing between the waters.

2)Notification of change of water shall take place no later than 1 hour before this. Notice shall be given for vessels covered by the electronic reporting of logbook data via this system. For other vessels, messages must be submitted via mobile phone applications or the website of the Swedish Environmental Protection Agency. Upon receipt, the master receives a receipt number to be entered in the logbook. The master is responsible for the change of waters not before the above registration number is entered in the logbook and before the notified date and that it takes place at the specified position. If no change of water has occurred within 1 hour after the notified date, a new message must be submitted. For vessels fitted with satellite surveillance equipment (vessel monitoring unit, FOE),

3) The commander must listen to the international emergency and call frequencies (VHF and medium wave), so that the Nature Agency may call the master for inspection at the notified border position.

ANNEX 6 SENDING NOTIFICATIONS OF CHANGED RULES AND TERMS OF FISHING

When issuing notifications of changed fishing conditions, the following procedure is applied:

1) The announcement is broadcast over Lyngby Radio, regardless of the waters for which the message applies. Notifications will be sent from the Nature Agency over Lyngby Radio on Mondays, Tuesdays, Wednesdays, Thursdays or Fridays in connection with traffic announcements at. 8.05 and kl. 18.05, but at. 7.05 and at. 17.05 in the summertime period.

2) The notification is sent to the organizations represented in the Business Fisheries Committee, per. e-mail on the broadcast date. Messages can also be viewed on the NaturErhvervstyrelsens website www.naturerhverv.dk immediately after the broadcast.

3) The date of entry into force is stated in the notice.

ANNEX 7 FISHING SPECIES, IT IS FORBIDDEN TO RESCIND IF THEY CAN BE LANDED LEGALLY

Blue whiting	turbot
tusk	Plain cowboy
sprat	Rokke
Blue ling	flounder
Norway lobster	Lemon sole
Northern shrimp	porbeagle
megrim	herring
smelt	Damage
Havgalt	grenadier
Monkfish	Scrub
halibut	witch
Horse mackerel	brill
Whiting	Sperling
Ising	Tobis
hake	Tongue
haddock	Cod
Salmon	Other species in the Norwegian zone
Lange	
Soldering	
Mackerel	
coalfish	

ANNEX 8 INFORMATION TO THE NATIONAL AGENCY FOR THE TRANSFER OF IOC SHARES AND ANNUAL AMOUNTS

To prove that the transfer of quota shares has taken place, cf. section 91 (1). 4 and that the terms of the transfer have been met, the following information must be given to the Swedish National Agency for Nature and Rural Development:

1) Date of transfer.

2) Vessels EU Identification Numbers, Names and Harbor Identification Numbers.

3) Seller and buyer's name.

4) Size of quota or amount of year and EU identification number, name and port number of the vessel (s) to which each quota share was allocated.

5) Information on the amount of fish caught with the quota share in this catch is until the date of the transfer.

6) Water in which the quota share is allocated.

7) Declaration that the parties commit to the trade concluded.

8) Declaration that the requirements regarding the ownership of the vessel and its influence on the utilization of quota shares, cf. section 7 2, and section 90 is complied with.

9) For IOC: The selling price of the sold quota share.

ANNEX 9 INFORMATION TO THE NATURE AGENCY IN CONNECTION WITH THE TRANSFER OF FKA AND ANNUAL QUANTITIES FOR CERTAIN SPECIES

To prove that the transfer of quota shares has taken place and that the conditions for the transfer have been fulfilled, the following information must be provided to the Swedish Environmental Protection Agency:

1) Date of transfer.

2) Vessels EU Identification Numbers, Names and Harbor Identification Numbers.

3) Provides and recipient's names.

4) Size of quota or amount of year and EU identification number, name and port number of the vessel (s) to which each quota share was originally allocated.

5) Information on the amount of quota fished in the current catches up to the date of the transfer.

6) Water in which the quota share is allocated.

7) Declaration that the parties commit to the agreement entered into.

8) Declaration that the requirements of the vessel's owners are met.

9) The value of the transferred quota share, cf. section 83.

ANNEX 10 LANDINGS OF COD, HAKE, HERRING, MACKEREL AND HORSE MACKEREL OVER A CERTAIN AMOUNT IN DESIGNATED PORTS

Vessels with more than 2,000 kg of cod and / or 2,000 kg of hake (live weight) aboard the North Sea, Skagerrak and Kattegat may only land in the following 16 ports in Denmark: Bønnerup, Esbjerg, Gilleleje, Grenå, Hanstholm, Hirtshals, Hundested, Hvide Sande, Lemvig, Lild Strand, Nørre Vorupør, Skagen, Strandby, Torsminde, Thorup Strand and Thyborøn.

Vessels with more than 10,000 kg of herring, mackerel and horse mackerel on board may only land in the following 7 ports: Esbjerg, Thyborøn, Hanstholm, Hirtshals, Skagen, Grenå and Gilleleje.

In the case of herring, the above conditions for catches taken in ICES divisions I, II, IIIa, IV, Vb, VI and VII apply. In the case of mackerel, the conditions for catches taken in ICES divisions IIa, IIIa, IV, Vb, VI, VII, VIII, IX, X, XII and XIV and horse mackerel shall be subject to the conditions for catches taken in ICES zones IIa, IV, Vb , VI, VII. , VIII, IX, X, XII and XIV.

Annex 11

List of deep sea species

Latin name	Commonly used name
Aphanopus carbo	Black saber fish
Apristuris spp.	Icelandic catshark
Argentina Silus	smelt
Beryx spp.	Alfonsinos
Centrophorus granulosus	Ru pighaj
Centrophorus squamosus	Dark pighaj
Centroscyllium fabricii	Fabricius' sorthaj
Centroscymnus coelolepis	Portuguese pigha
Coryphaenoides rupestris	grenadier
Dalatias licha	kitefin
Deania Calceus	Næbhaj
Etmopterus princeps	Great lantern shark
Etmopterus spinax	Sorthaj
Galeus melastomus	dogfish
Galeus murinus	Mouse catshark
Hoplostethus atlanticus	Orange savbug
Molva dypterigia	Blue ling
Phcis blennoides	Forkbeards
Centroscymnus crepidates	Long-legged pighaj
Scumnodon ringens	Haj (Scymnodon ringens)
Hexanchus griseus	Six-hailed shark
Chlamydoselachus anguineus	Frilled
Oxynotus paradoxus	Sparked triangle shark
Somniosus microcephalus	Greenland shark
Pagellus Bogaraveo	Exciting blankest
Chimaera monstrosa	chimaeras
Marcrourus berglax	Nord skolestad
Mora fun	poor cod
Antimora rostrata	Blue antimora
Epigonous telescope	Telescopic pomfret
Helicolenus datylopterus	Blue mouth
Conger conger	Common oatmeal
Lepidopus caudatus	Scabbard
Alepocephalus bairdii	Baird's sledding fish
Lycodes esmarkii	Esmark eelbrosme
Raja hyperborean	Polar Rokke
Sebastes viviparous	Little redfish
Hoplostethus mediterraneus	Middehavssavbug
Trahuscorpia cristulata	Dragonfly Fish (Trachyscorpia cristulata)
Raja nidarosiensus	Black bugged coat
Chaceon (Geryon) affinis	Deepwater crab (Chaceon (Geryon) affinis)
Raja fillets	Filled dresses
Hydrolagus mirabilis	Big island sea mice
Rhinochimaera atlantica	Havmus (Rhinochimaera atlantica)
Alepocephalus rostratus	Rissos glathoved fish
Polyprion americanus	Wreckfish

Annex 12

The percentage distribution of the individual quotas for which yarn or trawler vessels are allocated to loan-FKA in relation to, cf. section 73 based on the basis of calculation of the individual vessel, cf. section 72

		Trawl%	Yarn%
Hanstholm	Cod in the North Sea	10.68	51.2
	Cod in the Kattegat	0	0.03
	Cod in the Skagerrak	1.12	5.11
	Cod in the Baltic Sea area 22-24	0.01	
	Heavy in Skagerrak, Kattegat and the Baltic Sea	0.27	0.67
	Heavy in the North Sea	0.43	4.55
	Red pepper in the North Sea	4.2	12.08
	Plaice in the Kattegat	0.04	0
	Plaice in the Skagerrak	7.05	3.87
	Plaice in the Baltic Sea	0	0
	Norway lobster in Skagerrak, Kattegat and the Baltic Sea	2.62	
	Norway lobster in the North Sea (EU waters)	5.57	
	Norway lobster in Norway (Norwegian zone)	30.12	
	Mørksej in the North Sea, Skagerrak, Kattegat and the Baltic Sea	6.96	1
	Kuller in Skagerrak, Kattegat and the Baltic Sea	1.14	0.24
	Hills in the North Sea	1.11	2.15
	Deepwater reefs in the Skagerrak and Kattegat	1.16	
	Deepwater rains in the North Sea (Norwegian zone)	2.5	
	Kulmule Nordsøen (EU waters)	0.39	17.12
	Turbot and bristle in the North Sea (EU waters)	0.44	1.36
	Havtaske in the North Sea (Norwegian zone)	13.68	0.62
	Sprat in the North Sea (EU waters)	8.91	
	Sprat in Skagerrak and Kattegat	0.01	
	Sprat in the Baltic Sea	1.58	
Skagen	Cod in the North Sea	0.01	2.15
	Cod in the Kattegat	0.34	4.72

	Cod in the Skagerrak	13.63	31.74
	Cod in the Baltic Sea area 22-24	0.01	4.18
	Cod in the Baltic Sea area 25-32	0.16	1.13
	Heavy in Skagerrak, Kattegat and the Baltic Sea	1.45	26.68
	Heavy in the North Sea	0	
	Red pepper in the North Sea	0	0.01
	Plaice in the Kattegat	0.71	10.02
	Plaice in the Skagerrak	3.55	10.17
	Plaice in the Baltic Sea	0	0.01
	Norway lobster in Skagerrak, Kattegat and the Baltic Sea	58.67	
	Mørksej in the North Sea, Skagerrak, Kattegat and the Baltic Sea	10.76	7.64
	Kuller in Skagerrak, Kattegat and the Baltic Sea	1.86	1.52
	Hills in the North Sea	0	
	Deepwater reefs in the Skagerrak and Kattegat	6.84	
	Deep sea rains in the North Sea (EU waters)	0.03	
	Deepwater rains in the North Sea (Norwegian zone)	0.01	
	Kulmule Nordsøen (EU waters)		0.02
	Turbot and bristle in the North Sea (EU waters)	0	
	Sprat in Skagerrak and Kattegat	0.51	
	Sprat in the Baltic Sea	1.39	
	Herring in the Baltic Sea area 22-24	0.09	
North Sea	Cod in the North Sea	4.71	21.94
	Cod in the Kattegat	0.03	0.03
	Cod in the Skagerrak	0.28	0.5
	Cod in the Baltic Sea area 22-24	2.85	2.59
	Cod in the Baltic Sea area 25-32	1.29	0.31
	Heavy in Skagerrak, Kattegat and the Baltic Sea	0.39	2.39
	Heavy in the North Sea	0.69	27.51
	Red pepper in the North Sea	22.72	28.47
	Plaice in the Kattegat	0.16	0.37
	Plaice in the Skagerrak	4.79	2.55
	Plaice in the Baltic Sea	0.21	0.05
	Norway lobster in Skagerrak, Kattegat and the Baltic Sea	0.02	
	Norway lobster in the North Sea	10.13	

For additional analytical, business and investment opportunities information, please contact Global Investment & Business Center, USA at (703) 370-8082. Fax: (703) 370-8083. E-mail: ibpusa3@gmail.com Global Business and Investment Info Databank - www.ibpus.com

	(EU waters)		
	Norway lobster in Norway (Norwegian zone)	2.93	
	Mørksej in the North Sea, Skagerrak, Kattegat and the Baltic Sea	1.38	0.06
	Kuller in Skagerrak, Kattegat and the Baltic Sea	0.06	0
	Hills in the North Sea	1.02	0.12
	Kulmule Nordsøen (EU waters)	0.41	4.75
	Turbot and bristle in the North Sea (EU waters)	2.75	8.3
	Havtaske in the North Sea (Norwegian zone)	3.46	0.06
	Sprat in the North Sea (EU waters)	34.93	
	Sprat in Skagerrak and Kattegat	0.69	
	Sprat in the Baltic Sea	3.82	
	Herring in the Baltic Sea area 22-24	0.26	0
Skagerrak	Cod in the North Sea	6.55	26.63
	Cod in the Kattegat	0.05	0.03
	Cod in the Skagerrak	6	26.71
	Cod in the Baltic Sea area 22-24	1.6	0.8
	Cod in the Baltic Sea area 25-32	0.29	0.78
	Heavy in Skagerrak, Kattegat and the Baltic Sea	2.11	4.48
	Heavy in the North Sea	0.57	5.68
	Red pepper in the North Sea	2.77	8.28
	Plaice in the Kattegat	0.37	0.06
	Plaice in the Skagerrak	4.08	24.28
	Plaice in the Baltic Sea	0.19	0.03
	Norway lobster in Skagerrak, Kattegat and the Baltic Sea	9.9	
	Norway lobster in the North Sea (EU waters)	5.78	
	Norway lobster in Norway (Norwegian zone)	14.32	
	Mørksej in the North Sea, Skagerrak, Kattegat and the Baltic Sea	8.58	0.48
	Kuller in Skagerrak, Kattegat and the Baltic Sea	2.46	0.06
	Hills in the North Sea	0.67	0.13
	Deepwater reefs in the Skagerrak and Kattegat	23.01	
	Deep sea rains in the North Sea	0.18	

	(EU waters)		
	Deepwater rains in the North Sea (Norwegian zone)	0.89	
	Kulmule Nordsøen (EU waters)	0.22	0.94
	Turbot and bristle in the North Sea (EU waters)	0.63	0.63
	Havtaske in the North Sea (Norwegian zone)	6.53	0
	Sprat in the North Sea (EU waters)	0.44	
	Sprat in Skagerrak and Kattegat	1.67	
	Sprat in the Baltic Sea	0.09	
	Herring in the Baltic Sea area 25-32	0.05	
Kattegat	Cod in the North Sea	0.54	4.89
	Cod in the Kattegat	2.75	3.86
	Cod in the Skagerrak	4.6	10.09
	Cod in the Baltic Sea area 22-24	2.38	6.44
	Cod in the Baltic Sea area 25-32	0.8	0.93
	Heavy in Skagerrak, Kattegat and the Baltic Sea	15.57	46.74
	Heavy in the North Sea	0.23	1.99
	Red pepper in the North Sea	0.22	1.96
	Plaice in the Kattegat	3.53	11.16
	Plaice in the Skagerrak	1.72	10.11
	Plaice in the Baltic Sea	0.28	1.03
	Norway lobster in Skagerrak, Kattegat and the Baltic Sea	55.65	
	Norway lobster in the North Sea (EU waters)	0.15	
	Mørksej in the North Sea, Skagerrak, Kattegat and the Baltic Sea	3.33	0.38
	Kuller in Skagerrak, Kattegat and the Baltic Sea	0.63	0.16
	Hills in the North Sea	0	0
	Deepwater reefs in the Skagerrak and Kattegat	0.71	
	Kulmule Nordsøen (EU waters)	0	0.04
	Turbot and bristle in the North Sea (EU waters)	0.02	0.23
	Havtaske in the North Sea (Norwegian zone)	0.06	
	Sprat in the North Sea (EU waters)	0.01	
	Sprat in Skagerrak and Kattegat	6.68	
	Sprat in the Baltic Sea	0.16	
	Herring in the Baltic Sea area 22-		0

	24		
Baltic Sea area 22-24	Cod in the North Sea	0.58	1.71
	Cod in the Kattegat	0.98	0.37
	Cod in the Skagerrak	0.77	0.6
	Cod in the Baltic Sea area 22-24	33.96	67.62
	Cod in the Baltic Sea area 25-32	13.56	3.05
	Heavy in Skagerrak, Kattegat and the Baltic Sea	5.58	10.44
	Heavy in the North Sea	0.12	1.59
	Red pepper in the North Sea	0.64	3.25
	Plaice in the Kattegat	1.01	1.09
	Plaice in the Skagerrak	1.08	0.89
	Plaice in the Baltic Sea	3.42	8.05
	Norway lobster in Skagerrak, Kattegat and the Baltic Sea	12.88	
	Norway lobster in the North Sea (EU waters)	1.43	
	Mørksej in the North Sea, Skagerrak, Kattegat and the Baltic Sea	0.27	0.01
	Kuller in Skagerrak, Kattegat and the Baltic Sea	0.24	0.02
	Hills in the North Sea	0.01	0.02
	Kulmule Nordsøen (EU waters)	0.01	0.01
	Turbot and bristle in the North Sea (EU waters)	0.13	0.44
	Sprat in the North Sea (EU waters)	1.67	
	Sprat in Skagerrak and Kattegat	1	
	Sprat in the Baltic Sea	13.79	
	Herring in the Baltic Sea area 22-24	6.85	0.84
	Herring in the Baltic Sea area 25-32	0.01	
	Salmon in the Baltic Sea	0	0.02
Baltic Sea area 25-32	Cod in the North Sea	0.64	0.04
	Cod in the Kattegat	0.1	0
	Cod in the Skagerrak	0.31	
	Cod in the Baltic Sea area 22-24	12.4	16.36
	Cod in the Baltic Sea area 25-32	48.97	73.53
	Heavy in Skagerrak, Kattegat and the Baltic Sea	0.54	1.91
	Heavy in the North Sea	0.06	0.01
	Red pepper in the North Sea	5.64	0.13
	Plaice in the Kattegat	0.09	0

	Plaice in the Skagerrak	0.24	
	Plaice in the Baltic Sea	4.41	3.62
	Norway lobster in Skagerrak, Kattegat and the Baltic Sea	3.46	
	Norway lobster in the North Sea (EU waters)	12.99	
	Mørksej in the North Sea, Skagerrak, Kattegat and the Baltic Sea	0.32	0
	Kuller in Skagerrak, Kattegat and the Baltic Sea	0.08	0
	Hills in the North Sea	0.35	
	Deepwater reefs in the Skagerrak and Kattegat	0.01	
	Kulmule Nordsøen (EU waters)	0.21	0.03
	Turbot and bristle in the North Sea (EU waters)	0.7	0.09
	Havtaske in the North Sea (Norwegian zone)	0.55	
	Sprat in the Baltic Sea	2.85	
	Herring in the Baltic Sea area 22-24	0.52	0
	Herring in the Baltic Sea area 25-32	0.28	0
	Salmon in the Baltic Sea	4.25	4.28

ANNEX 13 FISHING WITH TRAWL AND / OR OTHER TOWING GEAR IN THE KATTEGAT

When fishing with trawl and / or other towing gear in the Kattegat, which is to be carried out with mesh sizes of 90 mm or more, a sorting panel as specified below must be used.

The window is inserted into the non-conical part with at least 80 open masks in the perimeter. The window will be inserted in the top panel. There must be no more than two open diagonal masks between the rear mask row in the side of the window and the joint. The window ends no more than six m from the dash. The joint ratio is two diagonal masks for a square mesh when the mesh size of the catch is at least 120 mm, five diagonal masks for two square meshes when the mesh size of the catch is at least 100 mm and below 120 mm and three diagonal masks for a square mesh when the mesh size of the catch is at least 90 mm and below 100 mm.

The window must be at least 3 m long. The masks must have a minimum opening of 120 mm. The masks should be square masks, ie. All four sides of the window are cut tipped. The net is mounted so that the posts are parallel to and perpendicular to the length of the codend.

The square mesh panel mesh should be knotless single yarn. The window is inserted so that the masks are always fully open when fishing. The window must not in any way be obstructed by devices on the inside or outside of the net.

Annex 14 Requirements for the selective catches to be used when fishing with trawls and / or other towing gear in Kattegat with a mesh size of 90 mm or more, cf. section 35 2

One of the following 3 types of selective catch bags must be used:

1) 4-panel catch bag with a 180 mm square-mesh sorting window mounted 4-7 meters from the dash.

2) 4-panel catch bag with a 270 mm diamond-mesh sorting window mounted 4-7 meters from the tie.

3) 2-panel catch bag with a 180 mm square-mesh sorting window mounted 4-7 meters from the dash.

Description of the 3 types of selective catch bags

All mesh dimensions are specified in inner full masks.

1) 4-panel catch bag with a 180 mm square-mesh sorting window mounted 4-7 meters from the dash.

The catch bag consists of a square panel section of 3 meters in length and 4 sides that are equally wide. The sides and the bottom are made of traditional diamond masks with a mesh size of at least 90 mm. There must be a maximum of 25 open meshes in width in one page. The top section must place a 3 meter wide screening window with square masks that end up to a maximum of 4 meters from the dot. The square mask with square mesh must have a mesh size of at least 180 mm and consist of 8 open square meshes in width. The screening window with square mesh must be done in a button-stable material. The tool's 90 mm diamond masks are joined to the 180 mm square mesh in the 3: 1 ratio. The principles are shown in the following figures.

2) 4-panel catch bag with a sorting window with a minimum mesh mask of at least 270 mm mounted 4-7 meters from the tie.

The capture bag is identical to Type 1, but the selection window consists of diamond masks with a mesh size of at least 270 mm. The diamond masks of at least 270 mm are fitted with Y masks and the joint ratio between the Cotton Bag mask and the 270 mm diamond mask of the selection window are 4 to 1 with the mesh size of at least 90 mm and less than 120 mm and 3 to 1 where the mesh size of the catch is 120 mm or more. The principles of the tool are shown in the following figures.

3) 2-panel catch bag with a 180 mm square-mesh sorting window mounted 4-7 meters from the dash.

The catch bag consists of a traditional 2-panel construction. Top and bottom sections are equally wide (maximum 50 open meshes in each section, see Council Regulation 850/98). The top section must place a 3 meter wide screening window with square masks that end up to a maximum of 4 meters from the dot. The square mask with square mesh must have a mesh size of at least 180 mm and consist of 8 open square meshes in width. The screening window with square mesh must be done in a button-stable material. The sorting window must be located in the middle of the top section so that there are equal openings between the two sides of the screen window and the two sides. The tool's 90 mm diamond masks are joined to the 180 mm square mesh in the 3: 1 ratio. The principles of the tool are shown in the following figures.

Mounting nets

A stop can be inserted into the selective catch bags (types 1-3). The minimum mask size provisions are not applied to the stopwatch. The front yarn's front attachment is at the rear of the sorting window and perpendicular to the longitudinal direction of the implement. The stop yarn is mounted in the codend post. The stop yarn must not overlap the sorting window.

Annex 15 Requirements for the selective tools to be used when fishing with trawls and / or other towed gear in Skagerrak, cf. Section 36.

1)   The tunnel / collection bag used in accordance with section 36 3 must have an opening of at least 23 cm and max 30 cm and be constructed of 120 mm square mesh or have a top panel with 120 mm square meshes. It must be at least 3 meters long and at least as wide as the sorting grid, cf. Figure 1.

2)   The sorting grid to be used in accordance with section 36 4, must comply with the following specifications and illustrated in Figure 2:

     a)   The sorting grid must be mounted in a trawl whose catch bag consists of square meshes with a mesh size of at least 70 mm. The catching bag must be at least 8 meters long. It is prohibited to use trawls of more than 100 square meshes in the circumference of the catch, excluding joints or snippets.

     b)   The grate shall be rectangular. The grate bars should be parallel to the longitudinal axis of the grate. The distance between the bars must not exceed 35 mm. It is permitted to use one or more hinges so that the grate can be more easily placed on the grid.

     c)   The grate must be mounted diagonally in the trawl with the upper edge of the grate pointing backwards and upwards. It can be mounted directly in front of the catch or farther forward in the extension piece. The grate must be attached to the trawlet on all sides.

     d)   In the top panel of the trawl, there must be an unblocked opening in which the fish can escape. The ejection opening must be as wide as the grid and at the front at a point where the sides are cut along the mask posts on each side of the grid.

     e)   It is permissible to attach a funnel-shaped device in front of the grate to guide the fish against the bottom of the trawl and the grid. The mesh size in the hopper must be at least 70 mm. The hopper must have a vertical opening at the grill of at least 15 cm. The trawl opening at the grate must be as wide as the grid.

3)   In the case of fishing pursuant to section 36, subsection 6 must be used one of the following 3 types of selective catch bags:

     a)   A panel with a minimum of 140 mm. square mesh in a 4-panel section, see Design 1 in Figure 3.

     b)   A panel with a minimum of 270 mm. diagonal masks in a 4-panel section, see Design 2 in Figure 3.

For additional analytical, business and investment opportunities information,
please contact Global Investment & Business Center, USA
at (703) 370-8082. Fax: (703) 370-8083. E-mail: ibpusa3@gmail.com
Global Business and Investment Info Databank - www.ibpus.com

c) A panel with a minimum of 140 mm. square mesh in a 2-panel section, see Design 3 in Figure 3.

A panel, as described in (a), (b) and (c), must be at least 3 meters long and be located no more than 4 meters from the strap. The section panel shall have the same width as the crosspiece of the trawl measured from nail to seam. If the panel is 270 mm. diagonal mask, it should be placed in a 4-panel section and fitted with a joint ratio of three 90-100 mm. Mask for one 270mm mesh or two 100-120mm stitches for one 270mm. mask, cf. Figures 4 and 5. Panels with 140 mm. square masks must be fitted with a joint ratio of three 90-100 mm. Mask to one 140 mm. square mesh, two 100-120 mm. Mask to one 140 mm. square mesh or five 100-120 mm. mesh for two 140 mm. square mask, cf. Figure 6.

Annex 16 Information to the National Agency for the transfer of kW days

To prove that the transfer of annual quantities of kW shares has taken place, cf. section 165, and that the conditions for the transfer have been met, the following information must be given to the NaturErhvervstyrelsen:

1) Date of transfer.

2) Seller and buyer's name.

3) Size of kW units or kW-days and EU identification number, name and port number of the vessel (s) of each kW share at the time of transfer.

4) The segment of the kW shares.

5) Declaration that the parties commit to the trade concluded.

6) Declaration that the requirements, if the owner of the vessel, cf. section 7 2 is complied with.

Annex 17 Maximum rates for shareholdings and quota shares, cf. section 86 and section 90

In the overview below, ownership interests concern the maximum limit of the amount of the individual quota a person can own. Quota shares concern the maximum limit for the amount of the individual quota a vessel may dispose of.

FKA quotas	Stakes	Fishing concessions
Cod in the North Sea	5%	5%
Cod in the Skagerrak	5%	5%
Cod in the Kattegat	5%	5%
Cod in the Baltic Sea area 25-32	10%	10%
Cod in the Baltic Sea area 22-24	5%	5%
Red peas in the North Sea	6%	6%

Plaice in the Skagerrak	7.5%	7.5%
Plaice in the Kattegat	7.5%	7.5%
Plaice in the Baltic Sea	5%	5%
Dark sea in all waters	10%	10%
Hills in the North Sea	10%	10%
Kuller in Skagerrak and Kattegat	10%	10%
Norway lobster in Skagerrak, Kattegat and the Baltic Sea	10%	10%
Norway lobster in the North Sea (EU waters)	10%	10%
Norway lobster in Norway (Norwegian zone)	10%	10%
Havtaske in the North Sea (Norwegian zone)	10%	10%
Heavy in the North Sea	10%	10%
Heavy in Skagerrak, Kattegat and the Baltic Sea	5%	5%
ITQ quotas	Stakes	Fishing concessions
Herring in the Baltic Sea area 22-24	15%	15%
Herring in the Baltic Sea area 25-32	15%	15%
Sprat in the Baltic Sea	15%	15%
Sprat in Skagerrak and Kattegat	15%	15%
Sprat in the North Sea	10%	10%
Tobis in the North Sea	10%	10%

SUPPLEMENTS

IMPORTANT CONTACTS

Note: The telephone country code for Denmark is 45 (excluding Greenland and Faroes). There are no city codes as such. All phone and fax numbers are 8-digit numbers.

EMBASSY OF THE UNITED STATES OF AMERICA

Address:
Dag Hammarskjölds Allé 24
DK-2100 Copenhagen
Denmark
Tel.: (+45) 3341 7100
After hours (+45) 3341 7400
Fax: (+45) 3543 0223
http://denmark.usembassy.gov/
U.S. Commercial Service
Tel.: (+45) 3341 7315
Fax: (+45) 3542 0175
e - mail: **copenhagen.office.box@trade.gov**
http://export.gov/denmark/

U.S. EMBASSY TRADE PERSONNEL:

Mr. Bjarke Castberg Frederiksen, Head of Commercial Section
Ms. Sabina Krøigaard, Commercial Specialist
Mr. Peter Strandby, Commercial Specialist
Ms. Maria Norsk, Commercial Assistant
Mr. Nicholas Kuchova, Regional Senior Commercial Officer (Resident in Stockholm)
Mailing address for mail from the United States of America:
FCS
5280 Copenhagen Pl
Washington, DC 20521-5280

DANISH GOVERNMENT AGENCIES

Ministry of Foreign Affairs
Asiatisk Plads 2
DK-1448 Copenhagen K
Tel: (+45) 33-920000
Fax: (+45) 31-540533
Web: **www.um.dk**
Ministry of Business and Growth
Slotsholmsgade 12
DK-1216 Copenhagen K
Tel: (+45) 33-923350
Fax: (+45) 33-123778
Web: **www.evm.dk**
Ministry of Food, Agriculture and Fisheries
Veterinary and Food Directorate
Moerkhoj Bygade 19
DK 2860 Soborg
Tel: (+45) 33-956000
Fax: (+45) 33-956001

For additional analytical, business and investment opportunities information,
please contact Global Investment & Business Center, USA
at (703) 370-8082. Fax: (703) 370-8083. E-mail: ibpusa3@gmail.com
Global Business and Investment Info Databank - www.ibpus.com

Web: **www.foedevarestyrelsen.dk**
Central Customs and Tax Administration
Customs Center Copenhagen
Snorresgade 15
DK-2300 Copenhagen S
Tel: (+45) 32-887300
Fax: (+45) 32-951874
Web: **www.skat.dk**
Miljostyrelsen (Danish Environmental Protection Agency)
Strandgade 29
DK-1401 Copenhagen K
Tel: (+45) 32-660100
Fax: (+45) 32-660479
Web: **www.mst.dk**
Patent- og Varemaerkestyrelsen (The Danish Patent Office)
Helgeshoj Alle 81
DK-2630 Taastrup
Tel: (+45) 43-508000
Fax: (+45) 43-508001
Web: **www.dkpto.dk**
Sundhedsstyrelsen (National Board of Health)
Amaliegade 13
DK-1256 Copenhagen K
Tel: (+45) 33-961601
Fax: (+45) 33-931636
Web: **www.sst.dk**
Laegemiddelstyrelsen (The Danish Medicines Agency)
Frederikssundvej 378
DK-2700 Bronshoj
Tel: (+45) 44-88-9111
FAX: (+45) 44-917373
Web: **www.laegemiddelstyrelsen.dk** ; **www.dkma.dk**
TRADE ASSOCIATIONS/CHAMBERS OF COMMERCE
The American Chamber of Commerce in Denmark
Christians Brygge 28
DK-1559 Copenhagen V
Tel: (+45) 33-932932
Fax: (+45) 33-130517
Web: **www.amcham.dk**
The Danish Chamber of Commerce
Borsen
DK-1217 Copenhagen K
Tel: (+45) 33-950500
Fax: (+45) 33-325216
Web: **www.hts.dk**
Confederation of Danish Industry
H.C. Andersens Boulevard 18
DK-1787 Copenhagen V
Tel: (+45) 33-773377
Fax: (+45) 33-773300
Web: **www.di.dk**
The Agricultural Council
Axeltorv 3
DK-1609 Copenhagen V

For additional analytical, business and investment opportunities information,
please contact Global Investment & Business Center, USA
at (703) 370-8082. Fax: (703) 370-8083. E-mail: ibpusa3@gmail.com
Global Business and Investment Info Databank - www.ibpus.com

Tel: (+45) 33-145672
Fax: (+45) 33-149574
Web: **www.landbrugsraadet.dk**
Danish Franchise Association
Lyngbyvej 20
DK-2100 Copenhagen O
Tel: (+45) 39-158282
Fax: (+45) 39-158010
Web: **www.dk-franchise.dk**

COMMERCIAL BANKS

Citibank International plc, Denmark Branch
Dagmarhus
H.C. Andersens Boulevard 12
DK-1553 Copenhagen V
Tel: (+45) 33-638383
Fax: (+45) 33-338333
Web: **www.citigroup.com**
Danske Bank A/S
Holmens Kanal 2-12
DK-1092 Copenhagen K
Tel: (+45) 39-440000
Fax: (+45) 39-185873
Web: **www.danskebank.com**
Nordea Bank A/S
Torvegade 2
DK-1786 Copenhagen V
Tel: (+45) 33-333333
Fax: (+45) 33-331212
Web: **www.nordea.com**
Jyske Bank A/S
Vestergade 8-16
DK-8600 Silkeborg
Tel: (+45) 89-222222
Fax: (+45) 89-222496
Web: **www.jyskebank.dk**

WASHINGTON-BASED U.S. COUNTRY CONTACTS

TPCC Trade Information Center
Washington DC
Tel: 1-800-USA-TRADE
Agricultural Export Services Div.
Foreign Agricultural Service (FAS)
U.S. Department of Agriculture
14th and Independence Ave, SW
Washington DC 20250-1000
Tel: (202) 720-7420
Fax: (202) 690-4374

U.S. Department of Commerce
Denmark Desk
Room H-3043
14th and Constitution Ave., NW
Washington, DC 20230
Tel: (202) 482-4414

Fax: (202) 482-2897

U.S.-BASED MULTIPLIERS RELEVANT FOR DENMARK

Royal Danish Embassy in Washington
3200 Whitehaven Street, N.W.
Washington, D.C, 20008-3683
Tel.: (202) 234-4300
Fax.: (202) 328-1470
E-mail: wasamb@um.dk
Homepage: **www.denmarkemb.org**

Royal Danish Consulate General in Los Angeles
10877 Wilshire Blvd., Ste. 1105
Los Angeles, CA 90024
Tel: (310) 443-2090
Fax: (310) 443-2099
E-mail: info@danishconsulate.org
Homepage: **www.danishconsulate.org**

Royal Danish Consulate General in Chicago/
Trade Commission of Denmark
211 East Ontario, Suite 1800
Chicago, Illinois 60611-3242
Tel: (312) 787-8780
Fax: (312) 787-8744
E-mail: infodk@consulatedk.org
Homepage: **www.consulatedk.org**

Royal Danish Consulate General New York
825 Third Avenue
New York, NY 10022-7519
Tel: (212) 223-4545
Fax: (212) 754-1904
www.denmark.org

Danish American Chamber of Commerce
825 Third Avenue, 32nd Fl.
New York, NY 10022
Tel: (212) 980-6240

Danish Mission to the UN
One Dag Hammerskjold Plaza
885 Second Avenue, 18th Floor
New York, NY 10017
Tel: (212) 308-7009
Fax: (212) 308-3384
Email: denmark@un.int
Homepage: **www.un.int/denmark**

Danish-American Chamber of Commerce in New York
One Dag Hammerskjold Plaza
885 Second Avenue, 18th Floor
New York, NY 10017
Tel: (212) 980-6240

**For additional analytical, business and investment opportunities information,
please contact Global Investment & Business Center, USA
at (703) 370-8082. Fax: (703) 370-8083. E-mail: ibpusa3@gmail.com
Global Business and Investment Info Databank - www.ibpus.com**

Email: jh@daccny.com
Web: **www.daccny.com**

TRADE EVENTS

Information on upcoming trade events. **http://www.export.gov/tradeevents/index.asp**

GREENLAND - STRATEGIC INFORMATION

GDP DKK 11,543 million
GDP - real growth rate -0.9%
Labor force 26,994 permanent residents, aged 18-64 (monthly average 2012)
Industries Fish processing (mainly prawns and Greenland halibut), handicrafts, hides and skins, small shipyards, mining
Agriculture products Sheep, cows, reindeer, fish
Exports DKK 2,761.1 million
Export commodities Provisions and livestock 90.5%
Export partners Denmark, Iceland
Imports 4,955.3 DKK million
Import commodities
Machinery and transport equipment, manufactured goods,
provisions and livestock petroleum products
Import partners EU (primarily Denmark and Sweden), Economic aid 3,587 DKK (2012) and 3,624 DKK (2013) million in subsidies

Main source: **Greenland in figures**

Greenland is the world's largest island, containing an area of 2,166,086 km2. Of this area, 303,252 km2, or approximately 14 % of the island, is free of ice. The climate in Greenland is primarily artic, meaning that the temperature does not exceed +10ºC even during the warmest months of the year. Greenland has a population of 56,282 (Jan. 2014) with 16,818 (Jan. 2014) living in the capital of Nuuk. Other important cities include Ilulissat, Kangerlussuaq, Sisimiut, and Qaqortoq, all of which are located on the western coast of the island. However, no roads or railways connect towns inside Greenland; therefore, transportation must be accomplished by air or sea. Despite the limitations on ground transportation, the island has a fairly sophisticated sea network, principally managed through concession by the **Royal Arctic Line** (RAL).

RAL transport and cargo vessels share ports with one of the most modern fishing fleets in the world today. Currently, seafood is the primary export industry in Greenland, comprising over 90% of the exports from the island. However, the mineral and petroleum industries are poised to become the dominant industries in Greenland as prospecting, exploration, and exploitation licenses have increased exponentially over the last decade despite a global economic slowdown.

POLITICAL ENVIRONMENT

Greenland has previously been a Danish colony and a constituent of the Danish Realm. Beginning in 1979, the island became the **Home Rule of Greenland** . This system transferred much of the Denmark's political responsibility to Greenlandic authorities. Among the powers transferred during this time were legislative and executive functions. Furthermore, Greenland assumed responsibility for an increasingly large number of administrative and financial powers during the 1980s and 1990s. During this period, the Home Rule of Greenland was supported by its own taxes and duties in addition to a large block grant from the Danish government.

For additional analytical, business and investment opportunities information,
please contact Global Investment & Business Center, USA
at (703) 370-8082. Fax: (703) 370-8083. E-mail: ibpusa3@gmail.com
Global Business and Investment Info Databank - www.ibpus.com

The island gained further autonomy on June 21, 2009 when the government changed its status from home rule to **self-government** under the Danish Realm. On this date (Greenland's national day), the Greenlandic government assumed control over a number of key areas, including the authority of the nascent mineral and oil industries, as well as any revenues thereof. However, in addition to still receiving the block grant from the Danish government, Greenland currently relies on Denmark for a variety of sovereign functions including foreign policy, defense, and the justice system.

The current representative government of Greenland is centered on the Landsting, an elected body of thirty-one members for a maximum term of four years. The Landsting embodies the supreme legislature of Greenland. The administrative arm of the national government is comprised of a cabinet of five to eight members elected by the Landsting. At the local level, the country is divided into four municipalities with elected governments discharging local political functions.

THE ECONOMY

The economy remains critically dependent on exports of shrimp and fish, income from resource exploration and extraction, and on a substantial subsidy from the Danish Government. The subsidy is budgeted to be about USD 650 million in 2012, approximately 56% of Greenlandic government revenues in 2012 for the year. The public sector, including publicly owned enterprises and the municipalities, plays the dominant role in Greenland's economy.

The Greenlandic economy has benefited from increasing catches and exports of shrimp, Greenland halibut and, more recently, crabs. Due to Greenland's continued dependence on exports of fish - which accounted for 89% of exports in 2010 - the economy remains very sensitive to foreign developments. International consortia are increasingly active in exploring for hydrocarbon resources off Greenland's western coast, and international studies indicate the potential for oil and gas fields in northern and northeastern Greenland.

Within the area of mining, olivine sand continues to be produced and gold production has resumed in south Greenland, while rare-earth and iron ore mineral projects have been proposed or planned elsewhere on the island. Tourism also offers another avenue of economic growth for Greenland, with increasing numbers of cruise lines now operating in Greenland's western and southern waters during the peak summer tourism season.

FORMS OF BUSINESS

There are a variety of business entities that can be established in Greenland to meet the needs of various operations. Among the more important business forms are the public limited company (aktieselskab or A/S); the private limited company (anpartsselskab or ApS); and the branch office (filial).

The Companies Act establishes the applicable regulations for both subsidiary corporations and registered branch offices. Joint ventures are also a possible form of doing business and can be achieved either through partnerships or joint shareholding of a corporation. However, it is important to note that partnerships are not defined by law, and it is therefore necessary to define the relationship in the agreement between the two parties.

Both A/S and ApS entities are limited liability forms of business, with shareholder liability limited only to invested capital. Formation of both types of companies must be accompanied by registration with the **Danish Commerce and Companies Agency** (DCCA). In addition, all forms of business must register with the **Greenland Business Register** (GER) and thereafter with the employer registration system if the entity wishes to employ staff. Before registration with the DCCA, any enterprise is not considered an independent entity, exposing the founders to personal liability for company activities. Oftentimes, companies wishing to do business immediately will circumvent the corporate founding process and purchase shares in a "shelf company," a registered company that has not carried out activities in its existence. The purchasing company then amends the articles of the shelf company to conform to the needs of the operation.

The two main differences that arise between A/S and ApS corporate models pertain to the requirements for share capital and founding members. A/S corporations require share capital of at least DKK 500,000 before being registered. This capital must be contributed either in cash or in kind. Asset contributions in kind must undergo a valuation report, typically prepared by a state authorized public accountant. In contrast, an ApS corporation requires only DKK 125,000 paid in a similar fashion. While an ApS does not have the option to hold its own shares, an A/S can hold up to 10% of its shares.

An A/S company requires at least one founder, and of the founders, at least one must be a resident of Greenland. These requirements can be met by a founder being a legal entity of Greenland. Additionally, the Ministry of Economic and Business can grant exceptions for the residency requirement. ApS companies necessitate at least one founding member but these members are not subject to a residency requirement.

Companies with lawfully registered home offices in the EU, the Nordic Countries, the U.S., or Canada have the option to establish a registered branch office in Greenland. These enterprises are entitled to carry out the business activities within the purview of the home office and must do so over a certain period of time. Conversely to A/S and ApS corporate models, home offices retain unlimited liability for the debts of branch offices as they are not considered to be an independent legal entity. Additionally, registered branch offices require registration with both the DCCA and the GER.

While branch offices are not subject to capital requirements, there are certain resident requirements for office managers. The branch office manager must be a resident of Greenland and any non-Greenland resident that wishes to be appointed manager must apply to the Government of Greenland before appointment.

TAXES

The corporate tax rate is 31.8%, levied against both resident corporations and registered branch offices. This rate also applies to capital gains which are subject to taxation. Companies which hold a license under the Mineral Resources Act are an exception to the corporate tax rate and are charged at a rate of 30%. Taxable income is computed as profit disclosed in the required annual report which has been adjusted to meet the applicable tax laws.

Profit distributions (dividends) for Greenlandic companies are levied at the personal income tax rate of the municipality in which the distributing company is registered. Currently the range of municipal income taxes varies from 37% to 45%. Again, an exception is made for those companies holding an exploitation license under the Mineral Resources Act; these companies are charged 37% on dividends regardless of physical location. Registered branch offices can remit profits to the foreign head office without paying withholding taxes to Greenland. Subject to approval, companies are eligible to deduct dividends paid from taxable income during the year of distribution.

Greenland has no VAT system but does maintain import duties on a variety of products such as motor vehicles, cigarettes, and alcohol. Additionally, products involved in the production of energy are levied with an environmental tax. As previously mentioned, the level of individual income tax varies by municipality; however, there is a nationwide AMA scheme requiring a contribution of 0.9% of payroll for post-education.

EMPLOYMENT

When sending employees to Greenland it is often required that these employees receive work and residence permits. Permission to employ foreign employees is granted by local employment offices. These offices differentiate between unskilled labor and skilled specialists when making their determinations. Generally, only Scandinavian workers are automatically afforded the right to work and reside in Greenland without further permits. Special attention should be paid to situations involving branch office managers and founders of corporations, which are usually required to be citizens of Greenland.

Typically, those individuals who obtain a permanent address or stay in Greenland for a period longer than six months are liable for unlimited taxation on their income. Individuals working in Greenland not meeting these characteristics may still be liable for limited tax liability.

MINING AND PETROLEUM INDUSTRIES

One of the more substantial changes made in the transition from home rule to self-government was the transfer of mineral and petroleum resource management. Due to the vital nature of these industries to Greenland's future, it was important for control of these fields to be among the first transferred to the new government in order for the transition to be significant. This reallocation involved handing over the Bureau of Minerals and Petroleum (BMP) to the Government of Greenland.

The BMP is working to improve the framework for mineral and petroleum exploration and exploitation in order to create a successful industry enjoying a healthy working relationship with the people of Greenland. The BMP is responsible for processing all the relevant licenses needed to operate within the mineral and petroleum industries. There is general political consensus that Greenland should move to make these the primary industries of the island in order to promote the economy, create jobs, and wean the Government's from it dependency on Danish grants. This push has been successful as active prospecting, exploration, and exploitation licenses increased in both petroleum and minerals during the first decade of the millennium, in some cases over fivefold.

To handle this uptick in of interest in mineral and petroleum exploitation, the new self-government of Greenland enacted the **Mineral Resources Act** to control the future of these industries. The Act is meant to create a unified approach to the manner in which the petroleum and mineral industries are managed, touching on topics as diverse as environmental concerns, technical requirements, and economic issues. Under the Act, enterprises that wish to explore and exploit within these industries are required to meet special requirements and criteria. For example, while branch offices are eligible to explore for minerals and petroleum, the shift from exploration to exploitation requires an exploitation license that can only be granted to Greenlandic-registered companies. Additionally, corporations and branches under the Mineral Resources Act are subject to special, sometimes favorable, taxation regimes.

Key Links:

Government of Greenland - **http://uk.nanoq.gl/**
Greenland Official Tourism site - **http://www.greenland.com/en/**
Sermersooq Business Council (Nuuk) - **http://www.business.gl/en/**

For additional analytical, business and investment opportunities information,
please contact Global Investment & Business Center, USA
at (703) 370-8082. Fax: (703) 370-8083. E-mail: ibpusa3@gmail.com
Global Business and Investment Info Databank - www.ibpus.com

Bureau of Minerals and Petroleum - **http://www.bmp.gl/**
The Employers' Association of Greenland - **http://www.ga.gl/tabid/1264/language/da-DK/Default.aspx**
Danish Ministry of Foreign Affairs background on Greenland - Danish Ministry of Foreign Affairs background on Greenland - Danish Ministry of Foreign Affairs background on Greenland - Greenland in figures -
http://www.stat.gl/publ/en/GF/2012/content/Greenland%20in%20Figures%202012.pdf

STRATEGIC CONTACTS IN DENMARK

Danish Trade Council, Ministry of Foreign Affairs, Asiatisk Plads 2, DK-1448 Copenhagen K Tel.: +45 33920000, Fax: +45 32540533, E-mail: **um@um.dk**, Web: **www.eksportraadet.dk**
Danish Chamber of Commerce, Børsen, DK-1217 Copenhagen K Tel.: +45 33950500, Fax: +45 33325216, E-mail: **mail@commerce.dk**, Web: **www.commerce.dk**
International Division of the Danish Chamber of Commerce, Børsen, DK-1217 Copenhagen K Tel.: +45 33950500, Fax: +45 33325216, E-mail: **handelskammeret@commerce.dk**, Web: **www.commerce.dk**
Confederation of Danish Industries, H C Andersens Boulevard 18, DK-1787 Copenhagen V Tel.: +45 33773377, Fax: +45 33773300, E-mail: **di@di.dk**, Web: **www.di.dk**
The Department for Intl. Trade and Market Development of the Confederation of Danish Industries, H C Andersens Boulevard 18, DK-1787 Copenhagen V Tel.: +45 33773377, Fax: +45 33773300, E-mail: **di@di.dk**, Web: **www.di.dk**
DI Export Contact Service, H C Andersens Boulevard 18, DK-1787 Copenhagen V Tel.: +45 33773377, Fax: +45 33773300, E-mail: **di@di.dk**, Web: **www.di.dk**
Association of Danish Fish Processing Industries and Exporters, Kronprinsessegade 8B, DK-1306 Copenhagen K Tel.: +45 33149999, Fax: +45 33327757, E-mail: **dfe@dfedk.dk**
Association of Danish Furniture Industries, Center Boulevard 5, DK-2300 Copenhagen S Tel.: +45 70268111, Fax: +45 70268332, E-mail: **mail@danishfurniture.dk**, Web: **www.danishfurniture.dk**
BYG, Federation of Danish Building Employers, Kejsergade 2, DK-1155 Copenhagen K Tel.: +45 70101113, Fax: +45 33740801, E-mail: **jensklarskov@byg.dk**, Web: **www.byg.dk**
Copenhagen Capacity, Gammel Kongevej 1, DK-1610 Copenhagen V Tel.: +45 33220222, Fax: +45 33220211, E-mail: **info@copcap.com**, Web: **www.copcap.com**
Danida, Asiatisk Plads 2, DK-1448 Copenhagen K Tel.: +45 33920000, Fax: +45 32540533
Danish Agency for Trade and Industry, Langelinie Allé 17, DK-2100 Copenhagen Ø Tel.: +45 35466000, Fax: +45 35466001, E-mail: **efs@efs.dk**, Web: **www.efs.dk**
Danish Agricultural Council, Axeltorv 3, DK-1609 Copenhagen V Tel.: +45 33145672, Fax: +45 33149574, E-mail: **landbrug@landbrug.dk**, Web: **www.landbrugsraadet.dk**

Danish Bacon and Meat Council, Axeltorv 3, DK-1609 Copenhagen V
Tel.: +45 33116050, Fax: +45 33116814, E-mail: **ds-dir@danskeslagterier.dk**, Web: **www.danskeslagterier.dk**

Danish Commerce and Companies Agency, Kampmannsgade 1, DK-1780 Copenhagen V
Tel.: +45 33307700, Fax: +45 33307799, E-mail: **eogs@eogs.dk**, Web: **www.publi-com.dk**

Danish Dairy Board, Frederiks Allé 22, DK-8000 Århus C
Tel.: +45 87312000, Fax: +45 87312001, E-mail: **ddb@mejeri.dk**, Web: **www.mejeri.dk**

Danish Design Center, H C Andersens Boulevard 27, DK-1553 Copenhagen V
Tel.: +45 33693369, Fax: +45 33693300, E-mail: **design@ddc.dk**, Web: **www.ddc.dk**

Danish Employers' Confederation, Vester Voldgade 113, DK-1790 Copenhagen V
Tel.: +45 33389000, Fax: +45 33122976, E-mail: **da@da.dk**, Web: **www.da.dk**

Danish Energy Agency, Amaliegade 44, DK-1256 Copenhagen K
Tel.: +45 33926700, Fax: +45 33114743, E-mail: **ens@ens.dk**, Web: **www.ens.dk**

Danish Export Group Association, Nygade 1B, DK-8600 Silkeborg
Tel.: +45 86813888, Fax: +45 86813114, E-mail: **export@dega.dk**, Web: **www.dega.dk**

Danish Federation of Small and Medium-Sized Enterprises, Amaliegade 31, DK-1256 Copenhagen K
Tel.: +45 33932000, Fax: +45 33320174, E-mail: **hvr@hvr.dk**, Web: **www.hvr.dk**

Danish Patent and Trademark Office, Helgeshøj Allé 81, DK-2630 Taastrup
Tel.: +45 43508000, Fax: +45 43508001, E-mail: **pvs@dkpto.dk**, Web: **www.dkpto.dk**

Danish Shipowners' Association, Amaliegade 33, DK-1256 Copenhagen K
Tel.: +45 33114088, Fax: +45 33116210, E-mail: **info@danmarksrederiforening.dk**, Web: **www.danmarksrederiforening.dk**

Danish Standards Association, Kollegievej 6, DK-2920 Charlottenlund
Tel.: +45 39966101, Fax: +45 39966102, E-mail: **dansk.standard@ds.dk**, Web: **www.ds.dk**

Danish Trade Association of International Transport, Omfartsvejen 1, DK-6330 Padborg
Tel.: +45 74671233, Fax: +45 74674317, E-mail: **itd@itd.dk**, Web: **www.itd.dk**

Danish Windturbine Manufactures Association, Vester Voldgade 106, DK-1552 Copenhagen V
Tel.: +45 33730330, Fax: +45 33730333, E-mail: **danish@windpower.dk**, Web: **www.windpower.dk**

Danmarks Nationalbank, Havnegade 5, DK-1093 Copenhagen K
Tel.: +45 33636363, Fax: +45 33637103, E-mail: **nationalbanken@nationalbanken.dk**, Web: **www.nationalbanken.dk**

Export Promotion Denmark, Gammeltorv 8, DK-1457 Copenhagen K
Tel.: +45 33321711, Fax: +45 33321910, E-mail: **info@ees.dk**, Web: **www.ees.dk**

IFU, IØ & IFV (Danish International Investment Funds), Bremerholm 4, DK-1069 Copenhagen K
Tel.: +45 33637500, Fax: +45 33322524, E-mail: **ifu@ifu.dk**, Web: **www.ifu.dk**

Invest in Denmark, Danish Trade Council, Asiatisk Plads 2, DK-1448 Copenhagen K
Tel.: +45 33920000. Fax: +45 32540533. E-mail: **info@investindk.com**. Web:

For additional analytical, business and investment opportunities information,
please contact Global Investment & Business Center, USA
at (703) 370-8082. Fax: (703) 370-8083. E-mail: ibpusa3@gmail.com
Global Business and Investment Info Databank - www.ibpus.com

www.investindk.com
LAU Exhibition & Promotion, Skodsborgvej 48, DK-2830 Virum Tel.: +45 45857677, Fax: +45 45854220, E-mail: **lau@lau.dk**, Web: **www.lau.dk**
Ministry of Trade and Industry, Slotsholmsgade 10-12, DK-1216 Copenhagen K Tel.: +45 33923350, Fax: +45 33123778, E-mail: **em@em.dk**, Web: **www.em.dk**
NCM EKR Credit Insurance, Gammel Kongevej 11-13, DK-1610 Copenhagen V Tel.: +45 33265000, Fax: +45 33265010, E-mail: **ncmekr@ncmgroup.com**, Web: **www.ncm.dk**
Statistics Denmark, Sejrøgade 11, DK-2100 Copenhagen Ø Tel.: +45 39173917, Fax: +45 39173999, E-mail: **dst@dst.dk**, Web: **www.dst.dk**
The Danish Plastics Federation, Nørre Voldgade 48, DK-1358 Copenhagen K Tel.: +45 33308630, Fax: +45 33308631, E-mail: **pd@plast.dk**, Web: **www.plast.dk**
The Danish Tourist Board, Vesterbrogade 6D, DK-1620 Copenhagen V Tel.: +45 33111415, Fax: +45 33931416, E-mail: **dt@dt.dk**, Web: **www.visitdenmark.com**
The Directorate for Food, Fisheries and Agro Business, Kampmannsgade 3, DK-1780 Copenhagen V Tel.: +45 33958000, Fax: +45 33958080, E-mail: **dffe@dffe.dk**, Web: **www.dffe.dk**
The National Forest and Nature Agency, Haraldsgade 53, DK-2100 Copenhagen Ø Tel.: +45 39472000, Fax: +45 39279899, E-mail: **sns@sns.dk**, Web: **www.sns.dk**
The Öresund Comitee, Gammel Kongevej 1, DK-1610 Copenhagen V Tel.: +45 33220011, Fax: +45 33220023, E-mail: **info@oerekom.dk**, Web: **www.oresundskomiteen.dk**
Wonderful Copenhagen, Gammel Kongevej 1, DK-1610 Copenhagen V Tel.: +45 33257400, Fax: +45 33257410, E-mail: **woco@woco.dk**, Web: **www.visitcopenhagen.dk**
Øresundsbro Konsortiet, Vester Søgade 10, DK-1601 Copenhagen V Tel.: +45 33416000, Fax: +45 33416102, E-mail: **info@oeresundsbron.com**, Web: **www.oeresundsbron.com**

GOVERNMENT AND BUSINESS CONTACTS

DENMARK MINISTRIES

Ministry of Finance, Christiansborg Slotsplads 1, DK-1218 Copenhagen K Tel.: +45 33923333, Fax: +4533328030, E-mail: **fm@fm.dk**, Web: **www.fm.dk**
Ministry of the Interior, Slotsholmsgade 6, DK-1216 Copenhagen K Tel.: +45 33923380, Fax: +4533111239, E-mail: **inm@inm.dk**, Web: **www.indenrigsministeriet.dk**
Ministry of Culture, Nybrogade 2, DK-1203 Copenhagen K Tel.: +45 33923370, Fax: +4533913388, E-mail: **kum@kum.dk**, Web: **www.kum.dk**
The Prime Minister's Office, Prins Jørgens Gård 11, DK-1218 Copenhagen K

Tel.: +45 33923300, Fax: +4533111665, E-mail: **stm@stm.dk**, Web: **www.stm.dk**
Ministry of Ecclesiastical Affairs, Frederiksholms Kanal 21, DK-1220 Copenhagen K Tel.: +45 33923390, Fax: +4533923913, E-mail: **km@km.dk**, Web: **www.km.dk**
Ministry of Education, Frederiksholms Kanal 21, DK-1220 Copenhagen K Tel.: +45 33925000, Fax: +4533925547, E-mail: **uvm@uvm.dk**, Web: **www.uvm.dk**
Ministry of Transport, Frederiksholms Kanal 27, DK-1220 Copenhagen K Tel.: +45 33923355, Fax: +4533123893, E-mail: **trm@trm.dk**, Web: **www.trm.dk**
Ministry of Social Affairs, Holmens Kanal 22, DK-1060 Copenhagen K Tel.: +45 33929300, Fax: +4533923998, E-mail: **sm@sm.dk**, Web: **www.sm.dk**
Ministry of Defence, Holmens Kanal 42, DK-1060 Copenhagen K Tel.: +45 33923320, Fax: +4533320655, E-mail: **fmn@fmn.dk**, Web: **www.fmn.dk**
Ministry of Justice, Slotsholmsgade 10, DK-1216 Copenhagen K Tel.: +45 33923340, E-mail: **jm@jm.dk**, Web: **www.jm.dk**
Ministry of Food, Agriculture and Fisheries, Holbergsgade 2, DK-1057 Copenhagen K Tel.: +45 33923301, Fax: +4533145042, E-mail: **fvm@fvm.dk**, Web: **www.fvm.dk**
Ministry of Economic Affairs, Ved Stranden 8, DK-1061 Copenhagen K Tel.: +45 33923322, Fax: +4533936020, E-mail: **oem@oem.dk**, Web: **www.oem.dk**
Ministry of Housing and Urban Affairs, Slotsholmsgade 1, DK-1216 Copenhagen K Tel.: +45 33926100, Fax: +4533926104, E-mail: **bm@bm.dk**, Web: **www.bm.dk**
Ministry of Trade and Industry, Slotsholmsgade 10-12, DK-1216 Copenhagen K Tel.: +45 33923350, Fax: +4533123778, E-mail: **em@em.dk**, Web: **www.em.dk**
Ministry of Environment and Energy, Højbro Plads 4, DK-1200 Copenhagen K Tel.: +45 33927600, Fax: +4533322227, E-mail: **mem@mem.dk**, Web: **www.mem.dk**
Ministry of Taxation, Slotsholmsgade 12, DK-1216 Copenhagen K Tel.: +45 33923392, Fax: +4533149105, E-mail: **skm@skm.dk**, Web: **www.skm.dk**
Ministry of Health, Holbergsgade 6, DK-1057 Copenhagen K Tel.: +45 33923360, Fax: +4533931563, E-mail: **sum@sum.dk**, Web: **www.sum.dk**
Ministry of Foreign Affairs, Asiatisk Plads 2, DK-1448 Copenhagen K Tel.: +45 33920000, Fax: +4532540533, E-mail: **um@um.dk**, Web: **www.um.dk**
Ministry of Labour, Holmens Kanal 20, DK-1060 Copenhagen K Tel.: +45 33925900, Fax: +4533121378, E-mail: **am@am.dk**, Web: **www.am.dk**
Ministry of Research and Information Technology, Bredgade 43, DK-1260 Copenhagen K Tel.: +45 33929700, Fax: +4533323501, E-mail: **fsk@fsk.dk**, Web: **www.fsk.dk**

DANISH GOVERNMENT AGENCIES

Ministry of Foreign Affairs
Asiatisk Plads 2
DK-1448 Copenhagen K.
Tel: 33 92 00 00
FAX: 31 54 05 33

Ministry of Business and Industry
Slotsholmsgade 12
DK-1216 Copenhagen K.
Tel: 33 92 33 50
FAX: 33 12 37 78

Danish Customs
Customs and Tax Region 1
Strandgade 100
DK-1401 Copenhagen K
DenMark
Tel: (45) 32-88-93-00
Fax: (45) 31-95-10-12

Danmarks Statistik (Danish Bureau of Statistics)
Sejerogade 11
DK-2100 Copenhagen O.
Tel: 39 17 39 17
FAX: 31 18 48 01

Dansk Standard (Danish Standards Association)
Kollegievej 6
DK-2920 Charlottenlund
Tel: 39 96 61 01
FAX: 39 96 61 02

Flyvematerielkommandoen (Air Materiel Command)
Flyvestation Vaerlose
P.O. Box 130
DK-3500 Vaerlose
Tel: 44 68 22 55
FAX: 44 66 25 33

Forbrugerstyrelsen (The National Consumer Agency of DenMark)
Amagerfaelledvej 56
DK-2300 Copenhagen S.
Tel: 31 57 01 00
FAX: 32 96 02 32

DSB (Danish State Railways)
Solvgade 40
DK-1349 Copenhagen K.
Tel: 33 14 04 00
FAX: 33 14 04 40

Haerens Materielkommando (Army Materiel Command)
Arsenalvej 55
DK-9800 Hjorring
Tel: 98 90 13 22
FAX: 98 90 06 23

Miljostyrelsen (The National Agency of Environmental Protection)
Strandgade 29
DK-1401 Copenhagen K.
Tel: 31 57 83 10
FAX: 31 57 24 49

Patentdirektoratet (The Patent Agency)
Helgeshoj Alle 81
DK-2630 Taastrup

For additional analytical, business and investment opportunities information,
please contact Global Investment & Business Center, USA
at (703) 370-8082. Fax: (703) 370-8083. E-mail: ibpusa3@gmail.com
Global Business and Investment Info Databank - www.ibpus.com

Tel: 43 71 71 71
FAX: 43 71 71 70

Sovaernets Materielkommando (Navy Materiel Command)
Holmen
DK-1433 Copenhagen K.
Tel: 31 57 22 55
FAX: 32 96 80 55

Statens Luftfartsvaesen (Civil Aviation Administration)
Luftfartshuset
Ellebjergvej 50
DK-2450 Copenhagen SV
Tel: 36 44 48 48
FAX: 36 44 03 03

Sundhedsstyrelsen (National Board of Health)
Amaliegade 13
DK-1256 Copenhagen K.
Tel: 33 91 16 01
FAX: 33 93 16 36

Laegemiddelstyrelsen
(The Danish Medicines Agency)
Frederikssundvej 378
DK-2700 Bronshoj
Tel: 44 88 91 11
FAX: 42 84 70 77

Dansk Godkendelse af Medicinsk Udstyr - DGM
(Danish Medical Devices Certification)
Kollegievej 6
DK-2920 Charlottenlund
Tel: 39 96 64 00
FAX: 39 96 64 01

Telestyrelsen (National Telecom Agency)
Holsteinsgade 63
DK-2100 Copenhagen O.
Tel: 35 43 03 33
FAX: 35 43 14 34

DANISH TRADE ASSOCIATIONS/CHAMBERS OF COMMERCE

Confederation of Danish Industries
H.C. Andersens Boulevard 18
DK-1787 Copenhagen V.
Tel: 33 77 33 77
FAX: 33 77 33 00

The Danish Chamber of Commerce
Borsen
DK-1217 Copenhagen K.
Tel: 33 95 05 00
FAX: 33 32 52 16

The Agricultural Council
Axeltorv 3
DK-1609 Copenhagen V
Tel: 33 14 56 72
Fax: 33 14 95 74

For additional analytical, business and investment opportunities information,
please contact Global Investment & Business Center, USA
at (703) 370-8082. Fax: (703) 370-8083. E-mail: ibpusa3@gmail.com
Global Business and Investment Info Databank - www.ibpus.com

American Club in Copenhagen
c/o PACE
Ny Ostergade 23
DK-1101 Copenhagen K.
Tel: 33 14 76 56
FAX: 33 11 97 47

Danish Franchise Association
Amaliegade 37,3
DK-1256 Copenhagen K
Tel: 33 15 60 11
FAX: 33 91 03 46

MARKET RESEARCH FIRMS

AIM Research A/S
Strandboulevarden 89
DK-2100 Copenhagen O.
Tel: 35 43 35 43
FAX: 35 43 26 34

Burson-Marsteller A/S
Ostergade 26
DK-1100 Copenhagen K.
Tel: 33 32 30 00
FAX: 33 32 30 01

Nielsen Marketing Research A/S
Strandboulevarden 89
DK-2100 Copenhagen O.
Tel: 35 43 35 43
FAX: 35 43 13 31

Vilstrup Research A/S
Rosenvaengets Alle 25
DK-2100 Copenhagen O.
Tel: 35 43 66 33
FAX: 35 43 66 16

COMMERCIAL BANKS

Citibank N.A.(Subsidiary of Citicorp)
Industriens Hus
Vesterbrogade 1-B
DK-1620 Copenhagen V.
Tel: 33 15 50 30
FAX: 33 32 88 73

Den Danske Bank A/S
Holmens Kanal 2-12
DK-1092 Copenhagen K.
Tel: 33 44 00 00
FAX: 31 18 58 73

Unibank A/S
Torvegade 2
DK-1786 Copenhagen V.
Tel: 33 33 33 33
FAX: 31 54 21 33

For additional analytical, business and investment opportunities information,
please contact Global Investment & Business Center, USA
at (703) 370-8082. Fax: (703) 370-8083. E-mail: ibpusa3@gmail.com
Global Business and Investment Info Databank - www.ibpus.com

A/S Jyske Bank
Vestergade 8-16
DK-8600 Silkeborg
Tel: 89 22 22 22
FAX: 89 22 24 96

U.S. EMBASSY TRADE PERSONNEL

Christian Reed
Senior Commercial Officer
American Embassy
Dag Hammarskjolds Alle 24
DK-2100 Copenhagen O.
Tel: 35 55 31 44
FAX: 35 42 01 75
usfcs@post4.tele.dk

WASHINGTON-BASED USG COUNTRY CONTACTS

TPCC Trade Information Center
Washington DC
Tel: 1-800-USA-TRADE

Agricultural Export Services Div.
Foreign Agricultural Service
U.S. Department of Agriculture
14th and Independence Ave, SW
Washington DC 20250-1000
Tel: 202-720-7420
Fax: 202-690-4374

U.S. Department of Commerce
Denmark Desk
Room H-3043
14th and Constitution Ave., N.W.
Washington, DC 20230
Tel: (202)-482-4414
Fax: (202)-482-2897

EXPORT-IMPORT AND TRADE SERVICES

 Danish American Chamber of Commerce
825 Third Avenue, 32nd Fl.
New York, NY 10022
Tel: (212)-980-6240
FAX: N/A

Commercial Counselor
Royal Danish Consulate General
825 Third Avenue
New York, NY 10022-7519
Tel: (212)-223-4545
FAX: (212)-754-1904

AGRICULTURAL SECTOR CONTACTS

Ministry of Food, Agriculture and Fisheries
Veterinary And Food Directorate
Rolighedsvej 25
DK-1958 Frederiksberg C
Danmark
Tel: (45) 31-35-60-00

**For additional analytical, business and investment opportunities information,
please contact Global Investment & Business Center, USA
at (703) 370-8082. Fax: (703) 370-8083. E-mail: ibpusa3@gmail.com
Global Business and Investment Info Databank - www.ibpus.com**

FAX: (45) 35-36-60-01

Services: Physical examination and control procedures applicable
to livestock and meat products for the Danish market.
Advice about legal compliance with legislation on artificial
aromas, additives.

American Embassy
Office of Agric. Affairs
Dag Hammarskj lds Alle, 24
DK-2100 Copenhagen O
Danmark
Tel: (45) 35-55-31-44 (Embassy)
Tel: (45) 35-26-10-81 (FAS)
FAX: (45) 35-43-02-78 (FAS)

Mailing address for mail from the U.S.A.:
Office of Agric. Affairs
PSC-73
American Embassy (FAS)
APO AE 09716-5000

Services: Commodity and other analytical market reports (see list
below); Danish retail food contacts; trade and other statistics;
administrative support for promotional events; marketing
background for selected retail food and agricultural products;
technical, tariff and excise duties, regulatory and food
labeling/additive information.

The Institute for Food Studies
& Agro-Industrial Development
Venlighedsvej 6
DK-2970 Horsholm
Denmark
Tel: (45) 42-57-05-82
Fax: (45) 45-76-58-60

Services: Conducts special food related studies.

TRADE COMMISSIONS

Australia, Trade Commission of Denmark, Suite 301, 434 St. Kilda Road, Melbourne VIC 3004 Tel.: +61 3 98678733, Fax: +61 3 98209086, E-mail: **dtcmelbourne@dtcmelb.org.au**, Web: **www.eksportraadet.dk/hand/melb**, Trade Commissioner Ole Malmgren
Canada, Trade Commission of Denmark, Suite 308-545 Clyde Avenue, West Vancouver, B.C. V7T 1C5 Tel.: +1 604 9268611, Fax: +1 604 9265569, E-mail: **dtovanc@axionet.com**, Trade Commissioner Bjarne Brynk Jensen
Canada, Délégation Commerciale du Danemark, 1350, Rue Sherbrooke Quest, Bureau 1410, Montréal, Quebec H3G 1J1 Tel.: +1 514 4992099, Fax: +1 514 4990767, E-mail: **dtcmont@cam.org**, Web: **www.eksportraadet.dk/hand/mont**, Trade Commissioner Morten Winther
Croatia, Trade Commission of Denmark, Andrije Hebranga 33/1, 10000 Zagreb Tel.: +385 1 4855299, Fax: +385 1 4854345, E-mail: **ole.gustafsson@za.tel.hr**, Trade

For additional analytical, business and investment opportunities information,
please contact Global Investment & Business Center, USA
at (703) 370-8082. Fax: (703) 370-8083. E-mail: ibpusa3@gmail.com
Global Business and Investment Info Databank - www.ibpus.com

Tel.: +51 1 4419143, Fax: +51 1 4419915, E-mail: **dtclima@protelsa.com.pe**, Trade Commissioner Per Ulrik Andersen

Poland, Trade Commission of Denmark, ul. Slaska 21, 81-319 Gdynia
Tel.: +48 39 124149, Fax: +48 39 124013, E-mail: **dtcgdy@key.net.pl**, Trade Commissioner Jesper Floyd Kristiansen

Poland, Trade Commission of Denmark, ul. Bukowska 12, 60-810 Poznan
Tel.: +48 61 8653900, Fax: +48 61 8653905, E-mail: **dtcpoznan@optimus.poznan.pl**, Trade Commissioner Michael Adam Czartoryski

Portugal, Delegação de Comércio e Indústria Dinamarquesa, Rua de Diu 312, 4150-272 Porto
Tel.: +351 22 6103331, Fax: +351 22 6103327, E-mail: **dtcporto@mail.telepac.pt**, Trade Commissioner Michael Steen Lunde

Saudi Arabia, Royal Trade Commission of Denmark, P.O. Box 5333, City Center Building, Tower B, 3rd floor, No. 6B, Kilo 4, Medina Road, Jeddah 21422
Tel.: +966 2 6630181, Fax: +966 2 6657743, E-mail: **rdtcjed@zajil.net**, Trade Commissioner Allan Jan Formann Kristensen

Saudi Arabia, Trade Commission of Denmark, City Center Building, Tower B, 3rd FL, No 6B, Kilo 4, Madina Road
Tel.: +966 2 6630181, Fax: +966 2 6657743, E-mail: **rdtcjed@zajil.net**

Slovakia, Trade Commission of Denmark, Bastova 7, 816 06 Bratislava 1
Tel.: +421 7 54419982, Fax: +421 7 54419981, E-mail: **dtobratislava@dtobratislava.sk**, Trade Commissioner Sven Aage Færch Nielsen

Slovenia, Trade Commission of Denmark, Trdinova 8, 1000 Ljubljana
Tel.: +386 61 1317371, Fax: +386 61 1317417, E-mail: **dtcljubljana@its.si**, Trade Commissioner Lennart Axen

Sweden, Danmarks Handelskontor, Lilla Bommen 1, 411 04 Göteborg
Tel.: +46 31 150450, Fax: +46 31 159660, E-mail: **dtcgothenburg@swipnet.se**, Trade Commissioner Helle Sejersen Myrthue

Turkey, Trade Commission of Denmark, Dilhayat Sokak No. 9, 80630 Etiler Istanbul
Tel.: +90 212 2658829, Fax: +90 212 2658828, E-mail: **dtcistanbul@iris.com.tr**, Trade Commissioner Gert Grønkjær

United Arab Emirates, Trade Commission of Denmark, P.O. Box 2988, Al Maidan Tower, Office no. 104, Al Maktoum Street, Deira, Dubai
Tel.: +971 4 2227699, Fax: +971 4 2235751, E-mail: **dtcdubai@emirates.net.ae**, Trade Commissioner Flemming Jensen

United Kingdom, Trade Commission of Denmark, 5th floor, Quay House, Quay Street, Manchester M3 3JH
Tel.: +44 161 8327740, Fax: +44 161 8320312, E-mail: **dtcmanchester@btinternet.com**, Trade Commissioner Helle Skaarup Larsen

United States, Trade Commission of Denmark, International Tower, 229 Peachtree Street, N.E. Suite 1010, Atlanta, GA 30303
Tel.: +1 404 5881588, Fax: +1 404 5881589, E-mail: **dtcseusa@bellsouth.net**, Web: **www.eksportraadet.dk/hand/atla**, Trade Commissioner Kent Horskjær Fallesen

United States, Trade Commission of Denmark, World Houston Plaza, 15710 JFK Boulevard, Suite 260, Houston, TX 77032-2346
Tel.: +1 281 4429004, Fax: +1 281 4429024, E-mail: **dantrade@msn.com**, Web: **www.eksportraadet.dk/hand/hous**, Trade Commissioner Lars Juul Øbro

EMBASSIES AND CONSULATES

Albania, Royal Danish Embassy, Rr. Nikolla Tupe No. 1, 4th Fl. Apt. 4, Tirana
Tel.: +355 42 57422, Fax: +355 42 57420, E-mail: **ambadane@icc.al.eu.org**

Algeria, Ambassade Royale de Danemark, 12 Avenue Emile Marquis, Lot. Djenane El-Malik, 16035 Hydra, Alger
Tel.: +213 2 693567, Fax: +213 2 692846, E-mail: **ambadane@eepad.com**

Angola, Royal Danish Consulate General, Rua Conego Manuel das Neves, no.s 104/106, C. Postel 1402, Luanda
Tel.: +244 2446724, Fax: +244 2449035, E-mail: **dansk@ebonet.net**

Antigua and Barbuda, Royal Danish Consulate, 54 High Street, P.O. Box 104, St. John's Antigua & Barbuda, West Indies
Tel.: +1 268 4803070, Fax: +1 268 4803076

Argentina, Real Embajada de Dinamarca, Av. Leandro N. Alem 1074, 1001 Buenos Aires
Tel.: +54 11 43126901, Fax: +54 11 43127857, E-mail: **ambadane@ambadane.org.ar**

Argentina, Real Consulado de Dinamarca, Calle 1, Muelle Carga General 8103, Ingeniero White, 8000 Bahía Blanca, Prov. de B.A.
Tel.: +54 291 4571590, Fax: +54 291 4570653, E-mail: **ahosch@agencia-martin.com.ar**

Argentina, Real Consulado de Dinamarca, Jujuy 2700, Los Vázquez, 4000 San Miguel de Tucumán, Prov. de Tucumán
Tel.: +54 381 4294150, Fax: +54 381 4294100, E-mail: **mercotuc@satlink.com**

Argentina, Real Consulado de Dinamarca, Nuñez del Prado 2484, B. Alto Verde, 5009 Córdoba
Tel.: +54 351 4810171, E-mail: **ebischoff@fiatauto.com.ar**

Argentina, Real Consulado de Dinamarca, Gutierrez 323, P.B.,, 5500 Mensoza, Prov. de Mendoza
Tel.: +54 261 4232610, Fax: +54 261 4203546, E-mail: **apulenta@impsat1.com.ar**

Argentina, Real Consulado de Dinamarca, Hipólito Irigoyen 10-5A, 7500 Tres Arroyos, Prov. de B. A.
Tel.: +54 2983 426286, Fax: +54 2983 430572

Argentina, Real Consulado de Dinamarca, Calle 51-No 1840, 7630 Necochea, Prov.de Buenos Aires
Tel.: +54 2262 432277, Fax: +54 2622 432277

Argentina, Real Consulado de Dinamarca, Estanislao Zeballos 2342, Casa "C", 2000 Rosario, Prov. de Santa Fé
Tel.: +54 341 4487969, Fax: +54 341 4850006, E-mail: **postmaster@fmurb.sld.ar**

Aruba, Vice-Consulate of Denmark, L.G. Smith Blvd. 82, P.O. Box 189, Oranjestad
Tel.: +297 8 24622, Fax: +297 8 21627, E-mail: **meta.corp@setarnet.aw**

Australia, Royal Danish Embassy, 15 Hunter Street, Yarralumla, A.C.T. 2600 Tel.: +61 2 62732195, Fax: +61 2 62733864, E-mail: **dkembact@dynamite.com.au**
Australia, Royal Danish Consulate General, Level 14, Gold Fields House, 1 Alfred Street, Sydney, NSW 2000 Tel.: +61 2 92472224, Fax: +61 2 92517504, E-mail: **sydgkl@sydgkl.um.dk**, Web: **www.dkconsul-sydney.org.au**
Australia, Royal Danish Consulate General, 40a Highfield Road, P.O. Box 167, Canterbury, Victoria 3126 Tel.: +61 3 98305944, Fax: +61 3 98304855, E-mail: **danconej@eisa.net.au**
Australia, Royal Danish Consulate, Minter Ellison, 15th Floor, AMP Building, 1 King William Street, Adelaide, S.A. 5000 Tel.: +61 8 2335555, Fax: +61 8 2127518
Australia, Royal Danish Consulate, 3rd Fl., National Australia Bank, Building, 180 Queen St., Brisbane QLD 4000 Tel.: +61 7 32218641, Fax: +61 7 32218646, E-mail: **osa@gil.com.au**
Australia, Royal Danish Consulate, 19 Phillimore Street, P.O. Box 393, Fremantle W.A. 6160 Tel.: +61 8 93355122, Fax: +61 8 94304141
Australia, Royal Danish Consulate, 18 Bender Drive, Derwent Park, Tasmania 7009 Tel.: +61 3 62730677, Fax: +61 3 62730932, E-mail: **danishconsul@incat.com.au**
Australia, Danish Vice-Consulate, 103 Outram Street, West Perth, P.O. Box 401, Nedlands, 6009 W.A. Tel.: +61 8 93353954, Fax: +61 8 93361886
Austria, Königlich Dänische Botschaft, Führichgasse 6, Postfach 298, 1015 Wien Tel.: +43 1 5127904, Fax: +43 1 5138120, E-mail: **dkembvie@ping.at**
Austria, Königlich Dänisches Generalkonsulat, Ferstelgasse 3/4, 1090 Wien Tel.: +43 1 4079188, Fax: +43 1 4022297
Austria, Königlich Dänisches Konsulat, Maria Theresien Strasse 42, 6020 Innsbruck Tel.: +43 512 582971, Fax: +43 512 5739514
Austria, Königlich Dänisches Konsulat, Roseggerstrasse 59 a, 4020 Linz Tel.: +43 732 651414, Fax: +43 732 651414, E-mail: **dkkonsliaut@merlin.at**
Austria, Königlich Dänisches Konsulat, Grieskai 12-14, 8011 Graz Tel.: +43 316 7030, Fax: +43 316 70388
Austria, Königlich Dänisches Konsulat, Imbergstrasse 15, 5020 Salzburg Tel.: +43 662 8714850, Fax: +43 662 8714856

FOREIGN EMBASSIES IN DENMARK

Algeria

Embassy of Algeria, Amaliegade 36, DK-1256 Copenhagen K Tel.: +45 33119440, Fax: +45 33115850, E-mail: **ambalda@post10.tele.dk**
Argentina
Embassy of Argentina, Borgergade 16, DK-1300 Copenhagen K Tel.: +45 33158082, Fax: +45 33155574, E-mail: **embardin@post1.tele.dk**
Australia
Australian Trade Commission, Strandboulevarden 122, DK-2100 Copenhagen Ø Tel.: +45 39292077, Fax: +45 39296077, E-mail: **dk@austrade.gov.au**, Web: **www.austrade.dk**
Austria
Embassy of Austria, Sølundsvej 1, DK-2100 Copenhagen Ø Tel.: +45 39294141, Fax: +45 39292086, E-mail: **austria@post7.tele.dk**
Commercial Counsellor's Office of Austria, Grønningen 5, DK-1270 Copenhagen K Tel.: +45 33111412, Fax: +45 33911413
Consular Section of the Embassy of Austria, Svanemøllevej 7, DK-2100 Copenhagen Ø Tel.: +45 39296672
Bangladesh
Consulate General of Bangladesh, Lundtoftegårdsvej 95, DK-2800 Kgs. Lyngby Tel.: +45 45263375, Fax: +45 45263330
Belgium
Embassy of Belgium, Øster Allé 7, DK-2100 Copenhagen Ø Tel.: +45 35250200, Fax: +45 35250211, E-mail: **ambelcph@inet.uni2.dk**
Commercial Section of the Embassy of Belgium, Walloon Region, Gothersgade 103, DK-1123 Copenhagen K Tel.: +45 33130211, Fax: +45 33136320, E-mail: **awex@image.dk**
Commercial Section of the Embassy of Belgium, Flemish Region, Gothersgade 103, DK-1123 Copenhagen K Tel.: +45 33130488, Fax: +45 33132802, E-mail: **vlev.kopenhagen@ibm.net**
Bolivia
Embassy of Bolivia, Amaliegade 16C, DK-1256 Copenhagen K Tel.: +45 33124900, Fax: +45 33124903, E-mail: **embodk-1@inet.uni2.dk**
Consulate General of Bolivia, Søllerød Slotsvej 4, DK-2840 Holte Tel.: +45 45802296, Fax: +45 45802296

For additional analytical, business and investment opportunities information,
please contact Global Investment & Business Center, USA
at (703) 370-8082. Fax: (703) 370-8083. E-mail: ibpusa3@gmail.com
Global Business and Investment Info Databank - www.ibpus.com

Bosnia and Herzegovina
Embassy of Bosnia-Herzegovina, Nytorv 3, DK-1450 Copenhagen K Tel.: +45 33338040, Fax: +45 33338017, E-mail: **ba-emb-dk-cph@mobilixnet.dk**
Brazil
Embassy of Brazil, Ryvangs Allé 24, DK-2100 Copenhagen Ø Tel.: +45 39206478, Fax: +45 39273607, E-mail: **ambassade@brazil.dk**
Bulgaria
Embassy of Bulgaria, Gamlehave Allé 7, DK-2920 Charlottenlund Tel.: +45 39642484, Fax: +45 39634923, E-mail: **bbb25387@vip.cybercity.dk**
Burkina Faso
Embassy of Burkina Faso, Svanemøllevej 20, DK-2100 Copenhagen Ø Tel.: +45 39184022, Fax: +45 39271886, E-mail: **amba@burkina.dk**
Burundi
Consulate of Burundi, Granskoven 8, DK-2600 Glostrup Tel.: +45 43434590, Fax: +45 43434049
Cameroon
Consulate of Cameroon, Hveensvej 6, DK-2950 Vedbæk Tel.: +45 45892000, Fax: +45 45893100, E-mail: **sattrac@get2net.dk**
Canada
Embassy of Canada, Kristen Bernikows Gade 1, DK-1105 Copenhagen K Tel.: +45 33483200, Fax: +45 33483220, Web: **www.canada.dk**
Chile
Embassy of Chile, Kastelsvej 15, DK-2100 Copenhagen Ø Tel.: +45 35385834, Fax: +45 35384201, E-mail: **embassy@chiledk.dk**, Web: **www.chiledk.dk**
China
Embassy of China, Øregårds Allé 25, DK-2900 Hellerup Tel.: +45 39460889, Fax: +45 39625484, Web: **www.chinaembassy.dk**
Commercial Section of the Embassy of China, Øregårds Allé 12, DK-2900 Hellerup

For additional analytical, business and investment opportunities information,
please contact Global Investment & Business Center, USA
at (703) 370-8082. Fax: (703) 370-8083. E-mail: ibpusa3@gmail.com
Global Business and Investment Info Databank - www.ibpus.com

Tel.: +45 39611013, Fax: +45 39612913
Colombia
Embassy of Columbia, Kastelsvej 15, DK-2100 Copenhagen Ø Tel.: +45 35263026, Fax: +45 35262297, E-mail: **emdinarmarca@colombia.dk**, Web: **www.colombia.dk**
Congo, Democratic Republic
Consulate of the Democratic Republic of Congo, Nørrebred 153, DK-2625 Vallensbæk Tel.: +45 43626810, Fax: +45 43626810, E-mail: **congo_consul@hotmail.com**
Costa Rica
Consulate General of Costa Rica, Kvæsthusgade 3, DK-1251 Copenhagen K Tel.: +45 33110885, Fax: +45 33937530
Croatia
Embassy of Croatia, Dronningens Tværgade 5, DK-1302 Copenhagen K Tel.: +45 33919095, Fax: +45 33917131, E-mail: **vpdk@koebenhavn.mail.telia.com**
Cuba
Embassy of Cuba, Carolinevej 12, DK-2900 Hellerup Tel.: +45 39401510, Fax: +45 39401510
Cyprus
Consulate General of Cyprus, Aurikelvej 22, DK-2000 Frederiksberg Tel.: +45 36462980, Fax: +45 33317141
Czech Republic
Embassy of the Czech Republic, Ryvangs Allé 14-16, DK-2100 Copenhagen Ø Tel.: +45 39291888, Fax: +45 39290930, E-mail: **copenhagen@embassy.mzv.cz**
Egypt
Embassy of Egypt, Kristianiagade 19, DK-2100 Copenhagen Ø Tel.: +45 35437070, Fax: +45 35253262
El Salvador
Consulate of El Salvador, Gartnervej 18, DK-2630 Taastrup Tel.: +45 43998530, Fax: +45 43998530, E-mail: **konsulatet@el-salvador.dk**, Web: **www.el-salvador.dk**

Estonia
Embassy of Estonia, Aurehøjvej 19, DK-2900 Hellerup Tel.: +45 39463070, Fax: +45 39463076, E-mail: **sekretar@estemb.dk**
Finland
Embassy of Finland, Sankt Annæ Plads 24, DK-1250 Copenhagen K Tel.: +45 33134214, Fax: +45 33324710, E-mail: **webmaster@finamb.dk**, Web: **www.finamb.dk**
Commercial Section of the Embassy of Finland, Toldbodgade 18, DK-1253 Copenhagen K Tel.: +45 33134114, Fax: +45 33132072, E-mail: **copenhagen@finpro.fi**, Web: **www.finpro.fi**
France
Embassy of France, Kongens Nytorv 4, DK-1050 Copenhagen K Tel.: +45 33155122, Fax: +45 33939752, Web: **www.amba-france.dk**
Commercial Section of the Embassy of France, Hammerensgade 6, DK-1267 Copenhagen K Tel.: +45 33934822, Fax: +45 33934866
Consular Section of the Embassy of France, Ny Østergade 3, DK-1101 Copenhagen K Tel.: +45 33325090, Fax: +45 33337570, E-mail: **consulat@amba-france.dk**
Germany
Embassy of Germany, Stockholmsgade 57, DK-2100 Copenhagen Ø Tel.: +45 35459900, Fax: +45 35267105, E-mail: **tyskeamba@email.dk**, Web: **www.tyske-ambassade.dk**
Ghana
Embassy of Ghana, Egebjerg Allé 13, DK-2900 Hellerup Tel.: +45 39628222, Fax: +45 39621652
Greece
Embassy of Greece, Borgergade 16, DK-1300 Copenhagen K Tel.: +45 33114533, Fax: +45 33931646, E-mail: **greekembcop@post.tele.dk**
Commercial Section of the Embassy of Greece, Store Kongensgade 24, DK-1264 Copenhagen K Tel.: +45 33148486, Fax: +45 33140235
Guatemala
Consulate of Guatemala. Immortellevei 4. DK-2950 Vedbæk

Tel.: +45 45891584, Fax: +45 45893322

Guinea

Guinea Conakry Konsulatet, Hveensvej 6, DK-2950 Vedbæk
Tel.: +45 45892000, Fax: +45 45893100, E-mail: **sattrac@get2net.dk**

Guinea-Bissau

Consulate of Guinea-Bissau, Mesterlodden 16, DK-2820 Gentofte
Tel.: +45 39658933, Fax: +45 39654126

Holy See (Vatican City State)

Apostolic Nunciature of the Holy See, Immortellevej 11, DK-2950 Vedbæk
Tel.: +45 45893536, Fax: +45 45661771, E-mail: **nunciature@inet.zitech.dk**

Honduras

Consulate General of Honduras, Telegrafvej 5, DK-2750 Ballerup
Tel.: +45 44973626, Fax: +45 44683304

Hungary

Embassy of Hungary, Strandvejen 170, DK-2920 Charlottenlund
Tel.: +45 39631688, Fax: +45 39630052, E-mail: **huemb.cph@teliamail.dk**

Hungarian Trade Centre, Møntergade 1, DK-1116 Copenhagen K
Tel.: +45 33134432, Fax: +45 33115617, E-mail: **hungcom@image.dk**

Iceland

Embassy of Iceland, Dantes Plads 3, DK-1556 Copenhagen V
Tel.: +45 33181050, Fax: +45 33181059, E-mail: **coph@utn.stjr.is**

India

Embassy of India, Vangehusvej 15, DK-2100 Copenhagen Ø
Tel.: +45 39182888, Fax: +45 39270218, E-mail: **indemb@euroconnect.dk**

Indonesia

Embassy of Indonesia, Ørehøj Allé 1, DK-2900 Hellerup
Tel.: +45 39624422, Fax: +45 39624483

Iran

**For additional analytical, business and investment opportunities information,
please contact Global Investment & Business Center, USA
at (703) 370-8082. Fax: (703) 370-8083. E-mail: ibpusa3@gmail.com
Global Business and Investment Info Databank - www.ibpus.com**

Embassy of Iran, Engskiftevej 6, DK-2100 Copenhagen Ø
Tel.: +45 39160071, Fax: +45 36160075

Ireland

Embassy of Ireland, Østbanegade 21, DK-2100 Copenhagen Ø
Tel.: +45 35423233, Fax: +45 35431858, E-mail: **irlemb_dk@yahoo.com**

Israel

Embassy of Israel, Lundevangsvej 4, DK-2900 Hellerup
Tel.: +45 39626288, Fax: +45 39621938, E-mail: **info@embassy-of-israel.dk**, Web:
www.embassy-of-israel.dk

Italy

Embassy of Italy, Gammel Vartov Vej 7, DK-2900 Hellerup
Tel.: +45 39626877, Fax: +45 39622599, E-mail: **italambcph@get2net.dk**

Consular Section of the Embassy of Italy, Engskiftevej 4, DK-2100 Copenhagen Ø
Tel.: +45 39183444, Fax: +45 39270106, E-mail: **italconscph@get2net.dk**

Italian Institute for Foreign Trade, Østergade 24B, DK-1100 Copenhagen K
Tel.: +45 33129200, Fax: +45 33933304, E-mail: **icecph@inet.uni2.dk**, Web:
www.ice.it/estero/copenaghen

Ivory Coast

Embassy of Côte d'Ivoire, Gersonsvej 8, DK-2900 Hellerup
Tel.: +45 39628822, Fax: +45 39620162, E-mail: **ambaivoire@mail.tele.dk**

Japan

Embassy of Japan, Pilestræde 61, DK-1112 Copenhagen K
Tel.: +45 33113344, Fax: +45 33113377, E-mail: **info@embjapan.dk**, Web: **www.embjapan.dk**

Jordan

Consulate of Jordan, H C Andersens Boulevard 9, DK-1553 Copenhagen V
Tel.: +45 33338677, Fax: +45 33338986

Korea, South

Embassy of the Republic of Korea, Svanemøllevej 104, DK-2900 Hellerup
Tel.: +45 39460400, Fax: +45 39460422

Commercial Section of the Embassy of the Republic of Korea, Holbergsgade 14, DK-1057
Copenhagen K

For additional analytical, business and investment opportunities information,
please contact Global Investment & Business Center, USA
at (703) 370-8082. Fax: (703) 370-8083. E-mail: ibpusa3@gmail.com
Global Business and Investment Info Databank - www.ibpus.com

Tel.: +45 33126658, Fax: +45 33326654

Kuwait

Consulate of Kuwait, Strandvejen 203, DK-2900 Hellerup
Tel.: +45 39611420, Fax: +45 39610677

Latvia

Embassy of Latvia, Rosbæksvej 17, DK-2100 Copenhagen Ø
Tel.: +45 39276000, Fax: +45 39276173, E-mail: **latemb@latemb.dk**

Lebanon

Consulate of Lebanon, Mantziusvej 18, DK-2900 Hellerup
Tel.: +45 39621816

Lesotho

Embassy of Lesotho, Strandvejen 64H, DK-2900 Hellerup
Tel.: +45 39624343, Fax: +45 39621538, E-mail: **ccc23925@vip.cybercity.dk**

Liberia

Consulat General of Liberia, Dampfærgevej 10, DK-2100 Copenhagen Ø
Tel.: +45 35262995, Fax: +45 35266995, E-mail: **gh@ghananordiv.dk**, Web:
www.ghananordiv.dk

Libya

Embassy of Libya, Rosenvængets Hovedvej 4, DK-2100 Copenhagen Ø
Tel.: +45 35263611, Fax: +45 35265606

Lithuania

Embassy of Lithuania, Bernstorffsvej 214, DK-2920 Charlottenlund
Tel.: +45 39636207, Fax: +45 39636532, E-mail: **lrambdan@inet.uni2.dk**, Web:
inet.uni2dk/home/ltembassydk/

Luxemburg

Embassy of Luxembourg, Fridtjof Nansens Plads 5, DK-2100 Copenhagen Ø
Tel.: +45 35268200, Fax: +45 35268208

Macedonia

Embassy of Macedonia, Kildegårdsvej 36, DK-2900 Hellerup

Tel.: +45 39766920, Fax: +45 39766923

Madagascar

Consulate General of Madagascar, Skodsborgvej 242, DK-2850 Nærum
Tel.: +45 45806266, Fax: +45 45806278

Malawi

Consulate General of Malawi, Agavevej 17, DK-2900 Hellerup
Tel.: +45 39627650

Malaysia

Consulat of Malaysia, Sundkrogsgade 10, DK-2100 Copenhagen Ø
Tel.: +45 39179333, Fax: +45 39179393

Mali

Consulate of Mali, Dampfærgevej 10, DK-2100 Copenhagen Ø
Tel.: +45 35262995, Fax: +45 35266995, E-mail: **gh@ghananordic.dk**, Web:
www.ghananordiv.dk

Malta

Maltas Konsulat for Sjælland, Skodsborg Strandvej 156, DK-2942 Skodsborg
Tel.: +45 45560099, Fax: +45 45560050

Mauritania

Consulate General of Mauretania, Frydendalsvej 26, DK-1809 Frederiksberg C
Tel.: +45 33223361, Fax: +45 33221842, E-mail: **oa@oveandersen.dk**

Mauritius

Consulate of Mauritius, Gothersgade 101D, DK-1123 Copenhagen K
Tel.: +45 33338182, Fax: +45 33330507

Mexico

Embassy of Mexico, Strandvejen 64E, DK-2900 Hellerup
Tel.: +45 39610500, Fax: +45 39610512, E-mail: **info@mexican-embassy.dk**, Web:
www.mexican-embassy.dk

Consular Section of the Embassy of Mexico, Gammel Vartov Vej 18, DK-2900 Hellerup
Tel.: +45 39295744, Fax: +45 39292792

For additional analytical, business and investment opportunities information,
please contact Global Investment & Business Center, USA
at (703) 370-8082. Fax: (703) 370-8083. E-mail: ibpusa3@gmail.com
Global Business and Investment Info Databank - www.ibpus.com

Monaco
Consulate General of Monaco, Aurehøjvej 11, DK-2900 Hellerup Tel.: +45 39626358, Fax: +45 39627476, E-mail: **vagn.jespersen@mail.tele.dk**
Mongolia
Consulate of Mongolia, Fiskerihavnsgade 6, DK-2450 Copenhagen Sv Tel.: +45 33148273, Fax: +45 33128373
Morocco
Embassy of Morocco, Øregårds Allé 19, DK-2900 Hellerup Tel.: +45 39624511, Fax: +45 39622449, E-mail: **sifamadk@inet.uni2.dk**
Nepal
Consulate General of Nepal, Aldersrogade 3A, DK-2100 Copenhagen Ø Tel.: +45 39273175, Fax: +45 39201245, E-mail: **janus@janus-as.dk**
Netherlands
Embassy of the Netherlands, Toldbodgade 33, DK-1253 Copenhagen K Tel.: +45 33707200, Fax: +45 33140350, E-mail: **nltrade@euroconnect.dk**, Web: **www.nlembassy.dk**
Niger
Consulate of Niger, Onsgårdsvej 37, DK-2900 Hellerup Tel.: +45 39624623
Norway
Embassy of Norway, Amaliegade 39, DK-1256 Copenhagen K Tel.: +45 33140124, Fax: +45 33140624, E-mail: **norge2@danbbs.dk**, Web: **www.norsk.dk**
Oman
Consulate of Oman, Strandvænget 5B, DK-8240 Risskov Tel.: +45 86175072, Fax: +45 86175058
Pakistan
Embassy of Pakistan, Valeursvej 17, DK-2900 Hellerup Tel.: +45 39621188, Fax: +45 39401070, E-mail: **parepcopenhagen@hotmail.com**
Panama

Consulate General of Panama, Amaliegade 42, DK-1256 Copenhagen K Tel.: +45 33113399, Fax: +45 33324625
Paraguay
Commercial Office of Paraguay, Vester Voldgade 96, DK-1552 Copenhagen V Tel.: +45 33150178, E-mail: **farremi@hotmail.com**
Peru
Embassy of Peru, Rosenvængets Allé 20A, DK-2100 Copenhagen Ø Tel.: +45 35265848, Fax: +45 35268406, E-mail: **perudk@post6.tele.dk**, Web: **home6.inet.tele.dk/perudk**
Philippines
Consulate General of the Philippines, Snorresgade 20, DK-2300 Copenhagen S Tel.: +45 32578641, Fax: +45 32574900, E-mail: **philcon@scan-group.dk**
Poland
Embassy of Poland, Richelieus Allé 12, DK-2900 Hellerup Tel.: +45 39467700, Fax: +45 39467766, E-mail: **ambaspol@post4.tele.dk**, Web: **www.ambpol.dk**
Commercial Counsellor's Office of the Embassy of Poland, Ryvangs Allé 46, DK-2900 Hellerup Tel.: +45 39622633, Fax: +45 39622554, E-mail: **brhdania@post10.tele.dk**, Web: **www.brh-dania.dk**
Portugal
Embassy of Portugal, Hovedvagtsgade 6, DK-1103 Copenhagen K Tel.: +45 33131301, Fax: +45 33149214, E-mail: **embport@get2net.dk**
Commercial Counsellor's Office of Portugal, Gammeltorv 4, DK-1457 Copenhagen K Tel.: +45 33127632, Fax: +45 33938885
Romania
Embassy of Romania, Strandagervej 27, DK-2900 Hellerup Tel.: +45 39407177, Fax: +45 39627899, E-mail: **roemb@mail.tele.dk**, Web: **www.romanianembassy.dk**
Russia
Embassy of Russia, Kristianiagade 5, DK-2100 Copenhagen Ø Tel.: +45 35425585, Fax: +45 35423741

Commercial Representation of Russia, Vigerslev Allé 161, DK-2500 Valby Tel.: +45 36462811, Fax: +45 36462982
Saudi Arabia
Embassy of Saudia Arabia, Lille Strandvej 27, DK-2900 Hellerup Tel.: +45 39621200, Fax: +45 39626009, E-mail: **s.a.embassy@mail.tele.dk**
Senegal
Consulate General of Senegal, Amaliegade 43, DK-1256 Copenhagen K Tel.: +45 33932710
Serbia and Montenegro
Embassy of Serbia-Montenegro, Svanevænget 36-38, DK-2100 Copenhagen Ø Tel.: +45 39297784, Fax: +45 39297919, E-mail: **bkb4913@vip.cipercity.dk**
Sierra Leone
Consulate of Sierra Leone, Strandboulevarden 33, DK-2100 Copenhagen Ø Tel.: +45 35265526, Fax: +45 35263211
Singapore
Consulate General of Singapore, Snorresgade 20, DK-2300 Copenhagen S Tel.: +45 32548360, Fax: +45 32548370, E-mail: **sincon@scan-group.dk**
Slovakia
Embassy of Slovakia, Vesterled 26-28, DK-2100 Copenhagen Ø Tel.: +45 39209911, Fax: +45 39209913, E-mail: **slovakiskamb@vip.cybercity.dk**, Web: **slovakiskamb.homepage.dk**
Slovenia
Embassy of Slovenia, Amaliegade 6, DK-1256 Copenhagen K Tel.: +45 33730120, Fax: +45 33150607
Somalia
Consulate General of Somalia, Snorresgade 20, DK-2300 Copenhagen S Tel.: +45 32544011, Fax: +45 32570411
South Africa
Embassy of South Africa, Gammel Vartov Vej 8, DK-2900 Hellerup

Tel.: +45 39180155, Fax: +45 39184006, E-mail: **saembassy@inform-bbs.dk**
Spain
Embassy of Spain, Kristianiagade 21, DK-2100 Copenhagen Ø Tel.: +45 35424700, Fax: +45 35263099, E-mail: **spain@post.cybercity.dk**
Commercial Section of the Embassy of Spain, Vesterbrogade 10, DK-1620 Copenhagen V Tel.: +45 33312210, Fax: +45 33213390
Swaziland
Embassy of Swaziland, Kastelsvej 19, DK-2100 Copenhagen Ø Tel.: +45 35426111, Fax: +45 35426300
Sweden
Embassy of Sweden, Sankt Annæ Plads 15A, DK-1250 Copenhagen K Tel.: +45 33360370, Fax: +45 33360395, E-mail: **ambassaden.kopenhamn@foreign.ministry.se**, Web: **www.sverigesambassad.dk**
Swedish Trade Council, Toldbodgade 18, DK-1253 Copenhagen K Tel.: +45 33155522, Fax: +45 33329499, E-mail: **danmark@swedishtrade.se**, Web: **www.swedishtrade.se**
Switzerland
Embassy of Switzerland, Amaliegade 14, DK-1256 Copenhagen K Tel.: +45 33141796, Fax: +45 33337551, E-mail: **vertretung@cop.rep.admin.ch**
Tanzania
Consulate of Tanzania, Gothersgade 21, DK-1123 Copenhagen K Tel.: +45 33164900, E-mail: **anni@post7.tele.dk**
Thailand
Embassy of Thailand, Norgesmindevej 18, DK-2900 Hellerup Tel.: +45 39625010, Fax: +45 39625059, E-mail: **thai-dk@inet.uni2.dk**
Commercial Affairs Office of Thailand, Hellerupvej 76, DK-2900 Hellerup Tel.: +45 39626999, Fax: +45 39626099, E-mail: **dep@thaicum.dk**
Turkey
Embassy of Turkey, Rosbæksvej 15, DK-2100 Copenhagen Ø Tel.: +45 39202788, Fax: +45 39205166, E-mail: **turkembassy@internet.dk**, Web: **www.turkembassy.dk**
Commercial Counsellor's Office of the Embassy of Turkey, Borgergade 42, DK-1300

Copenhagen K Tel.: +45 33122920, Fax: +45 33146346
Uganda
Embassy of Uganda, Sofievej 15, DK-2900 Hellerup Tel.: +45 39620966, Fax: +45 39610148, E-mail: **ug-embassy-denmark@inet.uni2.dk**
Ukraine
Embassy of Ukraine, Toldbodgade 37A, DK-1253 Copenhagen K Tel.: +45 33161635, Fax: +45 33160074
United Kingdom
Embassy of the United Kingdom, Kastelsvej 36-40, DK-2100 Copenhagen Ø Tel.: +45 35445200, Fax: +45 35445293, E-mail: **brit-emb@post6.tele.dk**, Web: **www.britishembassy.dk**
United States
Embassy of the United States of America, Dag Hammarskjölds Allé 24, DK-2100 Copenhagen Ø Tel.: +45 35553144, Fax: +45 35430223, Web: **www.usembassy.dk**
Venezuela
Embassy of Venezuela, Holbergsgade 14, DK-1057 Copenhagen K Tel.: +45 33936311, Fax: +45 33156911, E-mail: **emvendk@post5.tele.dk**, Web: **home7.inet.tele.dk/emvendk**

INVEST IN DENMARK'S REGIONAL NETWORK

Business Development
Centre West
Havnegade 1
DK- 6700 Esbjerg

Tel: +45 7512 1603
Fax: +45 7512 1607
E-mail: **bni@euvest.dk**
Internet:
www.euvest.com

Copenhagen Capacity
Gammel Kongevej 1, 1.
DK-1610 Copenhagen V

Tel: +45 3322 0222
Fax: +45 3322 0211
E-mail: **info@copcap.dk**
Internet:
www.copcap.com

Funen Industrial
Development Centre
Blangstedgårdsvej 1
DK-5220 Odense SØ

Tel: +45 6615 6531
Fax: +45 6615 6541
E-mail: **fer@fynerhv.dk**
Internet: **www.fynerhv.dk**

Future Invest
c/o Eura A/S
Vester Strandsberg 4A
DK-6950 Ringkøbing

Tel: +45 9732 5000
Fax: +45 9732 5044
E-mail: **eura@eura.dk**

Invest in Viborg County
Skottenborg 26
DK-8800 Viborg

Tel: +45 8727 1700
Fax: +45 8662 6862
E-mail:
crbbbm@vibamt.dk
Internet:**www.vibamt.dk/e
a/rifo/**

Investment Location
Region Aarhus Denmark
Aaboulevarden 3
DK-8000 Aarhus C

Tel: +45 8940 2660
Fax: +45 8940 2665
E-mail: **info@invloc.dk**
Internet: **www.invloc.dk**

The Investment Corridor
East Jutland
Tobaksgården 1
Allégade 10
DK-8700 Horsens

For additional analytical, business and investment opportunities information,
please contact Global Investment & Business Center, USA
at (703) 370-8082. Fax: (703) 370-8083. E-mail: ibpusa3@gmail.com
Global Business and Investment Info Databank - www.ibpus.com

Tel: +45 7562 8588
Fax: +45 7562 8599
E-mail:
korridoren@korridoren.c om
Internet:
www.korridoren.com

North West Zealand
Investment
Oesterled 28, Postboks 338
DK-4300 Holbaek

Tel: +45 5944 4268
Fax: +45 5944 4201
E-mail: **erh@reghol.dk**

NorthDenmark Invest
Niels Jernes Vej 10
DK- 9220 Aalborg Øst

Tel: +45 9635 4400
Fax: +45 9815 1944

E-mail: **bnn@njes.dk**
Internet:
www.northdenmark.com

South Jutland Regional
Business Development
Centre
Bjergparken, Bjerggade 4C
DK- 6200 Aabenraa

Tel: +45 7362 1010
Fax: +45 7362 1011
E-mail:
webmaster@sjec.dk
Internet: **www.sjec.dk**

Storstrom Business
Development Centre
Marienbergvej 80
DK- 4760 Vordingborg

Tel: +45 5534 0155
Fax: +45 5534 0355

E-mail: **sec@sec.dk**
Internet: **www.sec.dk**

Triangle Region Denmark
Regional Development
Fredericiagade 32
DK- 6000 Kolding

Tel: +45 7550 8383
Fax: +45 7550 0363
E-mail:
info@trekantomraadet.d k
Internet:
www.trekantomraadet.dk

Zeeland Gateway
Vestsjællands Erhvervsråd
Amerikakajen 1
DK-4220 Korsør

Tel: +45 5357 7200
Fax: +45 5357 7884
E-mail: **ve@ve.dk**

For additional analytical, business and investment opportunities information,
please contact Global Investment & Business Center, USA
at (703) 370-8082. Fax: (703) 370-8083. E-mail: ibpusa3@gmail.com
Global Business and Investment Info Databank - www.ibpus.com

ELECTRONIC AND HIGH TECH COMPANIES IN DENMARK

ACTE Denmark AS

Telefonvej 8
2860 Søborg
Tel: 39 57 71 00
Fax: 39 57 71 02
Email: **b.hoeg@acte.dk**
Web: **www.actenc.com**
Executive Assistant : Gitte Paalvast email: **b.hoeg@acte.dk**
Direktør : Jan Friis email: **j.friis@bbe.dk**
Økonomichef : Michael Norskov email: **m.norskov@acte.dk**

Sales and distribution of electronic components (active, passive, and electromechanical) and systems in Denmark, Finland, Norway and Sweden. Specialised within development and construction. Quality Assurance: ISO 9001.

Alcatel Danmark A/S

Lautrupvang 2
2750 Ballerup
Tel: 44 86 75 00
Fax: 44 86 75 01
Email: **info@alcatel.dk**
Web: **www.alcatel.com**

Direktør : Asger F. Knudsen email: **asger.knudsen@alcatel.dk**
Økonomichef : Jan Plenge email: **jan.plenge@alcatel.dk**
Engineering chef : Mikael Nadelmann email: **mna@alcatel.dk**
Logistikchef : Peter Knudsen email: **peter.knudsen@alcatel.dk**

Telecommunication equipment, digital PABXs, subsets, data terminals, cellular phones, telecommunication electronics, satellite equipment, and transport systems.

Alstom Signalling A/S

Priorparken 530
2605 Brøndby
Tel: 43 43 84 00
Fax: 43 43 84 01
Email: **sid@transport.alstom.com**

Direktør : Henrik Bækbo email: **henrik.baekbo@transport.alstom.com**

Electronic railway signalling equipment for interlocking, line block, level crossing and train detection. Design, installation and commissioning. Support of a full range of products for railway and mass transit.

APC Denmark A/S

Silcon Allé
Postboks 868
6000 Kolding
Tel: 75 54 22 55
Fax: 75 54 27 89
Email: **info@appc.com**
Web: **www.appc.com**
Kvalitets- og miljøchef : Yitzhak Shoshan email: **yshoshan@apcc.com**
Direktør : Søren Rathmann email: **srathman@apcc.com**
Adm. Direktør : Hans J. Nielsen email: **hnielsen@apcc.com**
Logistikchef : Susanne E. Sørensen email: **ssorense@apcc.com**
Personalechef : Marianne Lock email: **mlock@apcc.com**

UPS systems (DATAPOWER) 0,5-330 kVA. Inverters. Chargers. Frequency converters.

APW Power Supplies A/S

Smedevænget 1
5560 Aarup
Tel: 63 43 21 22
Fax: 63 43 21 60
Email: **info@apw-power.com**
Web: **www.apw-power.com**
Udviklingschef : Jens Vett-Larsen email: **jvl@danicasupply.com**
Produktionschef : Jørn Jespersen email: **jrj@danicasupply.com**
Teknisk direktør : Jørgen M. Lundbeck email: **jml@danicasupply.com**
Direktør : Jesper Bilde email: **jeb@danicasupply.com**

Stabilised power supplies, switch mode, bench and build-in models. DC/DC converters step up/step down.

Ascom Nordic A/S

Park Allé 295
2605 Brøndby
Tel: 43 43 43 95
Fax: 43 43 53 54
Direktør : Povl M. Knudsen email: **pmk@ascom.dk**

Manufacturers of public pay-phones and pay-phone management systems. Terminals for electronic funds transfer.

Bang & Olufsen A/S

Peter Bangs Vej 15
7600 Struer
Tel: 96 84 11 22
Fax: 96 84 11 44
Web: **www.bang-olufsen.com**
Direktør : Karsten Okholm Larsen email:
Teknologichef : Palle Nissen email: **nis@bang-olufsen.dk**
Direktør : Anders Knutsen email: **ajk@bang-olufsen.dk**
Direktør : Carl Henrik Jeppesen email: **cje@bang-olufsen.dk**
: Kent G. Christensen email: **kgc@bang-olufsen.dk**

Miljøchef : Jens Simonsen email: **jsi@bang-olufsen.dk**
Personalechef : Niels Mose Thorsted email: **nmt@bang-olufsen.dk**
Projektleder : Klaus Breinholt email: **klb@bang-olufsen.dk**
Direktør : Karsten Okholm Larsen email:

Consumer electronics and telecommunication equipment: Colour television, radio receivers, video and audio tape recorders, compact disc players, gramophones, pick-up cartridges, satellite receiving equipment, telephones.

BARCO AS

Emdrupvej 26
2100 København Ø
Tel: 39 17 00 00
Fax: 39 17 00 10
Email: **info.dk.bcs@barco.com**
Web: **www.barco.com**
Corporate Controller : Finn Holst email: **fho@re.dk**
Personalechef : Kirsten Neumann email: **kirsten.neumann@barco.com**
Direktør : Henrik Nørrelykke email: **henrik.norrelykke@barco.com**

Professional electronic equipment for communication. The product line includes broadcast quality digital video and audio codecs for telecommunication applications.

bb electronics a/s

Ane Staunings Vej 21
8700 Horsens
Tel: 76 25 10 00
Fax: 76 25 10 10
Email: **bbe@bbelectronics.dk**
Web: **www.bbelectronics.dk**
Planlægger : Flemming A. Olsen email: **fao@bbelectronics.dk**
Direktør : Bjarne Kvolbæk Jensen email: **bkj@bbelectronics.dk**
Økonomichef : Kim Lauridsen email: **kla@bbelectronics.dk**
Kvalitetskoordinator : Rikke Roden Jensen email: **rrj@bbelectronics.dk**

Printed circuit boards: single and double sided. Plated through holes. Multilayer boards. UL approval. ISO 9002. Electronics assembly: SMT assembly and soldering, capacity: 100,000 components/hour. Contract work. Assembly of complete units. In-circuit and function test. ISO 9002. X-ray inspection of the mounted PCB.

Bosch Telecom Danmark A/S

Industrivej 30
9490 Pandrup
Tel: 96 73 80 00
Fax: 96 73 80 01
Personalechef : Lone Broberg email: **lone.broberg@dk.bosch.com**
Direktør : Peter Hinrup email: **peter.hinrup@dk.bosch.com**
Sikkerhedschef : Niels Henrik Nielsen email: **niels-henrik.nielsen@dk.bosch.com**

Research, development, manufacture and distribution of wireless telecommunications products. The product range includes digital cellular telephones for GSM, DCS 1800 and 1900 networks.

Brüel & Kjær Sound & Vibration Measurement A/S

Skodsborgvej 307
2850 Nærum
Tel: 45 80 05 00
Fax: 45 80 71 92
Email: **info@bk.dk**
Web: **www.bk.dk**
Direktør : Henrik Håkonsson email: **hhakonsson@bk.dk**
Projekt- & Teknologidir. : Karl Kristian Nielsen email:
Personaledirektør : Henrik Bøje Svendsen email: **hbsvendsen@bk.dk**
Logistikchef : Finn Rasmussen email: **firasmusse@bk.dk**
Teknologidirektør : Knud Sørensen email: **ksorensen@bk.dk**
Att.: : Søren Jønsson email: **sjonsson@bk.dk**
Leverandøransvarlig : Bjarne Thomsen email: **bthomsen@bk.dk**

Test systems and components for evaluation of electroacoustic transmission performance and vibration testing of telephone terminals, audio equipment, and hearing aids.

C. Thiim A/S

Transformervej 31
2730 Herlev
Tel: 44 85 80 00
Fax: 44 85 80 05
Email: **thiim@thiim.com**
Web: **www.thiim.com**
Direktør : Søren Thiim email: **st@thiim.com**

Manufacture and Export: Full ranges of transducers. Relays for current voltages, frequency, phase failure, phase angle, phase sequence, temperature, level control, automatic engine starter, speed control, synchronizers, amplifiers for sensors, electronic motor brakes. Development, production and testing of special modules to customer specification.

CETEC

Niels Jernes Vej 10
9220 Aalborg Ø
Tel:
Fax:
Sekretær : Connie Hammenshøj email: **cetec@cetec.dk**

CETEC is a non-profit, commercial foundation with the purpose of strengthening research in the field of electrotechnical energy conversion. It is the aim of the foundation to initiate, to co-ordinate and to manage inter-disciplinary research and development projects in this field.

CETEC

Symbion IV
Vibevej 31, 305 v.
2400 København K

Tel: 96 35 44 35
Fax:
Email: **ch@cetec.dk**
Web: **www.cetec.dk**
Direktør : John Rosing email: **jr@cetec.dk**

Chemitalic A/S

Egebjergvej 128
8700 Horsens
Tel:
Fax:
Miljøchef : Inger Lise Lauritzen email: **ill@chemitalic.dk**
IT-chef : Torben Tambo email: **tt@chemitalic.dk**

IRCUIT electric as

Jens Juuls Vej 18
8260 Viby J.
Tel: 87 33 33 33
Fax: 87 33 33 34
Email: **mm@circuit.dk**
Web: **www.circuit.dk**
Direktør : Hans Finderup email: **hf@circuit.dk**
Salgschef : Mogens Meldgaard email: **mlm@circuit.dk**

Specialised in developing, projecting, producing and servicing within the following areas: Turnkey systems, power plants, low voltage distribution systems, marine plants, control console systems, PLC/PC-systems, computer-based process control systems, and motor control systems.

CorTech A/S

Bransagervej 30
Postboks 40
9490 Pandrup
Tel: 99 73 73 73
Fax: 99 73 73 72
Email: **cortech@cortech.dk**

Teknisk direktør : Ole Krogh Larsen email: **okl@cortech.dk**

Product development, hardware and software, cordless telephones and cordless telephone systems.

Damm Cellular Systems A/S

Møllegade 68
6400 Sønderborg
Tel: 74 42 35 00
Fax: 74 42 32 30
Email: **damm@damm.dk**
Web: **www.damm.dk**

For additional analytical, business and investment opportunities information,
please contact Global Investment & Business Center, USA
at (703) 370-8082. Fax: (703) 370-8083. E-mail: ibpusa3@gmail.com
Global Business and Investment Info Databank - www.ibpus.com

Direktør : Hans Damm email: **damm@damm.dk**
Salgs- og market.dir. : Moritz Hynkemejer email:

Manufacturer of Nordic Mobile Telephone Systems for NMT 450, NMT 450i and NMT 900, covering from 100 up to 50,000 subscribers and Radio Base Stations for MPT1327 and TETRA.

Danfoss A/S

Nordborgvej 81
6430 Nordborg
Tel: 74 88 45 10
Fax: 74 49 09 49
Email: **germann@danfoss.dk**

Produktionschef : Per Germann email: **germann@danfoss.dk**
Sektionsleder : Arendt Clausen email: **arc@danfoss.dk**
Direktør : Jørgen Mads Clausen email:

Frequency converters for speed and torque control of asynchronous motors. Automatic controls for heating, air-conditioning and refrigeration plants. Measuring equipment for industrial processes, sewage plants and marine applications, electrohydraulic controls.

Danfysik A/S

Møllehaven 31
4040 Jyllinge
Tel: 46 78 81 50
Fax: 46 73 15 51
Email: **brn@danfysik.dk**

Direktør : Bjarne Roger Nielsen email: **brn@danfysik.dk**
Afdelingsingeniør : Erik Steinmann email: **es@danfysik.dk**

Nuclear physics apparatus and instrumentation. Charged particle beam handling systems consisting of dipoles and quadrupole magnets with associated highly stabilized constant current power supplies and computer interfaces. Superconducting magnets. Current transducers. Beam diagnostic equipment for charged particle beams. Complete electrostatic accelerators and electromagnetic isotope separators and individual parts used for such equipment. Consultants in magnetostatic field calculation and generation. Consultants in optical calculation for charged particle beams. Industrial ion implanters.

Dantec Measurement Technology A/S

Tonsbakken 16-18
2740 Skovlunde
Tel: 44 57 80 00
Fax: 44 57 80 01
Email: **info@dantecmt.dk**
Web: **www.dantecmt.com**
Økonomichef : Henning Petersen email: **henning.petersen@dantecmt.com**
Salgschef : Edward Hayes email: **edward.hayes@dantecmt.com**
Account.Man. : Niels B. Bredal email: **niels.bredal@dantecmt.com**
Sekretær : Lisbet Axelgaard email: **lisbet.axelgaard@dantecmt.com**

Direktør : Kristian Askegaard email: **kristian.askegaard@dantecmt.com**

Dantec operates in three business segments: (1) Flow measurement: Systems for accurate measurement of flow patterns in air, gases and liquids. The systems are widely used in both scientific research and industrial applications such as the design of road vehicles, ships, aircraft and buildings, (2) Particle sizing: Particle-sizing instrumentation investigates the size, velocity and concentration of droplets, bubbles in liquids and solid particles in gaseous or liquid flows. In the design and manufacture of products such as spray nozzles, combustion chambers and fuel injectors, Dantec's equipment is used to optimise flow characteristics and particle-size distribution, (3) Process instrumentation: Dantec's non-intrusive measurement equipment provides valuable information (e.g. speed and length) in connection with paper production.

Dantrafo Horsens A/S

Islandsvej 28
8700 Horsens
Tel: 76 28 29 30
Fax: 76 28 29 31
Email: **dt@dantrafo.dk**
Web: **www.dantrafo.dk**
Direktør : Jørgen V. Larsen email: **jl@dantrafo.dk**
Udviklingschef : Kim Andersen email: **kla@dantrafo.dk**
Indkøbschef : Jørn Vendelbo email: **jev@dantrafo.dk**

Dantrafo is producing transformers in the followings fields: mains transformers, current transformers, line transformers, choke coils, transformers on ferrite cores, autotransformers, three-phase transformers, toroidal transformers, approved transformers, transformers with CCA certificate. CE-approved: plug-in transformers, AC/AC-AC/DC-AC/DC-stab, power supplies, battery chargers, transformers for lighting.

DEIF A/S

Frisenborgvej 33
Postboks 510
7800 Skive
Tel: 96 14 96 14
Fax:
Logistikchef : Niels Bækby email: **nib@deif.com**

DELTA

Dansk Elektronik, Lys & Akustik
Venlighedsvej 4
2970 Hørsholm
Tel: 45 86 77 22
Fax: 42 86 58 98
Email: **tg@delta.dk**
Web: **www.delta.dk**
Direktør : Torben Grønning email: **tg@delta.dk**
Divisionschef : Per Ølund Hansen email: **pha@delta.dk**
: Karsten Jensen email: **kj@delta.dk**
Cand.scient. : Michael Dybkjær Holbech email: **mdh@delta.dk**

Design, supply and testing of microelectronic components, optoelectronic systems, optical filters, light reflection measurement systems, smoke detectors, Internet technology, ATM broadband communications traffic simulation systems. Software programmes for sound and light design and analysis. Testing, evaluation, certification and CE-marking of electronics, software, light and sound products and components. ISO 9000 certification of electronics hardware and software developers, manufacturers and distributors. Software process test and improvement. Training courses in electronics hardware and software engineering, optics, light, acoustics, noise and vibration. AQAP-110 certification. DANAK and DKD accreditations.

Electrolux Hot Products Centre

Sjællandsgade 2
7000 Fredericia
Tel: 79 22 12 60
Fax: 75 91 42 80
Email: **christian.eskildsen@notes.electrolux.dk**

Direktør : Christian Eskildsen email: **christian.eskildsen@notes.electrolux.dk**

Electrolux Tech Centre is a technology center for component and system development.

EMRI A/S

Marielundvej 37 A
2730 Herlev
Tel: 44 91 82 04
Fax: 44 91 55 07
Email: **info@emri.dk**

Direktør : J. C. Nørtoft Thomsen email: **info@emri.dk**

Autopilots for ships. Manoeuvring systems for offshore supply vessels, passenger ships and cruise liners. Track control systems for hydrographic survey vessels. Fuel saving analog steering gear control systems. Rudder control systems. Propeller control systems. Rudder indicators. Subcontracts in development, documentation, production and testing.

Ericsson Diax A/S

Fælledvej 17
7600 Struer
Tel: 97 86 90 22
Fax: 97 85 44 22
Email: **dxd@dxd.ericsson.se**
Web: **www.ericsson.se/DK/DIAX**
Direktør : Jørgen Yde Jensen email: **joergen-yde.jensen@dxd.ericsson.se**
Økonomichef : Jes Henriksen email: **jes.henriksen@dxd.ericsson.se**
Kvalitetschef : Jens Villadsen email: **jens.villadsen@dxd.ericsson.se**
Development, manufacturing and marketing of digital telecommunication systems.

Ernitec a/s

Hørkær 22-24
2730 Herlev

Tel: 44 50 33 00
Fax: 44 50 33 33
Email: **ernitec@ernitec.dk**
Web: **www.ernitec.dk**
Direktør : Carsten Krogh email: **c.krogh@ernitec.dk**
Udviklingschef : Steen Ørsted email: **s.oersted@ernitec.dk**
Logistik- & admin.chef : Kåre Lund Pedersen email: **k.l.pedersen@ernitec.dk**
Regnskabschef : Anne Marie Dorph email: **a.m.dorph@ernitec.dk**

Development and manufacture of: video & control matrix systems, video transmission equipment and other products for CCTV.The product range is: lenses, camera houses, video matrixes and control systems, video transmission equipment - twisted pair equipment/fast scans B/W or colour, video motion detectors, passive infrared detectors.

Etronic Svendborg A/S

Rødeledsvej 95
5700 Svendborg
Tel: 62 21 38 50
Fax: 62 22 45 50
Email: **info@etronic.dk**
Direktør : E. Galsgaard email: **eg@etronic.dk**

LF amplifiers, power supplies, DC converters and charger rectifiers according to specification, TV marine antennas. Electronic measuring equipment for telephony. Communication equipment using the public telephone line.

EuroCom Industries A/S

Lautrupvang 4
2750 Ballerup
Tel: 70 13 70 00
Fax: 44 74 85 01
Email: **eci@eci.dk**

Personalechef : Annegrete Friis email: **af@eci.dk**
Direktør : Michael J. Peytz email: **mjp@eci.dk**
Techn. Marketing Man. : Peter Ole Jensen email: **poj@eci.dk**
Produktliniechef : Finn Sander email: **fsa@eci.dk**

Radio communications equipment and systems: MF/HF transceivers and receivers, DSC and radiotelex modems and scanning receivers, personal computers, mobile satellite terminals, radio consoles and remote controlled radio systems, VHF transceivers.

Ferroperm Magnetics A/S

Staktoften 22D
2950 Vedbæk
Tel: 45 65 05 70
Fax: 45 65 05 71
Email: **fm@ferropermmagnetics.com**

Direktør : Svend Holm email: **fm@ferropermmagnetics.com**

Magnetics materials. Powdered iron cores. Soft and hard ferrites. Iron-boron-neodymium.

Flux Transformerteknik A/S

Industrivangen 5
4550 Asnæs
Tel: 59 65 00 89
Fax: 59 65 21 20
Email: **sales@flux-int.com**
Web: **www.flux-int.com**
Direktør : Niels Overgaard Christensen email: **sales@flux-int.com**

Manufacturer of inductive components for high frequency purpose: switch mode magnetics, pulse- telecom and wideband transformers, cables, noise suppression, high voltage. Industrial grade as well as HiRel grade components.

FUTURE ELECTRONICS A/S

Hørskætten 14
2630 Tåstrup
Tel: 43 55 09 31
Fax: 43 55 09 32
Email: **mf@future-as.dk**

Direktør : Mads W. Fischer email: **mf@future-as.dk**
Logistikchef : Michael Ravn email: **mr@future-as.dk**

Global sales and distribution channel of electronic components. Special in sales and material logistic solutions. Quality Assurance ISO 9002.

Gåsdal Bygningsindustri A/S

Stålvej 7
6900 Skjern
Tel: 99 80 66 66
Fax: 99 80 67 89
Direktør : Jørgen Troelsen email:
Miljøkoordinator : Jens Ladefoged email: **jlc.gaab@velux.com**
Fr. : Merete Bildberg email:
Manufacturing of mechanical and electronic automation equipment.

GI Teamtec A/S

Porsbakken 6
7330 Brande
Tel: 97 18 22 00
Fax: 97 18 26 62
Email: **info@gi-teamtec.dk**
Web: **www.gi-teamtec.dk**
Direktør : Vilhelm N. Laursen email: **vnl@gi-teamtec.dk**
Q-koordinator : Lene Strejnicher email: **lsj@gi-teamtec.dk**
Forsyningschef : Ole Gregersen email: **og@gi-teamtec.dk**

Sub-supplier working in team-work with customers doing manufacturing, test and development of electronics, ranging from simple leaded PCB's to highly complex SMD mounted boards and complete electronics solutions. High supply capacity from 3 specialised factories for SMD technology, leaded production and mechanical assembly, including facilities for manufacturing of sensors and cables and for special protection of electronics placed in harsh environment.

GN Nettest as

Kirkebjerg Allé 90
2605 Brøndby
Tel: 7211 22 00
Fax: 72 11 23 50
Email: **com@nettest.dk**
Web: **www.gnnettest.com**
Direktør : Jens Maaløe email: **jm@nettest.dk**
Salgsdirektør : Frits Thaulow email: **tau@.nettest.dk**
Udviklingsdirektør : Peter Deichmann email: **pde@nettest.dk**
Produktionschef : Lars Harild email: **lha@nettest.dk**

Telecom, datacom and fibre-optical test equipment.

GN Store Nord as

Kongens Nytorv 26
Postboks 2167
1016 København K
Tel:
Fax:
Direktør : Jørgen Lindegaard email: **jl@gn.dk**

GN-Teknik

Rødegevej 12
Løgten
8541 Skødstrup
Tel: 86 99 32 92
Fax: 86 99 32 86
Email: **ign@gnteknik.dk**

Konsulent : Ib Glerup Nielsen email: **ign@gnteknik.dk**

Consultancy and training courses for te electronics industry within the following areas: - Environmental management, Design for environment; - Product reliability, Design for quality; - Project management

GPV Elbau Electronics A/S

Lyngsøvej 8
9600 Aars
Tel: 98 62 20 00
Fax: 98 62 47 65
Web: **www.gpv.dk**

Direktør : Jørgen K. Hansen email:
Kvalitetschef : Jesper Harvig email: **jeh@gpv-elbau.dk**

Strategic co-operation partner for contractual development and contractual production of electronics.

GPV Industri A/S

c/o GPV International A/S
Håndværkervej 3-5
6880 Tarm
Tel: 97 37 25 11
Fax: 97 37 27 50
Email: **bel@gpv.dk**
Web: **www.gpv.dk**
Direktør : Jørgen K. Hansen email: **jkh@gpv.dk**

Design and development, manufacturing, surface treatment, painting and assembly of mechanical parts and complete solutions to business areas such as electronics, communication, transport, defence etc.

Gronvaldt|DK

Vendersgade 26, st.
1363 København K
Tel: 33 33 92 25
Fax: 33 33 92 85
Email: **ib.grønvaldt@inet.uni2.dk**
Direktør : Ib Grønvaldt email: **ib.gronvaldt@ectel.org**
Consultancy for industry, industry associations, and public bodies, primarily in European public affairs, public relations, publicity. Management of independent review projects, support for mediation & arbitration.

Grundfos A/S

Poul Due Jensens Vej 7
8850 Bjerringbro
Tel: 86 68 14 00
Fax: 86 68 22 24
Email: **grundfos@grundfos.com**
Web: **www.grundfos.com**
Chefingeniør : Pierre Vadstrup email: **pvadstrup@grundfos.com**
Kvalitetschef : Henrik Hjortkjær email: **hhjortkjaer@grundfos.com**
Udviklingschef : Søren Louis Pedersen email: **slpedersen@grundfos.com**
: Torben Markussen email: **tmarkussen@grundfos.com**
Afdeling 5010 :email:
Miljøingeniør : Christina Monrad Nielsen email: **cmonradn@grundfos.com**
Environmental Engineer : Peter E. Hansen email: **pellekaerh@grundfos.com**
Fabrikschef : Ole Rudkilde email: **orudkilde@grundfos.com**
Afdelingsleder : Marjanne Grønhøj email:
Direktør : Poul Vesterbæk email: **pvesterbæk@grundfos.com**
Personaledirektør : Jørn Henriksen email:

Pump control systems for municipal water and irrigation, building services and industrial application. Induction motor speed control.

Hamann Electronics A/S

Rækmarken 6
Hørby
4300 Holbæk
Tel: 59 46 86 00
Fax: 59 46 86 05
Email: **hamann@hamann.dk**
Web: **www.hamann.dk**
Direktør : Knud P. Hamann email: **kph@hamann.dk**

Electronic and mechanical development and manufacturing. Testing - also according to military standards.

Hans Følsgaard A/S

Ejby Industrivej 30
2600 Glostrup
Tel: 43 20 86 00
Fax: 43 96 88 55
Email: **hf@hf.dk**
Web: **www.folsgaard.dk**
Direktør : Jørgen Linthoe email: **jl@hf.dk**
Salgsdirektør : Jørgen Stenberg email: **js@hf.dk**

Harnesses. Component assembling.

Hegmont ApS

Hegnsvej 82
2850 Nærum
Tel: 45 80 12 73
Fax: 45 50 58 01
Email: **hegmont@fon.egmont.com**

Direktør : Hans Egmont-Petersen email: **hegmont@fon.egmont.com**

Consultancy services mostly to companies actively engaged on the markets for electromedical equipment. Main issues are: Strategical positioning among competitors; Positioning in geographical sense; Markets and distribution channels within South East Asia

HI SEC International A/S

Tempovej 42
2750 Ballerup
Tel: 44 86 05 05
Fax: 44 86 05 00
Email: **dk@hisec.com**
Direktør : Martin Hildebrandt email: **mah@hisec.dk**

Design and development of high security systems: Access control systems, intruder alarm systems, fire alarm systems, video identification and video alarm systems.

Holm & Bertram

Generatorvej 8 F, 1.s.
2730 Herlev
Tel: 70 13 10 10
Fax: 70 13 10 11
Email: **post@holm-bertram.dk**
Web: **www.holm-bertram.dk**
Informatikchef : Bruno G. Jensen email: **post@holm-bertram.dk**
Direktør : Steen Holm email: **post@holm-bertram.dk**
Consulting within data communication.

I/O Consulting A/S

Lautrupvang 1B
Postbox 199
2750 Ballerup
Tel: 44 20 92 70
Fax: 44 20 92 71
Email: **rd@iocon.dk**
Web: **www.iocon.dk**
Direktør : Rune Domsten email: **rd@iocon.dk**

Technology Center doing contract development within ASIC, FPGA, Analog and Digital Hardware and embedded software. Technology focus on embedded internet connectivity, signal processing and implentation of advanced algorithms. Project experience within print servers, Radiolinks, Internet accessories, ultrasound systems, PABX and many more.

In-JeT ApS

Jeppe Åkjærsvej 15
3460 Birkerød
Tel: 45 82 13 24
Fax: 45 82 13 53
Email: **in-jet@get2net.dk**
Direktør : Jesper Thestrup email: **jesper.thestrup@get2net.dk**

Consultancy services to the electronics industry with overall strategy, product and technology strategy, product and technology strategy, marketing and IT strategy. In-Jet ApS has specialised in developing and implementing holistic strategy solutions, where single strategies are combined in an overall strategic environment. In-Jet Aps represents Apcosoft Infoway Ltd. of Bangalore, India. Apcosoft is one of India's fastest growing sofware houses and offers software development on a wide variety of software platforms. The services offered include: Client/Server Application Development services, Internet & E-Commerce, Euro Conversion Services, Software Migrating and Porting.

Industriselskabet Ferroperm A/S

Hejreskovvej 18A
3490 Kvistgård

For additional analytical, business and investment opportunities information, please contact Global Investment & Business Center, USA at (703) 370-8082. Fax: (703) 370-8083. E-mail: ibpusa3@gmail.com Global Business and Investment Info Databank - www.ibpus.com

Tel: 49 12 71 00
Fax: 49 13 81 88
Email: **pz@ferroperm.com**
Web: **www.ferroperm.com**
: *Karen W. Breumlund* email: **kbl@ferroperm.com**
Direktør : Jens Peter Holm email: **pz@ferroperm.com**
Økonomichef : Annette Winding email: **pz@ferroperm.com**
Teknisk direktør : Wanda W. Wolny email: **ww@ferroperm.com**
Salgschef : Bjørn Andersen email:

Piezoelectric ceramics. Thin film technologies. Optical interference filters.

Infocom A/S

Ellegårdvej 25
Postboks 282
6400 Sønderborg
Tel: 73 12 30 00
Fax: 73 12 30 01
Email: **info@infocom.dk**
Web: **www.infocom.dk**
Direktør : Bent Kristensen email: **bk@infocom.dk**

Sales, development, production, installation, delivery and service of customer specified information and communication systems to the public sector and private customers. This includes Digital audio/data systems. Integrated naval communication systems. Simulation and training systems. Mobile radio communication systems. Electronic display and information systems. Travelling information positioning systems. Resale of third party equipment, including communication equipment.

Judex Datasystemer A/S

Lyngvej 8
9000 Aalborg
Tel: 98 18 69 00
Fax: 98 18 80 19
Email: **eh@judex.dk**
Web: **www.judex.dk**
Direktør : Erling Henningsen email: **eh@judex.dk**

Medical computer systems for electromyography and electroencephalography. Medical computer systems for sleep and respiration analysis. Data conversion systems. Customer dedicated computer systems.

KIRK telecom A/S

Langmarksvej 34
8700 Horsens
Tel: 75 60 28 50
Fax: 75 60 28 51
Email: **kirk@kirktelecom.dk**
Web: **www.kirktelecom.dk**
Teknisk direktør : Erik Stridbæk email: **es@kirktelecom.dk**
Direktør : Peter Skov email: **ps@kirktelecom.dk**

Økonomichef : Claus W. Thomsen email: **cwt@kirktelecom.dk**
Produktionschef : Ole Christensen email: **oc@kirktelecom.dk**
Produktionsleder : Ida Rasmussen email:
Sælger : Jes Milton email:

Development, production and sales of telecommunication equipment. Telephone subsets, analogue and digital types for public network as well as PABX use. Cordless telephones according to DECT standards. Digital answering machines for Consumer and business application. Professional electronic subcontracting activities.

kk-electronic a/s

Cypresvej 6
7400 Herning
Tel: 97 22 10 33
Fax: 97 21 14 31
Email: **main@kk-electronic.dk**
Web: **www.kk-electronic.dk**
Direktør : Knud V. Jensen email: **main@kk-electronic.dk**
Udviklingschef : Henrik Simonsen email: **HS@kk-electronic.dk**

Development and manufacturing of customised microprocessor solutions, electronics, EMC test, SMD assembling, PC/PLC solutions, machine control systems, distribution boards, control panels, desk systems, windmill control systems.

L. M. Ericsson A/S

Sluseholmen 8
1790 København V
Tel: 33 88 33 88
Fax: 33 88 31 21
Email: **lmd@lmd.ericsson.se**
Web: **www.ericsson.dk**
Udviklingschef : Peer Kofod Andersen email: **peer.andersen@ericsson.dk**
Personalechef : Heidi Therkildsen email: **heidi.therkildsen@ericsson.com**
Direktør : Conni Simonsen email: **conni.simonsen@ericsson.dk**
Vicedirektør : Bo Stokholm email: **bo.stokholm@lmd.ericsson.dk**
Indkøbschef : Lars Trap Andersen email: **lars.trap@ericsson.com**

Communication networks solutions and servicesWireless/wired networks and devices, enabling voice, data, image and video communicationsSupport services and supporting systems

L. M. Ericsson A/S

Niels Jernes Vej 6B
9220 Aalborg Ø
Tel:
Fax:
Afdelingschef : Niels-Christian Gjerrild email: **lmdncg@lmd.ericsson.se**

Lucent Technologies Denmark A/S

Priorparken 680
2605 Brøndby

Tel: 43 45 88 88
Fax: 43 45 53 73
Email: **gknudsen@lucent.com**
Web: **www.lucent.com**
Direktør : Walter J. Ehmer email: **wjehmer@lucent.com**
Underdirektør : Gudmund Knudsen email: **gknudsen@lucent.com**
Miljøchef : Hanne Bertelsen email: **hbertelsen@lucent.com**
Ingeniør : Atle Søby email: **asoeby@lucent.com**
Sekretær : Anni Holm email: **aholm@lucent.com**

Development, production, and marketing of optical fibres, for Telecom, LAN and data applications as well as speciality fibres for lasers, amplifiers, and sensors.

Maxon Cellular Systems Denmark A/S

Niels Jernes Vej 8
Postboks 8440
9220 Aalborg Ø
Tel: 96 35 55 00
Fax: 96 35 56 00
Email: **lb@maxon.dk**
Web: **www.maxon.dk**
Udviklingschef : Lars Bonde email: **lb@maxon.dk**
Økonomiansvarlig : Else Bonde email: **er@maxon.dk**
Direktør : Claus Melgaard email: **cme@maxon.dk**
Development of cellular mobile telephones and associated equipment.

MEC A/S

Industriparken 23
2750 Ballerup
Tel: 44 97 33 66
Fax: 44 68 15 14
Email: **danmec@vip.cybercity.dk**
Web: **www.mec.dk**
Direktør : Ivan Gam Hansen email: **hansen@mec.dk**
Push button and toggle switches. Illuminated switches. Surface mount switches.

Memory Card Technology A/S

Sønderhøj 22
8260 Viby J.
Tel: 70 21 22 12
Fax: 70 21 22 11
Email: **john@memory-card-technology.com**
Web: **www.memory-card-technology.com**
Kvalitetschef : Kai-Lykke Mathiasen email: **kai-lykke@memory-card-technology.com**
Direktør : John Trolle email: **john@memory-card-technology.com**
Manager R&D : Henrik Lund-Olsen email: **henrik@memory-card-technology.com**

Computer equipment and systems. Contract development. Contract manufacturers. Development and production of electronic equipment.

Micro Matic Instrument A/S

For additional analytical, business and investment opportunities information,
please contact Global Investment & Business Center, USA
at (703) 370-8082. Fax: (703) 370-8083. E-mail: ibpusa3@gmail.com
Global Business and Investment Info Databank - www.ibpus.com

Industrivej 8
5471 Søndersø
Tel: 64 89 22 11
Fax: 64 89 21 94
Email: **mmi@micro-matic.instrument.dk**
Web: **www.micro-matic.dk**
Direktør : Kai Laursen email: **mmi@micro-matic.instrument.dk**

Electrical and electronic temperature measuring equipment for: marine and land installations, oil, petrochemicals, power plants, boilers, gas/diesel engines, district heating meters, compressors, cooling units, cold storage rooms, foods and beverages.

MIGATRONIC A/S

Aggersundvej 33
9690 Fjerritslev
Tel: 96 50 06 00
Fax: 96 50 06 01
Email: **migatronic@migatronic.dk**
Web: **www.migatronic.dk**
Direktør : Peter Roed email: **peter.roed@migatronic.dk**

Development, manufacture and distribution of equipment for arc welding and allied processes and automatic systems for arc welding. Arc welding power sources, wire feeders, water cooling units, transformers, inverters, control and monitoring equipment.

mikkelsen electronics as

Havremarken 3-5
3520 Farum
Tel: 42 95 43 22
Fax: 42 95 83 58
Email: **info@mikkelsen-electronics.dk**
Web: **www.mikkelsen-electronics.dk**
Direktør : Jürgen A. Haberl email: **juergen.haberl@mikkelsen-electronics.dk**
Underdirektør : Ejgild Nielsen email: **Ejgild.Nielsen@mikkelsen-electronics.dk**

Cable assemblies.

MODULEX ViewCom A/S

Kløvervej 101
7190 Billund
Tel: 72 19 34 00
Fax: 72 19 34 01
Email: **info@viewcom.dk**
Web: **www.viewcom.dk**
Adm. Direktør : John Larsen email: **jla@viewcom.dk**
Økonomichef : Rune Thomassen email: **rth@viewcom.dk**

Electronic visual display systems. Main segments airports, railway (stations, platforms, trains), bus terminals, banks, conference centres, courthouses and other public places. The product range includes information boards in all sizes, based on LCD or LED technology. Full graphic monitors can be supplied as CRT monitors or flat-screen plasma monitors. Software for integrated information systems for all segments is developed and implemented in turnkey deliveries to airports, railway stations, etc. Quality assurance according to ISO 9001 and in-house test facilities.

Modulohm A/S

Vasekær 6-8
Postboks 507
2730 Herlev
Tel: 44 94 70 11
Fax: 44 53 17 11
Email: **modulohm@modulohm.dk**
Web: **www.danweb.dk/modulohm**
Direktør : Børge Stentoft email: **modulohm@modulohm.dk**
Asst. Sales Manager : Anders Høgfeldt email:

Resistors: Wirewound resistors, all welded, manufactured from quite inorganic materials completely non-flammable. Ohmic value from R1-47K. Series A and E: Horizontal models with hot tinned print terminals. Series C: Vertical models with hot tinned print terminals with 10 mm spacing. Series K: Axial models with hot tinned terminals. Low ohm series from 6.8-100 milliohm for switch mode supplies.

Motorola A/S

Midtager 20
2605 Brøndby
Tel: 43 48 80 00
Fax: 43 48 80 01
Web: **www.motorola.com**
Direktør : John N. Palle email: **john.palle@motorola.com**
Teknisk direktør : Jens Kristiansen email: **tcv165@email.mot.com**
Udviklingschef : Ole Haslund email: **tgm211@email.mot.com**

Complete range of VHF and UHF, FM two-way radio communication equipment and paging systems. Fixed, portable and handheld transmitter/receivers including a wide range of selective calling equipment and with facilities for digital signalling, data transmission and encryption. Advanced radio communication systems for private mobile services designed to customer specifications encompassing a range of microwave link equipment. Public radio telephone systems in both analogue and digital techniques including a wide range of radio terminals and peripherals.

Müller Print A/S

Bredeløkkevej 17, Holtug
Postboks 29
4660 Store Heddinge
Tel: 56 50 02 00
Fax: 56 50 01 77
Email: **mp@as-mullerprint.dk**
Web: **www.as-mullerprint.com**
Direktør : Per Rinck-Henriksen email: **prh@as-mullerprint.dk**
Kvalitets- og miljøchef : Ellen Nielsen email: **mp@as-mullerprint.dk**

Printed circuit boards: Single- and double sided, non plated through PCB´s (NPT). Laminate types:FR2, CEM-1, FR4 standard, others on request. Special PCB´s for high current applications with 400 micron Cu, also for 3D appplications (routed or scored). Prototype service with supsequent deliviries of quantities. Silk screen printing with techniques for imaging, solder stop mask and ledgends. Line width/space to 0,20 mm. Electrical testing, drilling, routing, punching and scoring. CAD/CAM facilities. UL approval, ISO 9002.

Netman A/S

Vandtårnsvej 77
2860 Søborg
Tel: 39 66 40 20
Fax: 39 66 06 75
Email: **flb@netman.dk**

Direktør : Peter Keller-Andreasen email: **pka@netman.dk**

Development, integration and support of total solutions for the management and monitoring of networks and services across vendor platforms.

NH Electronics ApS

Orebyvej 183
4990 Sakskøbing
Tel: 54 70 00 64
Fax: 54 70 01 68
Email: **hjertholm@get2net.dk**
Web: **www.o2xygen.com**
Direktør : Niels Hjertholm email: **hjertholm@get2net.dk**

Independent distribution of electronic components. Development and implementation of leading-edge technology solutions, which allow our customers to effectively meet today's procurement challenges.

NIROS Telecommunication A/S

Hirsemarken 5
3520 Farum
Tel: 44 99 28 00
Fax: 44 99 28 08
Email: **niros@niros.com**
Web: **www.niros.com**
Udviklingsing. : Jens Rahbek email: **j.rahbek@niros.com**
Kvalitetschef : William P. Jensen email: **w.jensen@niros.com**
Direktør : Jørgen Lauritzen email: **j.lauritzen@niros.com**

NIROS Telecommunication A/S is a leading manufacturer of high-end portable and mobile radios, pagers and data radios for professional users. All products are characterised by a unique degree of flexibility and user-friendliness. Numerous features in the software make the radios suitable for a wide range of radio communication solutions.

Out:Con International

Nobisvej 64

3460 Birkerød
Tel: 45 82 11 44
Fax: 45 82 11 66
Email: **jorgen@outcon.com**

Direktør : Jørgen Staal email: **jorgen@outcon.com**

Consulting and practical assistance in outsourcing of electronics assembly and material sourcing from vendors particularly in Asia-Pacific. Services include outsourcing and sourcing consulting, program management and liaison. Electronics outsourcing activities comprise cost-reduction - and feasibility analysis as well as practical assistance in implementation of turnkey programs. Material sourcing activities are within standard components, printed circuit boards, plastic molded parts and sheet metal cabinets.Networking is provided to several international contract manufacturers including representations of professional EMS providers located in Singapore, Malaysia, Thailand, Indonesia, China, Mexico, USA and Hungary.

Pallas Informatik A/S

Rønne Allé 41
3450 Allerød
Tel: 48 10 24 10
Fax: 48 17 07 89
Email: **funder@pallas.dk**
Web: **www.pallas.dk**
Direktør : Karsten Funder email: **funder@pallas.dk**

Consultancy and software development, among others in the following fields: railway signalling and communication, fleet management systems, and farm control, hearing instrument control and management, electronic trade and information systems based on cd-rom, internet and satellite communication.

Partner Electric AS

Trekanten 15-17
6500 Vojens
Tel: 74 59 11 44
Fax: 74 59 11 75
Email: **pel@pel.dk**
Web: **www.partner-electric.com**
Kvalitets- og produktionschef : Tine Jul Jensen email: **tjj@pel.dk**
Direktør : Henry L. Pedersen email: **hlp@pel.dk**
Salgschef : Mogens Johansen email: **mj@pel.dk**
Økonomichef : Peter F. Hansen email: **pfh@pel.dk**
Udviklingschef : Søren Rosborg email: **sr@pel.dk**
Logistikchef : Benny Struck email: **bs@pel.dk**
Sælger : Michael Poewe email:

PABXs for small and medium size business use. ISDN terminal adaptors for voice communication. ISDN primary rate and basic rate diallers (LCR). Custom specified telephone equipment and systems. Complete Danish development and manufacturing.

Paul E. Danchell A/S

Lyngvej 8

**For additional analytical, business and investment opportunities information,
please contact Global Investment & Business Center, USA
at (703) 370-8082. Fax: (703) 370-8083. E-mail: ibpusa3@gmail.com
Global Business and Investment Info Databank - www.ibpus.com**

4450 Jyderup
Tel: 59 27 77 42
Fax: 59 27 72 14
Email: **danchell@danchell.dk**

Direktør : Flemming Justesen email: **fj@danchell.dk**

Subcontracting of units. High technology equipment for SMT mounting.

PentaCom A/S

Brundtland Center Denmark
Brundtlandparken 2
6520 Toftlund
Tel: 73 83 00 00
Fax: 74 83 00 39
Email: **pentacom@pentacom.dk**

Direktør : Bruno Lund Pedersen email: **blp@pentacom.dk**

Room temperature measuring using UHF radio techniques. Room temperature control systems are marketed on the European and North American markets under the brand name Genius.

PHI Fiberoptik

Lindeengen 2
2740 Skovlunde
Tel: 44 53 60 60
Fax: 44 53 60 06
Email: **sales@phi-fiber.com**
Web: **www.phi-fiber.com**
Direktør : Peter Hornung email: **peter.hornung@phi-fiber.com**

Connectorizing of fibre optic cables. Light sources: LD, LED, and ELED. Hand-held power meters. Variable attenuators and other equipment for fibre optic testing.

Powerlab A/S

Industrivej 45
2605 Brøndby
Tel: 43 63 43 44
Fax: 43 63 43 22
Email: **powerlab@powerlab.dk**
Web: **www.powerlab.dk**
Udviklingschef : Ole C. Thomsen email: **oct@powerlab.dk**

Development and production of standard and custom design power supplies and DC/DC converters based on switch mode technology.

PR electronics A/S

Lerbakken 10
8410 Rønde

Tel: 86 37 26 77
Fax: 86 37 30 85
Email: **pr@prelectronics.dk**
Web: **www.prelectronics.dk**
Udviklingschef : Stig Lindemann email: **develop@prelectronics.dk**
Direktør : Peter Rasmussen email: **prpriv@prelectronics.dk**
Kvalitetschef : Helle Grum email: **admin@prelectronics.dk**

Developer and manufacturer of a wide multi-purpose electronic modular system for signal conditioning, analogue as well as digital. Aimed at process instrumentation, transmitters, isolators, trip amplifiers, converters, power supplies, and displays can be applied both in hazardous areas (Ex) and normal industrial environments. QMS certified according to DS/EN ISO 9001. Fully equipped in-house EMC (Electromagnetic Compatibility) laboratory where all product designs are tested to meet CENELEC EN 50 081 and EN 50 082.

PRI-DANA Elektronik A/S

Odinsvej 2
8722 Hedensted
Tel: 75 89 23 11
Fax: 75 89 06 90
Email: **pridana@pridana.dk**

Direktør : H. C. Holmelund email: **pridana@pridana.dk**

Printed circuit boards: Multilayer boards (MLB), double-sided PCBs with PTH, PCBs for SMT, prototype service, quick service, simultaneous d/s electrical testing, bare board testing, laserplotting, CAD/CAM facilities. Specialities: Fine line boards, PCBs for SMT, with chemical nickel/gold, carbon ink printing, UL approval, ISO 9002.

Printca AS

Svendborgvej 3
Postboks 8120
9220 Aalborg Ø
Tel: 99 30 92 00
Fax: 99 30 92 99
Email: **puj@printca.dk**

Direktør : Peter Ulrik Jensen email: **puj@printca.dk**

Printed circuit boards: Multilayers and plated through holes. Technologies: Buried/blind via holes, copper-Invar-copper, mounting of press-fit connectors, rigid/flex. Quality assurance: DS/ISO 9002. Approvals: MIL-P-55110D, UL, ESA & CNES, AQAP 120.

ProTeleVision Technologies A/S

Skelmarksvej 4
2605 Brøndby
Tel: 43 29 23 00
Fax: 43 29 23 23
Email: **helpdesk@ptv.dk**
Web: **www.ptv.dk**

- 294 -

Direktør : Maurits van Tol email: **mvt@ptv.dk**
Udviklingschef : Torben Lund email: **tl@ptv.dk**
Indkøbschef : Poul Wachmann email: **pwa@ptv.dk**

Electronic test and measurement equipment for TV-studios, transmission and manufacturing of TV products (video test and pattern generators, colour analysers, modulators and demodulators, NICAM equipment).

Purup - Eskofot A/S

Sønderskovvej 5
8520 Lystrup
Tel: 87 43 43 43
Fax: 87 43 44 45
Direktør : William Schulin-Zeuthen email: **wsz@pe.dk**

PostScript based imagesetting systems for the graphic arts industry. The systems produce plate-ready films with integrated text, line art graphics and continuous tone pictures for forms, labels and packaging for advertisements, brochures, etc.

Radiometer A/S

Åkandevej 21
2700 Brønshøj
Tel: 38 27 38 27
Fax: 38 27 27 27
Direktør : Johan Schrøder email: **johan.schroeder@radiometer.dk**

Medical instruments: Blood gas analysers, blood electrolyte analysers. Instruments for oxygen saturation and haemoglobin pulse oximeters, transcutaneous monitors and electrodes, blood samplers, quality control systems, precision buffers and other fine chemicals, electrodes. OEM-supplies.

Radiometer Medical A/S

Åkandevej 21
2700 Brønshøj
Tel: 38 27 38 27
Fax: 38 27 27 27
Direktør : Peter Kürstein-Jensen email: **peter.kurstein@radiometer.dk**
Sektionschef : Bent Pedersen email: **bent.pedersen@radiometer.dk**
Logistikchef : Allan Svane email: **allan.svane@radiometer.dk**
Udviklingschef : Bjarne Sanddahl email: **bjarne.sanddahl@radiometer.dk**
: Michael Mikkelsen email: **michael.mikkelsen@radiometer.dk**

RAMBØLL

Bredevej 2
2830 Virum
Tel: 45 98 60 00
Fax: 45 98 69 27
Web: **www.ramboll.dk**
Direktør : Thorleif Mortensen email: **tm@ramboll.dk**
Afdelingsleder : Hans H. Hertz email: **hhz@ramboll.dk**

Overingeniør : Per H. Laursen email: **phl@ramboll.dk**
Afdelingsleder : Tonni Christiansen email: **toc@ramboll.dk**
*Kreditorbogholderiet :*email:

Consultancy for SCADA, RCC and automation systems and software development.

RAMTEX Engineering ApS

Skodsborgvej 346
Postboks 84
2850 Nærum
Tel: 45 66 45 80
Fax: 45 50 53 90
Email: **ramtex@ramtex.dk**
Web: **www.ramtex.dk**
Direktør : Peder Mousten email: **ramtex@ramtex.dk**
Salgsdirektør : Jan Kristoffersen email: **jkristof@ramtex.dk**

Consultancy, research and design of electronic equipment. Specialists in development of microprocessor based instruments and equipment. Development and sale of C/C + + software tools for embedded microprocessor programming. Migration of PC tools to the embedded industry.

RESON A/S

Fabriksvangen 13
3550 Slangerup
Tel: 47 38 00 22
Fax: 47 38 00 66
Email: **reson@reson.dk**

Direktør : Claus R. Steenstrup email: **crs@reson.dk**
Udviklingschef : Peter Koldgaard Eriksen email: **pke@reson.dk**
Økonomichef : Laust Nyvang email: **ln@reson.dk**
Udviklingschef : Steen G. Bruun email:

Specialists in underwater acoustic transducers and hydrophones for echo sounders. Multibeam sonars for hydrography, off-shore operations, minehunting and anti submarine warfare. Side scan systems. Calibration systems. Ultrasonic homogenizers for bitumen and heavy fuel oil. Ultrasonic filter technology and cleaning.

Scientific-Atlanta Arcodan A/S

Augustenborg Landevej 7
6400 Sønderborg
Tel: 73 12 21 50
Fax: 74 42 39 07
Email: **postmaster@sciatl.dk**
Web: **www.arcodan.com**
Direktør : Flemming Toft email: **ft@sciatl.dk**
: Kjeld Kleffel email: **kk@sciatl.dk**
Kvalitetschef : Jørgen N. Møller email: **jnm@sciatl.dk**
Salgschef : Benny Laursen email: **bl@sciatl.dk**

Logistikchef : Egon Jensen email: **ej@sciatl.dk**

Development, production and sale of: SMATV and CATV systems and equipment. Headend equipment for TV-Radio-Satellite reception. Broadband trunk and distribution amplifiers, splitters and taps. Analogue optical cable TV and telecommunications transmission systems.

SEM electronics a/s

Centervej Syd 1
4733 Tappernøje
Tel: 55 96 60 30
Fax: 55 96 60 69
Email: **rt@sem.dk**
Web: **www.sem.dk**
Direktør : Richard J. Toxværd email: **rt@sem.dk**

Strategic partner for all kinds of cable assembling including UL/CSA. Assembly of complete units for the electronic industry. ISO 9002.

Siemens A/S

Borupvang 3
2750 Ballerup
Tel: 44 77 44 77
Fax: 44 77 44 88
Email: **post @siemens.dk**
Web: **www.siemens.dk**
Direktør : Helmut Lengler email: **len@siemens.dk**
Direktør : Jimmy K. Nielsen email: **jmn@siemens.dk**
Divisionsdirektør : Jens Uffe Andersen email: **jua@siemens.dk**
Divisionsdirektør : Jørgen Thanning email: **jt@siemens.dk**
Økonomichef : Finn B. Hansen email: **fbh@siemens.dk**
Afdelingschef : Bjarne Jensen email: **bj@siemens.dk**
Personale- & kvalitetsdir. : Frank Olsen email:
Personaleadm.chef : Lene Petersen email: **lp@siemens.dk**

Development of software and hardware for mini- and microcomputer systems for data collection and -transmission, supervisory systems and process automation.

Simrad Shipmate AS

Østre Allé 6
9530 Støvring
Tel: 98 37 34 99
Fax: 98 37 38 07
Email: **Company@simrad-shipmate.dk**
Web: **www.simrad.no**
Direktør : John Larsen email: **john.larsen@simrad.no**
Økonomichef : Helle Nielsen email: **helle.nielsen@simrad.no**
Projektleder : Helge Lyngesen email: **helge.lyngesen@simrad.no**
Projektleder : Erik Rauff email: **erik.rauff@simrad.no**
Projektleder : Søren Lassen email: **soren.lassen@simrad.no**
Salgschef : Anders Knudsen email: **anders.knudsen@simrad.no**
Udviklingschef : Lars Nedergaard email: **lars.nedergaard@simrad.no**

Områdeleder : Jørgen Mølgaard email:

Simrad Shipmate is developing, manufacturing and selling maritime products within the following fields: VHFradio telephone, GPS satellitnavigation, Electronic chart systems, Echo sounders, Radar's and Integrated navigation systems.

STENTO Danmark A/S

Park Alle 350A
2605 Brøndby
Tel: 43 43 74 11
Fax: 43 43 75 22
Email: **info@stento.dk**
Web: **www.stento.dk**
Teknisk chef : Kim M. Hansen email: **kmh@stento.dk**
Direktør : Peter Borregaard email: **peb@stento.dk**
Sekretær : Wendy Bolmgren email: **wbb@stento.dk**

Sales, development, production, installation, delivery and service of customer specified communication systems to the public sector and private customers. This includes digital audio/data systems, mobile radio communication systems, resale of third party equipment, including communication equipment.

System & Software Engineering

Sandøgade 6
8200 Århus N
Tel: 86 10 07 07
Fax: 86 10 01 31
Email: **sw-eng@inet.uni2.dk**
Web: **www.sw-eng.suite.dk**
Direktør : Keld Hornbech Svendsen email: **sw-eng@inet.uni2.dk**

Consultancy and training courses in effective methods for project management and software development. The services include certified software process assessment and plan for improvements, project management, requirements and design specification. Services will be tailored for the actual need of the customer.

Teknologisk Institut

DTI Datateknik
Teknologiparken
8000 Århus C
Tel: 89 43 89 43
Fax: 89 43 89 89
Web: **www.data.dti.dk**
Centerchef : Jørgen Kunter Pedersen email: **jorgen.kunter.pedersen@dti.dk**

Training courses, consultancy services and implementation in the area of information technology focusing on four areas of specialisation: IT business development, software engineering, system integration and networks, and information engineering.

TELITAL R&D Denmark A/S

Østre Allé 6
9530 Støvring
Tel: 99 86 22 00
Fax: 99 86 22 01
Direktør : Tommi Sørensen email: **ts@telital.dk**

Development of cellular and cordless telephones.

Tellabs Denmark A/S

Lautrupbjerg 7-11
2750 Ballerup
Tel: 44 73 30 00
Fax: 44 73 30 01
Web: **www.dscc.com**
Personalechef : Aase Pedersen email: **aapeders@dscc.dk**
Direktør : Carsten E. Thomsen email: **carsten.thomsen@tellabs.com**
Adm. Direktør : Peter Viereck email: **pviereck@tellabs.com**
Civ.ing. : Flemming Gerdstrøm email: **fgerdstr@tellabs.com**
Souschef : Carsten Hede email: **chede@tellabs.com**
Senior Manager Ing. : Lars Lindqvist email: **llindqvi@tellabs.com**

Our mission is transmission. Transmitting is transporting. And at DSC Communications, we help facilitate the transmission of words, visuals and data via highly sophisticated optical and electronic equipment. We develop and market advanced telecommunications technology to private as well as public network, cable and utility operators all around the world.

TERMA Elektronik AS

Hovmarken 4
8520 Lystrup
Tel: 86 22 20 00
Fax: 86 22 27 99
Email: **terma.hq@terma.com**
Web: **www.terma.com**
Direktør : Johannes Jacobsen email: **jj@terma.dk**
Direktør : Per M. Borggaard email: **pmb@terma.dk**
Vice President : Finn Grydehøj email: **fg@terma.dk**
Udviklingsingeniør : Hans Jensen email: **haj@terma.dk**
Adm. leder : Heidi Carstensen email:

Design and manufacturing of military electronic equipment. Radar systems and communication equipment. Avionics equipment. Ballistic test instrumentation. Airport installations and services.

Topsil Semiconductor Materials A/S

Linderupvej 4
Postboks 93
3600 Frederikssund
Tel: 47 31 16 26
Fax: 47 31 42 69
Email: **topsil@topsil.com**

Direktør : David P. Meyer email: **dm@topsil.com**
Teknisk direktør : Hans Peter Mikkelsen email: **hm@topsil.com**

Monocrystalline float-zone silicon (neutron transmutation doped, high purity silicon, conventional float-zone & permium float zone) supplied in ingots or wafers (as cut, as lapped, as etched, as polished) for applications in high power electronic components.

TRIAX A/S

Bjørnkærvej 3
8783 Hornsyld
Tel: 76 82 22 00
Fax: 75 68 79 66
Email: **triax@micro-matic.triax.dk**

Direktør : Knud Chr. Jensen email: **triax@micro-matic.triax.dk**
Økonomichef : Jørgen Nederby email: **jnp@micro-matic.triax.dk**
General Sales Manager : Svend E. Kristensen email: **sek@micro-mativ.triax.dk**
Salgschef : Jens Hansen email: **jeh@micro-matic.triax.dk**

TV aerials. Satellite dishes. Amplifiers, filters, power supply units, distribution amplifiers, and outlet boxes. Satellite receiving equipment. Steel cabinets for gas, electrical, telephone and cable TV distribution. Contract production of electronics.

VIFA - Scan-Speak A/S

Stationsvej 5
Postboks 39
6920 Videbæk
Tel: 97 17 17 22
Fax: 97 17 16 96
Email: **vifa-speak@post4.tele.dk**

Eksportsælger : Allan Pedersen email: **vifa-speak@post4.tele.dk**
Salgsdirektør : Torben Søndergaard email: **vifa-speak@post4.tele.dk**
Direktør : Tonni Birk Sørensen email: **vifa-speak@post4.tele.dk**
Økonomichef : Jan Nielsen email: **vifa-speak@post4.tele.dk**

Development and manufacturing of high quality loudspeaker drive units. Wide range of 4-12 inch woofers, midrange dome and cone units, 3/4 and 1 inch soft and metal dome tweeters. Specialized in design of drive units according to customers' requirements.

Weibel Scientific A/S

Grusbakken 3
2820 Gentofte
Tel: 45 88 85 11
Fax: 45 88 65 58
Email: **main@weibel.dk**

Direktør : Erik T. Larsen email: **main@weibel.dk**
Direktør : Peder R. Pedersen email: **prp@weibel.dk**
Electro-optical equipment. Microprocessor systems.

For additional analytical, business and investment opportunities information,
please contact Global Investment & Business Center, USA
at (703) 370-8082. Fax: (703) 370-8083. E-mail: ibpusa3@gmail.com
Global Business and Investment Info Databank - www.ibpus.com

Window Master A/S

Skelstedet 13
2950 Vedbæk
Tel: 45 67 03 00
Fax: 45 67 03 90
Afdelingsleder : Jesper Darum email: **jda.wma-dk@velux.com**

For additional analytical, business and investment opportunities information,
please contact Global Investment & Business Center, USA
at (703) 370-8082. Fax: (703) 370-8083. E-mail: ibpusa3@gmail.com
Global Business and Investment Info Databank - www.ibpus.com

ATTORNEYS IN DENMARK

known to accept foreign clients can be found at http://go.usa.gov/3rzvx. This list of attorneys and law firms is provided by the American Embassy as a convenience to United States citizens. It is not meant to be a complete list of attorneys in Denmark, and the absence of an attorney from the list is in no way a reflection on competence. A complete list of attorneys in Denmark, Greenland and the Faeroe Islands may be found at the Danish Bar Association web site: www.advokatnoeglen.dk.

EMBASSY OF THE UNITED STATES OF AMERICA
Dag Hammarskjolds Alle 24
2100 Copenhagen, Denmark
Website: **http://denmark.usembassy.gov**
E-mail: **copenhagenACS@state.gov**
Telephone: +45-3341 7100; Fax: +45-3538 9616

BANKS: No American banks operate with branches in Denmark, but most Danish banks act as agents for American concerns. The three largest banks in Denmark are:

Danske Bank. www.danskebank.dk
Telephone: 7012 3456. danskebank@danskebank.dk SWIFT: DABADKKK
Nordea Bank Denmark. www.nordea.dk
Telephone: 7033 3333. Texting: 3333 2249. SWIFT: NDEADKKK
Jyske Bank, www.jbpb.dk
Telephone: 8989 6232. info@jbpb.dk

NOTARIES PUBLIC: In Denmark Notaries Public are deputy judges at the civil courts. The Ministry of Justice in Copenhagen may certify the signature of any appointed Notary Public.

Further information on Danish notary services may be obtained from: **Royal Danish Ministry of Justice** www.jm.dk Telephone: 3393 3340.

Apostille The Apostille is a validation stamp ensuring that a particular document is recognized in certain foreign countries (countries signatory to the Hague Convention of 5 October 1961 Abolishing the Requirement of Legalization for Foreign Public Documents. Denmark and the United States are both signatory countries to this Convention.) Apostilles (certifications) do not require further legalization by the U.S. Embassy in order to be recognized in the United States. **In Denmark Apostille certifications are administered by the Danish Ministry of Foreign Affairs, Asiatisk Plads 2, 1448 Copenhagen K. TEL: 3392 0000. The Embassy is not authorized to provide apostilles.**

PATENTS & TRADE MARKS: Applications for patents and trademarks can be filed by a Danish resident patent agent or an attorney. Three of the largest patent agents in Denmark are:

Hofman-Bang & Zacco, Hans Bekkevolds Alle 7, 2900 Hellerup. TEL: 3948 8000.
www.zacco.dk E-mail: **info.denmark@zacco.com**
Chas. Hude, H.C. Andersens Boulevard 33, 1780 Copenhagen V.
TEL: 3319 3400. **www.chashude.dk** E-mail: **chashude@chashude.dk**
Budde Schou A/S, Hausergade 3, 1128 Copenhagen K.
TEL: 7025 0900. **www.buddeschou.dk** E-mail: **info@buddeschou.dk**

BUSINESS INFORMATION:

Dun & Bradstreet Danmark A/S, Tobaksvejen 21, 2860 Søborg. TEL: 3673 8000;
www.dnb.com Email: **ks@dnbnordic.com**

COLLECTION & CREDIT REPORTING:

SVEA Finans, Torvestrædet 3, 3450 Allerød. TEL: (Finance) 7020 3300, (Collection) 7027 2500.
www.sveafinans.dk

DANISH BAR & LAW SOCIETY: Kronprinsessegade 28, 1306 Copenhagen K.
TEL: 3396 9798. **www.advokatsamfundet.dk**
Email: **samfund@advokatsamfundet.dk**
Web site lists lawyers throughout Denmark, Greenland and the Faroe Islands.

Free legal advice offices are available in most cities throughout Denmark. The local libraries
can advise you of the availability of free legal counseling in your area.

In Copenhagen:

Copenhagen Legal Aid (Københavns Retshjælp) Stormgade 20, 1555 Copenhagen V.
www.retshjaelpen.dk Telephone: 3311 0678.

Vesterbro Legal Aid (Vesterbro Retshjælp), Onkel Dannys Plads 1 1st. fl., 1713 Copenhagen V.
www.vesterbro-retshajelp.dk Email: **info@vesterbro-retshjaelp.dk** Telephone: 3322 3344.

Social Legal Aid (Den Sociale Retshjaelp), Bragesgade 10, 2nd. fl., Box 585,

2200 Copenhagen N. **www.socialeretshjaelp.dk** Email: **kbh@socialeretshjaelp.dk**

Telephone: 7022 9330.

In Aarhus:

Århus Legal Aid, Vester Alle 8, 8000 Århus C. **www.aarhusretshjaelp.dk** Email:
post@aarhusretshjaelp.dk Telephone: 8619 4700.

Aarhus Social Legal Aid, A. Hertzumsvej 2, 8000 Aarhus C. **www.socialeretshjaelp.dk** Email:
Aarhus@socialeretshjaelp.dk Telephone: 7022 9330.

In Aalborg: Advokatvagten, Rendsburggade 2, 9000 Ålborg.

Hours: Mondays 4:00 p.m. – 6:00 p.m. Only in person service.

ATTORNEYS - CITY OF COPENHAGEN

DANISH MINISTRY OF JUSTICE www.jm.dk

DANISH DEPARTMENT OF FAMILY LAW www.familiestyrelsen.dk

For additional analytical, business and investment opportunities information,
please contact Global Investment & Business Center, USA
at (703) 370-8082. Fax: (703) 370-8083. E-mail: ibpusa3@gmail.com
Global Business and Investment Info Databank - www.ibpus.com

DANISH DEPARTMENT OF FAMILY LAW LIST OF ATTORNEYS SPECIALIZING IN INTERNATIONAL CHILD ABDUCTION:

http://boernebortfoerelse.dk/oekonomisk-hjaelp/liste-over-advokater/

DANISH BAR ASSOCIATION www.advokatsamfundet.dk

ADVODAN: A chain of Danish law firms with 38 offices throughout the country. **www.advodan.dk** Copenhagen Office: Advodan, Havnegade 39, 1058 Copenhagen K. TEL: 7030 1006. Email: **Copenhagen@advodan.dk**

Aarhus Office: Advodan, Havnegade 2B, 8000 Aarhus C. TEL: 4614 6000. Email: **lasd@advodan.dk** *MAIN AREAS OF PRACTICE*: Employment & Work, Death & Division of Property, Cohabiting Couples, Taxes, Wills & Inheritance, Marriage, Construction Cases, Real Estate, Injuries & Damages, Divorce & Separation, Marriage Contracts.

ADVOKATERNE AMALIEGADE NO. 42: Amaliegade 42, 1256 Copenhagen K. TEL: 3311 3399; FAX: 3332 4625. Branch office in Paris, France.

www.amalex.com Email: **adv42@amalex.com** *MAIN AREAS OF PRACTICE*: Taking up Residence in Denmark, Mergers and Acquisitions, Setting up Business, Purchase-Sale-Leasing of Real Estate, Fiscal matters, IT, Employment Contracts, Fiscal Representation and Domiciliation, Agency-Distributorship-Franchise, Trademarks, Patents, Tenders-Construction Contrats, International Transportation, Financing-Securities, Debt Recovery, Insolvency, Foundation-Trusts-Estates, Marriage Contracts, Wills, Litigation – International Arbitration and Mediation.

ANDERSSON & TOFT LAW FIRM: Sankt Peders Stræde 39, 1st. fl, 1453

Copenhagen K. TEL: 3393 0300; FAX: 3312 9027. **www.advolaw.dk**

Email: **info@adv.dk**

SPECIALIZATION AND MAIN AREAS OF PRACTICE: Family Law. Separation/Divorce/Division of Joint Estate, Dissolution of Common Law Marriages, Voluntary and Involuntary Placement of Children in Foster Homes, Family Law Cases involving Danish Welfare Authorities, Child Custody and Visitation.

BECH-BRUUN LAW FIRM: Langelinie Alle 35, 2100 Copenhagen Ø. TEL: 7227 0000; FAX: 7227 0027. **www.bechbruun.com** Email: **info@bechbruun.com**

MAIN AREAS OF PRACTICE: Corporate, EU and Competition, Real Estate, Finance & Capital Markets, IP & Technology, Dispute Resolution, Public Law, Transport & Insurance.

BOELSKIFTE ATTORNEYS: Solbjergvej 3, 2000 Frederiksberg. TEL: 3816 0616; FAX: 3816 0626. **www.boelskifteadvokater.dk** Email: **advokat@takovda.dk**

General Practice, Family Law, Inheritance, Consumer Law. *SPECIALIZATION*: Criminal Law (defense), Real Estate, International Compensation, Administration of Condos and Co-ops.

BOUET LINDAHL LESCHLY LAW FIRM: Attorney Lise Bouet, Lindegårdsvej 51, 2920 Charlottenlund. TEL: 3963 4111; FAX: 3963 4101. **www.bouet.dk** Email: **bouet@bouet.dk**

MAIN AREAS OF PRACTICE: CHILDREN: Contact, Custody, Foster Care, Child Abduction.

MARRIAGE: Prenuptial Agreements, Separation, Divorce, Division of Joint Property. Wills, Purchase and Sale of Real Estate.

BRUUN & HJEJLE: Nørregade 21, 1165 Copenhagen K. TEL: 3334 5000; FAX: 3334 5050.

www.bruunhjejle.com

MAIN AREAS OF PRACTICE: Competition & EU, Employment & Labor, Mergers and Acquisitions, Banking & Finance, Real Estate and Construction., Dispute Resolution, Insolvency & Reconstruction, International Law, Tax Law.

DAVID FRANCIS LUBLIN LAW FIRM: Raadhuspladsen 16, 1550 Copenhagen V.

TEL: 2617 9739; FAX: 8896 8806. **www.dfllaw.dk** Email: **dfl@dfllaw.dk**

MAIN AREAS OF PRACTICE: Criminal Law.

JON PALLE BUHL LAW FIRM: Valkendorfsgade 16, 1151 Copenhagen K. TEL: 3348 0000; FAX: 3348 0048. **www.jpb.dk** Email: **adv@jpb.dk**
The firm provides assistance in general matter as well as the following *MAIN AREAS OF PRACTICE:* Bankruptcy Law, Company Law, Contracts, Corporate Finance and International Financing, Creditor Settlements, Criminal Law, Employment Law, Family Law and Estate Planning, including Marriage Contracts, Wills and Administration of Estates, Insurance Law, Intellectual Property Law, International Financing, Labor Law, Law of Succession, Litigation and Arbitration, Media Law, Mergers and Acquisitions, Public Law, EU Law, Real Estate, tax Law.

CPH LAW FIRM: Vester Voldgade 83, 1st. fl., 1552 Copenhagen V (next to City Hall Square.) TEL: 7022 4055; FAX: 7022 4065. **www.cphlawfirm.com** Email: **info@cphlawfirm.com**

MAIN AREAS OF PRACTICE: Corporate and Finance, IPR, Employment, IT and Telecom, Litigations.

ANJA CORDES: Vimmelskaftet 49, 1161 Copenhagen K. TEL: 3320 6020. **www.anjacordes.dk** Email: **ac@anjacordes.dk**

MAIN AREAS OF PRACTICE: FAMILY LAW: Separation, Divorce, Child Custody, Visitation Rights, Marriage Settlements, Cohabitation. International Family Law, Wills and Succession, Buying and Selling Property, Criminal Law, Mediation.

DELACOUR LAW FIRM: Langebrogade 4, 1411 Copenhagen K. TEL: 7011 1122;

FAX: 7011 1133. **www.delacour.dk** Email: **delacour@delacour.dk**

MAIN AREAS OF PRACTICE: Commercial Law, Collection of Debts, EU & Competition Law, International Law, IP, IT, Media and Gambling, Real Property, Finance and Banking, Insurance and Law of Torts, Horses, Veterinarians & Agriculture, Dispute Resolution, Insolvency and

Restructuring, Mergers & Acquisitions, Private Law, Maritime and Transport Law, Customs, VAT, Tax & Duty.

GORRISSEN FEDERSPIEL LAW FIRM: H.C. Andersens Boulevard 12, 1553 Copenhagen V. TEL: 3341 4141; FAX: 3341 4133. **www.gfklaw.dk**

Email: **contact@grissenfederspiel.com**

MAIN AREAS OF PRACTICE: Banking and Finance, Capital Markets, Corporate Mergers & Acquisitions, EU & Competition, Insolvency, IP & Technology, Labor & Employment, Shipping/Offshore/Transportation, Real Estate, Tax. Cross-Practice Groups: Aircraft & Rolling Stock, CSR-Corporate Social Responsibility, Environment, German Desk, Greenland Desk,

Insurance & Reinsurance, International Construction and Engineering Projects, Energy and Utilities, Media, Entertainment and Telecom.

HORTEN LAW FIRM: Philip Heymans Alle 7, 2900 Hellerup. TEL: 3334 4000;

FAX: 3334 4001. **www.horten.dk** Email: **info@horten.dk**

MAIN AREAS OF PRACTICE: Banking & Finance, Corporate & Commercial, Damages & Insurance, Employment & Labor Law, Energy & Supply Law, Environmental Law, EU, Public Procurement and Competition, German Desk, Insolvency & Restructuring, Intellectual Property Rights, IT, e-commerce & Telecommunications, Litigation, Arbitration and Mediation, Maritime, Air and Transportation, Media & Entertainment, Mergers & Acquisitions, Private Law, Public law, Real Estate & Construction, Tax.

KOCH/CHRISTENSEN: Sankt Annæ Plads 6, 1250 Copenhagen K. TEL: 3315 0800; FAX: 3315 5060. **www.kochchristensen.dk** Email: **kc@kochchristensen.dk**

MAIN AREAS OF PRACTICE: Administration of Estates, Building & Construction, Business Succession Processes, Contract Law, Company Law, Competition Law, Energy Law, Environmental Law, Housing Law, Real Property, Media Law, Labor & Employment Law, IT Law and e-commerce, Environmental Law, Criminal Law, Police Law, International Law issues. Provides legal advice to Greenland Business Firms and Danish and International Companies.

KROMANN REUMERT: Sundkrogsgade 5, 2100 Copenhagen Ø. TEL: 7012 1211;

FAX: 7012 1311. **www.kromannreumert.com** Email: **cph@kromannreumert.com**

Corporate and commercial practice with offices in Copenhagen, Aarhus, London and Brussels with a staff of 600 employees of which 320 are lawyers.

MAIN AREAS OF PRACTICE: Banking & Finance, Capital Markets, Commercial & Company Law, Competition Law, Compliance, CSR and Corporate Governance, Data Protection Law, Employment and Labor Law, Energy Law, Environmental Law and Public law, Financial Regulation and Asset management, German Desk, Greenlandic Law, Insolvency and Reconstruction, Insurance and Tort Law, IP, IT and Outsourcing, Litigation and Arbitration, Maritime and Transportation, Mergers & Acquisitions, Technology and Media, Outbound Services, Private Clients, Procurement, Purchase and Sale of SME, Real Estate & Construction Law, Shipping, Sports, Media & Entertainment, Succession Planning, Tax, Telecommunications.

KYED & JYBÆK LAW FIRM: Frederiksberggade 2, 1459 Copenhagen K. TEL 3314 5145; FAX: 3311 2741. **www.kjlaw.dk** Email: **mail@kjlaw.dk**

MAIN AREAS OF PRACTICE: Agricultural Law, Company Law, Corporate Law, Competition Law, Construction & Engineering, Family Law, EU Law, Mergers and Acquisitions, Succession, Bankruptcy & Reconstruction, Finance Law, Contracts, IT Law, Litigation, Employment Law, Real Estate, Rental Law, Inheritance and Wills, Professional Liability Law.

LASSEN RICARD LAW FIRM: Amaliegade 31, 1256 Copenhagen K. TEL: 3332 2012; FAX: 3332 2474. **www.lassenricard.dk** Email: **info@lassenricard.dk**

MAIN AREAS OF PRACTICE: Company Law and Directorship, Competition Law, Construction Law, EU Law, Finance Law, Intellectual Property Law, IT Law, Litigation, Media Law, Mergers and Acquisitions, Ownership Transition, Telecommunication.

LETT LAW FIRM: Rådhuspladsen 4, 1550 Copenhagen V. TEL: 3334 0000.

FAX: 3334 0001. **www.lett.dk** Email: **lett@lett.dk**

MAIN AREAS OF PRACTICE: Corporate Law, Mergers and Acquisitions, Aircraft Finance and Leasing, Liability & Insurance Law, Tax Law, Information Technology and Telecommunications Law, Employment Law, Competition Law, Intellectual Property Law, Public Procurement Law, Real Property and Construction Law, Lease and Real Property transfers Laws, Environmental Law, Food Law, Litigation and Arbitration.

LUND/ELMER/SANDAGER LAW FIRM: Kalvebod Brygge 39, 1560 Copenhagen V. TEL: 3330 0200; FAX: 3330 0299. **www.lundelmersandager.dk** Email: **info@lundelmersandager.dk**

MAIN AREAS OF PRACTICE: Company Law, Mergers and Acquisitions, Insolvency Law and Administration of Estates, Real Estate, Building, Rent Law/Construction Law, Labor Law and

Employment Law, Mediation/Conciliation, Competition Law, Intellectual Property Law, Contracts, Tax Law, Family Law, Litigation and Arbitration, Property Management.

MAZANTI-ANDERSEN, KORSØ JENSEN & PARTNERE: Amaliegade 10, 1256 Copenhagen K. TEL: 3314 3536; FAX: 3319 3737. **www.mazanti.dk** Email: **info@mazanti.dk**

MAIN AREAS OF PRACTICE: The company provides advice within all areas of company law, including: EU and Competition Law, Litigation and Arbitration, Mergers and Acquisitions, IP Law, Construction Law, Transportation Law, IT and Telecommunication, Public law, Environmental Law, Insolvency Law and Reconstruction, Employment Law, Franchising, Licensing and Distribution, Banking and Finance law.

MEELBERG BRUHN LAW FIRM: Hammerensgade 1, 2nd fl., 1267 Copenhagen K. TEL: 3393 6643; FAX: 33936640. **www.meelbergbruhn.dk** Email: **mm@meelbergbruhn.dk**

Attorney Mona Meelberg was born and raised in the United States.

MAIN AREAS OF PRACTICE: Criminal Law, Family Law: Divorce/Child Custody, Foster Care, Child Abuse, Child Abduction, Domestic Violence, Wills and Prenuptial Agreements, Estate Cases, Victim's Compensation Cases, Criminal Law.

MOLTKE-LETH LAW FIRM: Amaliegade 12, 1256 Copenhagen K. TEL: 3311 6511; FAX: 3311 4911. **www.moltke-leth.dk** Email: **law@moltke-leth.dk**

MAIN AREAS OF PRACTICE: Employment Law, Construction Law, Real Estate, Insurance Law, Family Law, Contracts, Disputes and Litigation, Agricultural and Forestry Law, Commercial Leasing Law, Environmental Law, Wills and Estates, Company Law, Criminal Law, Business Transfers.

NORRBOM & VINDING: Dampfærgevej 26, 2100 Copenhagen. TEL: 3525 3940; FAX: 3525 3950. **www.norrbomvinding.com** Email: **info@norrbomvinding.com**

SPECIALIST FIRM FOCUSED ON HR LAW – LABOR AND EMPLOYMENT LAW.

OSBAK LAW FIRM: Nørregade 30, 1165 Copenhagen K. TEL: 3314 4200; FAX: 3393 4209. **www.osbak.dk** Email: **osbak@osbak.dk**

MAIN AREAS OF PRACTICE: Real Estate, court Proceedings, Tenant Law, Criminal Law, Tort and Insurance Law, Salaried Employee Law, Handling of Estates of Deceased Persons, Inheritance, Wills, Immigration Law, Family Law.

KROER PRAMMING: Thoravej 11, 2400 Copenhagen NV. TEL: 7199 3131. **www.kroerpramming.dk** Email: **kontakt@kroerpramming.dk**

SPECIALIZATION: Personal Injury, Criminal Law (defense.) *OTHER AREAS OF PRACTISE:* Victim's Compensation Cases, Workmen's Compensation, Insurance & Torts, Litigation & Mediation, Family Law, Public Law & Debt Collection.

LONE REFSHAMMER LAW FIRM: Niels Hemmingsensgade 10, 5th fl, P.O. Box 15,

1001 Copenhagen K. TEL: 3393 0330; FAX: 3393 0310. **www.advokatrefshammer.dk**

Email: **lr@advokatrefshammer.dk**

MAIN AREAS OF PRACTICE: Legal proceedings (at all courts of law), Real Property, Owner-occupied Apartments, Family Law, Law of Succession, Access/Custody, Company Law, Contracts, Mergers & Acquisitions, Debt Collection, Criminal Law.

MARIANNE SIGFUSSON: Hauser Plads 16, 1127 Copenhagen K. TEL: 3311 2270; FAX: 3311 2236. **www.sigfusson.dk** Email: **Marianne@sigfusson.dk**

MAIN AREAS OF PRACTICE: National and International Taxation, National and International VAT and Duties, Expatriate Taxation – Global Transfer of Manpower, Setting up in Denmark, Administration of Companies (employment contracts, book keeping, payroll, etc.)

STAGETORN WENZEL LUND POULSEN ATTORNEYS: Store Strandstræde 21, 1255 Copenhagen K. TEL: 3312 4611; FAX: 3312 8445. **www.swlp.dk** Email: **info@swlp.dk**

MAIN AREAS OF PRACTICE: Criminal Law, Court appointed defense attorneys.

VESTERVOLD ATTORNEYS: Vester Voldgade 90, 1552 Copenhagen V.

TEL: 3315 8000. FAX: 3312 1533. **www.vestervoldadvokater.dk** Email: **info@vestervoldadvokater.dk** *MAIN AREAS OF PRACTICE:* Legal , Assistance to Foreign Business Clients, Construct Law, Commercial Law, Successions, Restructuring, Employment Law, Litigation and Arbitration, Construction Law, Estates, Divorce and Family Cases, Wills and marriage Contracts, Real Property and Rent Law, Public Administration, Penal Law.

PROVINCIAL TOWNS

9000 AALBORG (ÅLBORG)

BORGE NIELSEN LAW FIRM: Hasserisvej 174, 9000 Aalborg. TEL: 9812 9800.

Fax: 9812 9855. **www.abnlaw.dk** Email: **abn@abnlaw.dk**

MAIN AREAS OF PRACTICE: Corporate Law, Employment Law, Real Estate, Insolvency, Public Law, EU Law, Private Law, Law of Process.

HJULMAND & KAPTAIN: Badehusvej 16, 9000 Aalborg. TEL: 7015 1000;

FAX: 7221 1601. **www.hjulmandkaptain.dk** Email: **mail@70151000.dk**

MAIN AREAS OF PRACTICE: Employment Law, Risk Management, Mergers and Acquisitions, Environmental Law, Technology, Commercial Law, Directorship, Securities Law, Succession Planning, Commercial Law, Intellectual Property Law, Competition Law, EU Law, Corporate Structuring, Tax Law.

RYE-ANDERSEN LAW FIRM: Algade 33, 9100 Aalborg. TEL: 9816 1600. **www.rye-andersen.dk** Email: **info@rye-andersen.dk**

MAIN AREAS OF PRACTICE: General Practice, Family Law, Estate Cases, Trade Disputes, Criminal Cases, Commercial Law, Contracts, Insolvency, compensation Law.

8000 AARHUS (ÅRHUS)

ADVOKATERNE.COM: Aaboulevarden 3, 1st fl, 8000 Aarhus C. TEL: 8613 8833;

FAX: 8619 4010. **www.advokaterne.com** Email: **office@advokaterne.com**

MAIN AREAS OF PRACTICE: General Practice, Company Law, Contracts, Child Custody, Divorce, Unmarried partners, Estate Cases, Wills, General Family Law, Criminal Law, Torts, Insolvency, Compensation, Real Estate.

BECH-BRUUN LAW FIRM: Frue Kirkeplads 4, 8100 Aarhus C. TEL: 7227 0000;

FAX: 7227 0027. **www.bechbruun.com** Email: **info@bechbruun.com**

MAIN AREAS OF PRACTICE: Capital Markets, Company Law, Construction and Real Property Law, Corporate Consulting, Employment and Labor Law, Energy Supply, Environmental Law, EU and Competition Law, Insolvency and Restructuring, Intellectual Property Rights, International Law, IT Law and Telecommunications, Litigation, Media and Entertainment, Mergers and Acquisitions, Private Law, Public Law, Russian Law, Taxation, Tort & Insurance, Transport Law.

CLEMENS ADVOKATER: Sct. Clemens Stræde 7, 8100 Aarhus C. TEL: 8732 1250;

FAX: 8612 5012. **www.clemenslaw.dk** Email: **info@clemenslaw.dk**

MAIN AREAS OF PRACTICE: Company Law, Contracts, Employment Law, Corporate Transfers, Competition Law, Collection Law, Criminal Law, Insurance and Torts, Real Estate, Family Law, Inheritance.

DELACOUR LAW FIRM: Aaboulevarden 11, 8000 Aarhus C. TEL: 7011 1122; FAX: 7011 1133. **www.delacour.com** Email: **delacour@delacour.dk**

Offices in Copenhagen and Aarhus.

MAIN AREAS OF PRACTICE: Employment and Labor Law, Banking and Financing, Energy Law, Project Development, Family Law and Inheritance Law, Real Property Law, Environmental

Law, Insurance Law and Compensation, Horses and Veterinarians, Sports Law, Collection, Insolvency and Reconstruction, International Law, IT Law, Competition and Marketing, Lawsuits and Arbitration, Company Law, Criminal Law, Transportation and Maritime Law, Corporate Transactions.

GORRISSEN FEDERSPIEL: Silkeborgvej 2, 8000 Aarhus C. TEL: 8620 7500;

FAX: 8620 7599. **www.gorrissenfederspiel.com** Email: **contact@gorrissenfederspiel.com**

Offices in Copenhagen and Aarhus.

The firm offers advice within corporate, commercial and financial law.

MAIN AREAS OF PRACTICE: Banking & Finance, Capital Markets, Corporate/Mergers & Acquisitions, EU and Competition, IP & Technology, Labor & Employment, Litigation, Real Estate, Tax, Transportation.

KROMANN REUMERT: Raadhuspladsen 3, 8100 Aarhus C. TEL: 7012 1211; FAX: 7012 1411. **www.kromannreumert.com** Email: **arh@kromannreumert.com**

Corporate and commercial practice with offices in Copenhagen, Aarhus, London and Brussels with a staff of over 500 persons.

MAIN AREAS OF PRACTICE: Banking & Finance Law, Capital Markets, Commercial & Company Law, Competition Law, Compliance, CSR and Corporate Governance, Data Protection, Employment & Labor, Energy Law, Environmental & Public Law, Financial Regulation, German Desk, Greenlandic Law, Insolvency & reconstruction, Insurance & Tort, IP, IT & Outsourcing, Pharmaceuticals & Biotech, Litigation & Arbitration, Maritime &Transportation Law, Mergers & Acquisitions, Real Estate & Construction Law, Shipping, Sports, Media & Entertainment, Succession Planning, Tax Law, Telecommunications.

6700 ESBJERG

DAHL LAW FIRM: Dokken 10, 6700 Esbjerg. TEL: 8891 9000; FAX: 8891 9001. **www.dahllaw.dk** Email: **esb@dahllaw.dk**

Also offices in Copenhagen, Herning and Viborg.

MAIN AREAS OF PRACTICE: Corporate & Commercial, Construction Law, Real Property, Debt Collection, IT & IP, Competition Law, Insolvency & Reconstruction, Public law, Private Law, Litigation, Tax Law.

7500 HOLSTEBRO

SMITH KNUDSEN LAW FIRM: Store Torv 6, Postboks 1460, 7500 Holstebro.

TEL: 9742 6333; FAX: 9741 3400. **www.smithknudsen.dk** Email: **mail@smithknudsen.dk**

MAIN AREAS OF SPECIALIZATION: Commercial Law, Cross Border Agreements and Disputes, Negotiating and Drafting Contracts in English, EU Employment and Discrimination

Law. Advice is offered to English speaking clients in Family Law matters, Property Transactions, and Inheritance Law.

6000 KOLDING

TROLLE LAW FIRM: Kolding Aapark 2, 6000 Kolding. TEL: 7015 1532;

FAX: 7010 1029. **www.trolle-law.dk** Email: **info@trolle-law.dk**

MAIN AREAS OF PRACTICE: General Practice, Commercial Law, Estate Cases, Family Law, Insurance, Prenuptial Contracts, Divorce.

5000 ODENSE

LEXSOS LAW FIRM: Jernbanegade 4, 1st fl, 5000 Odense C.

TEL: 6612 7700; FAX: 6614 7712. **www.lexsos.dk** Email: **lexsos@lexsos.dk**

MAIN AREAS OF PRACTICE: Arbitration & Litigation, Employment, Intellectual Property, Leases, Building Contracts, Company Formation, Horticultural & Agricultural Law, Bankruptcy, Succession, Tax Law, Company Acquisitions and Disposals, Commercial Property, Agreements & Contracts, Company Law, EU Law, Debt Recovery.

DOMHUSGAARDEN LAW FIRM: Alabanigade 44, 2nd fl, 5000 Odense C. TEL: 7020 6898; FAX: 7020 6897. **www.domhusgaarden.dk/advokat-odense** Email: **office@Leckl.dk**

MAIN AREAS OF PRACTICE: Death & Estates, Divorce, Purchase & Sale of Real Estate, Wills, Tenants & Law on Lease.

8900 RANDERS

GRØNBÆK & HUUSE LAW FIRM: Raadhustorvet 4, 8900 Randers. TEL: 8915 2500; FAX: 8915 2501. **www.Ghadvokater.dk** Email: **mail@ghadvokater.dk**

MAIN AREAS OF PRACTICE: Real Estate, Debt Relief, Child Custody, Succession, Inheritance, Wills, Division of Property, Estates, Child Support, Immaterial Rights, Legal Counseling.

5700 SVENDBORG

ADVOKATHUSET SVENDBORG: Krøyers Stræde 3, 5700 Svendborg. TEL: 6221 2124; FAX: 6222 0966. **www.advokathuset-svendborg.dk** Email: **info@advokathuset-svendborg.dk**

MAIN AREAS OF PRACTICE: General Practice, Lawsuits, Arbitration & other Process, Real Estate and Construction, Company Law, Insolvency and Reconstruction, Immaterial Law, Patents, Design and Trademarks, Compensation and Insurance, Employment Law, Law in connection with Sports, Family Law, Inheritance Law, Estates, Collection and Foreclosure, Agricultural Law.

7100 VEJLE

SKOV ATTORNEYS: Havneparken 1, 7100 Vejle. TEL: 7640 7000; FAX: 7614 1401. **www.skovadvokater.dk** Email: **skov@skovadvokater.dk**

MAIN AREAS OF PRACTICE: General Commercial Issues, Mergers and Acquisitions, Commercial & Company Law, Tax Law, finance Law, Insolvency, Real Estate, Estate & Building Projects, Criminal Law, Construction, IT Law, Family Law, Law on Wills and Succession.

FAROE ISLANDS (FÆRØERNE)

(Telephone area code is +298)

DELACOUR DANIA INTERNATIONAL LAW FIRM:

Magnus Heinasonar Gøta 10, FO-110 Torshavn. TEL: +298-669900. FAX: +298-359901. **www.faroelaw.fo** Email: **faroelaw@faroelaw.fo**

MAIN AREAS OF PRACTICE: Company Foreign Law (Greenland Legal Matters, Russian Legal Matters, Faroese Legal matters), Bankruptcy and Insolvency, Capital Reorganization, Debt Collection, Commercial Agents, Distributors and Franchising, Finance, Mergers and Acquisitions, real Estate, Commercial Property, Oil & gas Law, Lease of Commercial Property, Building and Construction Law, Joint Venture, Employment Law, Intellectual property Law, Trademarks & Copyright, Marketing law, Project Development.

HEYGUM & PETERSEN ATTORNEYS:

Bøgøta 16, P.O. Box 164, FO-110, Torshavn. TEL: 298-351710. FAX: 298-351711. **www.adv.fo** Email: **hp@adv.fo**

MAIN AREAS OF PRACTICE: General Practice, Real Estate, Brokers Business, Collection of Debt, Divorce, Matrimonial Cases, Estate Cases, Bankruptcy, Taxation, Rental & Leasing, Forming and Winding up of Companies, Trade & Industry, Criminal Cases.

GREENLAND (GRØNLAND)

(Telephone area code is +299)

PAULSEN/KELDSEN LAW FIRM: Kissarneqqortuunnguaq 9, P.O. Box 510, 3900 Nuuk. TEL: (299)32 12 52; FAX: (299)32 58 77. **www.paulsen-law.gl** Email: **advokat@paulsen.gl**

MAIN AREAS OF PRACTICE: Agreements, Employment Law, Labor Law, Corporate Social Responsibility, Construction Law, Occupation/Business Counseling, Real Property, Corporate

Law, Debt Collection, Insolvency, Rental Law, Public Law, Litigation and Arbitration, Corporate Transfers. **LANGUAGES:** English.

MALLING & HANSEN DAMM: Aqqusinersuaq 27, Postboks 1046, 3900 Nuuk. TEL: (299) 32 34 00; FAX: (299)32 38 68. **www.malling-hansendamm.gl**

Email: **mhdlaw@malling-hansendamm.gl**

MAIN AREAS OF PRACTICE: General Practice, Greenland Law, Administrative Law, Energy & Mining Law, Business Law, Collection Cases, Estate Cases, Trade Disputes, Criminal Law. **LANGUAGES:** Greenlandic, English.

NUNA LAW FIRM: Qullierfik 2, P.O. Box 59, 3900 Nuuk. TEL: (299) 32 13 70; FAX: (299)32 41 17. **www.nuna-law.gl** Email: **email@nuna-law.com**

MAIN AREAS OF PRACTICE: Estate Cases, Administrative Law, Banking & Finance, Bankruptcy & Insolvency, Commercial Law, Company Law, Competition Law, Construction Law, Contract Law, Copyright, Criminal Law, Debt Collection, Employment & Labor Law, Environmental Law, Family law, Insurance Law, Intellectual Property Law, International Contracts, IT Law, Joint Ventures, Law of Torts, Law of Will & Succession, Litigation & Arbitration, Marketing Law, Mergers & Acquisitions, Oil, Gas & mineral Exploitation, Patents, Public Law, Real Property, Rent Law, Reorganization, Telecommunication, Trademarks, Transport & Maritime Law, Trust Law. **LANGUAGES**: Greenlandic, English.

The following U.S. based Family Law Specialist has expressed an interest in assisting Scandinavian resident clients:

ATTORNEY JOLENE WILSON-GLAH, 1105 Colquitt Street, Houston, Texas 77006. **www.wilson-glah.com** TEL: (713)862-7800; FAX: (713)862-7811. Email: **grogaard@aol.com**

Attorney Wilson-Glah is a fluent Norwegian speaker and able to communicate in the Danish and Swedish languages.

BASIC TITLES ON DENMARK

IMPORTANT!
All publications are updated annually!
Please contact IBP, Inc. at ibpusa3@gmail.com for the latest ISBNs and additional information

TITLE
Denmark A "Spy" Guide - Strategic Information and Developments
Denmark A Spy" Guide"
Denmark Air Force Handbook
Denmark Air Force Handbook
Denmark Banking & Financial Market Handbook
Denmark Banking & Financial Market Handbook
Denmark Business and Investment Opportunities Yearbook
Denmark Business and Investment Opportunities Yearbook
Denmark Business and Investment Opportunities Yearbook Volume 1 Strategic Information and Opportunities
Denmark Business Intelligence Report - Practical Information, Opportunities, Contacts
Denmark Business Intelligence Report - Practical Information, Opportunities, Contacts
Denmark Business Law Handbook - Strategic Information and Basic Laws
Denmark Business Law Handbook - Strategic Information and Basic Laws
Denmark Business Law Handbook - Strategic Information and Basic Laws
Denmark Business Law Handbook - Strategic Information and Basic Laws
Denmark Business Success Guide - Basic Practical Information and Contacts
Denmark Clothing & Textile Industry Handbook
Denmark Company Laws and Regulations Handbook
Denmark Company Laws and Regulations Handbook - Strategic Information and Basic Laws
Denmark Constitution and Citizenship Laws Handbook - Strategic Information and Basic Laws
Denmark Country Study Guide - Strategic Information and Developments
Denmark Country Study Guide - Strategic Information and Developments
Denmark Country Study Guide - Strategic Information and Developments Volume 1 Strategic Information and Developments
Denmark Criminal Laws, Regulations and Procedures Handbook - Strategic Information, Regulations, Procedures
Denmark Customs, Trade Regulations and Procedures Handbook
Denmark Customs, Trade Regulations and Procedures Handbook
Denmark Diplomatic Handbook - Strategic Information and Developments
Denmark Diplomatic Handbook - Strategic Information and Developments
Denmark Ecology & Nature Protection Handbook
Denmark Ecology & Nature Protection Handbook
Denmark Ecology & Nature Protection Laws and Regulation Handbook
Denmark Economic & Development Strategy Handbook
Denmark Economic & Development Strategy Handbook
Denmark Electoral, Political Parties Laws and Regulations Handbook - Strategic Information, Regulations, Procedures
Denmark Energy Policy, Laws and Regulation Handbook
Denmark Export Import & Business Directory
Denmark Export Import & Business Directory
Denmark Export-Import and Business Directory
Denmark Export-Import and Business Directory

For additional analytical, business and investment opportunities information,
please contact Global Investment & Business Center, USA
at (703) 370-8082. Fax: (703) 370-8083. E-mail: ibpusa3@gmail.com
Global Business and Investment Info Databank - www.ibpus.com

TITLE
Denmark Export-Import Trade and Business Directory
Denmark Export-Import Trade and Business Directory
Denmark Fishing and Aquaculture Industry Handbook - Strategic Information, Regulations, Opportunities
Denmark Foreign Policy and Government Guide
Denmark Foreign Policy and Government Guide
Denmark Government and Business Contacts Handbook
Denmark Government and Business Contacts Handbook
Denmark Immigration Laws and Regulations Handbook - Strategic Information and Basic Laws
Denmark Industrial and Business Directory
Denmark Industrial and Business Directory
Denmark Insolvency (Bankruptcy) Laws and Regulations Handbook - Strategic Information and Basic Laws
Denmark Internet and E-Commerce Investment and Business Guide - Strategic and Practical Information: Regulations and Opportunities
Denmark Internet and E-Commerce Investment and Business Guide - Strategic and Practical Information: Regulations and Opportunities
Denmark Investment and Business Guide - Strategic and Practical Information
Denmark Investment and Business Guide - Strategic and Practical Information
Denmark Investment and Business Guide - Strategic and Practical Information
Denmark Investment and Business Guide - Strategic and Practical Information
Denmark Investment and Business Profile - Basic Information and Contacts for Succesful investment and Business Activity
Denmark Investment and Trade Laws and Regulations Handbook
Denmark Investment, Trade Strategy and Agreements Handbook - Strategic Information and Basic Agreements
Denmark Labor Laws and Regulations Handbook - Strategic Information and Basic Laws
Denmark Land Ownership and Agriculture Laws Handbook
Denmark Land Ownership and Agriculture Laws Handbook
Denmark Mineral & Mining Sector Investment and Business Guide - Strategic and Practical Information
Denmark Mineral & Mining Sector Investment and Business Guide - Strategic and Practical Information
Denmark Mining Laws and Regulations Handbook
Denmark Recent Economic and Political Developments Yearbook
Denmark Recent Economic and Political Developments Yearbook
Denmark Recent Economic and Political Developments Yearbook
Denmark Starting Business (Incorporating) in....Guide
Denmark Tax Guide Volume 1 Strategic Information and Basic Regulations
Denmark Taxation Laws and Regulations Handbook
Denmark Telecom Laws and Regulations Handbook
Denmark Telecommunication Industry Business Opportunities Handbook
Denmark Telecommunication Industry Business Opportunities Handbook
Denmark Transportation Policy and Regulations Handbook
Denmark Wind Energy Production and Distribution Handbook
Denmark Wind Energy Production and Distribution Handbook
Denmark: How to Invest, Start and Run Profitable Business in Denmark Guide - Practical Information, Opportunities, Contacts

For additional analytical, business and investment opportunities information,
please contact Global Investment & Business Center, USA
at (703) 370-8082. Fax: (703) 370-8083. E-mail: ibpusa3@gmail.com
Global Business and Investment Info Databank - www.ibpus.com

FISHING AND AQUACULTURE
INDUSTRY HANDBOOK LIBRARY
(PRICE $99.95)

**Ultimate handbooks Fishing and Aquaculture
Industry laws and regulation in selected countries**

TITLE
Albania Fishing and Aquaculture Industry Handbook - Strategic Information, Regulations, Opportunities
Algeria Fishing and Aquaculture Industry Handbook - Strategic Information, Regulations, Opportunities
Angola Fishing and Aquaculture Industry Handbook - Strategic Information, Regulations, Opportunities
Antigua and Barbuda Fishing and Aquaculture Industry Handbook - Strategic Information, Regulations, Opportunities
Argentina Fishing and Aquaculture Industry Handbook - Strategic Information, Regulations, Opportunities
Armenia Fishing and Aquaculture Industry Handbook - Strategic Information, Regulations, Opportunities
Australia Fishing and Aquaculture Industry Handbook - Strategic Information, Regulations, Opportunities
Bahamas Fishing and Aquaculture Industry Handbook - Strategic Information, Regulations, Opportunities
Bahrain Fishing and Aquaculture Industry Handbook - Strategic Information, Regulations, Opportunities
Bangladesh Fishing and Aquaculture Industry Handbook - Strategic Information, Regulations, Opportunities
Barbados Fishing and Aquaculture Industry Handbook - Strategic Information, Regulations, Opportunities
Belarus Fishing and Aquaculture Industry Handbook - Strategic Information, Regulations, Opportunities
Belgium Fishing and Aquaculture Industry Handbook - Strategic Information, Regulations, Opportunities
Belize Fishing and Aquaculture Industry Handbook - Strategic Information, Regulations, Opportunities
Benin Fishing and Aquaculture Industry Handbook - Strategic Information, Regulations, Opportunities
Bolivia Fishing and Aquaculture Industry Handbook - Strategic Information, Regulations, Opportunities
Botswana Fishing and Aquaculture Industry Handbook - Strategic Information, Regulations, Opportunities
Brazil Fishing and Aquaculture Industry Handbook - Strategic Information, Regulations, Opportunities
Bulgaria Fishing and Aquaculture Industry Handbook - Strategic Information, Regulations, Opportunities
Burkina Faso Fishing and Aquaculture Industry Handbook - Strategic Information, Regulations, Opportunities
Burundi Fishing and Aquaculture Industry Handbook - Strategic Information, Regulations, Opportunities
Cabo Verde Fishing and Aquaculture Industry Handbook - Strategic Information, Regulations, Opportunities
Cambodia Fishing and Aquaculture Industry Handbook - Strategic Information, Regulations, Opportunities
Cameroon Fishing and Aquaculture Industry Handbook - Strategic Information, Regulations, Opportunities
Canada Fishing and Aquaculture Industry Handbook - Strategic Information, Regulations, Opportunities
Central African Republic Fishing and Aquaculture Industry Handbook - Strategic Information, Regulations, Opportunities
Chad Fishing and Aquaculture Industry Handbook - Strategic Information, Regulations, Opportunities
Chile Fishing and Aquaculture Industry Handbook - Strategic Information, Regulations, Opportunities
China Fishing and Aquaculture Industry Handbook - Strategic Information, Regulations, Opportunities
Colombia Fishing and Aquaculture Industry Handbook - Strategic Information, Regulations, Opportunities
Comoros Fishing and Aquaculture Industry Handbook - Strategic Information, Regulations, Opportunities
Congo Fishing and Aquaculture Industry Handbook - Strategic Information, Regulations, Opportunities

**For additional analytical, business and investment opportunities information,
please contact Global Investment & Business Center, USA
at (202) 546-2103. Fax: (202) 546-3275. E-mail: ibpusa3@gmail.com**

TITLE
Congo, Dem. Rep. of the Fishing and Aquaculture Industry Handbook - Strategic Information, Regulations, Opportunities
Cook Islands Fishing and Aquaculture Industry Handbook - Strategic Information, Regulations, Opportunities
Costa Rica Fishing and Aquaculture Industry Handbook - Strategic Information, Regulations, Opportunities
Croatia Fishing and Aquaculture Industry Handbook - Strategic Information, Regulations, Opportunities
Cuba Fishing and Aquaculture Industry Handbook - Strategic Information, Regulations, Opportunities
Cyprus Fishing and Aquaculture Industry Handbook - Strategic Information, Regulations, Opportunities
Czech Republic Fishing and Aquaculture Industry Handbook - Strategic Information, Regulations, Opportunities
Côte d'Ivoire Fishing and Aquaculture Industry Handbook - Strategic Information, Regulations, Opportunities
Denmark Fishing and Aquaculture Industry Handbook - Strategic Information, Regulations, Opportunities
Djibouti Fishing and Aquaculture Industry Handbook - Strategic Information, Regulations, Opportunities
Dominica Fishing and Aquaculture Industry Handbook - Strategic Information, Regulations, Opportunities
Dominican Republic Fishing and Aquaculture Industry Handbook - Strategic Information, Regulations, Opportunities
Ecuador Fishing and Aquaculture Industry Handbook - Strategic Information, Regulations, Opportunities
Egypt Fishing and Aquaculture Industry Handbook - Strategic Information, Regulations, Opportunities
El Salvador Fishing and Aquaculture Industry Handbook - Strategic Information, Regulations, Opportunities
Equatorial Guinea Fishing and Aquaculture Industry Handbook - Strategic Information, Regulations, Opportunities
Eritrea Fishing and Aquaculture Industry Handbook - Strategic Information, Regulations, Opportunities
Estonia Fishing and Aquaculture Industry Handbook - Strategic Information, Regulations, Opportunities
Ethiopia Fishing and Aquaculture Industry Handbook - Strategic Information, Regulations, Opportunities
Fiji Fishing and Aquaculture Industry Handbook - Strategic Information, Regulations, Opportunities
Finland Fishing and Aquaculture Industry Handbook - Strategic Information, Regulations, Opportunities
France Fishing and Aquaculture Industry Handbook - Strategic Information, Regulations, Opportunities
Gabon Fishing and Aquaculture Industry Handbook - Strategic Information, Regulations, Opportunities
Gambia Fishing and Aquaculture Industry Handbook - Strategic Information, Regulations, Opportunities
Georgia Fishing and Aquaculture Industry Handbook - Strategic Information, Regulations, Opportunities
Germany Fishing and Aquaculture Industry Handbook - Strategic Information, Regulations, Opportunities
Ghana Fishing and Aquaculture Industry Handbook - Strategic Information, Regulations, Opportunities
Greece Fishing and Aquaculture Industry Handbook - Strategic Information, Regulations, Opportunities
Greenland Fishing and Aquaculture Industry Handbook - Strategic Information, Regulations, Opportunities
Grenada Fishing and Aquaculture Industry Handbook - Strategic Information, Regulations, Opportunities
Guatemala Fishing and Aquaculture Industry Handbook - Strategic Information, Regulations, Opportunities
Guinea Fishing and Aquaculture Industry Handbook - Strategic Information, Regulations, Opportunities
Guinea-Bissau Fishing and Aquaculture Industry Handbook - Strategic Information, Regulations, Opportunities
Guyana Fishing and Aquaculture Industry Handbook - Strategic Information, Regulations, Opportunities
Haiti Fishing and Aquaculture Industry Handbook - Strategic Information, Regulations, Opportunities
Honduras Fishing and Aquaculture Industry Handbook - Strategic Information, Regulations, Opportunities
Iceland Fishing and Aquaculture Industry Handbook - Strategic Information, Regulations, Opportunities
India Fishing and Aquaculture Industry Handbook - Strategic Information, Regulations, Opportunities
Indonesia Fishing and Aquaculture Industry Handbook - Strategic Information, Regulations, Opportunities
Iran Fishing and Aquaculture Industry Handbook - Strategic Information, Regulations, Opportunities
Iraq Fishing and Aquaculture Industry Handbook - Strategic Information, Regulations, Opportunities
Ireland Fishing and Aquaculture Industry Handbook - Strategic Information, Regulations, Opportunities
Israel Fishing and Aquaculture Industry Handbook - Strategic Information, Regulations, Opportunities
Italy Fishing and Aquaculture Industry Handbook - Strategic Information, Regulations, Opportunities
Jamaica Fishing and Aquaculture Industry Handbook - Strategic Information, Regulations, Opportunities

For additional analytical, business and investment opportunities information,
please contact Global Investment & Business Center, USA
at (202) 546-2103. Fax: (202) 546-3275. E-mail: ibpusa3@gmail.com

TITLE
Japan Fishing and Aquaculture Industry Handbook - Strategic Information, Regulations, Opportunities
Jordan Fishing and Aquaculture Industry Handbook - Strategic Information, Regulations, Opportunities
Kazakhstan Fishing and Aquaculture Industry Handbook - Strategic Information, Regulations, Opportunities
Kenya Fishing and Aquaculture Industry Handbook - Strategic Information, Regulations, Opportunities
Kiribati Fishing and Aquaculture Industry Handbook - Strategic Information, Regulations, Opportunities
Korea Republic Fishing and Aquaculture Industry Handbook - Strategic Information, Regulations, Opportunities
Kuwait Fishing and Aquaculture Industry Handbook - Strategic Information, Regulations, Opportunities
Kyrgyzstan Fishing and Aquaculture Industry Handbook - Strategic Information, Regulations, Opportunities
Lao People's Dem. Rep. Fishing and Aquaculture Industry Handbook - Strategic Information, Regulations, Opportunities
Latvia Fishing and Aquaculture Industry Handbook - Strategic Information, Regulations, Opportunities
Lesotho Fishing and Aquaculture Industry Handbook - Strategic Information, Regulations, Opportunities
Liberia Fishing and Aquaculture Industry Handbook - Strategic Information, Regulations, Opportunities
Libya Fishing and Aquaculture Industry Handbook - Strategic Information, Regulations, Opportunities
Lithuania Fishing and Aquaculture Industry Handbook - Strategic Information, Regulations, Opportunities
Macedonia Fishing and Aquaculture Industry Handbook - Strategic Information, Regulations, Opportunities
Madagascar Fishing and Aquaculture Industry Handbook - Strategic Information, Regulations, Opportunities
Malawi Fishing and Aquaculture Industry Handbook - Strategic Information, Regulations, Opportunities
Malaysia Fishing and Aquaculture Industry Handbook - Strategic Information, Regulations, Opportunities
Maldives Fishing and Aquaculture Industry Handbook - Strategic Information, Regulations, Opportunities
Mali Fishing and Aquaculture Industry Handbook - Strategic Information, Regulations, Opportunities
Malta Fishing and Aquaculture Industry Handbook - Strategic Information, Regulations, Opportunities
Marshall Islands Fishing and Aquaculture Industry Handbook - Strategic Information, Regulations, Opportunities
Mauritania Fishing and Aquaculture Industry Handbook - Strategic Information, Regulations, Opportunities
Mauritius Fishing and Aquaculture Industry Handbook - Strategic Information, Regulations, Opportunities
Mexico Fishing and Aquaculture Industry Handbook - Strategic Information, Regulations, Opportunities
Micronesia Fishing and Aquaculture Industry Handbook - Strategic Information, Regulations, Opportunities
Moldova Fishing and Aquaculture Industry Handbook - Strategic Information, Regulations, Opportunities
Morocco Fishing and Aquaculture Industry Handbook - Strategic Information, Regulations, Opportunities
Mozambique Fishing and Aquaculture Industry Handbook - Strategic Information, Regulations, Opportunities
Myanmar Fishing and Aquaculture Industry Handbook - Strategic Information, Regulations, Opportunities
Namibia Fishing and Aquaculture Industry Handbook - Strategic Information, Regulations, Opportunities
Nauru Fishing and Aquaculture Industry Handbook - Strategic Information, Regulations, Opportunities
Nepal Fishing and Aquaculture Industry Handbook - Strategic Information, Regulations, Opportunities
Netherlands Fishing and Aquaculture Industry Handbook - Strategic Information, Regulations, Opportunities
New Zealand Fishing and Aquaculture Industry Handbook - Strategic Information, Regulations, Opportunities
Nicaragua Fishing and Aquaculture Industry Handbook - Strategic Information, Regulations, Opportunities
Niger Fishing and Aquaculture Industry Handbook - Strategic Information, Regulations, Opportunities
Nigeria Fishing and Aquaculture Industry Handbook - Strategic Information, Regulations, Opportunities
Norway Fishing and Aquaculture Industry Handbook - Strategic Information, Regulations, Opportunities
Oman Fishing and Aquaculture Industry Handbook - Strategic Information, Regulations, Opportunities
Pakistan Fishing and Aquaculture Industry Handbook - Strategic Information, Regulations, Opportunities
Palau Fishing and Aquaculture Industry Handbook - Strategic Information, Regulations, Opportunities
Panama Fishing and Aquaculture Industry Handbook - Strategic Information, Regulations, Opportunities
Papua New Guinea Fishing and Aquaculture Industry Handbook - Strategic Information, Regulations, Opportunities
Paraguay Fishing and Aquaculture Industry Handbook - Strategic Information, Regulations, Opportunities
Peru Fishing and Aquaculture Industry Handbook - Strategic Information, Regulations, Opportunities

For additional analytical, business and investment opportunities information,
please contact Global Investment & Business Center, USA
at (202) 546-2103. Fax: (202) 546-3275. E-mail: ibpusa3@gmail.com

TITLE
Philippines Fishing and Aquaculture Industry Handbook - Strategic Information, Regulations, Opportunities
Poland Fishing and Aquaculture Industry Handbook - Strategic Information, Regulations, Opportunities
Portugal Fishing and Aquaculture Industry Handbook - Strategic Information, Regulations, Opportunities
Qatar Fishing and Aquaculture Industry Handbook - Strategic Information, Regulations, Opportunities
Romania	Fishing and Aquaculture Industry Handbook - Strategic Information, Regulations, Opportunities
Russian Federation Fishing and Aquaculture Industry Handbook - Strategic Information, Regulations, Opportunities
Rwanda Fishing and Aquaculture Industry Handbook - Strategic Information, Regulations, Opportunities
Saint Kitts and Nevis Fishing and Aquaculture Industry Handbook - Strategic Information, Regulations, Opportunities
Saint Lucia Fishing and Aquaculture Industry Handbook - Strategic Information, Regulations, Opportunities
Saint Vincent/Grenadines Fishing and Aquaculture Industry Handbook - Strategic Information, Regulations, Opportunities
Samoa Fishing and Aquaculture Industry Handbook - Strategic Information, Regulations, Opportunities
Sao Tome and Principe Fishing and Aquaculture Industry Handbook - Strategic Information, Regulations, Opportunities
Saudi Arabia Fishing and Aquaculture Industry Handbook - Strategic Information, Regulations, Opportunities
Senegal Fishing and Aquaculture Industry Handbook - Strategic Information, Regulations, Opportunities
Seychelles Fishing and Aquaculture Industry Handbook - Strategic Information, Regulations, Opportunities
Sierra Leone Fishing and Aquaculture Industry Handbook - Strategic Information, Regulations, Opportunities
Slovakia Fishing and Aquaculture Industry Handbook - Strategic Information, Regulations, Opportunities
Solomon Islands Fishing and Aquaculture Industry Handbook - Strategic Information, Regulations, Opportunities
South Africa Fishing and Aquaculture Industry Handbook - Strategic Information, Regulations, Opportunities
South Sudan Fishing and Aquaculture Industry Handbook - Strategic Information, Regulations, Opportunities
Spain Fishing and Aquaculture Industry Handbook - Strategic Information, Regulations, Opportunities
Sri Lanka Fishing and Aquaculture Industry Handbook - Strategic Information, Regulations, Opportunities
Sudan Fishing and Aquaculture Industry Handbook - Strategic Information, Regulations, Opportunities
Suriname Fishing and Aquaculture Industry Handbook - Strategic Information, Regulations, Opportunities
Swaziland Fishing and Aquaculture Industry Handbook - Strategic Information, Regulations, Opportunities
Sweden Fishing and Aquaculture Industry Handbook - Strategic Information, Regulations, Opportunities
Syrian Arab Republic Fishing and Aquaculture Industry Handbook - Strategic Information, Regulations, Opportunities
Tanzania, United Rep. of Fishing and Aquaculture Industry Handbook - Strategic Information, Regulations, Opportunities
Thailand Fishing and Aquaculture Industry Handbook - Strategic Information, Regulations, Opportunities
Timor-Leste Fishing and Aquaculture Industry Handbook - Strategic Information, Regulations, Opportunities
Togo Fishing and Aquaculture Industry Handbook - Strategic Information, Regulations, Opportunities
Tonga Fishing and Aquaculture Industry Handbook - Strategic Information, Regulations, Opportunities
Trinidad and Tobago Fishing and Aquaculture Industry Handbook - Strategic Information, Regulations, Opportunities
Tunisia Fishing and Aquaculture Industry Handbook - Strategic Information, Regulations, Opportunities
Turkey Fishing and Aquaculture Industry Handbook - Strategic Information, Regulations, Opportunities
Turkmenistan Fishing and Aquaculture Industry Handbook - Strategic Information, Regulations, Opportunities
Tuvalu Fishing and Aquaculture Industry Handbook - Strategic Information, Regulations, Opportunities
Uganda Fishing and Aquaculture Industry Handbook - Strategic Information, Regulations, Opportunities
Ukraine Fishing and Aquaculture Industry Handbook - Strategic Information, Regulations, Opportunities
United Arab Emirates Fishing and Aquaculture Industry Handbook - Strategic Information, Regulations, Opportunities
United Kingdom Fishing and Aquaculture Industry Handbook - Strategic Information, Regulations,

For additional analytical, business and investment opportunities information,
please contact Global Investment & Business Center, USA
at (202) 546-2103. Fax: (202) 546-3275. E-mail: ibpusa3@gmail.com

TITLE
Opportunities
United States of America Fishing and Aquaculture Industry Handbook - Strategic Information, Regulations, Opportunities
Uruguay Fishing and Aquaculture Industry Handbook - Strategic Information, Regulations, Opportunities
Uzbekistan Fishing and Aquaculture Industry Handbook - Strategic Information, Regulations, Opportunities
Vanuatu Fishing and Aquaculture Industry Handbook - Strategic Information, Regulations, Opportunities
Venezuela Fishing and Aquaculture Industry Handbook - Strategic Information, Regulations, Opportunities
Vietnam Fishing and Aquaculture Industry Handbook - Strategic Information, Regulations, Opportunities
Yemen Fishing and Aquaculture Industry Handbook - Strategic Information, Regulations, Opportunities
Zambia Fishing and Aquaculture Industry Handbook - Strategic Information, Regulations, Opportunities
Zimbabwe Fishing and Aquaculture Industry Handbook - Strategic Information, Regulations, Opportunities

For additional analytical, business and investment opportunities information,
please contact Global Investment & Business Center, USA
at (202) 546-2103. Fax: (202) 546-3275. E-mail: ibpusa3@gmail.com

WORLD BUSINESS AND INVESTMENT OPPORTUNITIES YEARBOOK LIBRARY

World Business Information Catalog, USA: http://www.ibpus.com
Email: ibpusa3@gmail.com
Price: $99.95 Each

TITLE
Abkhazia (Republic of Abkhazia) Business and Investment Opportunities Yearbook Volume 1 Strategic, Practical Information and Opportunities
Afghanistan Business and Investment Opportunities Yearbook Volume 1 Strategic, Practical Information and Opportunities
Aland Business and Investment Opportunities Yearbook Volume 1 Strategic, Practical Information and Opportunities
Albania Business and Investment Opportunities Yearbook Volume 1 Strategic, Practical Information and Opportunities
Algeria Business and Investment Opportunities Yearbook Volume 1 Strategic, Practical Information and Opportunities
Andorra Business and Investment Opportunities Yearbook Volume 1 Strategic, Practical Information and Opportunities
Angola Business and Investment Opportunities Yearbook Volume 1 Strategic, Practical Information and Opportunities
Anguilla Business and Investment Opportunities Yearbook Volume 1 Strategic, Practical Information and Opportunities
Antigua and Barbuda Business and Investment Opportunities Yearbook Volume 1 Strategic, Practical Information and Opportunities
Antilles (Netherlands) Business and Investment Opportunities Yearbook Volume 1 Strategic, Practical Information and Opportunities
Argentina Business and Investment Opportunities Yearbook Volume 1 Strategic, Practical Information and Opportunities
Armenia Business and Investment Opportunities Yearbook Volume 1 Strategic, Practical Information and Opportunities
Aruba Business and Investment Opportunities Yearbook Volume 1 Strategic, Practical Information and Opportunities
Australia Business and Investment Opportunities Yearbook Volume 1 Strategic, Practical Information and Opportunities
Austria Business and Investment Opportunities Yearbook Volume 1 Strategic, Practical Information and Opportunities
Azerbaijan Business and Investment Opportunities Yearbook Volume 1 Strategic, Practical Information and Opportunities
Bahamas Business and Investment Opportunities Yearbook Volume 1 Strategic, Practical Information and Opportunities
Bahrain Business and Investment Opportunities Yearbook Volume 1 Strategic, Practical Information and Opportunities
Bangladesh Business and Investment Opportunities Yearbook Volume 1 Strategic, Practical Information and Opportunities
Barbados Business and Investment Opportunities Yearbook Volume 1 Strategic, Practical Information and Opportunities
Belarus Business and Investment Opportunities Yearbook Volume 1 Strategic, Practical Information and Opportunities

For additional analytical, business and investment opportunities information,
Please contact Global Investment & Business Center, USA
at (202) 546-2103. Fax: (202) 546-3275. E-mail: ibpusa3@gmail.com

TITLE
Belgium Business and Investment Opportunities Yearbook Volume 1 Strategic, Practical Information and Opportunities
Belize Business and Investment Opportunities Yearbook Volume 1 Strategic, Practical Information and Opportunities
Benin Business and Investment Opportunities Yearbook Volume 1 Strategic, Practical Information and Opportunities
Bermuda Business and Investment Opportunities Yearbook Volume 1 Strategic, Practical Information and Opportunities
Bhutan Business and Investment Opportunities Yearbook Volume 1 Strategic, Practical Information and Opportunities
Bolivia Business and Investment Opportunities Yearbook Volume 1 Strategic, Practical Information and Opportunities
Bosnia and Herzegovina Business and Investment Opportunities Yearbook Volume 1 Strategic, Practical Information and Opportunities
Botswana Business and Investment Opportunities Yearbook Volume 1 Strategic, Practical Information and Opportunities
Brazil Business and Investment Opportunities Yearbook Volume 1 Strategic, Practical Information and Opportunities
Brunei Business and Investment Opportunities Yearbook Volume 1 Strategic, Practical Information and Opportunities
Bulgaria Business and Investment Opportunities Yearbook Volume 1 Strategic, Practical Information and Opportunities
Burkina Faso Business and Investment Opportunities Yearbook Volume 1 Strategic, Practical Information and Opportunities
Burundi Business and Investment Opportunities Yearbook Volume 1 Strategic, Practical Information and Opportunities
Cambodia Business and Investment Opportunities Yearbook Volume 1 Strategic, Practical Information and Opportunities
Cameroon Business and Investment Opportunities Yearbook Volume 1 Strategic, Practical Information and Opportunities
Canada Business and Investment Opportunities Yearbook Volume 1 Strategic, Practical Information and Opportunities
Cape Verde Business and Investment Opportunities Yearbook Volume 1 Strategic, Practical Information and Opportunities
Cayman Islands Business and Investment Opportunities Yearbook Volume 1 Strategic, Practical Information and Opportunities
Central African Republic Business and Investment Opportunities Yearbook Volume 1 Strategic, Practical Information and Opportunities
Chad Business and Investment Opportunities Yearbook Volume 1 Strategic, Practical Information and Opportunities
Chile Business and Investment Opportunities Yearbook Volume 1 Strategic, Practical Information and Opportunities
China Business and Investment Opportunities Yearbook Volume 1 Strategic, Practical Information and Opportunities
Colombia Business and Investment Opportunities Yearbook Volume 1 Strategic, Practical Information and Opportunities
Comoros Business and Investment Opportunities Yearbook Volume 1 Strategic, Practical Information and Opportunities
Congo Business and Investment Opportunities Yearbook Volume 1 Strategic, Practical Information and Opportunities
Congo, Democratic Republic Business and Investment Opportunities Yearbook Volume 1 Strategic, Practical Information and Opportunities
Cook Islands Business and Investment Opportunities Yearbook Volume 1 Strategic, Practical Information and Opportunities
Costa Rica Business and Investment Opportunities Yearbook Volume 1 Strategic, Practical Information and Opportunities

For additional analytical, business and investment opportunities information,
Please contact Global Investment & Business Center, USA
at (202) 546-2103. Fax: (202) 546-3275. E-mail: ibpusa3@gmail.com

TITLE
Cote d'Ivoire Business and Investment Opportunities Yearbook Volume 1 Strategic, Practical Information and Opportunities
Croatia Business and Investment Opportunities Yearbook Volume 1 Strategic, Practical Information and Opportunities
Cuba Business and Investment Opportunities Yearbook Volume 1 Strategic, Practical Information and Opportunities
Cyprus Business and Investment Opportunities Yearbook Volume 1 Strategic, Practical Information and Opportunities
Czech Republic Business and Investment Opportunities Yearbook Volume 1 Strategic, Practical Information and Opportunities
Denmark Business and Investment Opportunities Yearbook Volume 1 Strategic, Practical Information and Opportunities
Djibouti Business and Investment Opportunities Yearbook Volume 1 Strategic, Practical Information and Opportunities
Dominica Business and Investment Opportunities Yearbook Volume 1 Strategic, Practical Information and Opportunities
Dominican Republic Business and Investment Opportunities Yearbook Volume 1 Strategic, Practical Information and Opportunities
Ecuador Business and Investment Opportunities Yearbook Volume 1 Strategic, Practical Information and Opportunities
Egypt Business and Investment Opportunities Yearbook Volume 1 Strategic, Practical Information and Opportunities
El Salvador Business and Investment Opportunities Yearbook Volume 1 Strategic, Practical Information and Opportunities
Equatorial Guinea Business and Investment Opportunities Yearbook Volume 1 Strategic, Practical Information and Opportunities
Eritrea Business and Investment Opportunities Yearbook Volume 1 Strategic, Practical Information and Opportunities
Estonia Business and Investment Opportunities Yearbook Volume 1 Strategic, Practical Information and Opportunities
Ethiopia Business and Investment Opportunities Yearbook Volume 1 Strategic, Practical Information and Opportunities
Falkland Islands Business and Investment Opportunities Yearbook Volume 1 Strategic, Practical Information and Opportunities
Faroes Islands Business and Investment Opportunities Yearbook Volume 1 Strategic, Practical Information and Opportunities
Fiji Business and Investment Opportunities Yearbook Volume 1 Strategic, Practical Information and Opportunities
Finland Business and Investment Opportunities Yearbook Volume 1 Strategic, Practical Information and Opportunities
France Business and Investment Opportunities Yearbook Volume 1 Strategic, Practical Information and Opportunities
Gabon Business and Investment Opportunities Yearbook Volume 1 Strategic, Practical Information and Opportunities
Gambia Business and Investment Opportunities Yearbook Volume 1 Strategic, Practical Information and Opportunities
Georgia Business and Investment Opportunities Yearbook Volume 1 Strategic, Practical Information and Opportunities
Germany Business and Investment Opportunities Yearbook Volume 1 Strategic, Practical Information and Opportunities
Ghana Business and Investment Opportunities Yearbook Volume 1 Strategic, Practical Information and Opportunities
Gibraltar Business and Investment Opportunities Yearbook Volume 1 Strategic, Practical Information and Opportunities
Greece Business and Investment Opportunities Yearbook Volume 1 Strategic, Practical Information and Opportunities

For additional analytical, business and investment opportunities information,
Please contact Global Investment & Business Center, USA
at (202) 546-2103. Fax: (202) 546-3275. E-mail: ibpusa3@gmail.com

TITLE
Greenland Business and Investment Opportunities Yearbook Volume 1 Strategic, Practical Information and Opportunities
Grenada Business and Investment Opportunities Yearbook Volume 1 Strategic, Practical Information and Opportunities
Guam Business and Investment Opportunities Yearbook Volume 1 Strategic, Practical Information and Opportunities
Guatemala Business and Investment Opportunities Yearbook Volume 1 Strategic, Practical Information and Opportunities
Guernsey Business and Investment Opportunities Yearbook Volume 1 Strategic, Practical Information and Opportunities
Guinea Business and Investment Opportunities Yearbook Volume 1 Strategic, Practical Information and Opportunities
Guinea-Bissau Business and Investment Opportunities Yearbook Volume 1 Strategic, Practical Information and Opportunities
Guyana Business and Investment Opportunities Yearbook Volume 1 Strategic, Practical Information and Opportunities
Haiti Business and Investment Opportunities Yearbook Volume 1 Strategic, Practical Information and Opportunities
Honduras Business and Investment Opportunities Yearbook Volume 1 Strategic, Practical Information and Opportunities
Hungary Business and Investment Opportunities Yearbook Volume 1 Strategic, Practical Information and Opportunities
Iceland Business and Investment Opportunities Yearbook Volume 1 Strategic, Practical Information and Opportunities
India Business and Investment Opportunities Yearbook Volume 1 Strategic, Practical Information and Opportunities
Indonesia Business and Investment Opportunities Yearbook Volume 1 Strategic, Practical Information and Opportunities
Iran Business and Investment Opportunities Yearbook Volume 1 Strategic, Practical Information and Opportunities
Iraq Business and Investment Opportunities Yearbook Volume 1 Strategic, Practical Information and Opportunities
Ireland Business and Investment Opportunities Yearbook Volume 1 Strategic, Practical Information and Opportunities
Israel Business and Investment Opportunities Yearbook Volume 1 Strategic, Practical Information and Opportunities
Italy Business and Investment Opportunities Yearbook Volume 1 Strategic, Practical Information and Opportunities
Jamaica Business and Investment Opportunities Yearbook Volume 1 Strategic, Practical Information and Opportunities
Japan Business and Investment Opportunities Yearbook Volume 1 Strategic, Practical Information and Opportunities
Jersey Business and Investment Opportunities Yearbook Volume 1 Strategic, Practical Information and Opportunities
Jordan Business and Investment Opportunities Yearbook Volume 1 Strategic, Practical Information and Opportunities
Kazakhstan Business and Investment Opportunities Yearbook Volume 1 Strategic, Practical Information and Opportunities
Kenya Business and Investment Opportunities Yearbook Volume 1 Strategic, Practical Information and Opportunities
Kiribati Business and Investment Opportunities Yearbook Volume 1 Strategic, Practical Information and Opportunities
Korea, North Business and Investment Opportunities Yearbook Volume 1 Strategic, Practical Information and Opportunities
Korea, South Business and Investment Opportunities Yearbook Volume 1 Strategic, Practical Information and Opportunities

For additional analytical, business and investment opportunities information,
Please contact Global Investment & Business Center, USA
at (202) 546-2103. Fax: (202) 546-3275. E-mail: ibpusa3@gmail.com

TITLE
Kosovo Business and Investment Opportunities Yearbook Volume 1 Strategic, Practical Information and Opportunities
Kurdistan Business and Investment Opportunities Yearbook Volume 1 Strategic, Practical Information and Opportunities
Kuwait Business and Investment Opportunities Yearbook Volume 1 Strategic, Practical Information and Opportunities
Kyrgyzstan Business and Investment Opportunities Yearbook Volume 1 Strategic, Practical Information and Opportunities
Laos Business and Investment Opportunities Yearbook Volume 1 Strategic, Practical Information and Opportunities
Latvia Business and Investment Opportunities Yearbook Volume 1 Strategic, Practical Information and Opportunities
Lebanon Business and Investment Opportunities Yearbook Volume 1 Strategic, Practical Information and Opportunities
Lesotho Business and Investment Opportunities Yearbook Volume 1 Strategic, Practical Information and Opportunities
Liberia Business and Investment Opportunities Yearbook Volume 1 Strategic, Practical Information and Opportunities
Libya Business and Investment Opportunities Yearbook Volume 1 Strategic, Practical Information and Opportunities
Liechtenstein Business and Investment Opportunities Yearbook Volume 1 Strategic, Practical Information and Opportunities
Lithuania Business and Investment Opportunities Yearbook Volume 1 Strategic, Practical Information and Opportunities
Luxembourg Business and Investment Opportunities Yearbook Volume 1 Strategic, Practical Information and Opportunities
Macao Business and Investment Opportunities Yearbook Volume 1 Strategic, Practical Information and Opportunities
Macedonia Business and Investment Opportunities Yearbook Volume 1 Strategic, Practical Information and Opportunities
Madagascar Business and Investment Opportunities Yearbook Volume 1 Strategic, Practical Information and Opportunities
Madeira Business and Investment Opportunities Yearbook Volume 1 Strategic, Practical Information and Opportunities
Malawi Business and Investment Opportunities Yearbook Volume 1 Strategic, Practical Information and Opportunities
Malaysia Business and Investment Opportunities Yearbook Volume 1 Strategic, Practical Information and Opportunities
Maldives Business and Investment Opportunities Yearbook Volume 1 Strategic, Practical Information and Opportunities
Mali Business and Investment Opportunities Yearbook Volume 1 Strategic, Practical Information and Opportunities
Malta Business and Investment Opportunities Yearbook Volume 1 Strategic, Practical Information and Opportunities
Man Business and Investment Opportunities Yearbook Volume 1 Strategic, Practical Information and Opportunities
Marshall Islands Business and Investment Opportunities Yearbook Volume 1 Strategic, Practical Information and Opportunities
Mauritania Business and Investment Opportunities Yearbook Volume 1 Strategic, Practical Information and Opportunities
Mauritius Business and Investment Opportunities Yearbook Volume 1 Strategic, Practical Information and Opportunities
Mayotte Business and Investment Opportunities Yearbook Volume 1 Strategic, Practical Information and Opportunities
Mexico Business and Investment Opportunities Yearbook Volume 1 Strategic, Practical Information and Opportunities

For additional analytical, business and investment opportunities information,
Please contact Global Investment & Business Center, USA
at (202) 546-2103. Fax: (202) 546-3275. E-mail: ibpusa3@gmail.com

TITLE
Micronesia Business and Investment Opportunities Yearbook Volume 1 Strategic, Practical Information and Opportunities
Moldova Business and Investment Opportunities Yearbook Volume 1 Strategic, Practical Information and Opportunities
Monaco Business and Investment Opportunities Yearbook Volume 1 Strategic, Practical Information and Opportunities
Mongolia Business and Investment Opportunities Yearbook Volume 1 Strategic, Practical Information and Opportunities
Montserrat Business and Investment Opportunities Yearbook Volume 1 Strategic, Practical Information and Opportunities
Montenegro Business and Investment Opportunities Yearbook Volume 1 Strategic, Practical Information and Opportunities
Morocco Business and Investment Opportunities Yearbook Volume 1 Strategic, Practical Information and Opportunities
Mozambique Business and Investment Opportunities Yearbook Volume 1 Strategic, Practical Information and Opportunities
Myanmar Business and Investment Opportunities Yearbook Volume 1 Strategic, Practical Information and Opportunities
Nagorno-Karabakh Republic Business and Investment Opportunities Yearbook Volume 1 Strategic, Practical Information and Opportunities
Namibia Business and Investment Opportunities Yearbook Volume 1 Strategic, Practical Information and Opportunities
Nauru Business and Investment Opportunities Yearbook Volume 1 Strategic, Practical Information and Opportunities
Nepal Business and Investment Opportunities Yearbook Volume 1 Strategic, Practical Information and Opportunities
Netherlands Business and Investment Opportunities Yearbook Volume 1 Strategic, Practical Information and Opportunities
New Caledonia Business and Investment Opportunities Yearbook Volume 1 Strategic, Practical Information and Opportunities
New Zealand Business and Investment Opportunities Yearbook Volume 1 Strategic, Practical Information and Opportunities
Nicaragua Business and Investment Opportunities Yearbook Volume 1 Strategic, Practical Information and Opportunities
Niger Business and Investment Opportunities Yearbook Volume 1 Strategic, Practical Information and Opportunities
Nigeria Business and Investment Opportunities Yearbook Volume 1 Strategic, Practical Information and Opportunities
Niue Business and Investment Opportunities Yearbook Volume 1 Strategic, Practical Information and Opportunities
Northern Cyprus (Turkish Republic of Northern Cyprus) Business and Investment Opportunities Yearbook Volume 1 Strategic, Practical Information and Opportunities
Northern Mariana Islands Business and Investment Opportunities Yearbook Volume 1 Strategic, Practical Information and Opportunities
Norway Business and Investment Opportunities Yearbook Volume 1 Strategic, Practical Information and Opportunities
Oman Business and Investment Opportunities Yearbook Volume 1 Strategic, Practical Information and Opportunities
Pakistan Business and Investment Opportunities Yearbook Volume 1 Strategic, Practical Information and Opportunities
Palau Business and Investment Opportunities Yearbook Volume 1 Strategic, Practical Information and Opportunities
Palestine (West Bank & Gaza) Business and Investment Opportunities Yearbook Volume 1 Strategic, Practical Information and Opportunities
Panama Business and Investment Opportunities Yearbook Volume 1 Strategic, Practical Information and Opportunities

For additional analytical, business and investment opportunities information,
Please contact Global Investment & Business Center, USA
at (202) 546-2103. Fax: (202) 546-3275. E-mail: ibpusa3@gmail.com

TITLE
Papua New Guinea Business and Investment Opportunities Yearbook Volume 1 Strategic, Practical Information and Opportunities
Paraguay Business and Investment Opportunities Yearbook Volume 1 Strategic, Practical Information and Opportunities
Peru Business and Investment Opportunities Yearbook Volume 1 Strategic, Practical Information and Opportunities
Philippines Business and Investment Opportunities Yearbook Volume 1 Strategic, Practical Information and Opportunities
Pitcairn Islands Business and Investment Opportunities Yearbook Volume 1 Strategic, Practical Information and Opportunities
Poland Business and Investment Opportunities Yearbook Volume 1 Strategic, Practical Information and Opportunities
Polynesia French Business and Investment Opportunities Yearbook Volume 1 Strategic, Practical Information and Opportunities
Portugal Business and Investment Opportunities Yearbook Volume 1 Strategic, Practical Information and Opportunities
Qatar Business and Investment Opportunities Yearbook Volume 1 Strategic, Practical Information and Opportunities
Romania Business and Investment Opportunities Yearbook Volume 1 Strategic, Practical Information and Opportunities
Russia Business and Investment Opportunities Yearbook Volume 1 Strategic, Practical Information and Opportunities
Rwanda Business and Investment Opportunities Yearbook Volume 1 Strategic, Practical Information and Opportunities
Sahrawi Arab Democratic Republic Volume 1 Strategic Information and Developments
Saint Kitts and Nevis Business and Investment Opportunities Yearbook Volume 1 Strategic, Practical Information and Opportunities
Saint Lucia Business and Investment Opportunities Yearbook Volume 1 Strategic, Practical Information and Opportunities
Saint Vincent and The Grenadines Business and Investment Opportunities Yearbook Volume 1 Strategic, Practical Information and Opportunities
Samoa (American) A Business and Investment Opportunities Yearbook Volume 1 Strategic, Practical Information and Opportunities
Samoa (Western) Business and Investment Opportunities Yearbook Volume 1 Strategic, Practical Information and Opportunities
San Marino Business and Investment Opportunities Yearbook Volume 1 Strategic, Practical Information and Opportunities
Sao Tome and Principe Business and Investment Opportunities Yearbook Volume 1 Strategic, Practical Information and Opportunities
Saudi Arabia Business and Investment Opportunities Yearbook Volume 1 Strategic, Practical Information and Opportunities
Scotland Business and Investment Opportunities Yearbook Volume 1 Strategic, Practical Information and Opportunities
Senegal Business and Investment Opportunities Yearbook Volume 1 Strategic, Practical Information and Opportunities
Serbia Business and Investment Opportunities Yearbook Volume 1 Strategic, Practical Information and Opportunities
Seychelles Business and Investment Opportunities Yearbook Volume 1 Strategic, Practical Information and Opportunities
Sierra Leone Business and Investment Opportunities Yearbook Volume 1 Strategic, Practical Information and Opportunities
Singapore Business and Investment Opportunities Yearbook Volume 1 Strategic, Practical Information and Opportunities
Slovakia Business and Investment Opportunities Yearbook Volume 1 Strategic, Practical Information and Opportunities

For additional analytical, business and investment opportunities information,
Please contact Global Investment & Business Center, USA
at (202) 546-2103. Fax: (202) 546-3275. E-mail: ibpusa3@gmail.com

TITLE
Slovenia Business and Investment Opportunities Yearbook Volume 1 Strategic, Practical Information and Opportunities
Solomon Islands Business and Investment Opportunities Yearbook Volume 1 Strategic, Practical Information and Opportunities
Somalia Business and Investment Opportunities Yearbook Volume 1 Strategic, Practical Information and Opportunities
South Africa Business and Investment Opportunities Yearbook Volume 1 Strategic, Practical Information and Opportunities
Spain Business and Investment Opportunities Yearbook Volume 1 Strategic, Practical Information and Opportunities
Sri Lanka Business and Investment Opportunities Yearbook Volume 1 Strategic, Practical Information and Opportunities
St. Helena Business and Investment Opportunities Yearbook Volume 1 Strategic, Practical Information and Opportunities
St. Pierre & Miquelon Business and Investment Opportunities Yearbook Volume 1 Strategic, Practical Information and Opportunities
Sudan (Republic of the Sudan) Business and Investment Opportunities Yearbook Volume 1 Strategic, Practical Information and Opportunities
Sudan South Business and Investment Opportunities Yearbook Volume 1 Strategic, Practical Information and Opportunities
Suriname Business and Investment Opportunities Yearbook Volume 1 Strategic, Practical Information and Opportunities
Swaziland Business and Investment Opportunities Yearbook Volume 1 Strategic, Practical Information and Opportunities
Sweden Business and Investment Opportunities Yearbook Volume 1 Strategic, Practical Information and Opportunities
Switzerland Business and Investment Opportunities Yearbook Volume 1 Strategic, Practical Information and Opportunities
Syria Business and Investment Opportunities Yearbook Volume 1 Strategic, Practical Information and Opportunities
Taiwan Business and Investment Opportunities Yearbook Volume 1 Strategic, Practical Information and Opportunities
Tajikistan Business and Investment Opportunities Yearbook Volume 1 Strategic, Practical Information and Opportunities
Tanzania Business and Investment Opportunities Yearbook Volume 1 Strategic, Practical Information and Opportunities
Thailand Business and Investment Opportunities Yearbook Volume 1 Strategic, Practical Information and Opportunities
Timor Leste (Democratic Republic of Timor-Leste) Business and Investment Opportunities Yearbook Volume 1 Strategic, Practical Information and Opportunities
Togo Business and Investment Opportunities Yearbook Volume 1 Strategic, Practical Information and Opportunities
Tonga Business and Investment Opportunities Yearbook Volume 1 Strategic, Practical Information and Opportunities
Trinidad and Tobago Business and Investment Opportunities Yearbook Volume 1 Strategic, Practical Information and Opportunities
Tunisia Business and Investment Opportunities Yearbook Volume 1 Strategic, Practical Information and Opportunities
Turkey Business and Investment Opportunities Yearbook Volume 1 Strategic, Practical Information and Opportunities
Turkmenistan Business and Investment Opportunities Yearbook Volume 1 Strategic, Practical Information and Opportunities
Turks & Caicos Business and Investment Opportunities Yearbook Volume 1 Strategic, Practical Information and Opportunities
Tuvalu Business and Investment Opportunities Yearbook Volume 1 Strategic, Practical Information and Opportunities

For additional analytical, business and investment opportunities information,
Please contact Global Investment & Business Center, USA
at (202) 546-2103. Fax: (202) 546-3275. E-mail: ibpusa3@gmail.com

TITLE
Uganda Business and Investment Opportunities Yearbook Volume 1 Strategic, Practical Information and Opportunities
Ukraine Business and Investment Opportunities Yearbook Volume 1 Strategic, Practical Information and Opportunities
United Arab Emirates Business and Investment Opportunities Yearbook Volume 1 Strategic, Practical Information and Opportunities
United Kingdom Business and Investment Opportunities Yearbook Volume 1 Strategic, Practical Information and Opportunities
United States Business and Investment Opportunities Yearbook Volume 1 Strategic, Practical Information and Opportunities
Uruguay Business and Investment Opportunities Yearbook Volume 1 Strategic, Practical Information and Opportunities
Uzbekistan Business and Investment Opportunities Yearbook Volume 1 Strategic, Practical Information and Opportunities
Vanuatu Business and Investment Opportunities Yearbook Volume 1 Strategic, Practical Information and Opportunities
Vatican City (Holy See) Business and Investment Opportunities Yearbook Volume 1 Strategic, Practical Information and Opportunities
Venezuela Business and Investment Opportunities Yearbook Volume 1 Strategic, Practical Information and Opportunities
Vietnam Business and Investment Opportunities Yearbook Volume 1 Strategic, Practical Information and Opportunities
Virgin Islands, British Business and Investment Opportunities Yearbook Volume 1 Strategic, Practical Information and Opportunities
Wake Atoll Business and Investment Opportunities Yearbook Volume 1 Strategic, Practical Information and Opportunities
Wallis & Futuna Business and Investment Opportunities Yearbook Volume 1 Strategic, Practical Information and Opportunities
Western Sahara Business and Investment Opportunities Yearbook Volume 1 Strategic, Practical Information and Opportunities
Yemen Business and Investment Opportunities Yearbook Volume 1 Strategic, Practical Information and Opportunities
Zambia Business and Investment Opportunities Yearbook Volume 1 Strategic, Practical Information and Opportunities
Zimbabwe Business and Investment Opportunities Yearbook Volume 1 Strategic, Practical Information and Opportunities

For additional analytical, business and investment opportunities information,
Please contact Global Investment & Business Center, USA
at (202) 546-2103. Fax: (202) 546-3275. E-mail: ibpusa3@gmail.com